STONES CLOUDS MILES

A RICHARD LONG READER

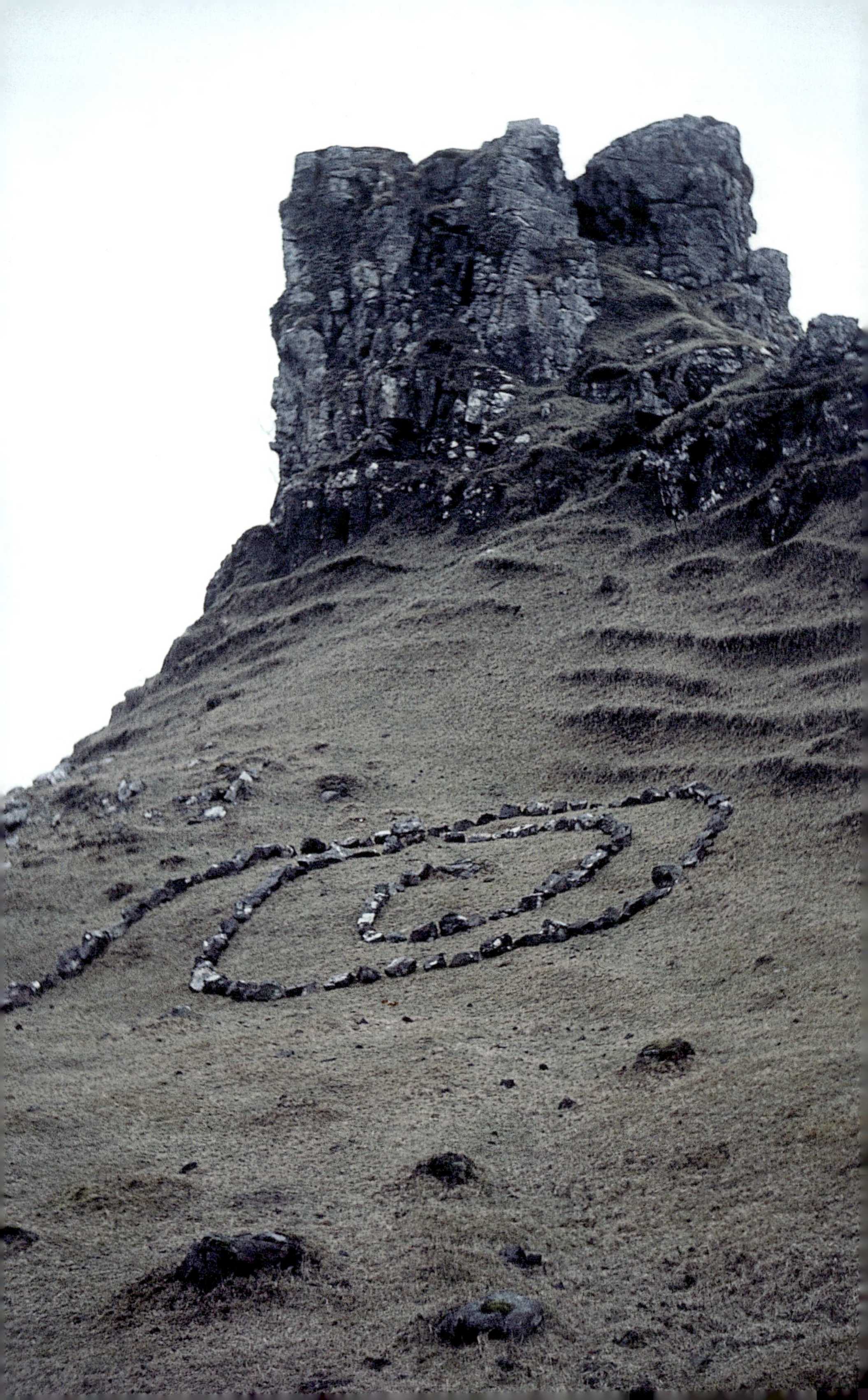

STONES CLOUDS MILES

A RICHARD LONG READER

Edited by Clarrie Wallis

Ridinghouse

Contents

Artist Writings

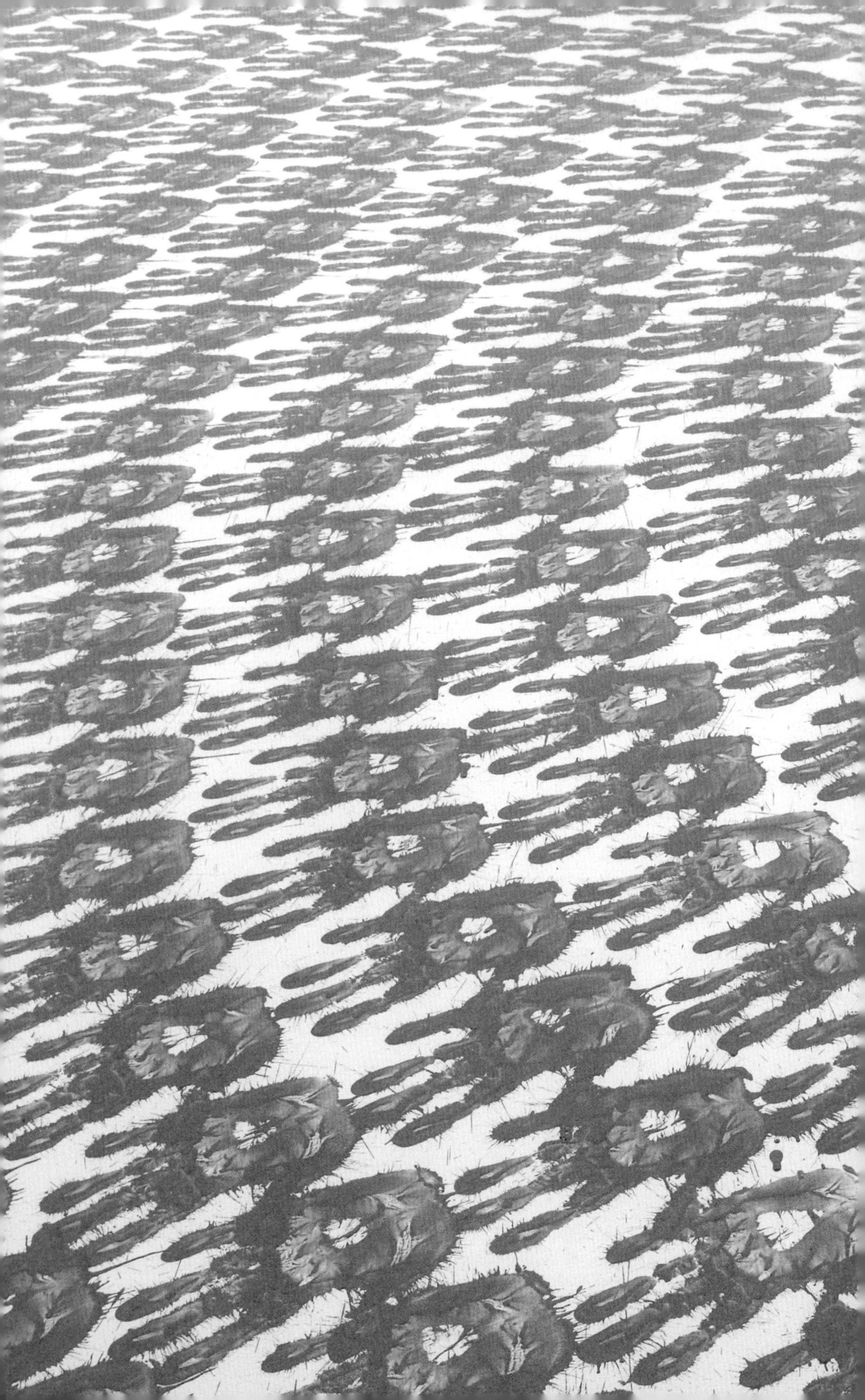

With thanks to

all the authors
Sarah Auld
Nicola Bion
Katherine Borkowski
Eileen Daly
Dorothy Feaver
Ann Gallagher
Doro Globus
Louisa Green
Daniel Griffiths
Liz Hallam
Sophic Kullmann
Philip Lewis
Tom Rowland
Karsten Schubert
Kate Sloss
Kostas Synodis
Tate Library staff
Joanna Thornberry
Gerard Vermeulen
Will Wallis
Andrew Wilson
Angela Westwater

FRONTISPIECE
Stones on Isle of Skye 1970

OPPOSITE
Whirlpool, Spike Island, Bristol 2008 (detail)

PAGES 14–15
Richard Long walking on Dartmoor with
his father 1968

Introduction

CLARRIE WALLIS

Richard Long's art is grounded in his direct engagement with the landscape. Born in Bristol in 1945 he first came to prominence in the late 1960s and is part of an international generation of artists who extended the possibilities of sculpture beyond traditional materials and methods. This anthology brings together a selection of texts about his work, as well as statements by the artist, which chart Long's impressive career and are key to an understanding of a body of work that encompasses sculpture, language, mudworks and printed matter. Collectively, they reflect on how the art is rooted in Long's love of nature and the revolutionary implications of using walking as a medium. As the articles in this volume confirm, what is striking is both the early stage at which Long established the formal parameters within which his work would develop, making art directly connected with the landscape, and the unwavering continuity of his approach. This new form of art was not only located in the landscape but was made from landscape itself.

The texts gathered together here are arranged chronologically to enable an appraisal of the different ways in which Long's art has been received over the last 40 years. Interspersed between the texts is a selection of photographs of key exhibitions. Remarkably, the idea-based approach of Long's mature work is already well established in his student work at St Martin's School of Art where he studied from 1966 to 1968. In his last term, the German gallerist Konrad Fischer wrote to Long inviting him to have an exhibition at his gallery in September 1968,[1] and at Fischer's suggestion, Long took the train to Amalfi in Italy and participated in *III Rassegna di arti figurative: Arte Povera + azioni povere*, (RA3: Third Amalfi Exhibition: Arte Povera + azioni povere). This was an annual event, which in 1968 consisted of an exhibition in the old Arsenale and three days of actions and collective works by artists and writers including Ger van Elk, whose commentary of the event is included here (pp.16–17).

In retrospect, the works made in Amalfi form a microcosm of the radical new approaches to materials and forms being explored by a number of European and American artists, including Richard Long.

They were intent on exploring new ideas about sculpture. By the early 1970s critics would describe these approaches in different ways such as 'process-orientated', 'anti-form', 'earthworks', 'Conceptual' and 'post-Minimal'. Long's presence in exhibitions such as *Op Losse Schroeven, situaties en cryptostructuren* and *Live in Your Head: When Attitudes Become Form (Works-Concepts-Processes-Situations-Information)* (both 1969) highlight the rapidity with which his work achieved international recognition. John Perreault's review of Long's exhibition at the John Gibson Gallery, New York, 1969 (p.17) together with Elizabeth Baker's review of his show at the Dwan Gallery, New York in 1970 (p.26) give an insight into how Long's practice was discussed at the time in relation to these new categories of work. Likewise, Paul Wember's catalogue essay for Long's first institutional exhibition at the Museum Haus Lange, Krefeld in 1969 (where he realised three works on the lawn), offers an early attempt to position his work alongside other international artists who took art beyond the studio (pp.19–21).

From the beginning of his career, Long developed two distinct but complementary aspects of making: the outdoor sculptures and walks, and the sculpture installations, photo, map and textworks. Photography was always important to him, as it was a practical way of showing people what he had made in the landscape. As Andrew Wilson's text notes, Long soon became interested in the different ways he could put work into the world: a photograph, a postcard, a sculpture, a text, or an artist's book were all possibilities, and all could be given equal status (pp.225–233). Long's first textwork, which treats language in a neutral way, was created for the exhibition *Live in Your Head: When Attitudes Become Form*. After completing a walk in the Alps near Bern his work for the exhibition that followed consisted of a printed poster pasted to the wall, which read: 'Richard Long, March 19–22, 1969, A Walking Tour in the Berner Oberland.'[2] In Ian Tromp's text he considers the use of poetry and language in Long's work that began with this work in 1969 and has continued to be a crucial element in Long's work since (pp.188–201). In 1970, at the Dwan Gallery in New York, Long walked a spiral on the floor with muddy boots, a work that he thought of as a two-dimensional sculpture. Later he realised that he could use the same material in a liquid state and apply it directly onto the wall with his hands.

Long's use of the natural environment meant that in early reviews, particularly by critics from the United States, he was often associated with Land art, a practice that emerged in the late 1960s and integrated aspects of Minimalism and Conceptualism with works made in the American West. While Long acknowledges a kinship with the artists Carl Andre (see Alistair Rider's text 'The "Curve Over the Crest of the Hill": Carl Andre and Richard Long,' pp.252–267) and Lawrence Weiner, he has always rejected any connection with the American Earth artists. Long's interventions in the landscape are of a very different nature to the machine made, monumental permanent works of the North American Land artists, works such as Michael Heizer's *Double Negative* (1969–70), or Robert Smithson's *Spiral Jetty* (1970). A journey provided Long with the dimensions of time and distance and encompassed a very different philosophical approach from that of the earthworkers. Long has only ever used his own hands and feet and the earth's natural, raw materials, and the scale of his sculptures has always been determined by his response to each chosen place or landscape along a walk. He uses the materials he finds there and his rearrangements are discrete marks of passage. As Long's walks are often many hundreds of miles long, their scale extends far beyond that of any monument.

In 1971 he participated in the Guggenheim International Award exhibition at the Solomon R Guggenheim Museum, New York and in 1972 exhibited in the Projects gallery at the Museum of Modern Art, New York (p.34). That same year, and again in 1982, Long was invited to participate in *Documenta 5* and *7* in Kassel (see statements p.293 and p.298). Long represented Britain at the Venice Biennale in 1976 and over the next decade this was followed by further high-profile exhibitions, including a major retrospective at the Solomon R Guggenheim Museum in 1986. In 1989 he was awarded the prestigious Turner Prize in London and in 2009 Japan's Praemium Imperiale in the field of sculpture.

The first stone circle was made while walking in the Andes in 1972. As Anne Seymour notes in her review of his inaugural exhibition at the Lisson Gallery in 1973, Long sought the means to go beyond the limitations of traditional representation, to develop a practice that is the result of a simple and direct experience of the land (pp.44–46). During this period he held to the belief that his work should speak for itself. In 1980, when faced with persistent misreadings of his work, Long felt it was important to clarify his position. His first statement, *Five, six, pick up sticks Seven, eight, lay them straight* was published by the Anthony d'Offay Gallery in 1980. Since then he has occasionally written statements to coincide with exhibitions, or in the case of *Riverlines* (2006) (p.308) and *Slate Oasis* (2007) (p.309) to address specific works. A selection of these statements, chosen by the artist, are included in this volume (pp.292–327). In the statement *Words after the fact*, written to coincide with his exhibition at the Arnolfini, Bristol in 1983, Long describes his approach as 'abstract art laid down in the real spaces of the world', (pp.298–299). He considers himself to be a realist. His work is always a balance between the patterns of nature, and his repeated use of a limited number of archetypal forms: the line, the circle, the cross and the spiral. This, as Michael Craig-Martin notes 'is not to imply mystical engagement on Long's part. His use of the land is matter-of-fact and practical' (pp.65–9).

Long's interest is in both art and nature, but not in formal issues or art theory. Many of these articles – including an interview with Richard Cork (pp.119–132) and Sean Rainbird's essay 'Crossing Place' (pp.160–166) – highlight the importance to the artist of Bristol and the River Avon, the places where Long grew up. They acknowledge that in the mid-sixties he felt that the art world had not fully engaged with the natural landscape or used the experiences that these places could offer. Beginning from his home in the South West of England and gradually spreading further afield, his work has always explored this potential.

For Long, walking can be both a physical and intellectual pleasure. His sense of the importance of experience and intuition has something in common with Zen Buddhism's concept of the here and now, of being in the moment, and is discussed in the interview with Colin Kirkpatrick (pp.166–178). Long has found that walking has proved to be an ideal means for him to explore relationships between time, distance, geography and measurement. And it is through the cumulative effect of each walk and the recording of simple sculptures made along the way, that the uniqueness of the world is revealed. Long's work is about his own physical engagement, exploring the order of the universe and nature's elemental and cosmic forces. And in this sense it is about being a body in the world and about measuring that world.

1 Long showed a sculpture of sticks cut from trees along the River Avon, laid in straight lines end-to-end on the gallery floor, converging towards the visual horizon of the far wall.

2 His original instructions before starting the walk were to have further copies of the textwork printed and displayed around the show, but in the event only one copy was on display.

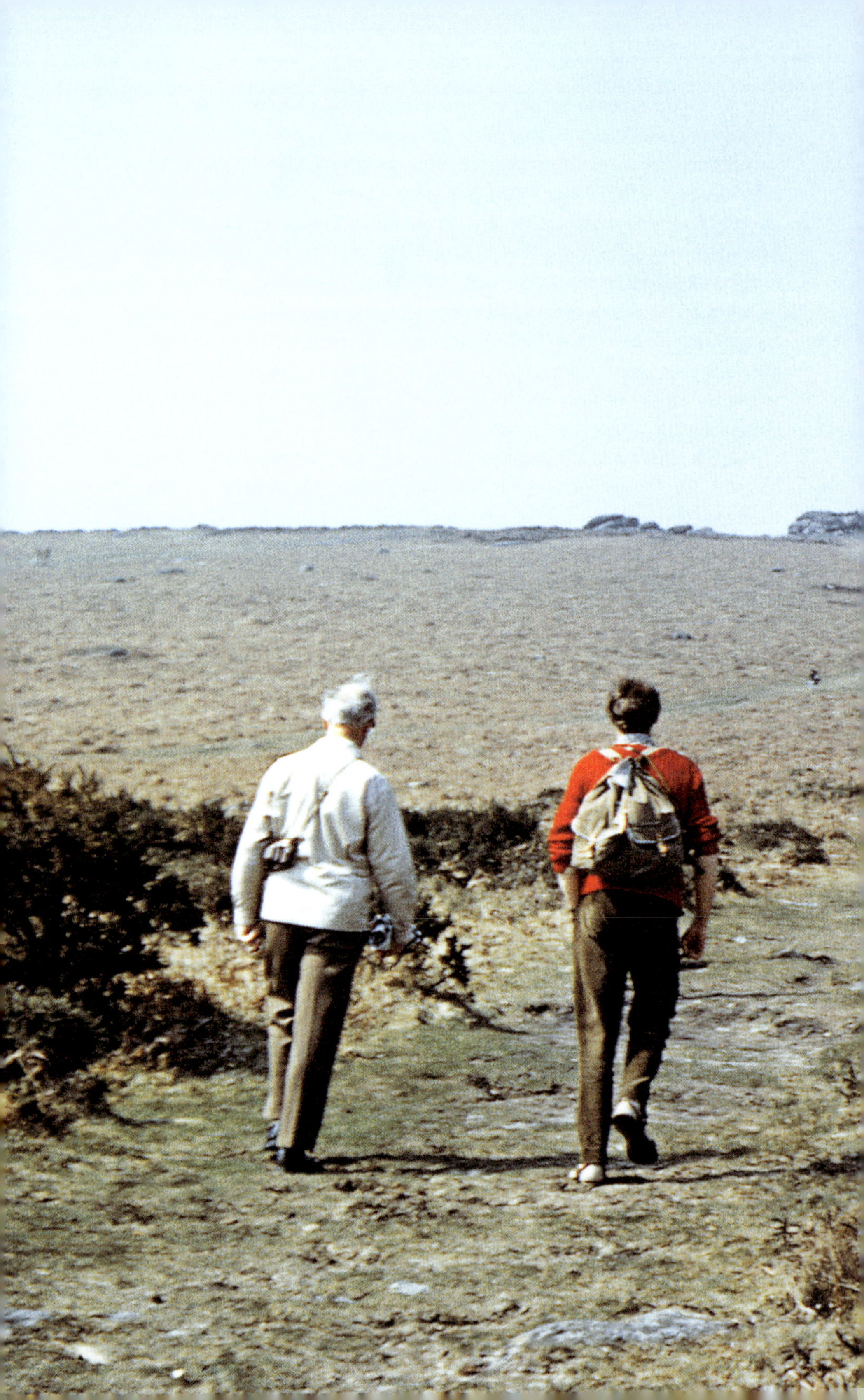

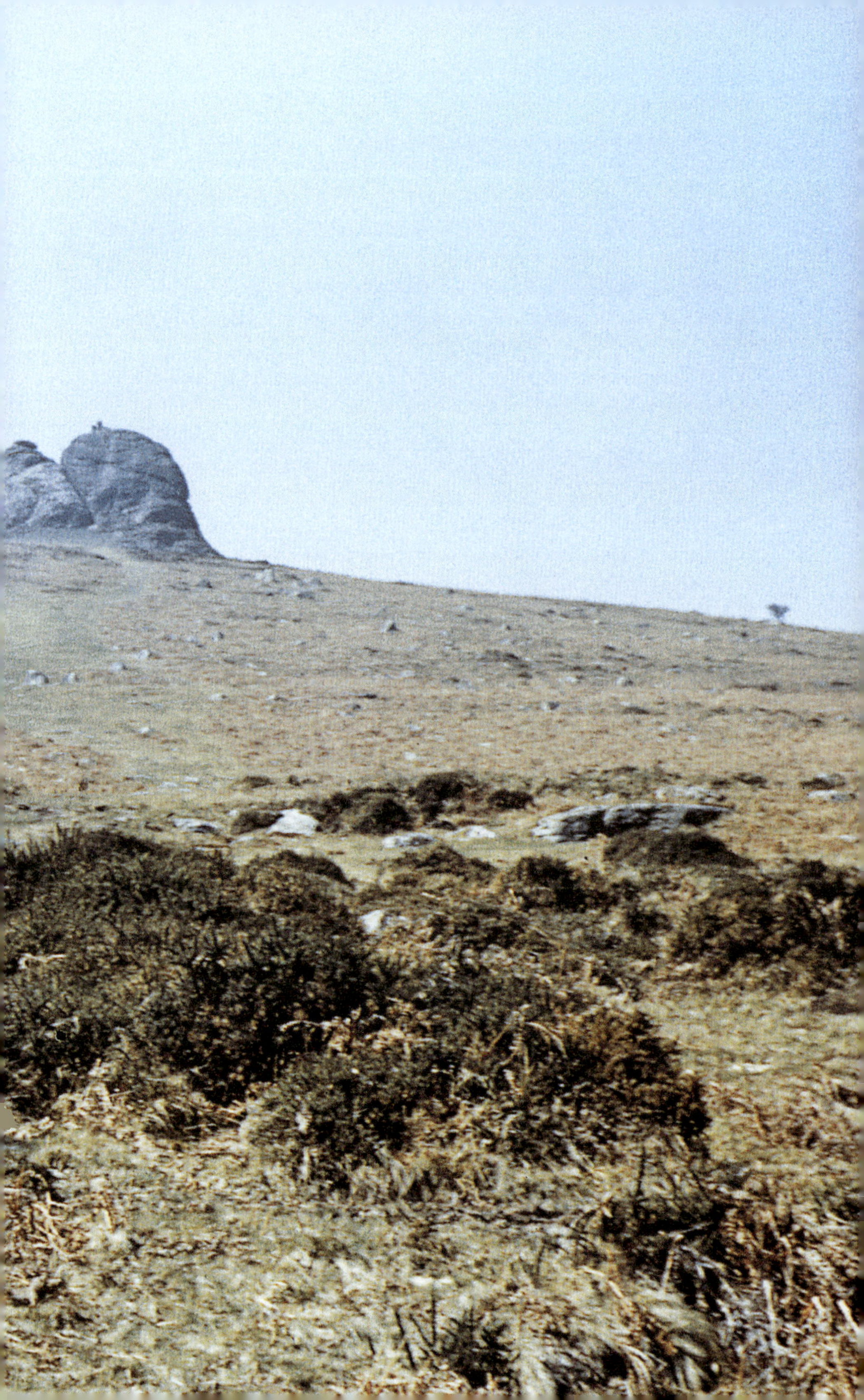

GER VAN ELK

Amalfi: Arte Povera in Azione Povere

Amalfi, 4 – 6 October 1968

On 4, 5, and 6 October in Amalfi, a small tourist resort between Salerno and Naples, a meeting was held between the artists of the Italian Arte Povera – a group centered around the Galleria Sperone in Turin – and a number of others: Italians not connected with galleries, and foreigners, whose art is indicated by Piero Gilardi as 'micro-emotive'.

The Italians present were: Giovanni Anselmo, Alighiero e Boetti, Mario Merz, Michelangelo Pistoletto, Gilberto Zorio, Emilio Prini, Pier Paolo Calzolari, Paolo Icaro, Piero Gilardi, Plinio Martelli, Gianni Piacentino; Jannis Kounellis and Pino Pascali had sent in work.

Of the foreigners invited, Richard Long, Jan Dibbets, Gerry Schum (of the Television Gallery in Dusseldorf) and myself attended. Marinus Boezem, who had also been invited, was unfortunately unable to come due to his teaching job, but sent an exhibit in the form of a weather forecast. The critics present were Henry Martin for *Art and Artists*, and Tommaso Trini for *Domus*. This third *Rassegna d'arte figurativa* was organised by M Rumma, a teacher, collector and critic, whose aim is to present to the public the new movements in Southern Italy. The first two exhibitions, which were dedicated to Pop art and Hard Edge, were sponsored by the Italian Socialist Party but this one was not since they were unsuccessful in the latest elections.

The exhibition, which was housed in the old arsenal building of the medieval republic Amalfi – a gigantic, gothic construction hewn out of rock – comprised, among many other objects, a wet rag, a cowhide stretched across a window by Kounellis, and an environment by Boetti. Long adapted his contribution to the Mediterranean climate; on the first day he painted two beams he came across white, and departed on foot with them to the top of the highest mountain rising out of the sea. That evening, on his return from the exhausting journey, he pointed to the result: a little piece of wood, at that distance no more than a matchstick. He shook hands with everyone he showed it to, as a congratulation for the success of having seen it.

An important feature of the event were the open discussions with the art critics, who together with the artists seek new pictorial possibilities – an example it would be wise to follow in the Netherlands.

As a joint project, Long, Dibbets and I also contributed a 'football scene' to liven up the discussions which withered somewhat almost as soon as they began.

Although the manifestation seemed somewhat confused, there were sufficient exhibits surprising enough in themselves to make the event a success, and many artists would benefit by coming into contact with art critics and museum people in an atmosphere of work.

Museumjournaal, February 1969, vol.14, no.1, pp.34–37.

JOHN PERREAULT

Richard Long at John Gibson Gallery

New York, 22 February – 14 March 1969

Richard Long is a talented 23-year-old English man who showed photo-documents of some of his work since 1963; sod-removal, geometrical cuts in the land, minimal, portable sculptures that he has bicycled and placed anonymously throughout the British countryside. One piece consisted of inscribing an 'X' in a meadow by snipping off the heads of flowers. Another was a path worn into the grass by walking back and forth for several hours. The new Earth art is obviously not limited to US homegrown examples nor to bravado exploits; Long's work is gentle, very English and very good.

Art News, vol.68, no.2, April 1969, pp.18–19.

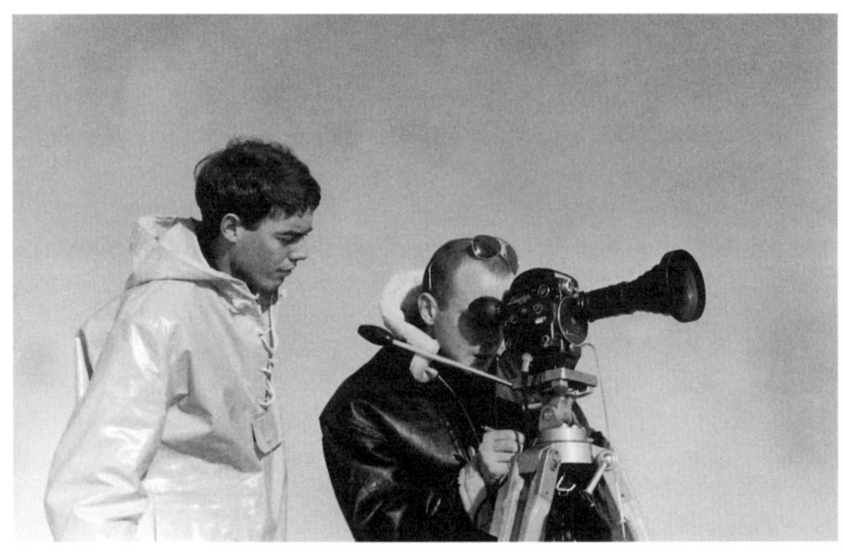

Richard Long and Gerry Schum during the making of *Walking a Straight 10 Mile Line Forward and Back Shooting every Half Mile* 1969

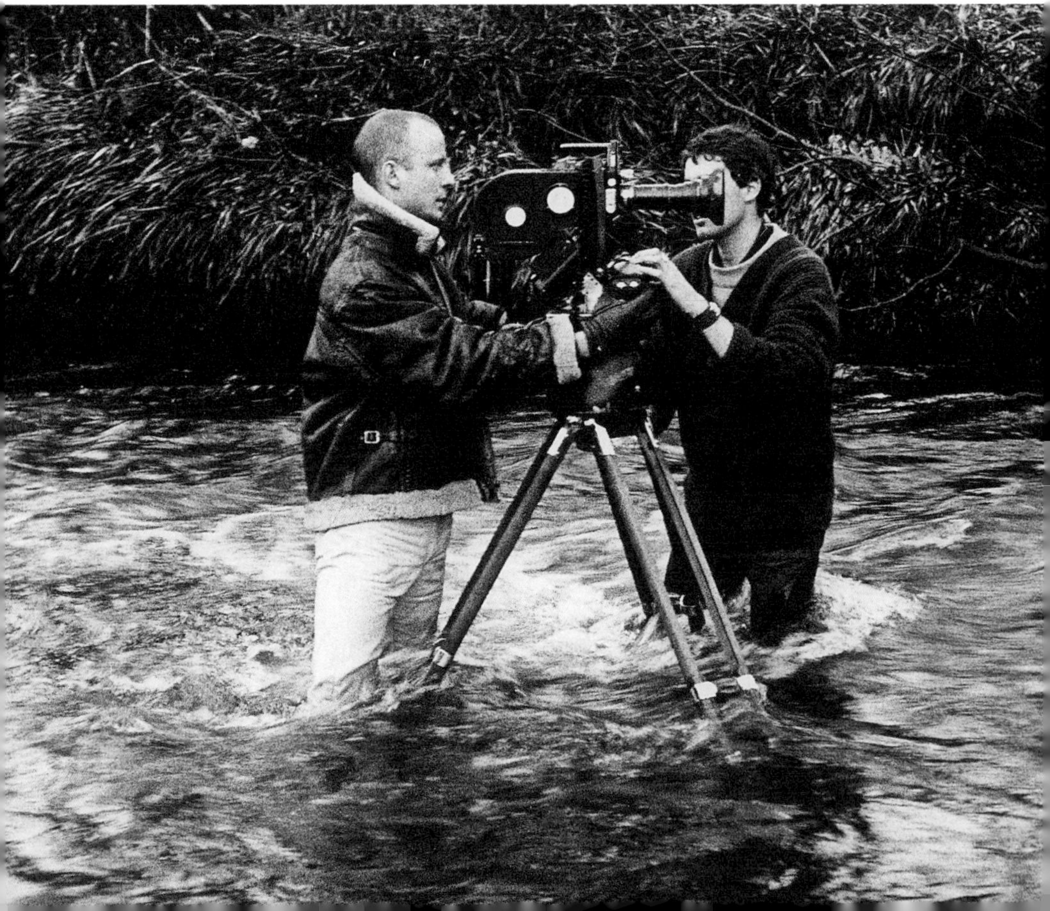

PAUL WEMBER

Richard Long in the Gardens of Museum Haus Lange

Valley
Hill
Mound
Land art in the Museum

In the exhibition *When Attitudes Become Form* in May and June 1969 the English Land artist Richard Long was represented by several of his actions.

Represented, but only in the sense of information. How otherwise could one represent the plan and the tracks of a walk through the English countryside? One can photograph the landscape; one can map out the way and make it clear and evident. Like Pop art, though in a different way, Land art is concerned with the coincidence of art and life. The tracks of a walking tour mean little; but still they are the free forms created by a human activity.

This action and expression, however, are not the whole of Land art. It has other types of activity and above all better ways of making itself comprehensible. While the above exhibition was going on, Richard Long was working in the park behind Haus Lange, like a gardener, a gardener architect, a garden-planner. He worked on the open lawn, which is ringed with trees and bushes, and created according to his own conception *Valley*, *Hill* and *Mound*[1] (all 1969). On that part nearest the house he laid out, with great skill, a 'valley' some 20 metres long, followed by a triple series of hollows. He wheeled the earth which he dug out over a plank walk to the south-west side of the lawn and built there a wide, raised ring some 37 metres in diameter. The 'Valley' lies close to the bushes on one side, whereas the ring or 'Hill' is in an open space, well away from the trees. From the latter, one discovers the 'Mound', an irregular tract almost 22 metres long on the south-east side of the lawn. It is made up of two mounds and two shallow depressions. The distances between the three works are, from *Valley* to *Hill* about ten and from *Hill* to *Mound* about 18 metres. Long raised the sods carefully. He used some of them in the larger hollow of the *Valley*, but the greater part on the walls of the ring. The rest of the walls were sowed with fresh seed, which sprouted quickly during the summer. From this point on, the function of the garden itself was continuously modified. When the exercises with Franz Erhard Walther's *Objects* took place in June 1969, it was already possible for the visitors to use the ring as a kind of amphitheatre.

There is no need to hang photographs in Museum Haus Lange in order to give a picture of the grounds. But for those who cannot inspect the alterations to the park and want to know what they look like, why should photographs not be sufficient? If one cannot go to Amsterdam to see Rembrandt's *The Night Watch* (1642), one looks at a photo of it or a colour reproduction. It is true that film, photography and TV have a special task in relation to many objects of Land art. Just as not everyone can travel to Amsterdam, most of us cannot journey into the desert, into the mountains or down to the sea to experience the works of Land art which may be there. But it is not quite true, that Land art has only become possible with the existence and by the services of film and TV. Nor does Land art necessarily mean a flight from the museum into the virgin landscape. This is only the case in part. As our example shows, it can enrich the immediate environment too; and here museums and public galleries are the sole institutions which can serve it. Only for the larger projects, in the desert, sea and mountains, are film and TV necessary interpreters.

The most important thing remains Land art itself, art in the landscape and by means of the landscape. Insofar as its media are ephemeral, photography, film and TV gain in importance as historical documentation. But they are conserves of Land art, not Land art itself. If they themselves are art, then it is the art of the film.

Land art itself is the problem. Everything else is helpful but incidental. John Anthony Thwaites wrote in a review of Gerry Schum's film *Land Art* (1969): 'the earth becomes a canvas and the elements the instruments with which it is marked.' And again: 'one experiences the straight line clearly, even dramatically.' In relation to Long's walk and to the film Thwaites remarks that 'the main actor is the plan of the line in Long's head.' Applied to our example this would be the plan of transforming the earth, also in Long's head.

The earth remains. One of the most convincing of all demonstrations of Land art was probably when Walter De Maria filled one room of a gallery with soil. Perhaps Earth art is an art without art. It is not transportable, one cannot hang it on the wall or put it on a pedestal. It cannot really be reproduced. In comparison with the gigantic works

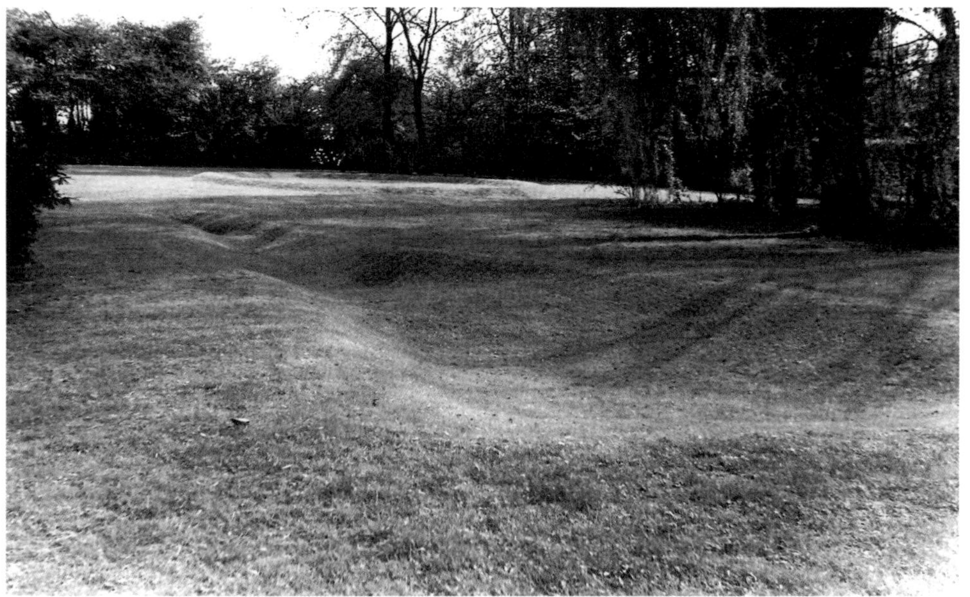

Valley, Museum Haus Lange, Krefeld 1969

in the desert, Long's *Valley, Hill* and *Mound* in Museum Haus Lange are only miniatures. Nevertheless, ownership is impossible. Land art is a new form of communication. It exists only because the visitor to Haus Lange can see it, walk round and over it, experience it in the act of walking.

That which Minimal art does with geometric and architectonic forms and Pop art with the things of everyday life, Land art does with land and landscape. Ideologically it is closest to the Pop mentality. It seeks the same immediacy as Pop art. It is also related to the Happening. The Land artist is not a maker of objects but the interpreter of a new conscious experience of Nature. The exodus from the museum is beginning, gradually. It begins for us in the garden, with the games of Franz Erhard Walther and the *Valley, Hill* and *Mound* of Richard Long.

Richard Long Land Art im Museum Haus Lange, JA Thwaites (trans), exh. cat., Museum Haus Lange, Krefeld 1970, n.p.

1 The work referred to in this text as 'Mound' is the work *Turf Circle* (1969).

4 Skulpturen

Städtisches Museum Abteiberg, Mönchengladbach,
16 July – 30 August 1970

All works untitled

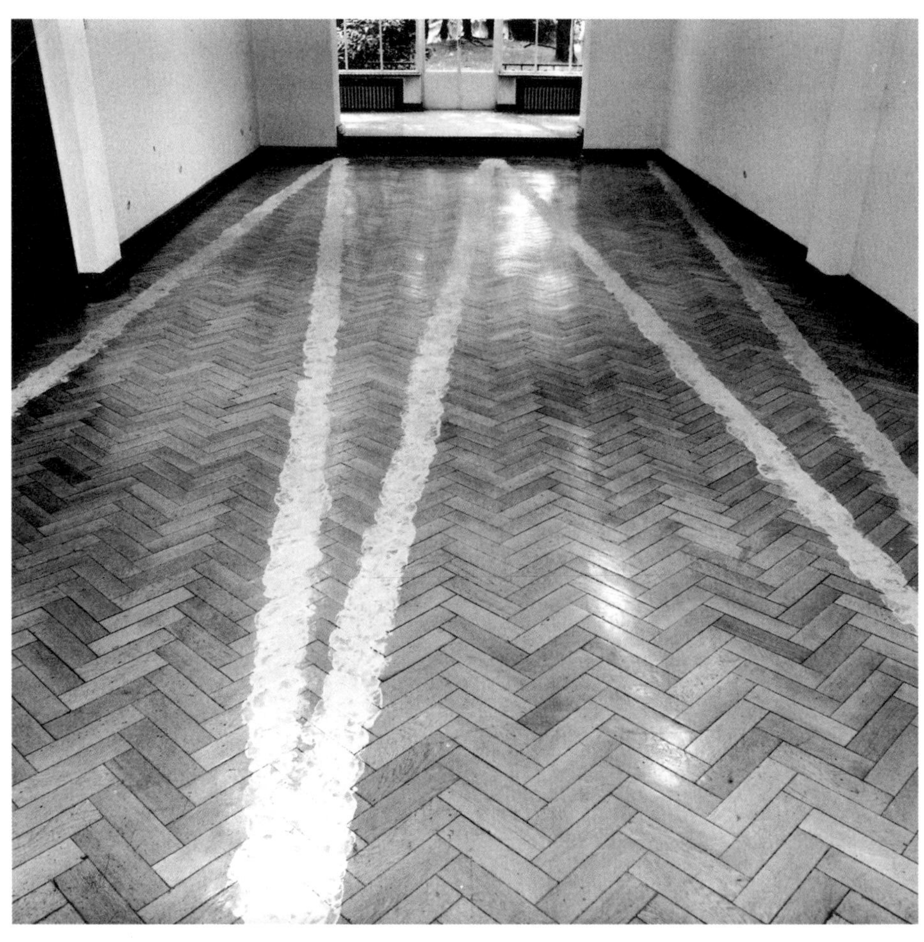

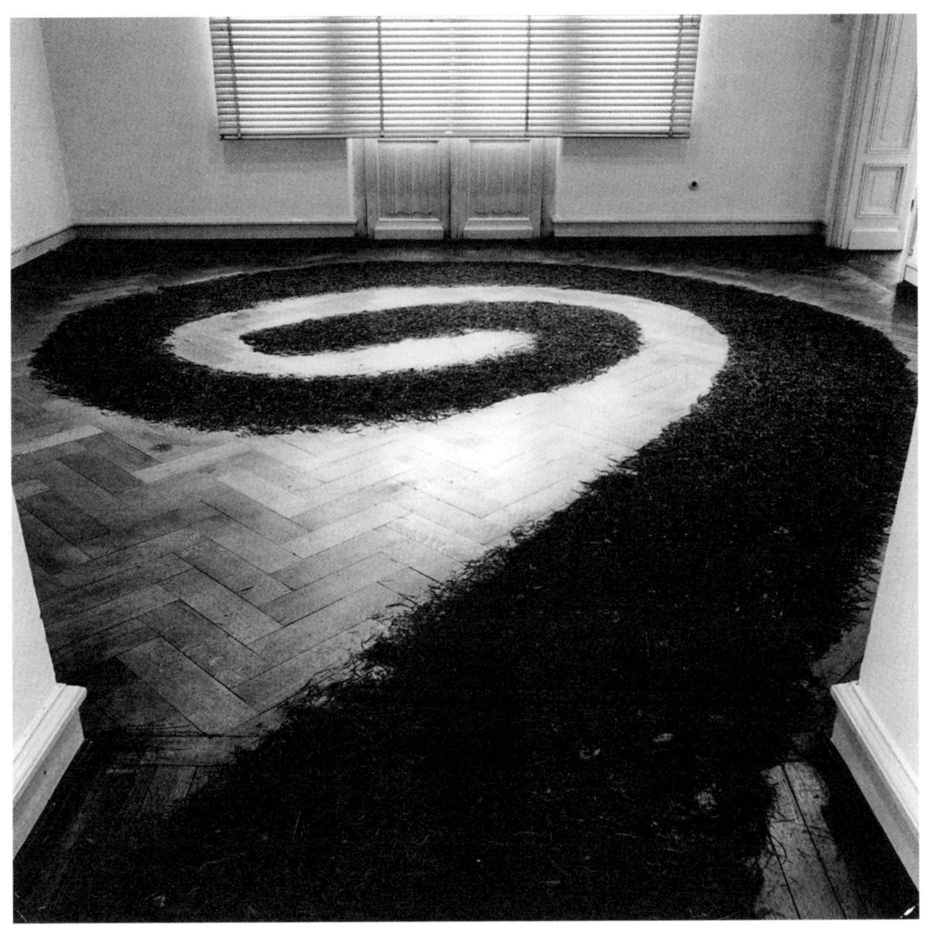

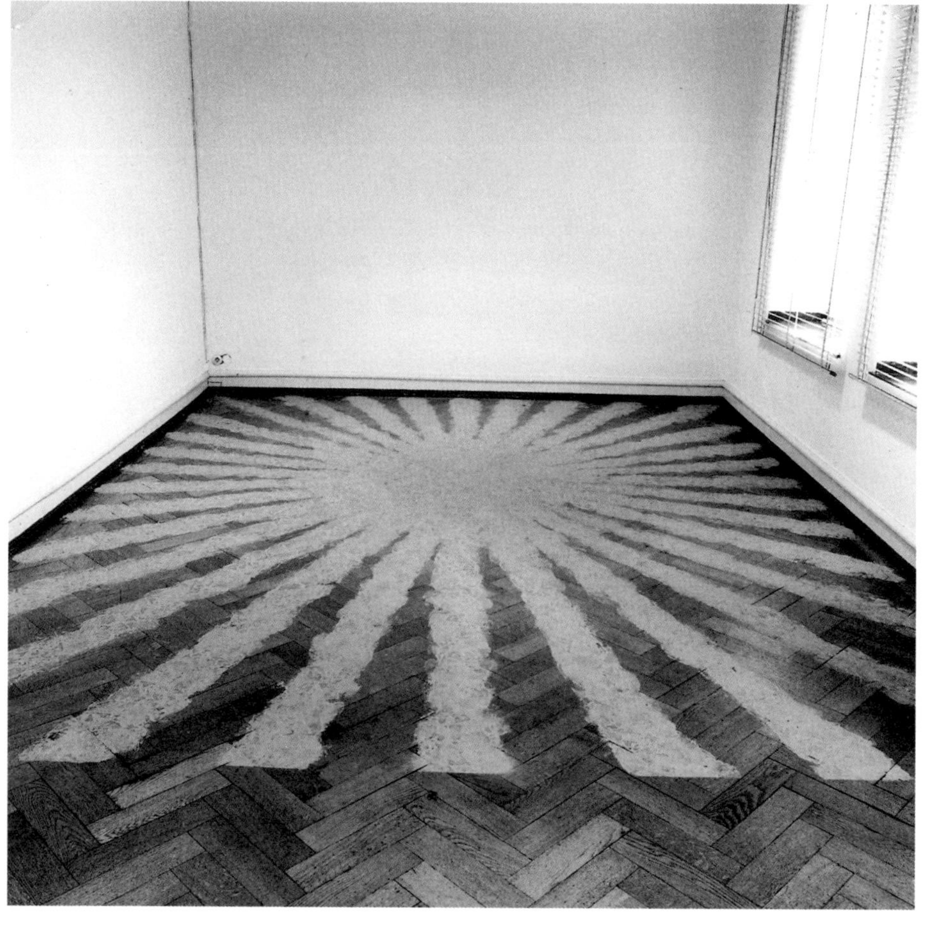

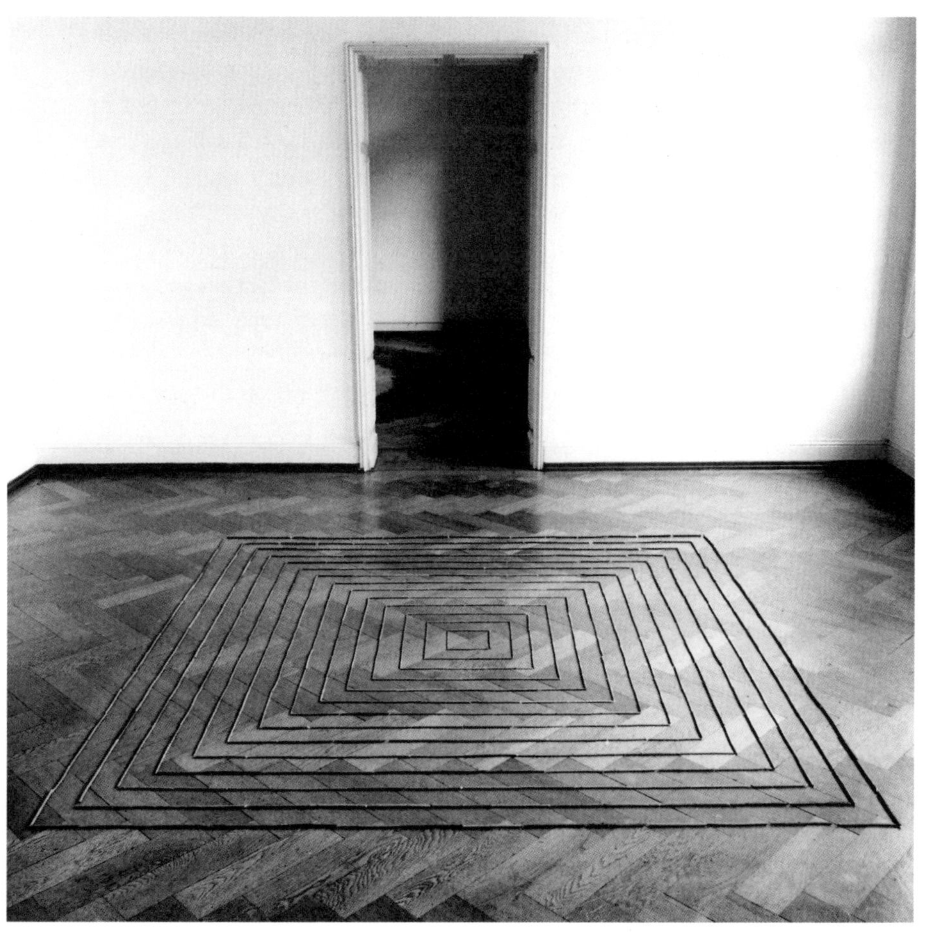

ELIZABETH BAKER

Richard Long at Dwan Gallery

New York, 3 – 29 October 1970

[The] young English artist, Richard Long, has evolved an unusually complex and personal mode among the international contingent of earthworkers. In his new show were two characteristically understated, lyrical and multi-referential pieces, both closely related to his more familiar landscape-sited works. One was a pale grey clay track of Long's footprints, wound up into a spiral nicely filling the confines of the room. The track was walked over several times, the footprints casually but quite neatly superposed. The track refers to a real outdoor situation: Silbury Hill, a prehistoric mound, the largest man-made hill in England. It has been partly excavated but nothing has been found – its purpose and origins are unknown. Long has included a local legend about the hill on his exhibition announcement. (The devil intended to set the hill down on a town; the town's most virtuoso liar tricked the devil into dropping it in an open space instead.) Long's walked spiral is the exact length of a path from the bottom to the top of Silbury Hill. The concept of duration, of distance, of walking, of traces of the artist's presence in a specific locale are all important factors in Long's thinking. The peculiar balance between an arbitrary visual form and a perhaps whimsical but completely specific 'subject' or place, the modest physicality and moderate scale, all contribute to the personal quality of what Long does. Many of his pieces, in fact, seem 'English' – subtly picturesque, even pastoral. Spectators may walk at will over the clay foot-track – while the clay is tenacious, the piece is ultimately ephemeral. The other work in the show is off-limits for wandering, intended just to be seen, and will continue to exist: it comprises concentric circles laid out on the floor – thin contours formed of wooden sticks. The circles are a variant of a recurrent formal motif which he has insinuated into numerous landscape situations (grass, woods, hillside, beach pebbles, etc.). The placement flat on the carpet is as straightforward as, say, a Carl Andre floor piece, but the sensibility is more fragile and the piece far more dematerialised than Andre even at his most linear.

Art News, vol.69, no.7, November 1970, p.22.

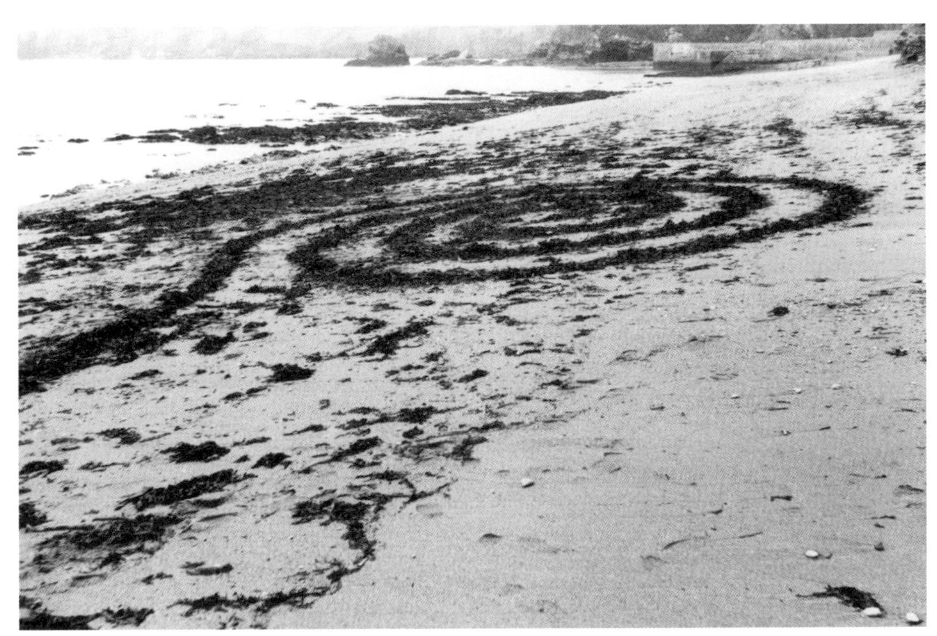

A SCULPTURE LEFT BY THE TIDE
CORNWALL 1970

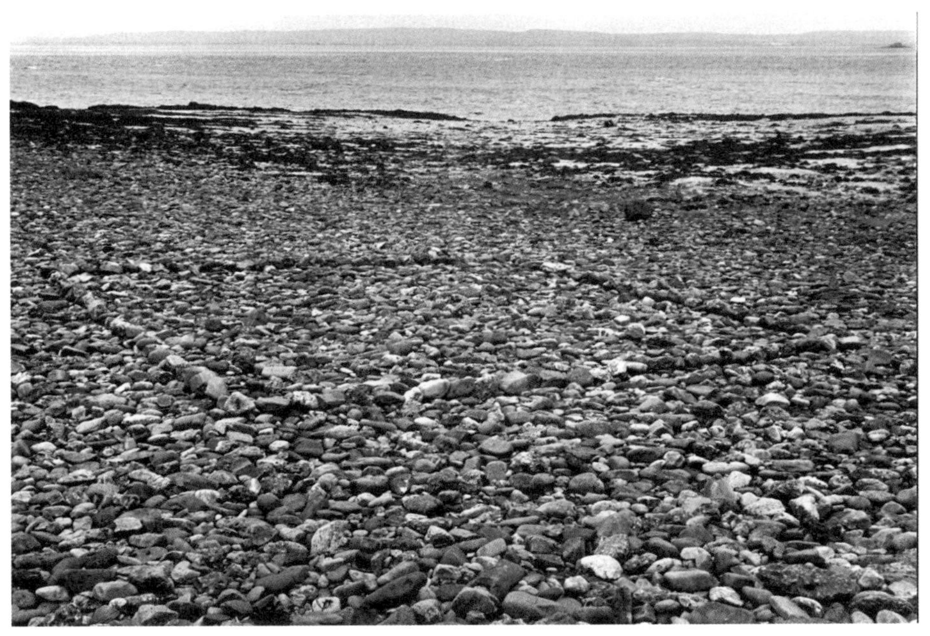

A SOMERSET BEACH
ENGLAND 1968

CAROLINE TISDALL

Richard Long at the Whitechapel Gallery

London, 9 – 21 November 1971

From a mountain top in Africa
To a Tennessee riverbed brushing
through the hoar frost
Magic signs, secret journeys,
A portrait of the artist touching
the earth.[1]

Richard Long is an artist who has spent most of the past four years walking. The lines above, he feels, should act as a key to his work. He is concerned with ritual and myth, with the abstract demarcations man makes on the surface of the earth, and the traces he leaves of his passing. The landscape itself provided the material for his sculpture, and to it he applies geometry, and concepts of time and space.

He shrugs off the label 'conceptual', if anything 'land' artist would be more appropriate, and as such he is recognised particularly by other artists in the United States and Germany as England's leading exponent. The exhibition at the Whitechapel with photographic records of his past four years' activity and two specially constructed pieces is his first showing in this country. Nothing is random in Long's approach, though he has several different ways of working that complement each other, and following his line of thought should be helpful for those who are perplexed by this sort of activity. The most traditional is to set up on a rocky beach, say a circle of wood, or to drape over the peak of Mount Kilimanjaro lengths of cloth. In these, whatever the artist does is largely dictated by the formation of the land – the rocks interrupt the circle of wood and the mountain directs the flow of the material. It is not so very different from the placing of a traditional piece of sculpture in a landscape.

The material of the landscape itself may be redistributed: turf is cut and built into a raised ring; seaweed on a Cornish beach is arranged into one of the spirals that crop up again and again in the work of artists who have 'turned to the land': each site and material used has a different time connotation; the next tide will wash away the spiral on the beach, or cover the cross cut in a mudflat, but the turf circle becomes part of the landscape.

The most transient are the traces left in grass. They represent the number of times the artist passes over the same spot. The more times the deeper the trace. The only trace left once the grass straightens will be the photographic record, the measure of an activity. Permanent marks left by transient land on the landscape, traces, motions of time, all these are indications of Long's feeling for prehistory and the recurring images that link the legend and myth of primitive peoples. The labyrinthine pattern carved by a craftsman in Connemara, Ireland in 2000BC is laid out anew in stone on a larger scale so that it becomes a walkable labyrinth. The spiral laid out in the gallery traced in plastery footsteps echoes this ritual pattern-making, though enclosed and without the natural context, the result is less evocative.

The abstract demarcations of land that man respects become another theme. The equator is an ideal example. When Long reached it in Africa he did a little dance, zigzagging backwards and forwards across it, from one hemisphere to another. The photographic record is juxtaposed with a distant shot of a Masai tribesman glimpsed at a distance standing on one leg and frozen against a desert background. That, Long says, is how he would like people to come across him going about his activities – captured in the eye for an instant.

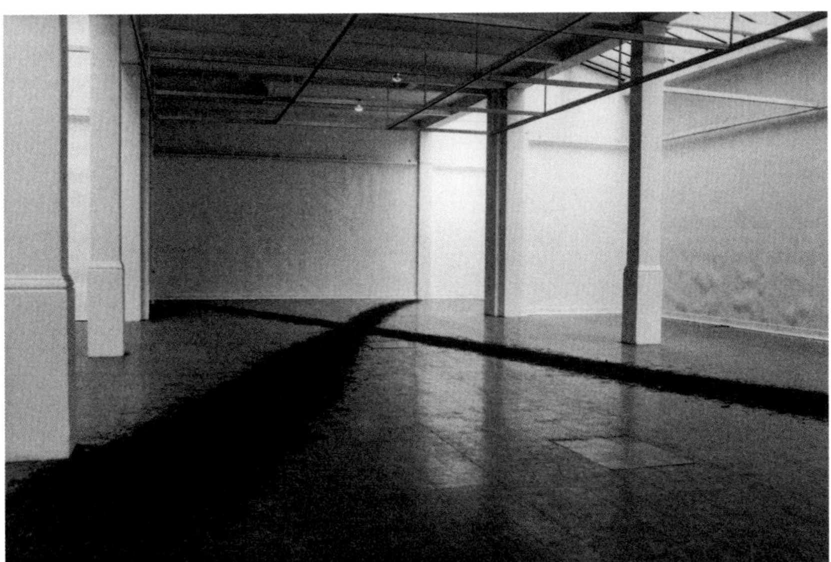

Pine Needles, Whitechapel Gallery, London 1971

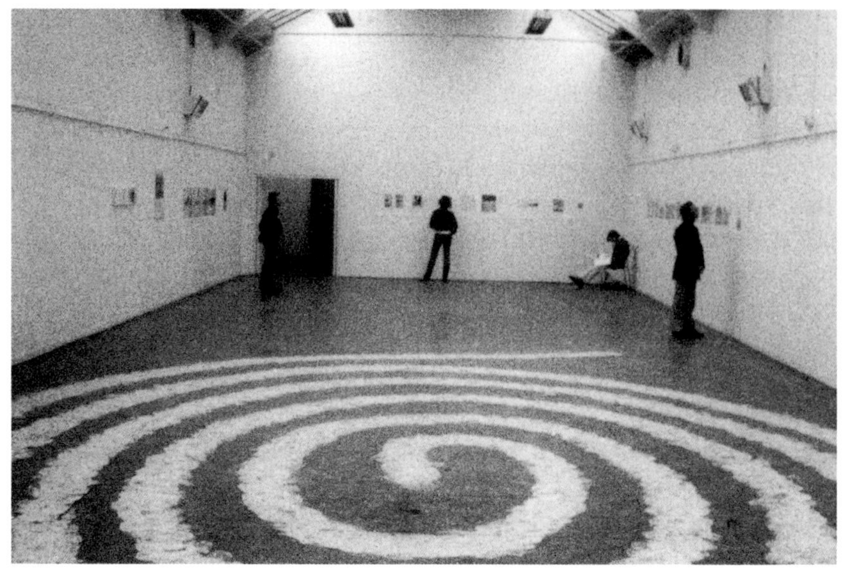

A Line the Length of a Straight Walk from the Bottom to the Top of Silbury Hill, 1970, Whitechapel Gallery, London 1971

The natural camouflage of animals, the stripe of the zebra echoed on the soil; an old Tennessee Indian's belief in the power of a circle to keep wolves out: for Long all these things are bound in time, space and geometry, and it only needs one man's vision to provide the link.

The Guardian, 16 November 1971, p.8.

1 From a statement by the artist, see pp.292.

CHARLES HARRISON

Richard Long at the Whitechapel Gallery

London, 9 – 21 November 1971

The majority of Richard Long's 'sculpture'[1] displays a narrow repertoire of basic configurations: straight lines (walked in grass, over landscapes – as recorded on survey maps etc.), circles (in white-painted wood on grass or sand, depressed or elevated in grass or sod), squares (in stones among stones on a beach, walked in Wiltshire etc.), crosses (in stones among stones on a riverbed, in pine needles, 'reserved' by picking off the heads of daisies in a field or by removing seaweed from a beach, walked in dust on grass), triangles (on sand in Kenya) and spirals (in seaweed on a tidal beach, in footprints of dried clay on a gallery floor, in rocks on the Isle of Skye). The evident and uncomplicated geometricality of the form asserts its origin in human activity and thus prepares the spectator for consideration of the 'interaction' between artist and environment.[2]

So far as the sculptures themselves are concerned, Long's sense of occasion has almost always been impeccable – since his first public appearance at the *Young Contemporaries* in 1968.[3] His floor pieces employing small sticks as units in basically geometric and linear patterns are comparatively self-contained and have characteristically been devised for gallery or other indoor situations.[4] Several more recent works like those at the Whitechapel consist of 'paths' of dried muddy footprints or carpets of pine needles; in these some more or less specific reference is made to features and contexts of landscape and to origins in more or less specific places. The out-of-door works are the least easily circumscribed and the most problematic in terms of conventional notions of 'arthood' and 'spectatorship', but there can be no question of their originality and attractiveness.

In every case the particular configuration is carefully related to the context in which it is to be seen; or rather, in the outdoor works, the 'character' – geology, flora, climate, history (subjective in personal association or objective in record) etc. – as it impinges upon the artist, decisively influences him in the selection, placing and 'construction' of his configurations. In certain outdoor works of 1966–67, Long used easily transported and easily assembled wooden elements, or the ubiquitous sticks. But it seems that to an increased extent Long's outdoor 'sculptures' have been 'realised' in materials which not only came readily to hand in a given context, but which can be seen as conveying what has been for him the essential in the 'character' of that context.

The materialist observer of sculpture might feel it desirable to be able to assert that the recognition of potential in a given material 'ingredient of the scene' is what renders a 'place' suitable to enshrine a sculpture. The (presumably) opposite position to take would be that in which the 'feel of the place' is seen as being the stimulus to a search for the material which would most effectively embody that sensation in an appropriate configuration.

Neither approach in isolation would be likely to offer much purchase upon the singular nature of Long's involvement with landscape – nor indeed upon any art in which such an involvement is of paramount importance (though of course it has previously only made sense in the Western tradition to apply to painting the notion of a first-order involvement with landscape).

What seems to me distinctive in the more successful of Long's activities is the intensity, consistency and detail of his experience and observation of place. It is the distinction of the man who knows the mark upon every tree along a given path; knows how his world changes with the seasons; has as his norms of distance specific distances travelled in particular known places, and as norms of scale similarly particularised memories of seeing, relating and traversing.

When such a person travels, he carries with him habits of observation sharpened over long periods through intimate acquaintance with a place he is leaving. There is a particularly English kind of nostalgia which we associate with such journeys and the resulting travelogues. It is a mood which can be identified with aspects of certain traditions, most of them insular and most of them literary, at best involving a rare blend of original imagination and acute and educated observation. Against Long's work the gigantisms of Michael Heizer, the pseudo-mythologising obsessions of Robert Smithson and the self-documenting desecrations of Dennis Oppenheim seem like the works of boors and egotists.

The comparative discreteness of Long's work generates a certain reserve in the presentation. 'Supportive' information is kept to a minimum. But any transmission from one medium to another involves the possibility of 'interference', and while Long's indoor works pose no real problems in this respect (for the 'educated' contemporary viewer), the indoor representation of outdoor works necessitates the use of maps and photographs. The result is an inevitable confusion in the ontology of the thing viewed,[5] which, insofar as one can see no possibility of clarification within the existing range of conventional relationships between 'work' and 'viewer', implies a far wider confusion as to what can justifiably be claimed about what 'is' the 'art ingredient' in any situation in which these relationships pertain.

Nowadays few dealers or collectors can afford entirely to respect even common-sense notions about the relative status and inherent uniqueness or reproducibility of the different ingredients in the artists' output (as 'art', as 'evidence', as 'documentation', as 'record', as 'working drawing', as rubbish or whatever). Long has been far more stringent in these matters than the majority of artists working frequently in the landscape, and this might be justified as an observation implying relative quality in his work – if nothing else, it's a sign of self-respect. But even Long's work raises questions of status in the end result which are critical, and which can never, for all Long's comparative fastidiousness, be divorced from the circumstances – cultural, social and economic – in which 'value' (of any kind) is attributed.

If these questions remain unanswered, or even unacknowledged, the work will remain isolated or isolationist. The status of the primary art object is culturally entrenched by a long tradition of financial and transubstantiating transactions which involve recognition of that object's uniqueness – its non-reproducibility. The 'documentary record' – photograph-plus-signature or whatever – of the otherwise evanescent or non-material 'work' has no such inherent historicity, no consequent 'special privileges', and no real custom of appropriate transactions to set precedents for evaluation. We might come to decide that the proliferation of short-term art histories and of fundamentally dubious criteria of worth is too high a price to pay to maintain a situation in which artists can ignore many of the most critical aspects of their own function.

Studio International, vol.183, no.940, January 1972, pp.33–43.

1 Long's usage. The less orthodox alumni of the St Martin's sculpture course seem to cling to this term with a mixture of devotion and irony which must irritate many of their former mentors.
2 Long has referred to his work as, 'A portrait of the artist touching the earth.'
3 His work had been independent for two years before this date. He was a highly influential student at St Martin's and became at once an internationally influential artist after his first one-man exhibition, at Konrad Fischer Galerie in Dusseldorf in September 1968. Carl Andre was among those who saw and admired this exhibition.
4 Usually about eight inches long and of nearly uniform thickness. They are cut from Leigh Woods near Long's home in Bristol.
5 Long's *A Ten Mile Walk* (1968) in the film *Land Art* (1969) (TV Galerie Gerry Schum) is an exception; it is also one of the few works made on film so far with a structure which one might be prepared to identify as 'proper' to the 'plastic arts'.

APRIL KINGSLEY

Projects: Richard Long, The Museum of Modern Art

New York, 14 March – 17 April 1972

Richard Long's seven concentric rectangles of red mud on the floor of a small gallery relate directly (as did his spiralling mud footpaths at the Guggenheim) to the surrounding architectural space. The result resembles something like an Indian sand painting based on a Frank Stella configuration, and does not resonate as sculpture. It does, by virtue of having been walked into existence, relate to the other, more conceptual works included in this mini-retrospective. In an odd way, many of these works – collages of juxtaposed statements, maps, diagrams and photographic documentation – have more sculptural connotations than the mud pieces. This is especially true of the earlier ones, such as *Ben Nevis Hitchhike* (1967), which obviously depends upon the same systems developed by Douglas Huebler for presenting a sculptural idea for a work which could never be perceived directly. The documentation enables the viewer to grasp the structure of the work conceptually. More recent works (in spite of a fey-Wordsworthian flavour which is reminiscent of Gilbert & George) have a new poeticism which seems to express Long's intentions more explicitly. As his various 'X's, spirals and rectangles 'walked into' the landscape over the years seem to indicate, it appears that Long wants to defy Pablo Picasso's dictum that 'Art is what nature isn't' by fusing art and nature in a manner much like that of the builders of Stonehenge, though far less permanently. The configurations he imposes on the landscape can't have that meaningful longevity, but their ephemeral beauty is touching.

Art News, vol.71, no.3, May 1972, p.52.

MARINA VAIZEY

Ideas into Art – Richard Long at the Lisson Gallery

London, 23 January – 24 February 1973

Ideas into art is a particularly relevant phrase at the moment, when a large part of the avant-garde is coping with what has come to be called Conceptual art. A remarkable exhibition of the work of the young British artist, Richard Long, has just opened at the Lisson Gallery, London. Richard Long does not like making statements or talking about his work, rather obviously feeling that it is all there to be seen. And so it is; he is concerned with two aspects of the same activity, that is, either himself making marks, trails, traces in landscape, or finding the marks, traces and age-old things other civilisations have left. What he presents, with great clarity, is a collection of aide-memoire, of souvenirs, of such activity.

This aspect of his work is presented in a series of photographs and maps. In a recent visit to Peru, he found in the high desert, lines in the crumbled rock left by a civilisation we know very little about. Some of these lines he walked again, and photographed the marks in landscape of his work. Or he made a water sculpture in desert sand, by pouring water to make a cross-shaped or 'X' indentation in the surface of the sand, and photographing that before evaporation made his 'sculpture' invisible again. Or he made a circle of stones in landscape, or arranged branches in such a way that his arrangement formally echoed the apparently haphazard natural arrangement of the spiky desert growths. There is a photograph of some strange and weathered upright rocks, linked by a horizontal rock slab, the link was made by some ancient civilisation, a miniature Peruvian Stonehenge.

Interspersed among this immaculately presented photographic record of marks and trails and paths made in and out of landscape by ancient Peruvian civilisations, and by Long himself, are traces left by the artist nearer home. But these, in the shape of the recording of walks such as *A Walk of Four Hours and Four Circles* (1972) marked on a map of Dartmoor Forest, or another walk in the shape of an 'X' marked on a map of Fernworthy Forest, are again juxtaposed by the photographic record of marks by other peoples in landscapes such as the Cerne Abbas Giant.

Richard Long's work is concerned with the interaction of man and landscape, not in the usual conventional sense of man as farmer, man as settler, but man acting out ritual; and leaving in fields of grass or in miles of desert, marks related to magic, and religion. One of the photographs shows, for instance, a Richard Long arrangement of campfire ash in the shape of a zigzag line arranged on a piece of rock, an echo in ritualistic intensity of the Inca Rock which is the subject of the other photograph contained in the same picture frame.

Richard Long either photographs what is there already, in terms of man-made traces of some long-ago magical-religious activity, or makes his own traces, in terms of walks, or arrangements of stones in spirals or circles. But he also makes things out of natural untreated materials such as the floor sculpture made out of pine needles which was shown at the Whitechapel; and there is a stone sculpture at the Lisson, made up of 198 weathered large seaside pebbles, which are beautiful things in themselves, although our awareness of the subtleties of the stone colours, sometimes almost rosy, sometimes greyish-yellow, depends in part on the fact of coming upon these

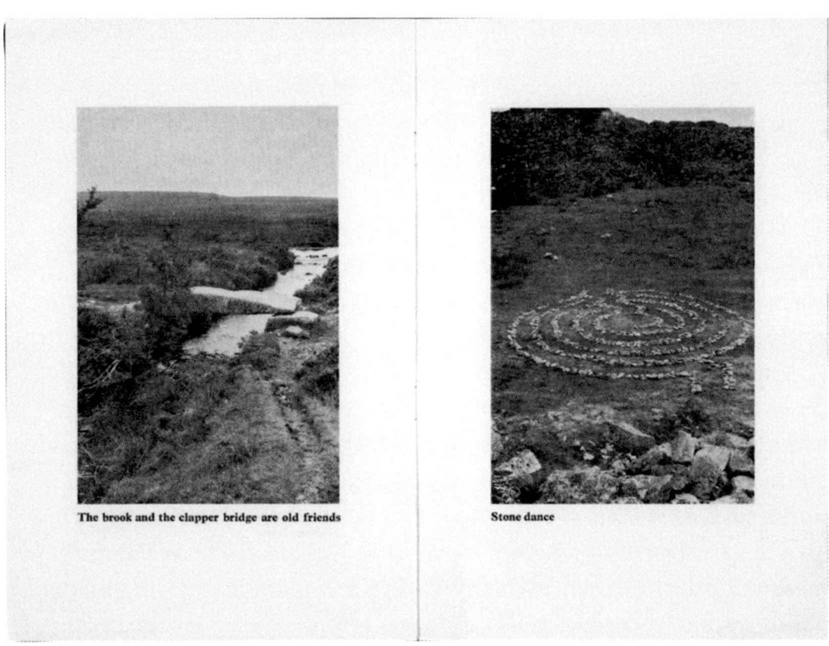

Two sheepdogs cross in and out of the pasing shadows
The clouds drift over the hill with a storm 1971

stones in an art gallery. The stones are arranged in two open-ended ziggurats, which are terminated by the walls of the gallery room, linked one to the other by a line of stones extending from the middle of each base, or top, depending on how one wants to look at it.

His work is the use of natural materials, so natural that we often overlook them, in a ceremonial, ritualistic manner, and where others have anthropomorphised animals, Richard Long touches on some deeply primitive chord in the manner in which he infuses landscape elements with a kind of vitality we assume as the perogative of animate life. This is abundantly clear in his book of photographs with captions such as 'The hilltop can see the sea on a fair day,' or 'The stones move a little every day towards a meeting place,' or 'The brook and the clapper bridge are old friends', published by the Lisson in 1971, with the title *Two sheepdogs cross in and out of the passing shadows The clouds drift over the hill with a storm*. By flinging himself into landscapes apparently deserted by man, by finding traces of man's ritualistic activity in these landscapes, and by making his own marks and traces in these unpopulated areas or sections of landscape, whether they be Peruvian deserts, English forest, or Scottish island, Richard Long jogs our vision of the natural world and certain aspects of the human relationship to that world in a manner analogous, despite all the startling difference of technique and method, to the great landscape *painters* of the past. He extracts art from landscape by virtue of his own physical activity in landscape, or by using the camera to record the traces of other human activity in the making of marks in landscape.

Like all apparently revolutionary art, what Long does is to give a twist to our vision by communicating what he sees and finds; the crucial difference between his art and other more traditional modes is that Long doesn't transform or transmute what he finds, but by using the raw materials of a particular landscape – grass, pine needles, stones, whatever – makes things which in a singularly intense manner act as analogues for human activity in landscape, and he also records with maps or photographs the actual traces of such activity. Like much present-day art, his activity is intensely self-conscious; but like all meaningful art, it 'works' because it touches on some atavistic response in the human psyche. His mode of presentation is startling, and refreshing; yet it too is but another example of 'attitude into form' that infuses those two very different exhibitions at the Royal Academy.

The Financial Times, 30 January 1973, p.3.

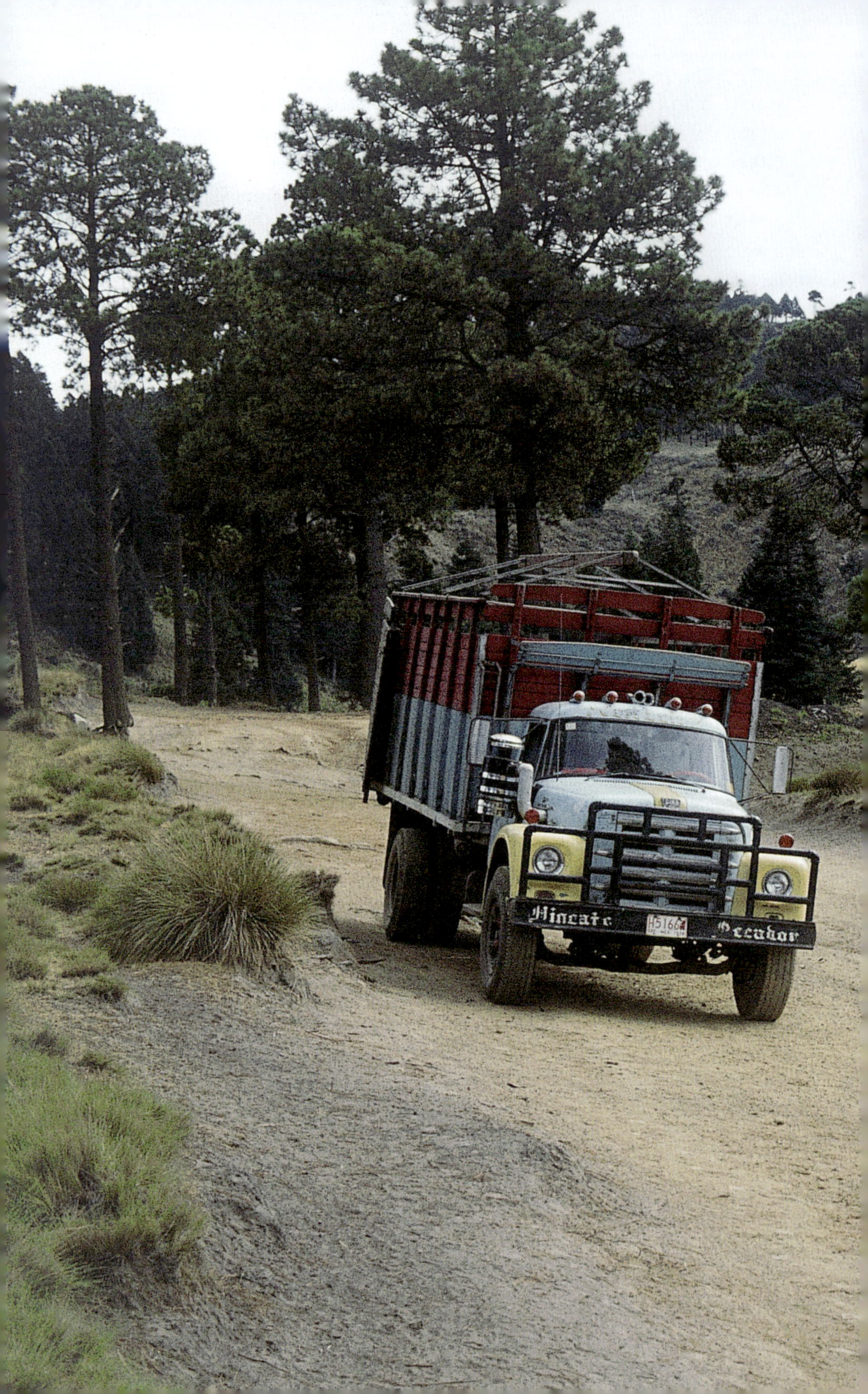

Richard Long, Mexico 1979

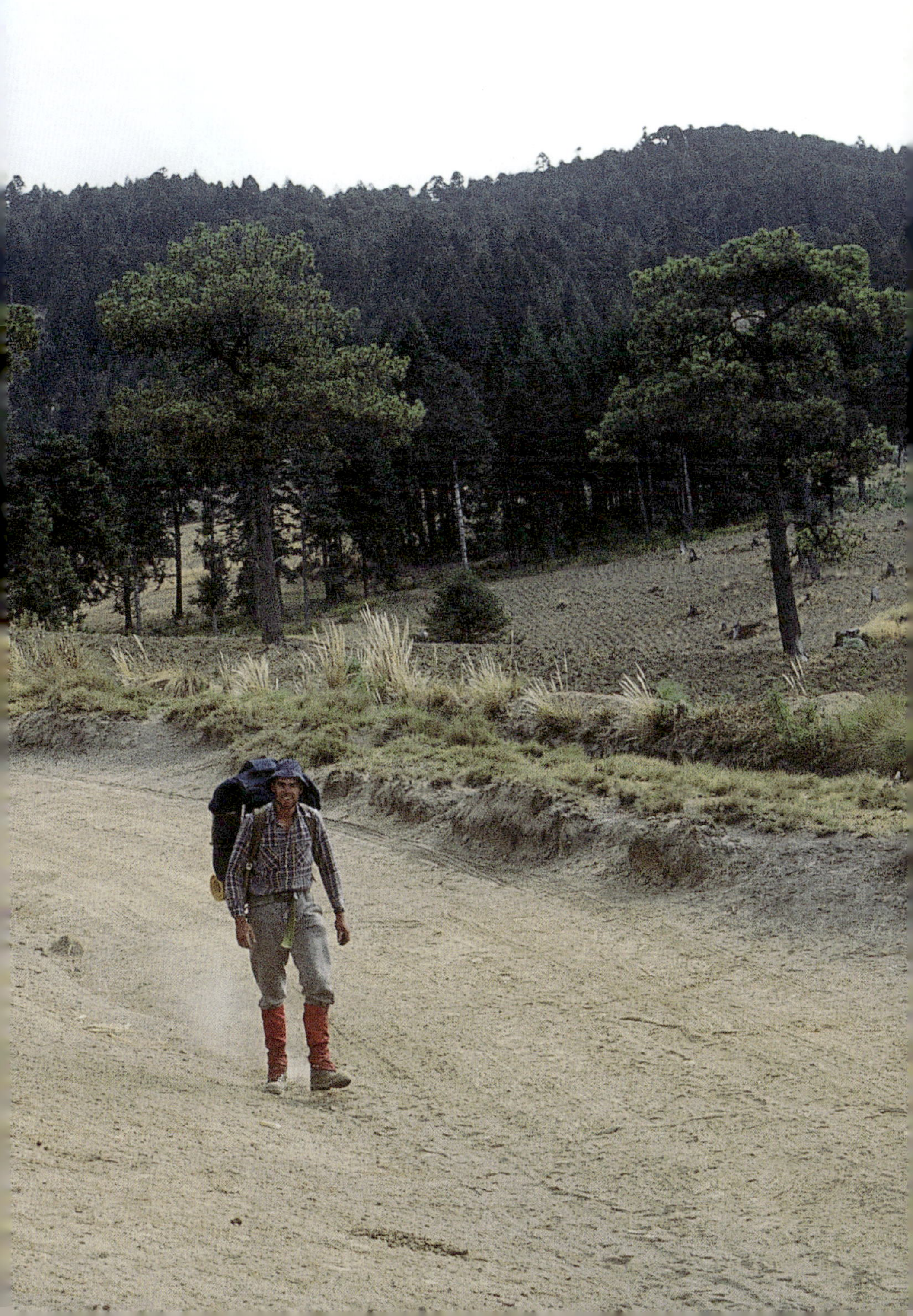

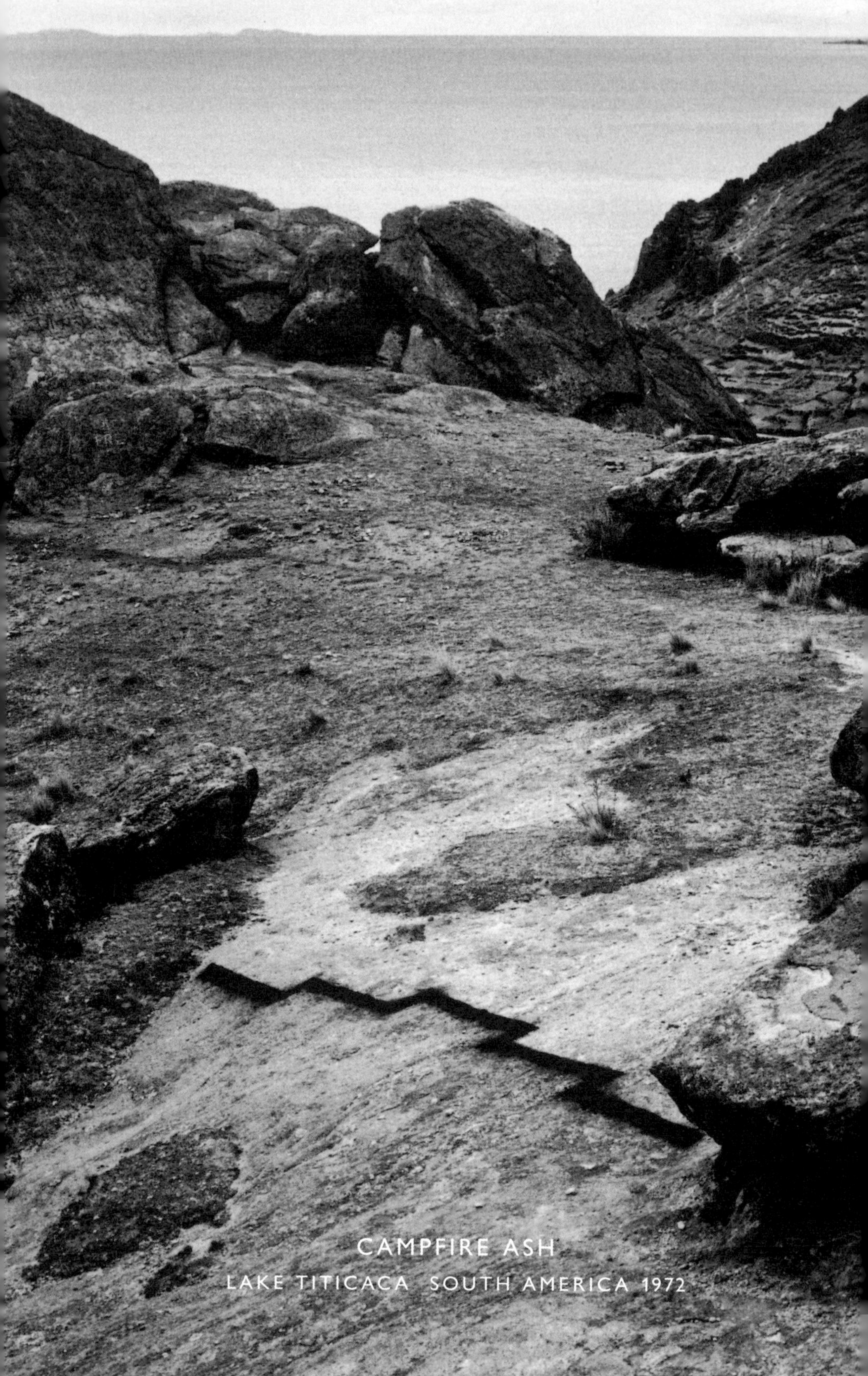

CAMPFIRE ASH
LAKE TITICACA SOUTH AMERICA 1972

RICHARD CORK

Long's Stony Road to Success

Lisson Gallery, London, 23 January – 24 February 1973

Richard Long has always called himself a sculptor. But his determination to leave the studio, move into the land and make his work out of the natural elements which he finds there, would seem above all to rebel against sculpture as most people know it.

Or so I thought when I wrote about his last London exhibition at the Whitechapel just over a year ago, and concluded that he had mounted a frontal attack on so many aspects of our sculptural tradition.[1]

Now, however, Long's new show at the Lisson Gallery appears to me to contain no hint of controversy or dissent: his activities are as simple and direct as those anonymous prehistoric men who like him, carved their ideas and emotions into the chalk hillsides of the English countryside.

The sense of isolation and privacy is still strong, certainly; yet the overriding feel of his work is gentle rather than militant, and only implies a rejection of other sculptors' conventions by quietly pursuing its single-minded aims.

In contrast with many other Land artists, who are tempted by the sheer scale of the territory they employ to indulge in overblown gestures and an almost boorish disregard for their chosen locations, Long takes his cue from the possibilities inherent in his site. As sensitive as a hunter to the spoor left behind by his animal prey, he never blunders into a landscape and imposes preconceived ideas regardless of their setting.

On a recent trip to South America he camped near a huge stone gateway erected by the Incas on a dramatic hilltop overlooking a panoramic expanse of water; but he was not tempted to vie with that spectacle and erect an alternative colossus nearby.

He simply took a photograph of the existing structure, cropped it halfway down to emphasise the way in which the Incas also managed to preserve the natural character of the stones they used, and then joined it to another photograph of an angular shape which he formed out of ash from the campfire.

The juxtaposition of these two images, ostensibly so different in their intentions, is thereby left to impinge on the viewer. And quietly, without any prodding on Long's part, they become linked through their shared understanding of what the place itself demands. He does not even presume to disrupt the landscape with materials of his own: they arise out of the given situation as surely as the stepped pattern assumed by the scorch-marks of the ash.

More often than not, Long's sculpture is rooted to such a self-effacing degree in the scene he selects that it seems as much a part of nature as the strata of a rocky outcrop or the meandering path pursued by a stream.

ROMANCE

A photograph of a stone circle lying in front of a mountain range hardly appears to have been arranged by him at all: it looks entirely inevitable, reflecting Long's realisation that all he needed to do was reveal an existing form by extracting some stones from the middle of the ring. Any suggestion of artifice is therefore dispelled, and along with it all trace of the sculptor as a maker of assertive, breast-beating declarations of personal power and authority.

Long's art stands at the very opposite pole from those who seek to impress with bulk, solidity and monumental excess.

He makes most other sculpture look melodramatic or clumsily overweight, even though his involvement with the romance of walks, journeys and 'sacred places' could easily lead a less disciplined temperament to lose his way in clouds of mystical rhetoric. The romanticism is there all right, allied to a feeling for communion between man and the earth which connects immediately with a time-honoured English love of travel, exploration, even discovery.

And yet there are no pioneering heroics attached to Long's wanderings. The prevailing mood tempers imaginative insight with the understatement of an artist who knows precisely how little is needed to convey the full immensity of his response.

There could easily be something simple-minded, precious or inadequate about his decision to walk across one line of a mysterious tracery of indentations left in the Peruvian desert generations ago by a forgotten tribe. But the result, photographed from a viewpoint which shows it as one soft stroke of white whispering its way across the ground until it tapers into a range of hills behind, combines certitude and poetry to a rare degree.

Treading, subtracting, disclosing, sifting, trailing, supplementing, pointing, touching, laying, imparting: these are a few of the strategies which Long more than anyone else I know has added to the language of sculpture.

He pares his intervention down to a limpid essence that threatens to become feebly passive and low-key, but manages instead to convey an epic intensity. Even when he leaves the landscape altogether and installs a floor-space in a gallery the understanding of scale, shape and particular materials is carried over intact from the rural to the urban environment.

The tightly organised sequence of rectilinear relationship charted with pebbles on the Lisson's white floorboards represent a pattern which has been at once inspired by Long's South American experiences and aroused by the space he was presented with here.

ENJOYMENT

What happens, however, to the Lisson's pebble installation once it is purchased by a collector and placed in a totally different setting?

That such questions do not rankle as much as they should or impede our enjoyment of the work is a tribute to Long's quality. But I hope that eventually he will go some way towards clarifying them, because every instinct tells me that here is a man set fair to become one of the finest artists England has ever produced.

The Evening Standard, 1 February 1973, p.28.

1 Review published in *The Evening Standard*, 18 November 1971.

ANNE SEYMOUR

Earthworks – Richard Long at the Lisson Gallery

London, 23 January – 24 February 1973

The Lisson Gallery is not a grand or very public place, but for the moment its white two-part space houses some of the finest pieces of sculpture on view in London today. Richard Long has an important place in the early-to-mid-sixties movement in which artists all over the world independently began to take what they were doing out into the context of real time and space, to work directly with the earth, with everyday objects, photographs, maps, ordinary language. This exhibition still retains some of the excitement of that radical step forward; but it also provides a clearer picture of the artist, because his work is broadening out and because there is less need now for aggressiveness about the context in which it has been achieved.

Long's concern is with things at their rawest, their simplest, their most pure. Though he works with the surface of the earth he doesn't cut it about in the lavish way some contemporary sculptors have. Perhaps this is something to do with being English. Perhaps it's indoor men who get apocalyptic out of doors. In any case, his endeavour is to see things in proportion, to look the ground in the eye. He has described what he does as a philosophical dialogue between the artist and the earth. The works which record his own actions – going for a walk, say – have a purposefulness which is essentially mysterious. In Kenya he spotted a tribesman standing on one leg watching something, ignoring chance passers-by, intent on his own business. Long seems to feel his presence should be regarded in the same way: private, a given part of the scheme of things.

One of his basic approaches is to take a simple geometrical shape and, instead of changing it physically according to a feeling for the place, as Barbara Hepworth might do, impose it whole upon the chosen site. The two things fuse, yet their separate identities remain distinct. The location imposes its modulations upon the geometrical form to produce a perfect shape which is also a kind of cast of the place, an image in its own likeness. Long's intuition of the essence of the place, his stringent selection of medium and configuration, produce something as unfathomable in origin as it is unerring in execution.

Working indoors, one way he creates an interpenetration of images is by transferring elements from his own environment to a particular site: sticks from woods near Bristol went to his 1968 show in Dusseldorf, stones from Westward Ho to the Hayward Gallery, the dimensions of Silbury Hill to New York. This time, in the small right-hand room in the Lisson, he has laid down a branching line of stones from a Somerset beach to form a double back-to-back South American ziggurat shape, the joining line starting in the middle of the room on the long axis and angling its downward path out to its farthest extremities where it runs along the walls. The pinkish stones, neat and graspable in size, give warmth and fullness to the small, totally bare secluded space. Their turning lines counterpoint the construction of the rectangular room and its relation to the rest of the gallery.

The photographs and maps which record the execution of physical actions without producing the actual results of those actions for inspection have been regarded more suspiciously, although it is probably in them that Long makes his most radical contribution. They contain possibilities beyond the wildest dreams of conventional sculpture. Not that Long is interested in an expanded scale in terms of size – it's the potential switches and juxtapositions of time and space, speed and terrain which are so astonishing in a traditional context.

The left-hand space at the Lisson Gallery is devoted to this kind of work. Six pieces, in wide white mounts and elegantly conservative

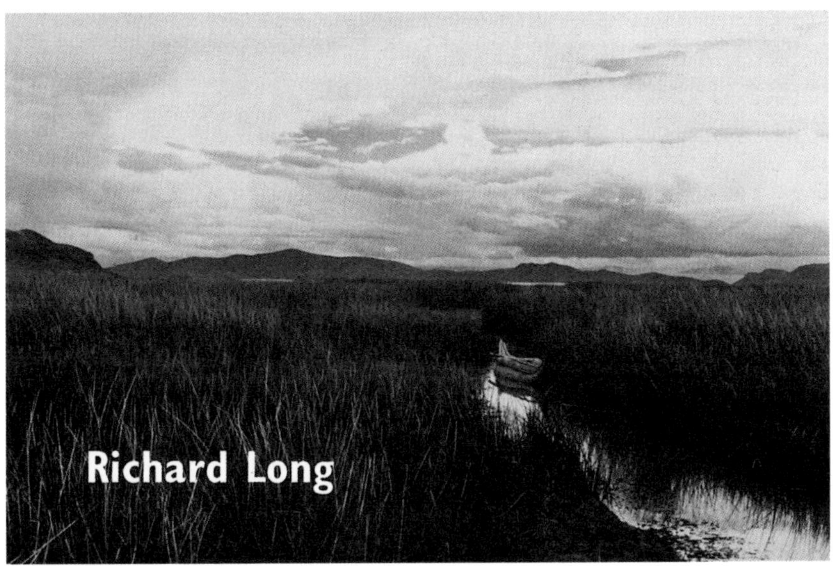

Exhibition invitation card, Lisson Gallery, London 1973

brown frames, are the fruit of Long's recent South American trip, which is the main subject of the show, but also included, giving them context, are three from home ground. A couple are maps recording specific walks on Dartmoor. One is made up of four concentric circles, each representing an hour's walk conditioned by the chosen terrain and the artist's own particular height, weight and build. The other is about the intersection of two walks: a photograph of an ancient monument called Bennett's Cross standing in a circular pool of rain has been stuck onto a square of Ordnance Survey map near the place where it is marked. Here on the map two diagonal lines representing two walks meet and pass one another at this signpost to many different levels of the past.

The relation of one image to another, creating a specific human situation, is the key to Long's work. But till now he seems to have made few pieces involving the direct correspondence of two photographs. There are several Peruvian and Bolivian pieces of this kind: for example a photograph of the geometrical pattern of his campfire ash juxtaposed with one of an Inca Rock silhouetted against the hills dropping down to Lake Titicaca. In another a feathery rectangle of pieces of llama-feed contrasts with a cross scuffed among discarded reeds near a place where they make reed boats; a creek with a boat close under the bank cuts its way through the marshes behind.

As the Saxon Giant of Cerne Abbas has his parallels with the great astronomical drawings at Nazca, the images in the South American pieces have their English counterparts; there are certain constant themes which have become part of Long's handwriting as an artist. But walking a line in the Peruvian desert is not the same as walking a line on English grass, the Pill Ferry is not the same as a Bolivian reed boat, a circle of stones in the Andes is very different from a circle of stones in Scotland. It is the touching and meaning of the touching that matters, respect for the area and the materials in the terms of presenting the area. Long can walk over the earth, rearrange it, drop pebbles on its back, and some may stick; the specific place is always the more important part of the sculpture.

There is magic in it perhaps, and strong medicine. The geometric symbols Long uses are part of the magic because they stand as signs and are not analysed as forms. After all, there is something disturbing about squares and circles. They were among the first things used by man and they will be among the last.

The New Statesman, 2 February 1973, p.173.

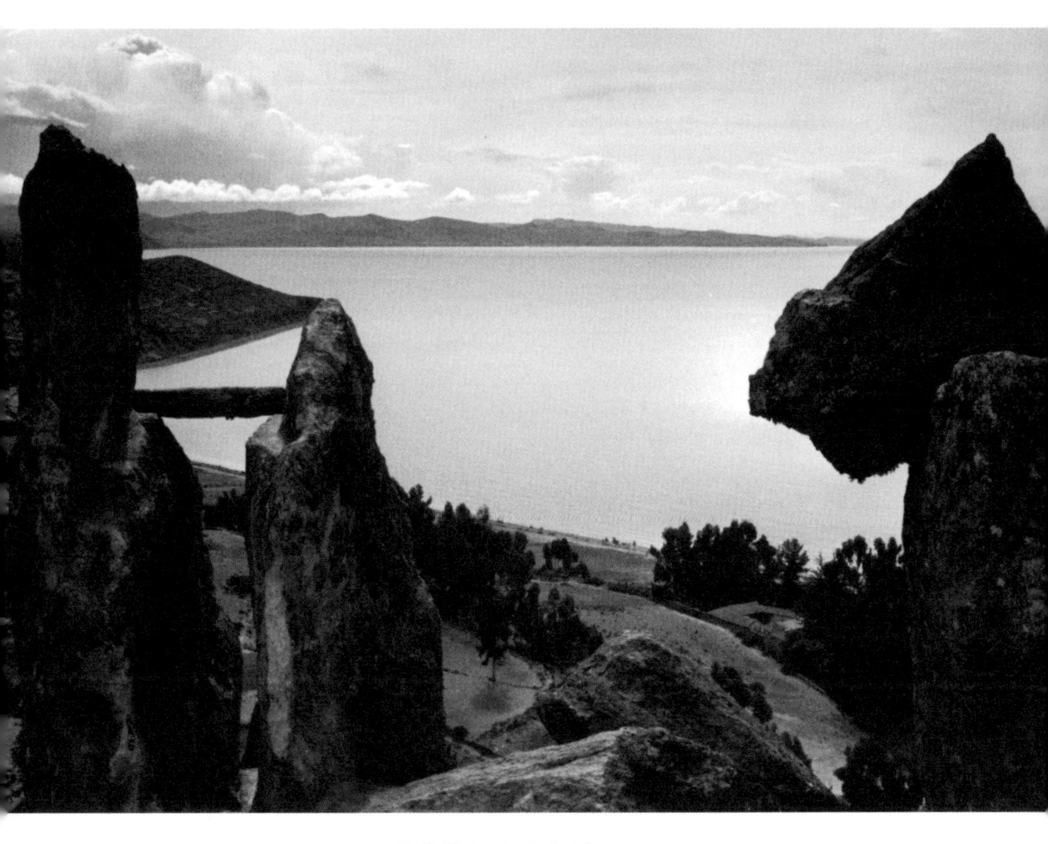

INCA ROCK

1972

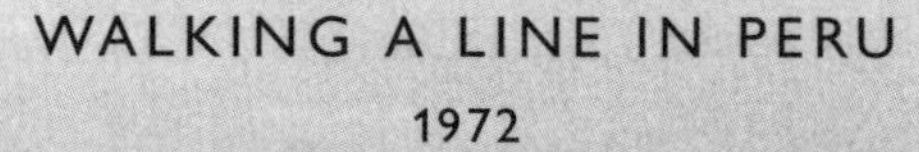

WALKING A LINE IN PERU

1972

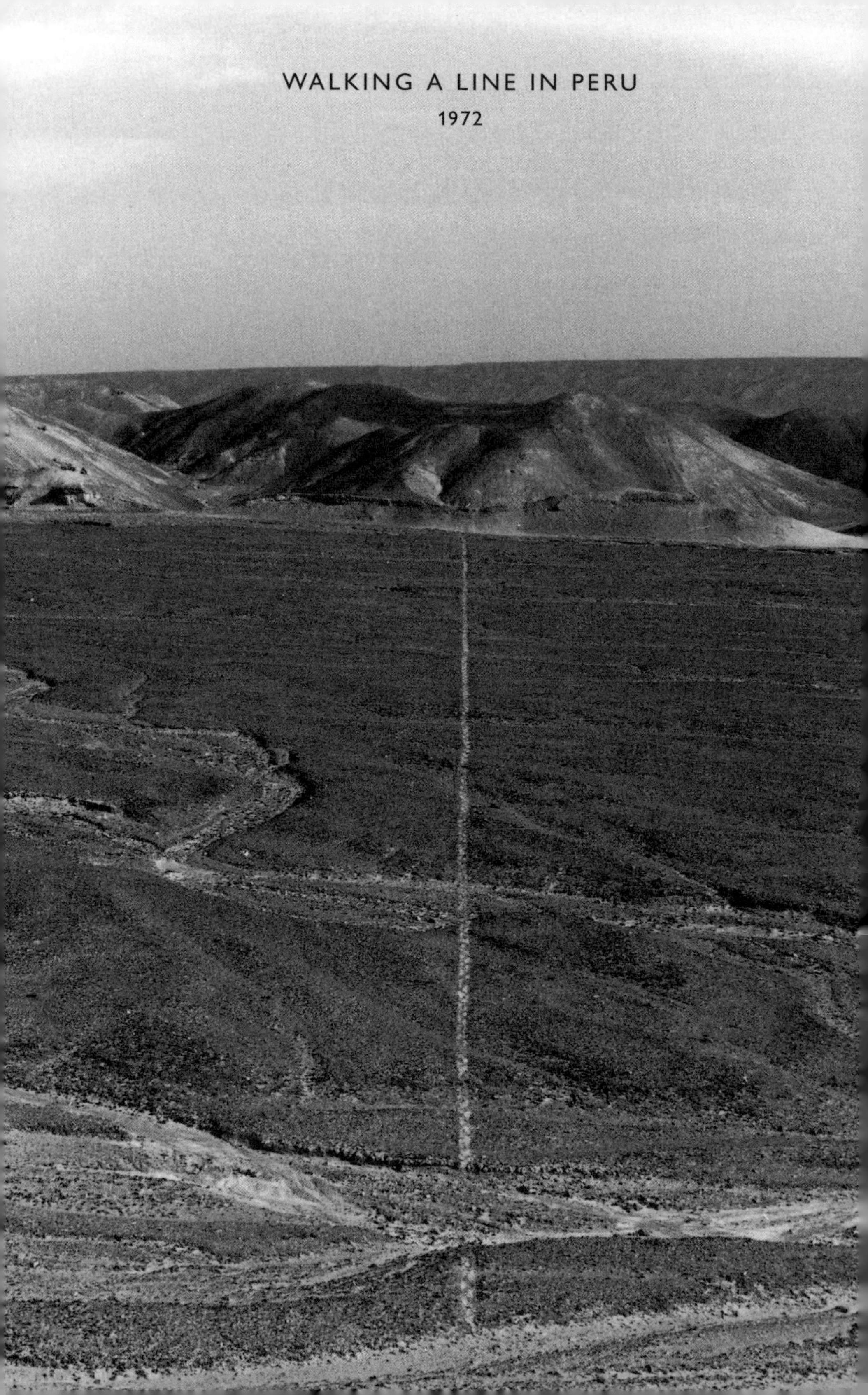

SIMON FIELD

Touching the Earth

Lisson Gallery, London, 23 January – 24 February 1973

> They inscribe a human meaning upon the hostile wastes of nature, in a graphic record of a forgotten but once important ritual. They are an architecture of two-dimensional space, consecrated to human actions rather than to shelter, and recording a correspondence between the earth and the universe… They are an architecture of diagram and relation, with the substance reduced to a minimum.
>
> George Kubler on the Nazca Lines, *The Shape of Time*, 1962

The redesigned Lisson Gallery has two spaces, separated by a single doorway. In Richard Long's recent show the one was occupied entirely by a sculpture of stones, the other by nine photographic and map pieces, the majority of them made on a recent trip to Bolivia and Peru; of the remainder, two were of Dartmoor walks, the third of the Cerne Abbas Giant in Dorset. The nine pieces, like Long's previous work, were photographs of places, usually where he had traced one of his 'sculptures': walked a line, a cross or made a circle of stones. As in the past, there was no explanatory material, just a simple evocative caption: *Two Sacred Places* (1972) or the briefest information: *A Walk of Four Hours and Four Circles* (1972).

One is left entirely alone to gauge Long's concerns, left with images and a presence that are extremely poetic, expressive of particular places, scale and time. The peculiar strength of Long's work is that behind this immediate poetry is a resonance that carries far beyond the gallery in which we stand, each work implies and involves all his others and furthermore, in this show, take their strength from and interlock with an even larger network of 'earthworks' from another time and another place.

Walking a Line in Peru (1972) is on the surface a simple piece. The photograph is taken from one side of a wide valley. Into the depth of the image and across the floor of the valley goes a thin walked line that disappears into the foothills in the distance. As in many of Long's photographs, scale is there but it's elusive, one can't judge how long

the walk would be. It's almost a lunar landscape, dry but with the marks of water, one wonders how long the line will remain.
The simplicity of the forms that Long uses has several consequences: not only are the line, the circle, the square, the cross fundamental to art, and common in ancient earthworks, but used as he uses them, they have three particular qualities that relate to that simplicity, which can be made clearer by a description of an earlier piece of Long's – bearing *Walking a Line in Peru* in mind. That earlier piece, another straight line, was done in 1968 at Redcliffe Bay in Somerset. On a very stony beach, the piece consisted of a single line of stones 14 feet long. With only a glance at the photograph it is hardly discernible against the haphazard shingle. The first distinctive quality is that the relationships are not between its component parts but directed outwards, thus its placement activates the whole environment, just as the first mark on a canvas activates the whole picture surface. Related to this is a second quality – made clear if one contrasts Long's work with that of say, Michael Heizer or Robert Smithson – of just 'touching the earth', simply arranging some stones, treading out a line. Unlike a Heizer hole or a Smithson jetty, the imposition is slight, a single man-made mark that draws attention to its context and the processes around it and not to itself (although inevitably the piece will be caught up in those processes: washed or blown away, grown over). It balances delicately in nature. Thirdly, each line sculpture relates to and echoes all of Long's other line sculpture, joined mentally through space, Peru to England; and through time, 1972 to pieces of 1967 and 1968. To illustrate Long's awareness of this: in 1967 he did a sculpture in eastern England – '16 similar parts placed irregularly surrounding an area of 2401 square miles. Near each part was a notice giving the information. Thus a spectator could only see one part (no information being given to locate the others), but have a mental realisation of the whole'. Similarly, each line sculpture can be seen as relating through space to all the others.

To return to *Walking a Line in Peru*: it carries these resonances and more, for Long was in that particular walk reactivating an old line and, by implication, a whole system of lines that cover the desert in this particular area of southern Peru and that have remained there since the first millennium and the Nazca culture that created them. It's worth quoting here at length from George Kubler, for the line that Long retraced is part of...

> an immense network of lines, stripes, spirals and effigies, all executed on a colossal scale upon the barren table lands above the Polpa and Ingencio rivers, in an area about 60 miles long and several miles wide. The weather-worn surface of small stones is dark, but the sand and gravel just underneath are much lighter in colour. The lines and stripes were formed by piling the dark surface stones along the side of the exposure. Many straight lines strike across the plateau and rise without lateral deflection up precipitous slopes to vanish inexplicably, going between points of no particular distinction without any pretence of serving as paths or roads. Certain modular measurements recur: lengths of 26m and 182m (seven times 26) have been ascertained. Miss Maria Reiche, who has patiently plotted and computed the plans and their possible use as astronomical sighting-lines, finds that some mark solstical and equinoctial points upon the horizon. Others may point to the rising and setting of certain stars, such as one in the constellation of Ursa Major, which coincided with the annual flood season in November at the beginning of the agricultural cycle.[1]

In a beautiful reciprocal act, Long in that walk reanimates and pays tribute to that extraordinary Nazca project and at the same time, with the same gesture incorporates it into his own. Their use of the shallow surface, the simple moving of stones, echoes Long's own methods and, one would imagine, appealed to him not least for its invisibility as a total structure. Not only are there lines, but the forms of a bird, a monkey, a tree and only visible from 30,000 feet up in the air, a point from which their creators could never have seen them. (Long had another piece in the Lisson show incorporating one of these lines which are almost invisible except when seen longitudinally – the piece is two photographs and entitled *Two Sacred Places* (1972) – the line in the desert is below, above it is Lake Titicaca with a contrasting climate and atmosphere. Near Titicaca is Tiahuanaco: 'no doubt a station for observations of the solar year, and as such it was the centre of the cosmos'.)[2]

Long's work centres around interrelationships and processes as implied by titles from an earlier piece: *Two sheepdogs cross in and out of passing shadows The clouds drift over the hill with a storm* (1971).[3] Not only a small or local scale, just around a piece that may or may not last – a cross made in seaweed – but through the fact that the pieces are open-ended on to a much larger scale. This is incorporated by this linking into systems, structures of a society that had elaborated a whole cosmology – a structure and balanced relationship between man, his earth and its universe. Both the Nazca and unknown builders of Stonehenge in 1850 BC (needing brains the equivalent of Einstein's according to Fred Hoyle) created monuments that are essentially sculpture locked into a whole system of thought and harmonised most particularly through reading of the stars with space and time, creating a calendar and a means of accurately calibrating time. The measurements of Silbury Hill, now being recognised as another 'gigantic sundial to determine the seasons and the true length of the year',[4] were incorporated by Long into a spiral at the Whitechapel.

Traditionally, sculpture has involved time in three dimensions: the time inscribed in its making, the time taken to look at it (incorporating its space) and its entry into the 'eternal' future time endowed upon the enduring art object. It's not hard to see how, in common with a number of other contemporary sculptors, Long's work reflects a complete upsetting of this situation (and with it of course other notions about the relationship between art, its objects and its galleries and museums) and how his work particularly, incorporates new aspects of time (and of states of being – a mark in campfire ash juxtaposed with an Inca Rock). That space and time are central to his work is implied by his caption to a photograph of the Cerne Abbas Giant:

> His eyes watch over a country mile
> The giant
> Walks on the hill
> One step
> For ever

and by the piece *A Walk of Four Hours and Four Circles* – the circles – on Dartmoor in an area with ancient circles – are concentric so the speed will be varied. In another earlier walking piece Long walked for one hour then marked the distance travelled on a map. Then on following days he walked that distance in four, eight, 16 then 32 hours. In the context of the rest of his work one can see how this is not simply a conceptual piece, but one that would involve an increasingly close knowledge of a repeatedly covered piece of ground, of its light, its colours and the changes, of its weather and, of course, its length of night and day, its balances of nature. The sculptor would have found himself in the essentially same relationship with his earth as the builders of Stonehenge, with no city or electricity or speed to alienate him from it.

The dimensions of time involved in pieces are natural durations. A cross at half-tide at Bertraghboy Bay will last little time at all, the circle in a dried-out lake in Bolivia could remain until the lake refills, or longer. A cross made by removing buttercup heads will exist until the other flowers die, the redrawn line in Peru could exist in a time dimension continuing way beyond the end of 'Western Civilisation'. Some exist (are brought back into existence?) now, as you read.

Certainly, the sculpture of stones in the gallery no longer exists in the form it did – and the form depends upon the place, the 'sculpture' is inseparable from its space. The sculptures indoors are distinct from the others, for rather than drawing attention to a place and its processes they draw in energy from their sources. Formally they act like minimal 'sculpture', a simple structure activating the space in which it exists – all the indoor pieces, at the Lisson, Hayward and Whitechapel, completely fill their allotted space, the spectator is inevitably involved in their dimensions. However, unlike minimal sculpture, they are not 'blank' or unrelated to anything but previous sculptural developments. The Lisson sculpture with its regular two-to-three-inch stones is in a stepped form reminiscent of Inca decorations – a form echoed in the campfire ash mark – like that mark, the drawing is recent, but the reference is back into history, the stones that shape the form are from a Somerset beach (perhaps Redcliffe Bay?) and carry with them their own time and form sculpted by the processes of a beach. The sculpture held in delicate, meditative balance with its own surroundings brings together widely differing spaces and times. One is reminded of literary critic Hugh Kenner's comment on the vortex: 'For the vortex is not the water but a patterned energy made visible by the water.' It is an apt analogy for the way Richard Long's sculptures operate.

Art & Artists, vol.8, no.1, April 1973, pp.15–19.

1 George Kubler, *Art and Architecture of Ancient America*, Penguin Books, Harmondsworth, 1962.
2 *Ibid.*
3 *Two sheepdogs cross in and out of the passing shadows The clouds drift over the hill with a storm*, Lisson Gallery Publications, London, 1971.
4 Andrew Davidson, *Silbury Hill in Britain – A Study in Patterns*, RILKO, 1971.

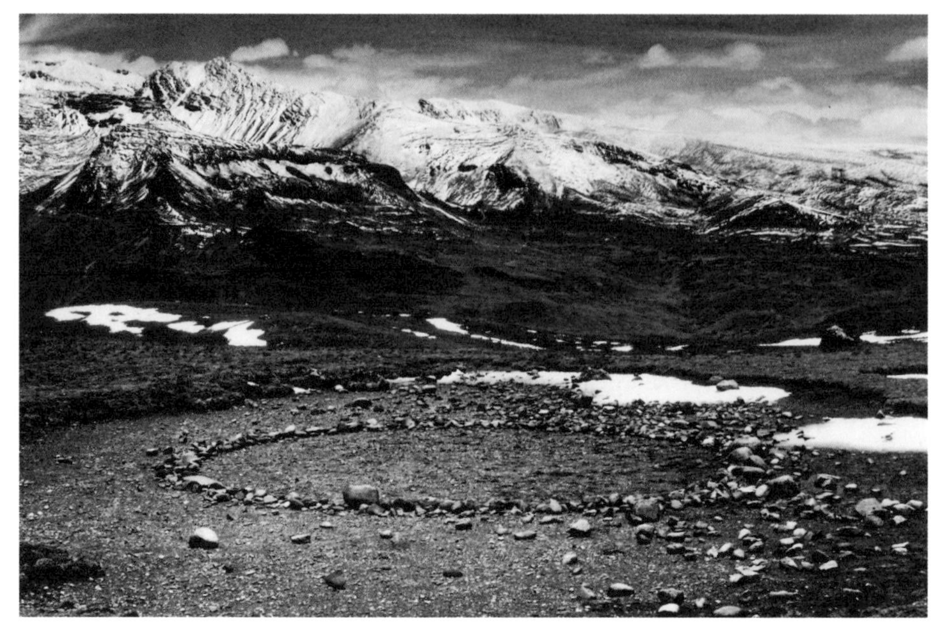

CIRCLE IN THE ANDES
1972

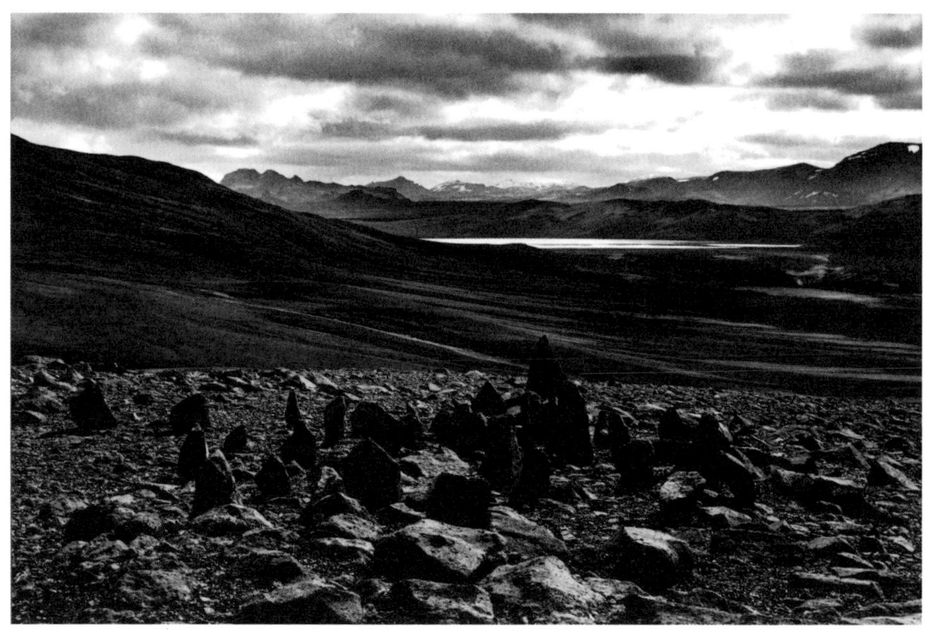

STONES IN ICELAND
1974

RH FUCHS

Memories of Passing: A Note on Richard Long

> Out at the sea the dawn wind
> Wrinkles and slides. I am here
> Or there, or elsewhere.
>
> TS Eliot, 'East Coker', *Four Quartets*, 1940

Richard Long's recent work *A Rolling Stone, Resting Places Along a Journey* (1973)[1] consists of ten photographs, each separately framed with wide margins. The series (the order of which is fixed) is preceded by a 'title page' similarly presented. The basic or most explicit proposition of the work is: *here I sat as I restlessly wandered along*.[2] This proposition, however, is framed by a cultural context of art, which adds to the semantic complexity of the work.

Each photograph, taken on a journey, presumably in Scotland (though that hardly matters), is a close medium shot of a configuration of stones either laid out on slopes or on wide, flat ground between distant mountains. With the exception of a regular circle in the last photograph of the series, the grouping of the stones is highly irregular, as if the result of idle play. In some cases the grouping seems so accidental that there can be some doubt whether the stones have been touched by human hands at all. (This does not matter either.) Contrary to the behaviour of classical sculpture, which claims a site absolutely for its own by *confronting* the space around, the configurations of stones mix gently with the surrounding area. They are there as discrete signs of passing (instead of monuments of staying, as conventional sculptures) – a campsite left, never to return, existing only in the traveller's memory.

But the last photograph is different. It presents a circle of rocks on a downward slope. A circular marking like this suggests, by virtue of its closed form, either permanence or completion. The circle puts an end to the indecision of passing through, it is the perfect coda to the journey as articulated by the preceding, irregular, almost hasty markings – a final farewell.

The medium of Richard Long's art is travelling, which means either staying at one place or going to another place. The formal signs used by him for marking the moments of a journey can therefore be logically sub-divided as signs of stay (circle, cross, square) or signs of movement (line, spiral, zigzag). And if a photograph is illusionistic, working as a recollection of a place once known or a track once walked, so is a piece presented indoors, in a gallery or a museum, an illusionistic recollection too: of the same? Its shape denotes the activity (staying or moving), its material (rocks, sticks, pine needles, sand) denotes its place, though naturally not as precisely as a photograph.[3]

This suggests that in Long's oeuvre there is no functional difference between a photograph and an 'actual' piece. Both are instruments of recollection; through them one is able to share Richard Long's memories.[4] That is what his art is about, and to me that seems a rather classic mode of apprehension.

Looking at art always entails sharing something (seldom something very specific) with the artist: his feeling, his intelligence, his understanding of the world. What one is invited to share with Richard Long seems quite evident: a contemplation of nature. Now this happens within a certain cultural context in which the concept of nature is qualified, and is carrying a set of connotations like, for instance, purity and stillness and isolation. Those connotations are all part of Richard Long's work; it is what the works transmit because they have been felt and perceived in that connotational frame, and fused into a perfectly matching, legible form of presentation.

Studio International, vol.187, no.965, April 1974, pp.172–73.

1 *A Rolling Stone* (1973) was recently acquired by the Stedelijk Museum, Amsterdam.

2 For those unfamiliar with English idiomatic usage: a rolling stone is figurative for restless wanderer. Also part of the meaning of the work's title is a popular saying: 'a rolling stone gathers no moss'. The playfulness of the title in relation to the material used for the markings (stones) is of course obvious.

3 In some cases the relation between a presentation in a gallery and a walk executed somewhere, is very precise. Long's exhibition in the Stedelijk Museum, Amsterdam, December 1973 – January 1974, contained a spiral of clay footprints which was the same length as a straight line walked to the top of a hill near Glastonbury, Somerset. So that spiral is almost a reproduction of that walk, differently presented because of the different conditions.

4 Because the work is about memories, it is of no real importance whether a mark somewhere (a 'sculpture') remains in existence or not.

ANN-SARGENT WOOSTER

Richard Long at the John Weber Gallery

New York, 4 – 29 May 1974

Although his gestures and composition are distinctly the product of the late 1960s and early-1970s sensibility, I cannot get over the feeling when seeing Richard Long's work that I am in the nineteenth century. Long's involvement with nature and his way of using it as material come out of the early Romantic period, when, before industrialisation and the automobile, the walk was a social institution. Aesthetes thought nothing of spending their summer vacations hiking through the Alps with wife, rucksack, walking stick and best friend. One can readily think of serious journals of experiences on long walks such as William Wordsworth's *Guide Through the Lakes in the North of England* (1835) or Henry David Thoreau's *Cape Cod* (1865), in which the writers sought to map both the physical facts and spiritual reverberations of their ambulations. Long comes out of this Romantic tradition but, curiously, reverses this writerly process: whereas the poet's journal suggests through its length and sequentiality the duration of the trip, Long reduces his experience to – at most – a phrase, a map and a photograph. This shorn document may, with the viewer's collaboration, expand outward from the nodule of the fact towards recreation of the artist's experience.

Long's most recent show in New York had an air of paucity. The four usual categories of his work were present:

1 A location or a moment – captioned with words situating it and suggesting its implications.
2 The pure walk documented with map, photographs and/or words.
3 The mark on the land – either created by Long through repetitive walking, making grooves or furrows in the earth or grass, or by reversing this technique, retracing a pre-existing line by walking on it.
4 Documentation of what might be called public monuments. This is an elusive category. Such works may be natural or geological phenomena, or a work constructed by Long. The ambiguity is important. One such work is *A Line of Sticks in Somerset* (1974); here, Long gathered together a group of sticks, approximately the same size, from the site of the piece, then laid them on the ground in a wide line (somewhat resembling fossil bones deposited by a river) and photographed it. The work is temporary, subject to the action of nature; but as long as it exists it can be experienced by everyone. *A Line in Ireland* (1974) is another work of this type.

Long exhibited two forms of the walk. In one he documents the discrepancy between an abstract mark on a two-dimensional surface

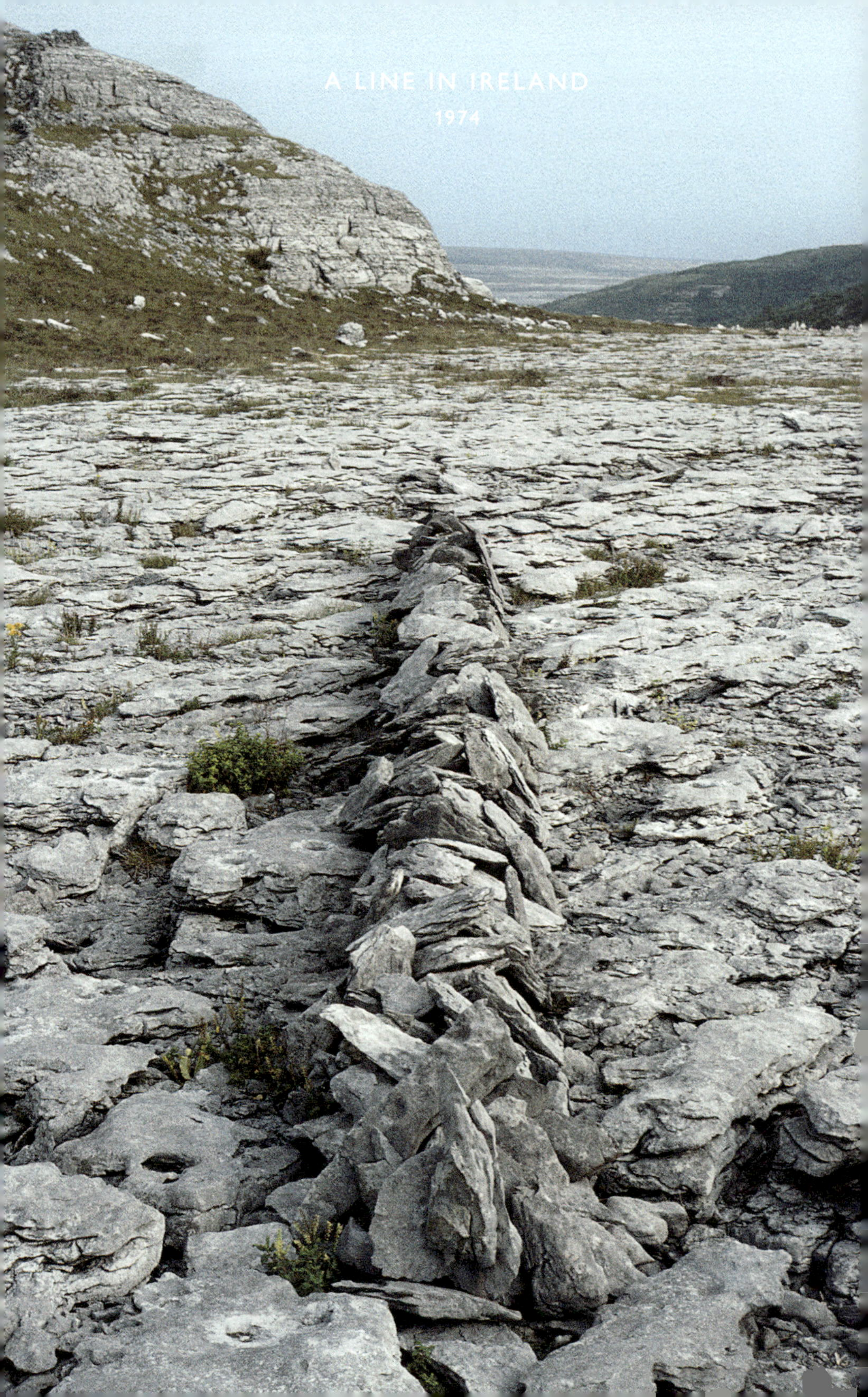

A LINE IN IRELAND
1974

and the variability of actual experience. In *Eight Walks* (1974), he drew an eight-line grid on a map and then walked the lines in the real landscape. Although they were of equal length and the landscape was fairly uniform, the length of time or the completion of each line-walk varied slightly (across: 60, 62, 66, 61 minutes; down: 62, 70, 64, 65 minutes). Long recorded the time at the end of each line.

In another work the walk becomes more like medieval or Inca roadbuilding. In *A Line of 164 Stones A Walk of 164 Miles* (1974), Long combines monument-making – the line of stones – with purported experience. The piece has a distinct composition: above a frontally shot photograph of a curving road with a stone in the right foreground are the words of the title; the viewer makes the two lines – of the words and the road – into a simile. Directly under the photograph Long states the experience he is allegedly documenting: 'A walk across Ireland, placing a nearby stone on my path at every mile along the journey.' He further emphasises his veracity by logging in a vertical list, the number of stones left in each place: 'Clare 49 Stones/Tipperary 38 Stones/Kilkenny 27 Stones/Leix 9 Stones/Carlow 20 Stones/Wicklow 21 Stones.' A work like this asks two questions: What is the meaning of photography – is it documentation or evocation of the whole experience? And what is the function of the words – are they like a magazine caption (in, say, the *National Geographic*), or are they a form of poetry in which experience is distilled?

Walking a Line in Peru (1972) sums up the new direction Long is taking. There is withdrawal from marking or scratching the land. In contrast to his earlier, vigorous manipulation of the landscape, the new work is more detached and the act of making art may now be seen as almost a residue of this former attitude. In *Walking a Line in Peru*, a photograph of a plain closed by distant mountains, with almost no horizon, is bisected by a single white line; the words of the title appear underneath it. Long deliberately uses the active verb 'walking' to indicate the process represented by the photograph. In this piece Long walked one of the prehistoric Nazca Lines, carved into the land over great distances, which date from before the Incan empire and are thought to have magical implications of the same order as Druidic constructions in England. Reversing his normal procedure of making his own mark on the land, by walking the Nazca Lines, Long retraces a mark that is aeons old. Here, the line itself makes a 'mark' on Long's body/mind through his experiencing of its length, site and historical implications.

Art in America, vol.62, no.4, July–August 1974, pp.83–84.

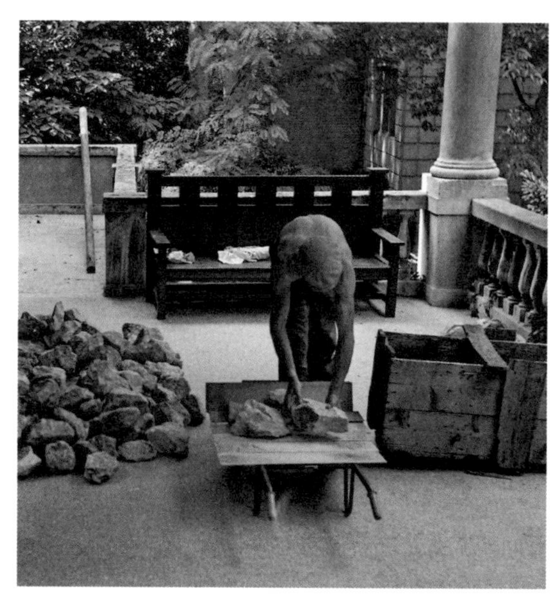

Richard Long
in Venice 1976

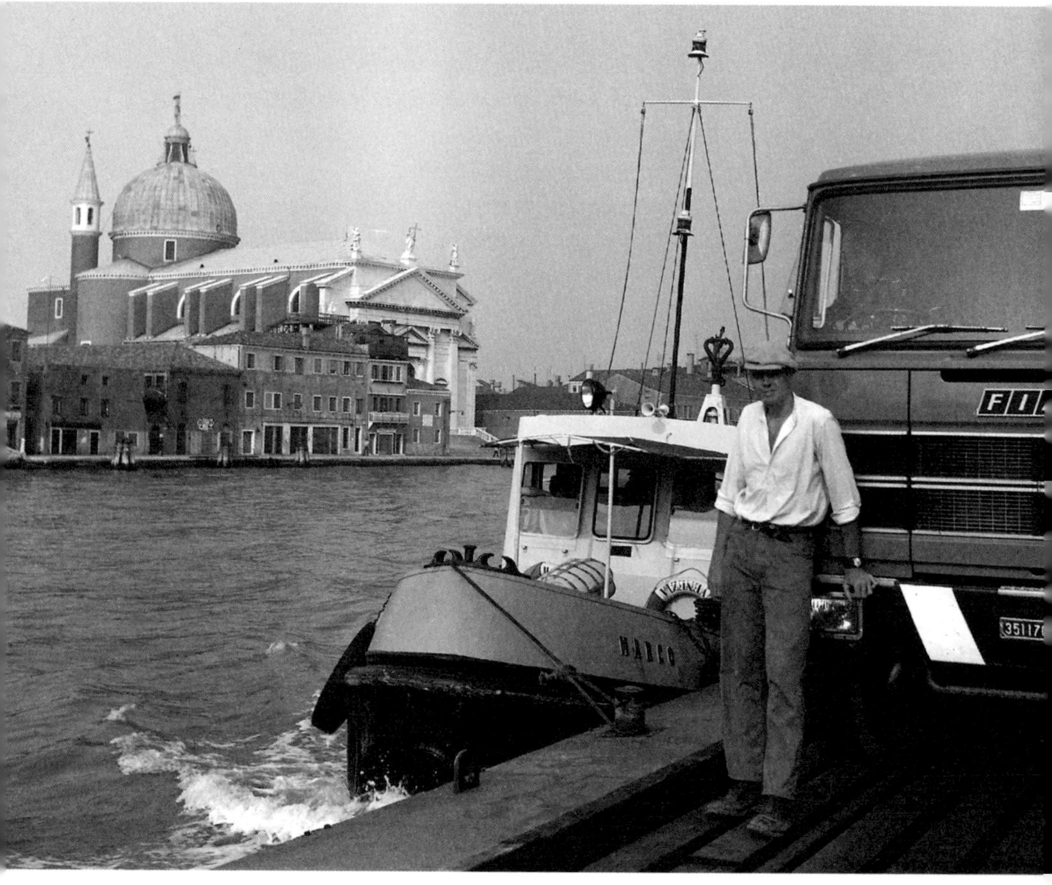

Venice Biennale XXXVII

British Pavilion, 18 July – 10 October 1976

A Line of 682 Stones 1976

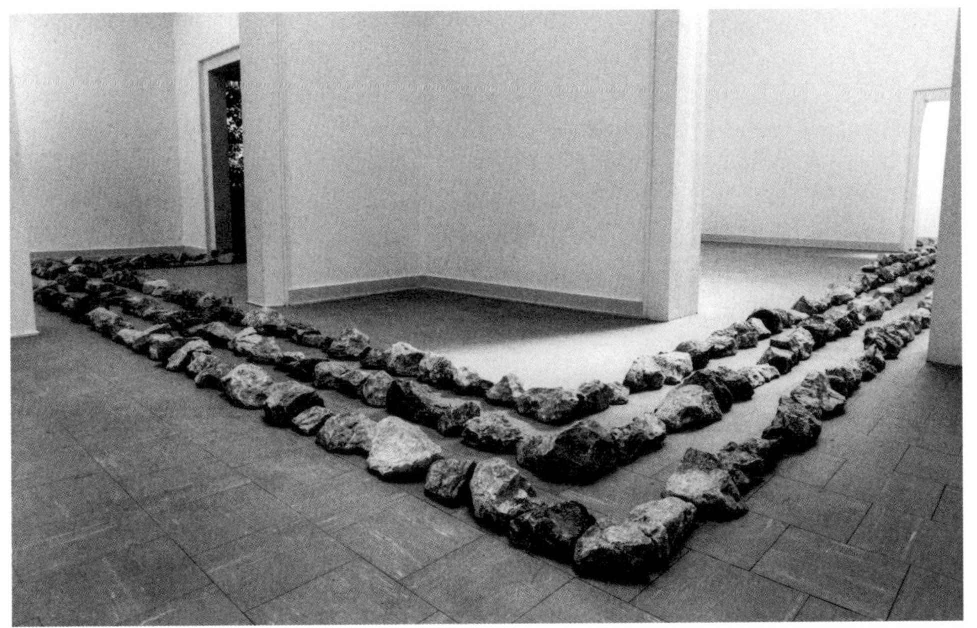

ROBERTA SMITH

Richard Long at Sperone Westwater Fischer

New York, 30 September – 28 October, 1978

Richard Long has a light, pure touch and his work a romantic, reticent solitariness which makes him something like the Agnes Martin of sculpture. Just as Martin's pencilled lines and thin washes barely, but irrevocably, turn a piece of canvas into a painting, Long delicately imposes the concept of 'art', of artistic decision and order, on natural found materials which he uses 'as is', and, in the larger sense, on the landscape, or nature, itself. Long's pieces often consist simply of a walk through the countryside from one place or point to another, documented with a laconically captioned map or photo of the country passed through (usually somewhere in England or Scotland; Long is British). His more tangible work consists of circles, lines and spirals of sticks or stones arranged either where he finds them (in which case the photo-document becomes the final work of art here, too), or in galleries and museums.

Long showed both kinds of work in his recent exhibition here: four circles, ten, 12, 13 and 16 feet in diametre, made respectively of pieces of charred wood, red slate from Vermont, driftwood from the River Avon and bluestone, plus five photoworks documenting various walks and pieces done elsewhere (*A Line in Australia* (1977), *A Circle in Africa* (1978)). Each part separate and distinct, the whole self-contained, the flat circles occupy space much like handmade, primitive Carl Andres – but somewhat less accommodating (you can't walk on them), somewhat more evocative of places and processes outside the gallery. The obvious care with which their components are selected and placed (each circle is spaced differently), conveys a sense of a deliberate aesthetic ritual which is also a communion of sorts with nature. It was instructive to compare the differing colour, scale and character of each circle: the wood made shrunken and smooth by fire or water, the large flat flagstones of red slate and, most imposing, the rough-cut rectangular chunks of bluestone. On the debit side, I think Long's pieces function best alone, dominating an entire space or series of spaces. Presented together, these works tended to diminish each other, becoming isolated like traditional art objects.

A fuller sense both of what inspires Long and of what he aspires to comes across in his photoworks. The large, greyish-brown prints have the look of nineteenth-century landscape photography, and the images themselves – usually rolling hills leading away to distant horizons – give us a nature which is all-encompassing, relatively unspoiled and benignly tolerant of Long's mild incursions. It's a landscape whose vastness and innocence has more to do with Thomas Hardy's Wessex than with Long's contemporaries, American earthworkers.

One of the best of these photoworks is titled *Dart Tamar Exe* (1978). The photograph shows us only one of the triangle's 'points', an inauspiciously trickling spring which is one of the three rivers' sources, and the country beyond, while the caption tells us that the triangle was 34, 41 and 44 miles on a side and that it took Long into the counties of Devon, Cornwall and Somerset. Lovely and serene as the image is (and as Long's walk presumably was), the piece or the 'art' resides as much in the caption as in the photograph and perhaps in our minds most of all. Because finally it's on our minds more than anywhere else that Long imposes his artistic concepts, and his poetic experience and ironic encapsulation of nature. In this case, Long implants a series of successive, resonating triangles, geometric, geographic and metaphoric: three points and lines, three locales and counties, and, finally, three small beginnings leading to the sea.

Art in America, vol.67, no.2, March–April 1979, pp.151–152.

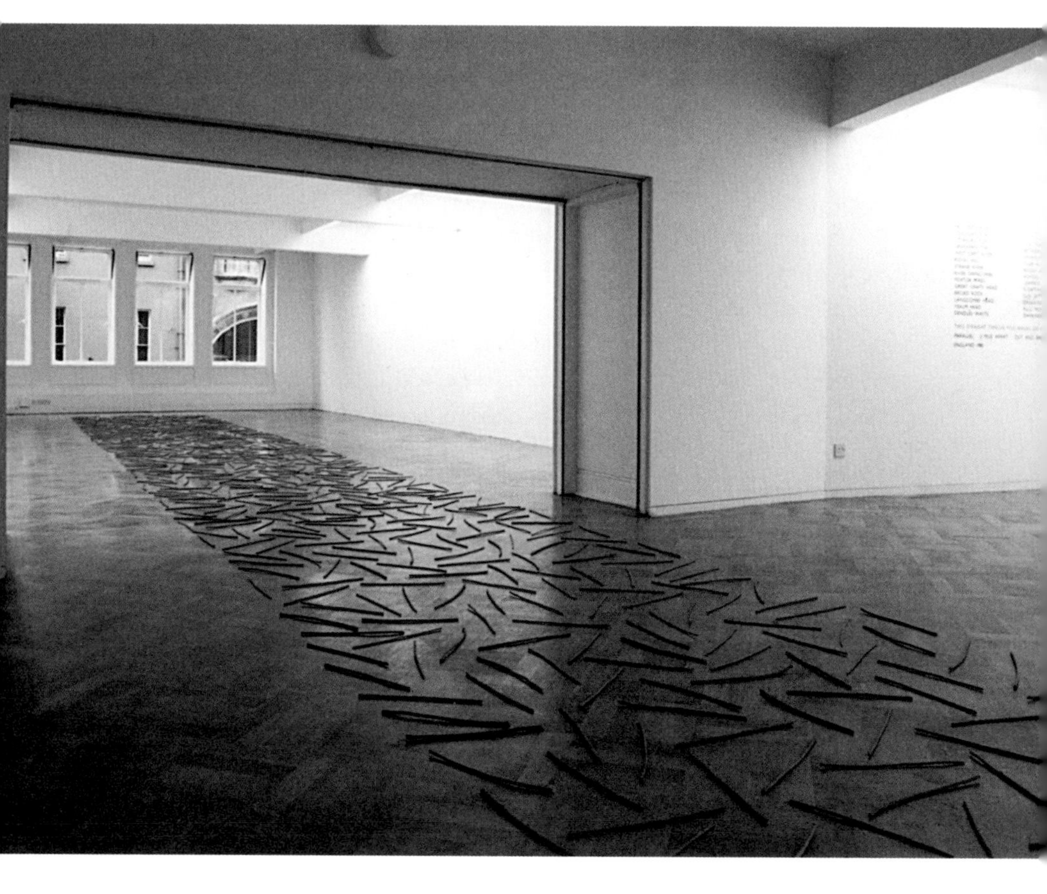

Somerset Willow Line 1980

MICHAEL CRAIG-MARTIN

Richard Long at Anthony d'Offay Gallery

London, 17 September – 16 October 1980

Although the work of Richard Long does not have characteristics I associate with much English art, it seems profoundly English. It is not whimsical or eccentric, parochial or derivative, self-expressive or rhetorical, intellectualised or mystifying. Other English characteristics are evident here: clarity and precision of language, deeply felt emotion expressed with reserve, straightforwardness and quiet authority. Despite having the landscape as its source, Long's work is not romantic, as is often assumed, but classical. Simple, orderly and clear, it uses lines, circles, parallels, numbers and measurements of time and space. On the other hand, the work is neither cold nor impersonal. It is both physically and emotionally instinctive, an intensely evocative art, an inclusive art.

Richard Long's exhibition at Anthony d'Offay presented recent work of the various types he has established over the past decade: works employing photographs, maps and texts, and a floor sculpture called *Somerset Willow Line* (1980). The ideas and themes which underlie Long's work have remained comparatively constant since he first began to exhibit. Those developments occurring in the form and content of the work have always been implicit in the previous work and have emerged as new avenues of approach rather than changes of direction.

The role of walks is the most radical and signal aspect of Long's work and has been the most misunderstood. The walks are made alone by the artist, sometimes in the cultivated English countryside familiar to him, particularly the West Country where he grew up and still lives. Here he follows the roads, paths and public ways available to everyone. Long has said that every artist first is a local artist and his own art is clearly rooted in his home territory and his childhood experience. Other walks are made in various parts of the world, often vast but isolated places, comparatively untouched by society – common land, the moors, the Scottish Highlands, the Andes, the African plains, the Australian Bush. In such places, his walks take considered patterns unique to himself, not routes taken by other travellers. The territory covered by these walks is often unfamiliar to the artist, sometimes physically dangerous and challenging. On these walks, Long achieves an extraordinary degree of identification between himself and the land. He becomes physically part of the landscape: he is within it and not a detached observer. His sense of the land is like that of the nomad or the Indian in relation to their sustaining terrain, without alienation. This is not to imply mystical engagement on Long's part. His use of the land is matter-of-fact and practical. The natural world has its own rhythms of contour and climate, space and time, to be accepted and respected. Long's actions lay across the land the human geometries of straight lines and circles, days and miles. He considers the walks to be works of art in themselves, 'three-dimensional traces'. Sometimes on the walks, he marks a certain place by making a simple structure, perhaps by upturning a circle of stones. In these circumstances, Long considers the sculpture to be the place itself, the whole place 'as far as the eye can see from the sculpture'.[1] Although these works are formally similar to ancient stone monuments, their meaning is fundamentally different ('modern ideas in the only practical places to take them').

Neither casual nor functional ('walking without travelling'), the walks are done not for pleasure or challenge, survival or discovery, though these may be aspects of the artist's experience. They are gratuitous, done for themselves, for and as art. They are structured to have form and visibility, if only in the imagination. They have physical identity without physical permanence, and emphasise time as much as space. Their scale is immense. Long lays claim to the whole surface of the earth, not as property as defined by society, but as inherently his, by nature, right and reciprocity, as it belongs to the stones, and to each of us. Such works neither challenge nature (no conquests) nor romanticise it (nothing picturesque or spectacular). For Long, every place on the surface of the earth is equal. He chooses the ones he does because they are 'extreme, neutral, uncluttered: good places to work'.

Richard Long was the first artist to do what has become known as Land art. But his work is significantly different from that of the Americans Robert Smithson, Walter De Maria or Michael Heizer. Their work is often simply large-scale sculpture done in the landscape and their attitude to the land is often alienated. None has Long's sustained commitment to the land. Either he is the only Land artist or not one at all.

The walks and outdoor sculptures are presented in the gallery in documentary form using photographs, maps and texts. 'Documentary' is perhaps misleading, with its implications of disinterested reportage.

Long's intention is to bring his private experience to the walks and the remoteness of the outdoor sculptures within the imaginative realm of the public. But Long makes these referential works independent and self-sufficient. No matter what the form or material or location, he gives each work the same weight and consideration, 'all the works and all the places being equal'. In this exhibition there were several works using photographs. Long does not consider himself a photographer seeking beautiful subjects for the perfect picture. He takes photographs on his walks to note aspects of importance to himself and to record outdoor sculptures done on route. They are black-and-white prints mounted on cream or white card and framed in simple wooden frames. The photographs are always accompanied by concise verbal texts written on the mount which take the form of single words, phrases and lists. They give details of the walks – country, year, location, distance covered, duration, the shape described. There are also brief descriptions of things seen, sculptures made, terrain covered. These words act as direct triggers to the imagination, to feelings, ideas and memories. Meaning arises from the conjunction of image, text and presentation. Everything about them is direct and purposeful.

Water Circle Walk (1980) consists of a framed photograph and a similarly framed map. The photograph shows a view looking forward along the walk in the Scottish Highlands accompanied by a brief description of its nature and duration. The map is a standard Ordnance Survey map of the area with the walk's circular route drawn onto it. In four places, the circle is broken by lakes and at each, the line indicates that the walk has digressed around the perimeter of the lake until the circle could be joined again. The imposed geometry of the circle is strikingly different from all the other lines of the map. The circle is easily drawn, but to make a circular walk on such uneven terrain would be a different matter.

Also in the exhibition were works consisting solely of text. They are printed in black and red on thin white paper, adhering directly to the wall. The content of these works and the use of single words and phrases is as in those works using texts and photographs. But they are conceptually self-sufficient and their structure often reflects that of the walk described. *Two Straight Twelve Mile Walks on Dartmoor, England* (1980) records parallel walks by presenting two parallel lists down which the reader travels. One is of the names of the places on the walk's route, the other a list of things seen or done along the way.

The richness and poetry of the place names is extraordinary, as are the descriptions in their variety of images and evocative power. This visually austere work exposes the remarkable potency of basic language to evoke sensual experience.

Long's indoor sculptures are arrangements on the floor of multiple units of simple, natural materials such as stones, sticks, driftwood, laid out in lines and circles. Sometimes such units are arranged to form perimeters or circumferences – linear works. Others are planar with the material units covering the whole interior space described. Of these planar works, some have the units abutting each other, creating a visually stable surface. In others the units are arranged as to create a visually charged configuration. Only one material is used in each sculpture – if stones, from a single source; if sticks, from a single species of tree. They are not constructions, and rest on the floor everywhere, equally, with no vertical dimension other than that of the single units of material. Each sculpture reveals itself as a whole immediately and no part is significantly different from or more interesting than any other, though each unit is clearly unique. These sculptures present a visual field rather than a figurative focus in a way similar to the paintings of Jackson Pollock. They are without illusion but rich in allusion. They use real materials, real space, real time. They are not just in the space of the gallery but part of it. Made in the space, paralleling the floor, such works cease to exist when gathered up and taken away, until they are reassembled.

Somerset Willow Line is a rectangular line two metres wide and 16.5 metres long made of hundreds of thin willow sticks. It is drawn along the floor from one end of the gallery to the other. The work seems to float on the floor's surface, nowhere touching a wall, leaving space to circulate around it. The sticks are randomly placed, not touching each other, barkless, cleanly cut at each end, reddish in colour and with no obvious inflection. They are nearly straight, like slightly crooked lines, of almost identical length (about 35 centimetres), and echo the shape of the work as a whole. They appear dry and brittle, almost weightless.

The polished parquet floor, similar in colour to the sticks, forms the intervals between them, the intervals forming a much greater surface area than the sticks. The floor slips up to the sculpture, through and beyond it, physically supporting it and visually part of it. This is a sculpture without a fixed or preferred view and one tends to look at it by walking round it, in a minutely scaled reflection of the artist's walks. Though virtually the same everywhere across its surface: the work's appearance changes as one's point of view changes. Viewed up its length, it is dramatically perspectival, with the sticks seeming to get denser in the distance. Viewed along its length, it fills one's peripheral vision in both directions and appears flat and endless. This changing aspect in viewing the same thing is the same as the visual experience of moving through a landscape.

The feeling of the work is both quiet and dramatic. It is resonant in associations with nature, unmistakable through the use of the willow sticks whose simple presence alludes to the countryside, woodlands and waterways. The sculpture recalls the transparent and reflective surface of water, gently agitated with implications of restrained internal energy, fragile but vigorous.

Long's indoor sculptures have much in common with Minimalism, with the sculpture, for example, of Carl Andre or the paintings of Robert Ryman. But while each particular work of Long's, as with the Minimalists, seeks to be taken as a thing in itself and uses simple geometric shapes and repeated similar units, his work is different in that he is overtly referential in a way that relates it more to European contemporary art, particularly that of Joseph Beuys. In the end, his work is neither American nor European but, like England itself, somewhere in between. Innovative and original, Long's works presents a contemporary view of the world in contemporary language.

The essence of Richard Long's work lies in its intensely emotional and physical evocation of the natural world. The essence of his aesthetic is in his ability to allow expression to surface through the means at his disposal. He does not make the stones and words and images speak, he lets them. He allows them their own inherent power. There is no ego here, no cleverness, manipulation or distortion. It is as though the artist was at the disposal of his materials, not them at his. On the walks, he accepts the requirements of the terrain; in the exhibited works, he accepts the requirements of the gallery.

Long is in continuous dialogue with the world through his art and through it with us. He does not impose himself on his materials but allows them their own voice. He does the same with us.

The Burlington Magazine, vol.CXXII, no.932, November 1980, pp.790–92.

1 All quotations from the artist's statements published to coincide with the exhibition *Richard Long* at Anthony d'Offay Gallery, London, 17 September – 16 October 1980 (see pp. 294–297).

SASKIA BOS

Richard Long, Art & Project

Amsterdam, 23 January – 20 February 1982

In his recent work, Richard Long unexpectedly appears as a kind of painter. On the white walls of the gallery are huge monochrome circles, two in brownish grey and one in a warmer reddish-brown; within the circles the white wall is left visible at intervals, thus implying not only a flat ornament but also structure and depth. Long painted with his hands, dipping his fingers in mud and clay with which he then covered the walls in a tense, rhythmic motion. Because of the supple and continuous movement of his fingers, the paintings have an overall structure that is both dynamic and controlled. On the one hand, their patterns remind one of intricate latticework; on the other, they recall the organic feeling of old landscape etchings.

The connections with Long's past work – especially with the book in which he used mud from the River Avon on the pages, enabling the viewer to 'read' the river – are obvious. *River Avon Mud Circle* (1982) and *Red Clay Circle* (1982) also relate to the circles of driftwood that Long has made for many years. What distinguishes them from these earlier sculptures is the suppleness and sensuousness of the new medium, which enable Long to convey different moods and sensations. Making an abstract image of nature out of nature's own materials, Long evokes the rhythms of flowing water and of moving earth in a river by using mud from the river itself.

In this impressive show, in which Long made his largest mud circles so far (previous works were presented in London and Lyons), he created a complement to his landscape photography. Both strongly evoke nature, but in quite different ways. It is always fascinating to see an artist find new formulations while remaining true to his central concerns; this is the more welcome in a period when eclecticism seems to be the only avenue for most 'new' painters.

Artforum, vol.20, no.10, June 1982, p.95.

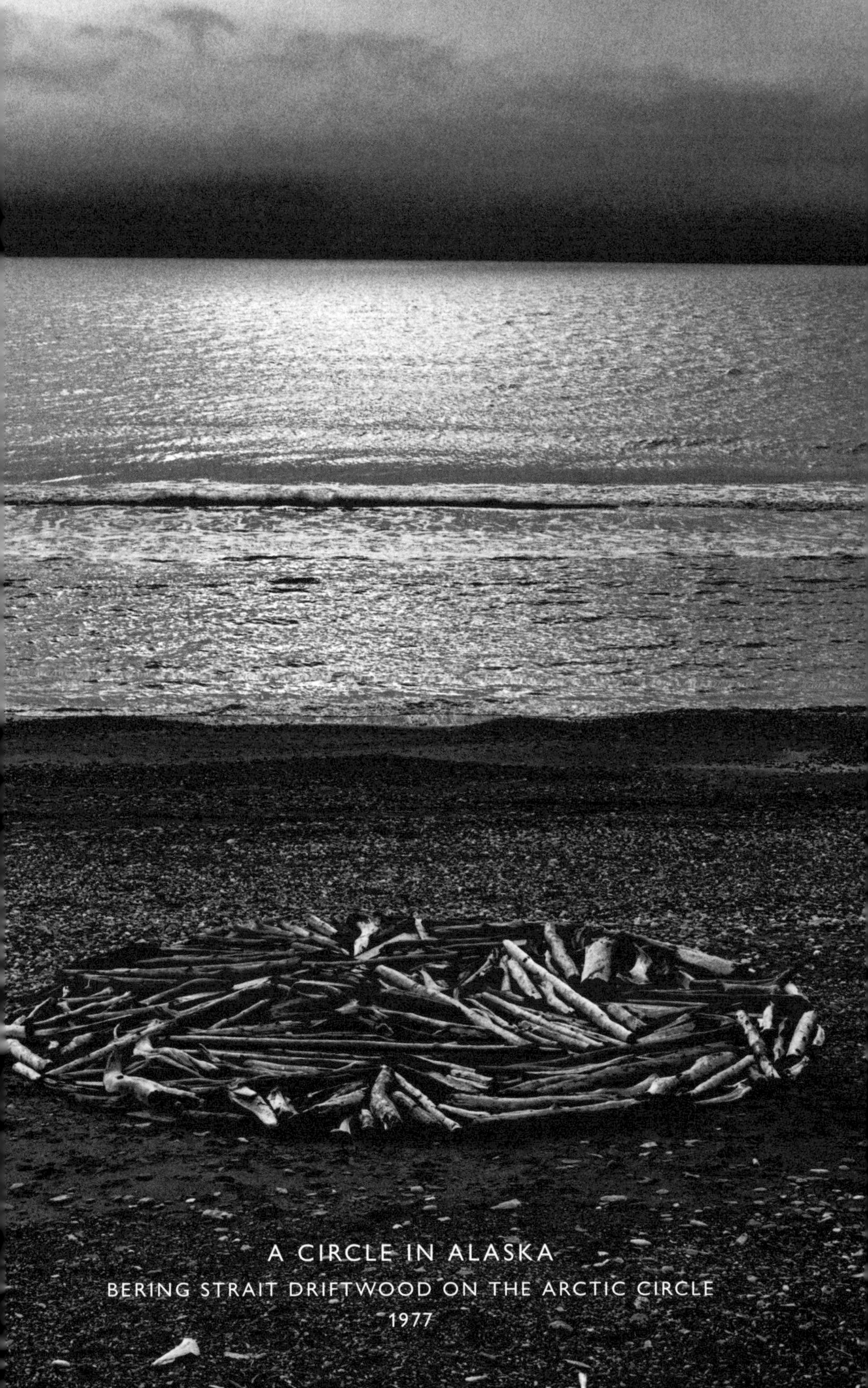

A CIRCLE IN ALASKA
BERING STRAIT DRIFTWOOD ON THE ARCTIC CIRCLE
1977

WILLIAM FURLONG AND RICHARD LONG

Interview

WF *Your work seems to divide down into groups. I don't know whether you see the distinctions as being very important?*

RL Well, I see my work as having the kind of freedom to work in the world in many different ways. I think formally my work is very open-ended because, as you say, the art that I produce may be a stone or a photograph or a word or a map. I see myself working always in the same direction; it's just that I happen to use different forms.

WF *When you go out into the landscape to make a work, to make a piece of sculpture as opposed to a walk...*

RL Actually, often the two happen together; the sculpture is found by being on the walk. In other words I discover the landscape through walking through it and then often I will find the place of the sculpture just by chance along the walk but I perhaps wouldn't have any preconceived idea about when the work could occur.

WF *Would you define that moment as being purely a moment determined by chance?*

RL No, I might have a preconceived idea which might actually often get changed by the circumstances of the walk. For example I went to Central Africa with the idea in my head first of all to make a circle of stones high on a mountain in Malawi, and when I climbed up on to the mountain I realised that even though it's a big mountain, because there's no ice or snow there were no actual screes or snow on the ground, everything was smooth rock. So obviously I had to change my plan and I ended up by making a circle of burnt cactuses which had been burnt in lightning storms which play around the mountain. So that's just an example of the actual place changing an original idea. In fact I made a circle, but of a material which I would never have thought about without having been there. Often, the best works occur completely out of the walk so that I come back having done something which I'd never have thought about before the walk started.

WF *Works such as the one you've described could in a sense be seen as the sort of index of your relationship with the location and the factors that you're responding to in the location.*

RL Yes, I suppose it's a crossing place between the place and me being there, with my ideas and my sensibility and it's just a record of that meeting place.

I made a walk in Scotland which was *As the Crow Flies, Scotland* (1979), a 12-hour walk in a straight line across the Highlands. I chose the location by looking at maps very carefully; finding rolling moorland which would provide me with a very practical place in which I could actually physically walk in a straight line for 12 hours continuously. So looking at a map beforehand in that work was very crucial to choosing the place. With the daisy work, *England 1968* (1968), I had the idea first of making my own pattern on top of a natural pattern. So having had the idea, I had to think of all the good places that I knew that might be possible to make such a work. There, the idea came first and I had to actually find the place and then make the work.

Other times chance might play a greater part. For example, when I went to Alaska we were flying into Fairbanks and we looked down and we saw what was interesting country from the plane and so for the first two days we went south. This was with my friend Hamish (Fulton). We were kind of stumbling through this fir forest and I think we both realised after a couple of days that this wasn't actually the sort of classic tundra landscape that we had come to Alaska to look for, so we went back into Fairbanks and thought of getting a little plane up north, up to Point Barrow. But the girl on the ticket desk said, 'well, I wouldn't go up there if I were you because a couple of white people were killed there last weekend, a sort of little Friday night drinking trouble'. She said, 'why don't you go over to the west coast, to Kotzebue, where it's really good tundra landscape but the local Eskimo tribe are much more friendly?' So it was really by those circumstances that we ended up on the west coast of Alaska which is how I came to be close to the Arctic Circle, which gave me the chance to make a driftwood circle actually on the Arctic Circle.

WF *I suppose one very fundamental definition of art could be purely the presence of a human being or the evidence of the presence of the human being. I'm talking about the very remote works you make where, as you say, a shepherd may not think it's an artwork but there is some feeling of a presence there or intervention by a human being.*

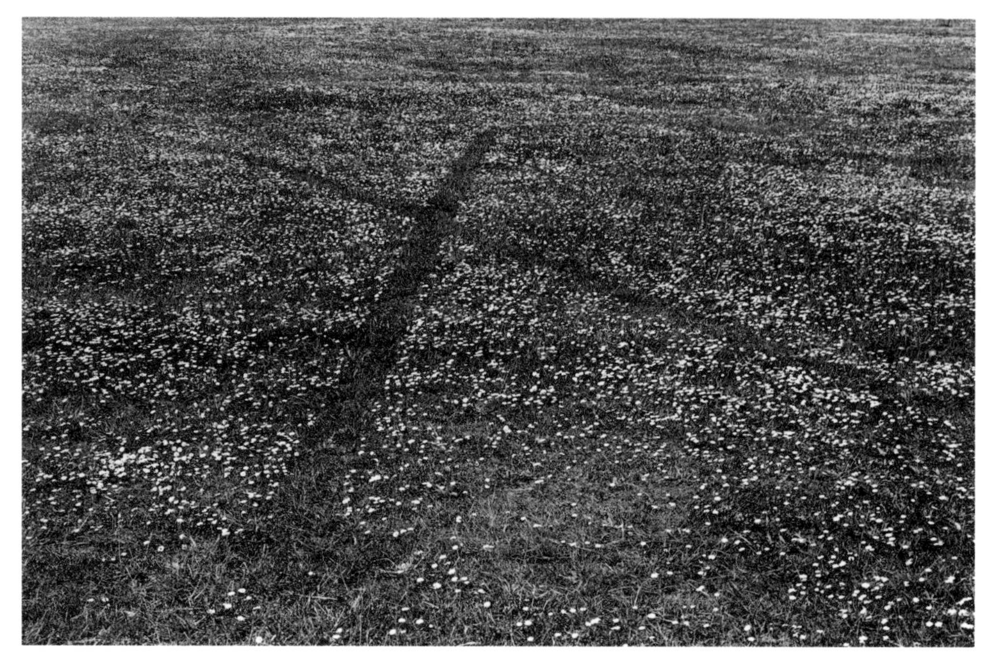

ENGLAND 1968

RL Yes, although I don't actually think like that when I'm making the work. It's really just that I might be in such a terrific, beautiful place and the materials to hand are such that it inspires me to make a work. It's crazy to feel that you shouldn't make art in a place just because you know it's not part of the art world. It's just that I should make a work whenever I have the idea, and if it just happens to be out in the middle of nowhere then so be it.

WF *Without labouring the point, would it be unacceptable to you to think in terms of one of those remote spots, where you might make a work, being designated as the site of one of your pieces of art?*

RL Well, that would be wrong. I mean one of the points is that the place should be anonymous in the art world. Really the only thing that reaches the art world is the image of the work and I might just call it, say like *A Line in Iceland* (1982) so the title is very abstract. It's not important to know where it is, it's only important just to have some knowledge of it through what the photograph looks like. I'm not interested in making permanent works which would turn into a famous site. In fact a lot of the landscape works you might only see by standing in the position where the photograph was taken from. If you stood to one side you wouldn't see the line; in a way the photograph makes it visible. In the space of the landscape the piece is almost invisible, it's only when you see it in the photograph that you kind of have that focus of attention. When I was in Mexico once, down one of the canyons of the Sierra Madre, I just did a water drawing on a riverbed down a rock face and I was stood back, just taking one of my usual photographs, and this Mexican came up the riverbed using it as a footpath (nice idea) and we sort of said good morning to each other and he sort of walked past the water drawing and he looked at the rock but he didn't actually see the work at all. It was like it was invisible to him. It was somehow only visible to me because I had made it. So that's just an example of how even a strong image back in the art world might, at the place, to someone walking by, be unnoticeable. There's no moral to that story, it's just the way it is.

WF *Going into the works which depend on words, how do you see the words functioning, how do you approach the use of words?*

RL Well, the first word piece I did was a sort of strange one-off in 1969 which was about a walk in the Alps, but after that there was a gap and

I suppose I started making word pieces again maybe five or six years ago. I think I really wanted another way of expressing the whole idea of a walk or even a sculpture. Sometimes, I would use the photograph to represent the idea of a walk but that was just like one moment and so, sometimes I thought I could use words to give the whole complete total idea. An example is a work I did in England in 1994, which was just to record in words all the different surfaces that I had walked over, you know, like roads, earth, sand, heather, rock, path.

I didn't see it as a literary way to use words or even poetic, just a very particular specific art way.

WF *The words become elements; they become discrete meanings that work against other words.*

RL Yes, it's like the line of words actually written on the page almost become like the line of my walk. For example, one of my sculptures was to cross Dartmoor and along the walk move one object to another object. And you can express that whole idea very well using words but it would be very complicated to try and take a photograph. So the best way of actually expressing that work is to use words: pinecone to sheep turd to jaw bone, stuff like that. It becomes a very pure way to express that work.

WF *One thing that one notices in a lot of the photo pieces is the very deliberate consideration of how they are photographed and how they are visually organised, which makes you very presumably concerned with perception and taking a fixed viewpoint as opposed to the idea of sculpture being in the round and being seen from any point of view.*

RL In 1967 I actually made a sculpture where the position of the spectator was part of the work. The work was three elements; it was a circle on the hillside, a black frame and then the place of the viewer, and the work came together when the three things were in line. That was a very formal work but I think in general I've tried to make my photographs very straightforward, very simple and direct in the spirit of the work and also usually from my eye level, no airplanes, no fancy lenses. I think that would distract the attention to the wrong place. I hope there is a consistency or straightforwardness in my photographs so you end up by concentrating on the work itself. Also in a very practical way, as I said before, sometimes the best way to see a line sculpture is by standing at one end and looking straight down it.

WF *So when you use photography, the photograph actually becomes the work?*

RL Yes, it does, it becomes art in a different way. And the handwritten text underneath it gives the photograph a different meaning than it would have if the photograph was just a photograph.

WF *One other way you've worked is through the publication. What role or function do you see your books as having?*

RL Well, that's another way of putting the work out in the world. It just does that job; it makes the ideas available to the people very cheaply and easily. The work is not about possession; so to say 'to know it is to possess it' is not quite right. But it's like people can know a fact of life, that knowledge is common to everyone, no one actually possesses it on their own.

WF *It reminds me, what you're saying, of Australian aboriginal concepts which don't actually include the concept of possession but of place and location and site.*

RL Well, I would hope my works were close to that same spirit. It was never really my intention that my early landscape works could be owned or possessed. I was attracted to the idea that you could make art with almost no means at all in the parts of the world which were free for everyone to use. So in some sense being English and being British and having the great National Parks like Dartmoor and the Highlands was quite important as well.

I mean also the kind of tradition in England of the countryside in some ways belonging to everyone, so that you can actually walk footpaths across fields as long as you respect the farmers' land and closed gates and stuff like that. A lot of my walking pieces would not be possible in America, for example, because they have a completely different attitude to the land. In fact I went to America because I had this idea to make a straight 100-mile walk on a landscape which was grassy plains, almost like a sea of grass. I hitchhiked through South Dakota and Wyoming and Montana looking for this landscape to make this work in and one day I was going down this track in Montana and a farmer came and told me that if I kept on down another 100 yards the next farmer would shoot me dead on his land. So in fact I ended up by going over into Canada which had the same landscape but a different mentality and I felt more relaxed about being there and making such a work as *The High Plains, A Straight Hundred Mile Walk on the Canadian Prairie* (1974).

WF *Going on from that, you live in Bristol and presumably when you make works in England you can feel an instant sympathy for the context and surroundings. When you go to places like the Andes and remote deserts do you have a problem in really appreciating the actual significance of the space and the objects and elements within it?*

RL Well, I remember the first time I went to East Africa in 1969 I did feel quite overwhelmed just by the vastness and difference of the landscape and of the culture. I felt very small and insignificant and sort of European. I think it does take a long time to really become absorbed into different landscapes and to kind of understand them in a way which has some meaning. I think it's something that I've hopefully learnt through experience to become at one in a different and new landscape and become absorbed by it and get into a state of mind where I feel very relaxed and that I'm not using it and I'm not making the work in the wrong way. But I think that's something that I've really had to learn and often I have to be in a landscape on a walk, sometimes I don't do a work until near the very end, it takes me that long to somehow come to terms with the differences and try and understand it. One of the works I made in Nepal recently was to brush a footpath. With a leafy branch I cleared maybe 50 yards of the footpath of all leaves and twigs and everything so it was just a bright earth image. So in a way that's a work which is right at the centre of the social life of the place, it's not a work which is removed from the people of the area, people will be passing and walking over that work as they go on their way. That's an example of the way that a work can share in the life of the local people rather than being removed from it.

WF *There's a piece that you made,* A Line Made by Walking *(1967), where you seem to be pressing down daisies within a field.*

RL Yes, it's really a line which is visible because the grass is trodden down by my footsteps and the flattened grass reflects the sunlight, so the sunlight is actually making the mark. I think that work was important because it really revealed to me the idea that how visible the art is just depends on how many times you do it. It was evident that if a line walked once was practically invisible, walked ten times it would leave a trace, and walked 1,000 times it would make a fairly permanent mark. Also, as its status as art was the same in each case, that enabled me to control the degrees of visibility or invisibility, and the permanence or impermanence, of any subsequent walking works.

WF *Up until quite recently you've been fairly reluctant or unwilling to write about your work or talk about it. Do you now feel more confident or do you feel that you should be talking about it?*

RL Well, you know doing something like this is a struggle. In the early years I had this naive idea that the work should speak for itself, but of course it doesn't actually work like that. I think if the work becomes well known to a certain extent then people start writing about it anyway and it's a bit like Chinese whispers. If there are only a few articles written by misinformed people, if that's all there is about you, then those articles take on an importance that they shouldn't have. So I did my first piece of writing in a way to try and set the record straight. That was the reason for doing the statements, the *Five, six, pick up sticks Seven, eight, lay them straight* (1980). I think art is a very moral activity, it doesn't threaten people, it doesn't use people, it sort of humanises us, I hope. My work really is just about being a human being and living on this planet, using nature as its source. On another level it's also about making art by doing things that I enjoy. You know it's not really about a struggle. I enjoy ideas. I actually enjoy camping and being on my own and the whole business of lighting fires, or choosing a campsite or sleeping on the ground. I always get my best sleep on some stony patch somewhere. I love the whole ritual and rhythm, the simple rhythm of being on a walk, like getting up with the sun and making breakfast and walking all day and being very tired in a very physical simple way. Apart from anything else it's just a very good way to live life. Somehow I've found a way to make it into art.

WF *And presumably that is really the source of your work, that physical involvement in and with nature.*

RL Yes, it is, you said it.

From an interview conducted in London in February 1984.
Originally published as an audiotape by *Audio Arts*, London 1985.

ANNE SEYMOUR

Old World New World

The first thing that seems to distinguish Richard Long's work when one tries to write about it, is its capacity to resemble a smooth round stone. Each aspect slides imperceptibly into another. Wherever you begin, before you have got very far, you find yourself discussing something else. There is clearly an organic philosophy which binds it together, but there is also a lightness of touch and a magic quality which defy investigation.

Long has often emphasised the simplicity of his undertaking, comparing it on one occasion to the way Samuel Beckett's hero Molloy kept his 16 sucking stones in his pocket and just moved them around, because it seemed the right thing to do. And indeed Long has much in common with Beckett, most anti-egotistical of writers, who shuns enquiries about himself and insists his readers look at his work for what it is.

Grand simplicity is easy to appreciate from the outside; you can develop a taste for it without enquiring further. To isolate the spiritual values and to discern the complexities within is rather more demanding. And Long's work does demand it – at least it doesn't 'demand', it gently but insistently draws the viewer into a meditation of extraordinary depth. Despite a similar emphasis on freedom, like Beckett, Long also has a pedagogical streak. For a number of years, his characteristic inclination to precision, accuracy and control over every aspect of his work, led him to allow very little to be published about it. However, Long has always responded generously to student enquiries and recently has also begun to deal with more public misconceptions, even to working with the media of film and TV. Looking back from the standpoint of accumulated experience, past actions and intuition become conscious, in his statements *Five, six, pick up sticks Seven, eight, lay them straight* (1980), and *Words after the fact* (1982), he has ensured there is now no excuse for misunderstanding the general principles of his art.

It is almost impossible not to begin with Richard Long's own starting point: 'The source of my work is nature.' The roots of this response, instinctive and inherited and helped by environment, were already growing in childhood, as he has shown in *Childhood Abiding*

Places (1983), redolent of the close-up, physical involvement Long felt as a boy with his surroundings in Bristol in the west of England, where he was born in 1945 and still lives. Typically these responses were not to the streets of the port on the banks of the River Avon, but to the grassy, rocky, reedy, woody, often secret places of the Avon Gorge and nearby countryside, each with a special individual meaning relating to a particular activity or past event.

Like so many artists Long was obviously going to be concerned with art virtually from the beginning, and it is equally clear in his first student days that his most interesting and personal works were those which involved nature in one way or another. Significantly they never seem to have been direct studies in the old-fashioned sense, they always had something to say, and among the most prophetic were a snowball drawing, a model of the River Avon, a plaster landscape incorporating the figure of a walking man and an installation involving a path through a room.

The first pieces Long made working directly with nature in the sense of with the land itself, were done by digging holes in it. This seems to have been during the months he spent working on the roads and in a paper mill, between being asked to leave the West of England College of Art (he never found our why) in the spring of 1965, and beginning at St Martin's School of Art in London, in the autumn. Within three years he had emerged as a key figure in the international mainstream of art.

Looking back on this time in *Words after the fact*, Long wrote: 'In the mid-sixties the language and ambition of art were due for renewal. I felt art had barely recognised the natural landscapes which cover this planet, or had used the experiences those places could offer. Starting on my own doorstep and later spreading, part of my work since has been to try and engage this potential.' Though no doubt it was not as clear as this what was happening at the time, the calm, matter-of-fact simplicity of the statement in contrast to the enormity of the proposition is characteristic, as is Long's effortless ability to range between small and large, nearness and distance, past and present.

Young artists can feel they do not have much to lose, but at that period striking out into 'nature', in the sense of real-life landscape, though logical, was unquestionably brave in many ways. The two most spectacularly novel aspects of it, which we shall come back to, were Long's direct use of the context of reality within the work, and the fact that he was following his own vision and predilections, taking no account of established forms of expression, or the accepted categories of painting and sculpture. But there were other things too. For one, nature, in the sense of pure landscape, has tended to be something of a second-class citizen in painting, even in the context of British art noted for its landscape tradition. For another, a major reaction among younger artists was in full swing against the neo-Romanticism of the forties and the landscape-based abstraction of the fifties. The prevailing direction of the time was specifically urban-based. Most young artists and critics had their sights fixed, if not on New York, then on London, and had in general not the faintest idea of the complex realities nature in the wild could offer, or that in fact it still covers most of this planet. On the contrary, they considered it positively inappropriate to modern society. Landscape was identified with the past and with being British; there was a feeling that to be modern and international you had to be urban. In the context of mainstream modern art, British art was generally regarded as of secondary importance, so to be British and involved in landscape would seem to make an international contribution doubly unlikely.

Obviously things are never as simple as they appear, and what can feel like a big shift in close-up can be seen to be infinitesimal from further away. However, it does seem at this point that the tide, which had in fact been turning for some time, even right back through the previous century, did make a powerful surge – though possibly not in quite the direction that was first perceived. Abstract formalism, which was the successful mode of the moment, was attacked by an even more anti-materialist wave of ephemeral art. Breaking down the distinctions between established categories like painting, sculpture and drawing, it relied more on giving conceptual form to ideas and less on physical monumentality. It used real space as part of itself in a much more complex way and on its own terms, ordinary objects as it found them, unimportant materials, words, photographs. Land art, Arte Povera, Conceptual art were names given to parts of what emerged. The movement was worldwide and Long was immediately recognised as one of the leading young exponents of the tendency in Britain. Unfortunately, as so often happens, the idea of a movement overshadowed what the artists were really doing. The medium was once again seen as all of the message. The individual personalities, preoccupations, and the subtlety and revolutionary importance of what these artists had to say were obscured, as were the connections with the mainstream of great art that had preceded them.

That man is part of nature, and can only live in harmony with his surroundings and realise his potential through understanding and reciprocity, are age-old ideas, which in the press for progress periodically get forgotten and remembered again. It seems to go in cycles, or maybe waves. There are personal ones and ones which involve whole civilisations. They seem to act like a kind of brake, a system of balances, a way of putting things in perspective, for they also tend to coincide with the expression of revolutionary new ideas. Traditionally the artist has always been the mediator between man and his surroundings, and his concern to reveal mystic truths about the relationship. But perhaps the world has looked different since the idea became rooted in man's mind that he can get off it. He has begun to distance himself from it and to be aware that he is made from the same natural substances and operates in the same rhythms as the universe surrounding him. As world thought has developed during the century the perspective on man's role in the scheme of things has changed somewhat. He has acquired a new consciousness in this respect, not only in the scientific, historical and regional view, but even in the cosmic context. Just as, apart from political obstructions, the whole world is spatially open to him, it is also available through a vast information explosion in terms of knowledge and ideas. Science and philosophy have moved closer together again and Eastern and Western approaches are no longer regarded as mutually exclusive, but are often revealed to be saying the same things and to have the same sources. Time and space have acquired a slightly different relativity and ancient can now be seen as equally applicable to modern and vice versa.

One of the most widely registered of recent influences from the old world or the East, which has for a long time crept insidiously into the Western subconscious, has been that of Zen Buddhism and its related customs and philosophies, especially those of Japan. It has had a powerful effect on many aspects of the Western arts generally, and in particular in connection with the idea of art as a total way of life. Among those belonging to Long's context in the postwar period, whose work demonstrates a link of this kind, can be included the writer Samuel Beckett; the composer John Cage, who studied with the Japanese philosopher DT Suzuki; and the artist Yves Klein, prematurely dead in 1962, who combined Zen with Rosicrucianism and a then revolutionary understanding of modern media. No doubt following ideas which were in the air, Long too came in contact with Zen some time in the later sixties, and though the direction of his art was well formed by then, must surely have found there remarkable confirmation of his ideas and extraordinary perceptive abilities in the face of nature. As Ezra Pound once said, 'Generalisation generally follows action in the arts.' Long's work is in essence intuitive and practical and it should not be thought to be based either on Zen or on Japanese art. Nothing could be further from the truth – or, for that matter, further from Zen advice, which encourages us not to follow any higher example, but only to look directly into the mystery of our own being, which is reality itself. Long's art is strictly based on nature and on reality. What is interesting in this context is that, when looked at through Zen, and Zen-related ideas, our understanding of it can be enormously enhanced.

Long is first and foremost a modern artist, a modernist in the pioneering, evolutionary, European sense of the word. He is also that rare thing, an English artist with a world view, who, like John Keats reading Homer or Cortez looking at the Pacific, suddenly found himself looking down a vast vista of possibilities in his chosen field, because he happened to be standing in the right place at the right time with the right sort of equipment. However the wild surmise is tempered not by the conventions of judgement but a firm grasp of reality. Long recognises his position as an Englishman living in the West, and he also sees that modern technology shares the world with other simultaneous parallel cultures. From the Tuareg to the Tibetan Buddhists all share the same nature, the same sun, the same world. It is an important aspect of Zen asceticism that it does not deny desires or instincts, and in actually making his art in the natural world and making it part of that world Long responded to personal inclination and pleasure in his actions and surroundings. His approach also corresponds with the Zen view, which recognises human nature as one with objective nature, in the sense that nature inhabits us and we nature and, unless we remove all artificial barriers between nature and ourselves, we can neither see into the real heart of it nor dwell there with love and understanding.

In recent history, perhaps this process began in earnest with JMW Turner and John Constable. Following their energetic response to the continuous flux of nature the Impressionists took their canvases out of doors. Auguste Rodin said 'I do not correct nature. I incorporate myself within it.' In penetrating beneath the surface of nature Long is also, in a sense, doing something similar to Paul Cézanne or Piet Mondrian, Henry Moore, Willem de Kooning, Pablo Picasso, Jackson Pollock or Jasper Johns, in looking beyond the outward appearance of things, at all the unseeable sensualities of life as well as the invisible energies and patterns beneath it. But in the last 30 years or so a new element has come into it – a bigger arena – that of real life, real space and real time. Yves Klein attempted literally to fly from his window. Joseph Beuys not only penetrated nature metaphorically and intellectually he also incorporated himself into an ongoing mixture of art and life involving art, science, politics and education. Gilbert & George made a similar leap in their capacity as Living Sculpture and the dedication of their whole lives to art and to humanity. Richard Long has not only penetrated more deeply into the world of natural landscape than anyone since Turner, he has taken abstract art with him, creating a new art which allows all parties to retain their full identities. Throughout the centuries artists have worked to extend the spiritual and material dialogue with the reality inhabited by the viewer, to dissolve the barriers between material and immaterial, subject and object. By bringing art into the sphere of real time and space, the artists of the last few decades have opened up possibilities for a new subtle expression of sensuality, idea and argument which has hardly begun to be explored.

Perhaps the single really necessary item or luggage for any journey should be respect. Respect is a vital condition in Long's relationship with nature. It is perhaps a somewhat Eastern expression of the feeling which in an older age would have been called love. This contrasts strongly with some of the more grandiose violations of nature perpetrated by American 'Land' artists of the sixties and seventies. 'I use ... nature with respect and freedom', Long wrote, 'I hope to make work for the land, not against it.' Just as, according to Zen, the things of heaven and earth are of the same root and substance, and one should not treat nature as something to be conquered, but as a friend whose inner being is similar to one's own.

Richard Long exhibits humility and delicacy in his attitude to nature. In working with it he does not shift great quantities of earth. He is not aiming for a memorial, or to make permanent, monumental works which will become visited sites. Indeed he often replaces, or stands down the stones he has used to make a work, after taking a photograph of it. Despite a great physical and personal engagement with the land and the potential to make art by walking on an unprecedented scale, he leaves merely a trace of his presence, a line of footsteps, some stones or sticks rearranged in a way measurable in terms of time, his own forces and nature's working together. Such marks, the pattern of his walks, are just one more layer upon thousands of crisscrossings of natural space by animals and humans. Long makes use of both footpaths and animal trails, he may re-use old fireplaces or sitting stones where others have rested before him. He will often pass stone circles made by other hands and for other purposes at various ncar and distant times. He wishes his work to reflect the impermanence and constant change of the processes of nature; a water drawing disappears as it dries, while other works are reabsorbed into nature in their own time. It is also his intention that the work should be regarded as part of a timeless continuum of marks, not just something to do with a specific present. Long is the first to acknowledge 'Nature has more effect on me than I on it.' In respecting and following the disciplines of nature, by abdicating his egoism in her presence, it seems that he is given insight into the meanings of her processes. Both artist and nature thus have freedom of movement and freedom of expression, and it is there, according to Zen that beauty is to be found.

Long has abandoned none of the traditional disciplines of art, it is just that his methods are different. The more freedom beckons, the greater the need the artist discovers for discipline. Kandinsky, a pioneer in this respect wrote in 1913, 'The freedom of an unfettered art can never be absolute ... Every age achieves a measure of freedom, but beyond the boundaries of its freedom the mightiest genius cannot go.' Long takes his freedom seriously. He talks of using nature 'with respect and freedom.' He says it is 'a great freedom won for art and for the viewer' that 'art can be made anywhere, perhaps seen only by a few people or not recognised as art when they do.' He emphasises how important to the work is the freedom to use 'all degrees of visibility and permanence'. Long's use of nature is thus primarily to be seen as emancipatory not retrogressive. He is not primitivising or going back to nature, but with other artists of his time taking huge steps forward. However, although he found the whole world spatially and temporally at his disposal, Long moved cautiously into his new territory. In essence his work has changed little from the start – indeed he seems to feel there is much enlightenment to be found in the experience of doing something again and again – but the grand coherent whole we see now, which has grown so consistently in depth and cross-reference, is only so coherent because every decision, however intuitive, has been taken with care in the context of the whole. Paradoxically it is the simple repetitive acts, such as walking, the repetition of circles or lines in time and space, which reveal the uniqueness of the fabric of the world, that every cell, every blade of grass, every stone, every river, every day is different. Long cannot but have been conscious of the great freedom to be felt in jettisoning unnecessary luggage, or that in the euphoria of abandon which swept art in the sixties many artists threw the baby out with the bath water.

In Zen freedom and creativity are synonymous. Freedom is attained through the discipline of enlightenment, and enlightenment means emancipation – i.e. freedom. What inhibits this state is the intellect. It is only when every intellectual or conscious deliberation is exhausted and all selfish interests abandoned that the inner being, source of the only true knowledge, reveals its secrets. The idea is that religion involves the moral sphere, but both art and the divine transcend morality. If we abandon the ego, we also have no moral responsibility. Thus to be free from all conditions and rules has to be the essence of the religious or artistic life, but equally this state has to exist without consciousness or purposeful intention or freedom is still not attained.

In Japan nature, having no visible purpose, is regarded as a perfect example of art. Long uses nature 'whole', unaltered. As Molloy moved his 16 stones around, Long has said he has no conscious understanding of why he likes walking or stones, or why he chooses to make marks in lines and circles. The latter are just a simple human idea and like the stones belong to no one, neither to him nor to anyone else. The wild, pure substances he works with, stones, sticks, mud, water, fire, can suggest freedom (and life) in themselves, but they also impose the pattern which he finds for them. Long's presence in nature can seem almost synonymous with freedom, but it is a freedom highly controlled and disciplined by nature in terms of both idea and action, as is his revolutionary choice of walking as a medium, which gives him potential access to the entire planet and enormously extends his and our consciousness of the capacity of walking as a human action and what it can reveal. Traditionally, walking has had religious, poetic and even healing connections. Apparently it can actually improve eyesight and mental powers. Among the peripatetic musicians and poets of history the great Japanese haiku poets like Matsuo Bashō were wandering artists. Haiku like Zen abhors egoism, artifice and ulterior motives. These poets are passive instruments for the expression of their inspiration and they have to ensure that nothing comes between them and their subject. Long's understanding of the dual aspect of freedom, and of the achievements possible in surrendering to nature, is perhaps nowhere more clearly and poetically expressed than in his photographic work *Reflections in the Little Pigeon River* (1970). Here the cross of stones he has made, from and within the stones of the riverbed beneath the water, is accompanied by a quotation from a song sung by Johnny Cash:

> I keep a close watch on this heart of mine
> I keep my eyes wide open all the time
> I keep the ends out for the tie that binds
> Because you're mine,
> I walk the line.

As the Zen swordsman, operating at the peak of unconsciousness, compares his art with the moon's reflection in water, so the artist continually walking the line, makes his mark on the flow of nature by giving up his identity to it. But it is reflected back to him again in the work. The spectator identifies with the artist and recognises that these worlds are mutually dependent and that each is dedicated to the other.

The eternal movement of nature is at the heart of the Zen appreciation of it, and movement is central to Long's art and one of its most revolutionary aspects. Because he is working with the total continuum of nature, his work can be as peaceful or active in as many ways as nature itself. Contrary to popular misconception, Zen does not espouse tranquillity as such; this would not only prevent the continuous motion of nature, it would indeed, as DT Suzuki has put it, be going so far as to embrace its dead corpse. Tranquillity has to be dynamic in order to transcend the duality of life and death. The idea of the energetic forces of life reflected and harnessed in art is one of its most basic concepts and at the bottom of all notions of creativity. The art of the twentieth century has perhaps distinguished itself among all others in its varied response to such considerations.

For Richard Long there is a kind of stopping place within this energetic continuum surrounding him where all things seem to be in balance. It may be only for a moment. But there is a place where everything seems to come together, almost by chance, which seems to be the source of what Long would call a 'good work', where place, image and idea are all held briefly in dynamic balance. Perhaps Long's is the purest contemporary solution, because, through the medium of his body, it presents the energetic body of nature in all its tangibility and intangibility, virtually unaltered and within the real space-time dimension we see as life. His philosophical dialogue with nature has an existence that is no less part of it than the context in which the work is created.

From early on Long was clearly fascinated by the relative movement of things in space and time. He even wrote a short thesis on Albert Einstein's theory of relativity at art school. Movement, time and measurement in ways dependent on substance and sensory perception move in inextricable harmony in his work and they are the means which bind him to it. He is the passive agent through which they express themselves. However, although Long is aware of the scientific and mystical implications of such concepts as that all knowledge already exists, that everything is cyclical, that it is matter that moves along while time just 'is', that everything is in dynamic movement and in some way connected, his primary concern is with a more direct form of approach. His concern is with allowing a natural flow from one form to another, with keeping things simple, making spontaneous use of the elements of intuition and chance. When it comes to time, matter and space it is his 'engagement' with it as such which provides his only understanding of it.

Thus while we are conscious that in Long's work nothing has existence outside time and that everything created involves movement, this does not mean that the time factor is obvious or intrusive. He has never made those sometimes bizarre, and most often dull, quasi-scientific works, which involve an artist going through the motions of doing something relentlessly, without pleasure, or for the sake of it. That is the opposite of freedom in the Zen sense, rather a kind of mechanical purposelessness where there is no mystery and no art. However far and strenuously Long has walked, it always seems easy and enjoyable. His approach to time, however factual, is always poetic, never imposed from the outside, but an organic characteristic of the idea which occurs to him. The poetry comes from its truth to nature and absence of self. Though his activity is, in a sense, purposeless, it is never gratuitous. It may be the result of chance, but it is made for and with nature, following the natural movements of both and according to nature's principle of minimal effort. By following her inclination towards non-resistance he achieves a lightness of touch, which can only be reached by mental and bodily understanding of the environment he is working with.

Walking has become Long's trademark. It seems like the literal fulfilment of the condition that beauty is felt where there is freedom of motion and freedom of expression. Often considered the most idiosyncratic of his activities it is also specifically lacking in egoism. It is simply the most straightforward, ordinary activity which distinguishes him as a human being, that is to say one who can roam the world at will with consciousness as his only burden. In setting out alone on foot he abandons status, material luggage and ego. There is an interesting parallel in this with the Japanese Noh play *Yama-uba*. It recounts the story of the Buddha's wandering through the countryside helping the peasants in the disguise of an old woman, whose good works are manifest but who always vanishes into nowhere. Similarly Long passes on his invisible way, leaving only the evidence of his goodwill to demonstrate the benign relationship between man and nature. In a sense it is Long's personal absence rather than his presence which is characteristic of his stance, whereas in Beuys's or Gilbert & George's work there is an aspect of their presence (though in the art not the personal sense) which is of primary importance, They see nature through man, whereas Long sees man through nature.

Long is able to reveal ideas about nature and about the pattern of life through the forms of his walks and the stopping places along them, partly because, like the Zen swordsman or priest, he has superb discipline and training as well as an extraordinary, intuitive, all-over view of life and of the traditional nature and structure of art. But as he is not an intellectual, neither is Long a mountaineer, a climber or an athlete. He is simply an ordinary very fit person, a first-class walker and countryman. He is at home in this element; walking a precise compass reading is normal and practical for him. His is a kind of purposeless walking, which stands in sharp contrast to the kind of purposeful but meaningless travelling most of us madly indulge in today, without perceiving anything very much.

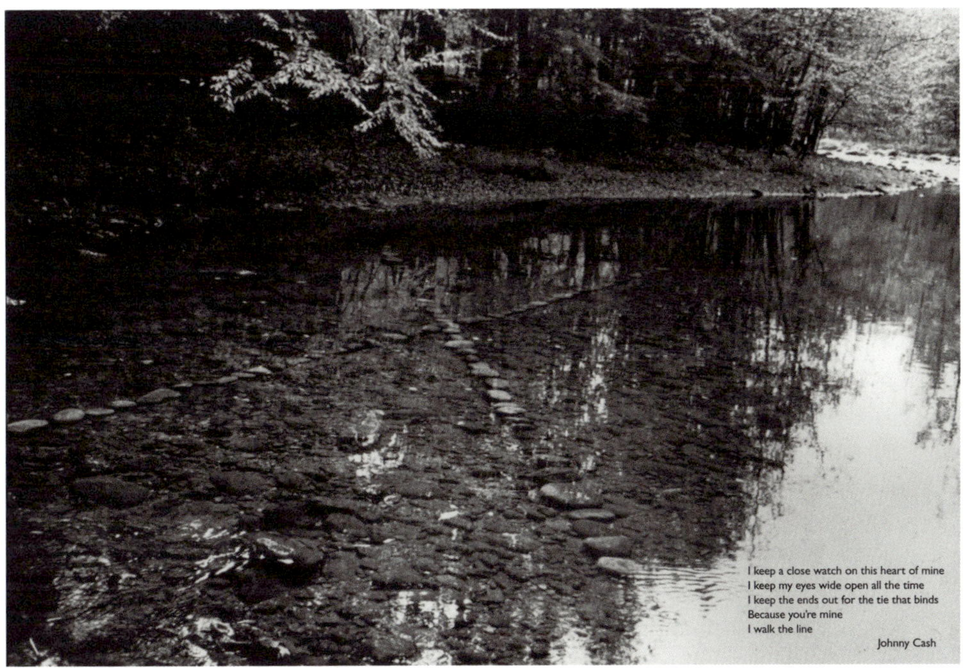

REFLECTIONS IN THE LITTLE PIGEON RIVER GREAT SMOKEY MOUNTAINS TENNESSEE 1970

From all these generalisations, from Richard Long's careful, pared-down statements about walking: 'A walk moves through life, it is physical, but afterwards invisible ... The freedom to use precisely all degrees of visibility and permanence is important to my work', we get only the smallest glimpse of the grandeur of the conception and of the actuality of the walks themselves, the kind of physical forces incorporated in them, the imaginative structures by which he causes places to reveal their essences. Nor do we immediately realise that there are hundreds of these enormous works in existence, works which have been made all over the free world. Even if one were to know only of the works Long has made on Dartmoor, relatively near his home, they would amount to an extraordinary contribution to the history of sculpture. *Four Hours and Four Circles* (1972), involved walking each of four concentric circles in the space of one hour, at speeds varying from slow in the centre to fast on the outside. In 1970 he walked a line from east to west on the moor for six consecutive nights in which, 'The sculpture becomes slower and slower, from day to day, day to night, day night day, motionless.' In 1976 he made *A Hundred Tors in a Hundred Hours*, a 114-mile walk on Dartmoor, and in 1978 *Dartmoor Riverbeds*, a four-day walk along all the riverbeds within a circle on Dartmoor. These are only a few examples at random from the nearest wild place to Long's home in Bristol.

For him a walk is an 'open system' capable of using an infinite number of ideas. It concerns his human scale and at the same time it can intersect a whole country. It can be about pace, about the geometry of places and time. It can be about rivers, about the desert, about wind, about sleeping under the stars. A walk can be a meandering journey, it can also be the ritual repetition of a straight line or a circle. Walking a straight line for an hour, while noting the first word that comes to mind at one-minute intervals, is a way of making a word line. Whichever it is, a line of stones, words or footsteps, all are equal and complementary and part of the overall dynamic balance of opportunities he finds in nature.

There is a strange magic by which the quiet, controlled embodiment of these ideas in maps, photographs and words, as we grasp their individual natures, suddenly triggers our realisation of the intense physicality of Long's art, whether it refers to things visible or invisible, permanent or impermanent. In that moment we comprehend its concern with the heart-stopping beauties of nature in the widest view of pure sensation, from sucking the icicles from the grass stems of Dartmoor, to the colour and texture of River Avon mud, from the sound of the river's roar in the Himalayas to the mists of MacGillycuddy's Reeks in Ireland, or water splashed on a sunny rock in Mexico.

We realise that his solution to passing on this experience is not to attempt its representation, but to encapsulate the essence of it in a way which involves making available to us, as simply as possible, knowledge of his actions and the circumstance of them. In one way this reification of the idea is the equivalent of a Japanese haiku. But in another it is an extension of the traditional, formal and analytical ideas of Western art since the Renaissance, only on a different and more directly realistic scale of time, space and perception. Yet a third aspect involving the viewer concerns both of these and produces a different kind of reification. For there is an important sense in which each of Long's works, however linear in time or wide-ranging in space and experience, becomes if not exactly monolithic, at least something with a precise shape. Even though it may be nothing like anything you have ever held in your hands before, you can at least mentally and metaphorically examine it there, as a whole, and see how it is made and marvel at the crisp precision at the execution. It is sculpture in the old-fashioned sense. When Long dipped paper in the Avon mud, bound it up and handed it back to us as a book, so that we could hold and read the river in our hands, he was involving us in the literal equivalent of something like this.

'Time passes, a place remains.' The artist moves through time at his pace, leaving only the faintest traces of his passing, such as footsteps, or a stone moved here or there, nature moves at hers. Though the two are related they each have their own roles. On a walk the two meet and converse, they even dance together, and where there is a stopping place there may be a blossoming, a celebration. This is the moment of well-being, of sunlight, cloud or shadow, of identification with a particular horizon or energy. 'A sculpture', Long has said, 'is still, a stopping place, visible.' Walking is the means of finding the place. In *Reflections in the Little Pigeon River* artist and viewer seem to look down into the water and see their lives and nature, reflected and intermingled metaphorically and actually in the simple cruciform arrangement of stones on the riverbed. At such a stopping point the activity of artist and nature seems to be doubly charged, as it were, by electricity. A different kind of energy is produced. Nature seems to respond to the touch of the artist who approaches her in her own language. As Long has said, 'It's the touching and the meaning of the touching that matters.' This is the essence of sculpture. On a Cornish beach he rearranged the seaweed into a spiral, which would be swept into nature's own pattern again by the incoming tide. On the shores of the Arctic Circle he brought driftwood together into a solid circle which seems to be clinging to its own kind, washed there by the currents of the water, a sort of pendant on the desolate necklace which encircles the neck of the world. In Africa he created a circle from lightning-blackened cactus, an African-style sacred place in British art in another continent. There are infinite simple ways of making a temporary mark on the surface of the earth, from picking the heads off the daisies in a field in England, to ploughing a spiral in the barren sand of the Sahara with the heel of your boot.

Sometimes when the artist reaches an appropriate pausing place on a walk, instead of making a sculpture with his hands he walks one, like the circle walked on a pass among the mountain tops of Ladakh, creating a portrait of that dual meeting place. On a desert plain he might mark the ground by walking a line ritualistically back and forth emphasising the flatness of that place. In walking Long is touching the earth in a different way from that in which he makes a sculpture with his hands, but the same sort of specific surge of energy is involved. A walk can be a meandering journey or a repeated ritual. It may be created by a long line of footsteps, an invisible spider's-web portrait of a particular place which, if it is on roads or footpaths, overlays the passing of generations of walkers who have gone that way before, making an accumulation of countless footsteps, a line of time constantly renewed.

In single lines, back and forth, round and round concentrically, in squares and meanders, fast and slow, across islands, through deserts and rivers, over moorland and mountain and gallery floor, Long is his own superbly organic pair of calipers. Walking is his pencil and his chisel, his way of delineating, of measuring time and space and existence. Through it he marks his progress through time creating a living web of his activities across the world, not in order that we should focus upon his life as such, but that, by identifying with his actions, the reality of things should be revealed to us, as it is to him. Walking bridges the gap between artist and non-artist and gives the latter a strangely immediate perspective through that identification. Long's journey becomes all our journeys, like past and present, yin and yang, simply different facets of the same thing. The ultimate goal is perhaps the sense of belonging, of being in touch with the living energy of the world.

These are 'images and ideas' which, as Long hopes, 'mark the earth and the mind'. There are related thoughts behind other contemporaneous work, Anselm Kiefer's treatment of the land, for example, where painting equals burning. Beuys equated sculpture with birch and insulated his energy with felt. For Long, whose work as a whole 'has become a simple metaphor of life', and himself 'a figure walking down his road making his mark', walking actually does equal sculpture, not once but throughout his existence. And within each walk he carries with him the memories of all the others. So that as time has gone on, the ideas behind them have grown in complexity and the categories intermingled. Stones small enough to be carried do not always remain in one place, but can be formed into lines many miles in length. A walk recorded in words on paper may take the same form as a circular slate floor piece or present itself like the petals of a flower, incorporating the making of several small sculptures within its circumference.

Richard Long has said that whereas photographs and text works feed the imagination, sculptures feed the senses. Walking and work made actually in the landscape are only half the story. He also makes works from materials which he selects from natural sources and transports to his other fields of action all over the world, the museum, art gallery or private house. And in a sense these are stopping places too in a wider totality.

He has said, 'My inside and outside sculptures are made in the same spirit. The urban and rural worlds are mutually dependent, and they both have equal significance in my work.' If against all odds we have persisted in the romantic view of Long as an artist, perhaps it will become clear now that Long is a realist working with the sublime. If a mountain vista does not, a bucket of mud thrown at a gallery wall may bring this home. The personas of stones and sticks and muddy water are brought bodily into the professional art context. Stones among stones in their own context they become like ambassadors in this one, reversing Long's role as traveller. The civilisation of the wild is thrust into direct confrontation with the habitat of man. Even indoors nature is a great cutter-down-to-size. Our attention is focused into inward meditation by the physical presence of the materials before us, which involve us in a confrontation equally direct, but more traditional, than accessibility through maps or photographs or words, embodying the essence of vast dimensions. In the gallery we are brought into a kind of close-up with substance which suggests the scale of nature in another way, by measuring the rocks or sticks against our watching human presence. Because there is nowhere to wander, no wider landscape, nothing but a single, simple image, the relationship between art and audience is ruthlessly concentrated. There is nothing to distract the mind contemplating the image from egolessness. Thus we perhaps, like Long or like Bashō, may also do the equivalent of sitting looking into the pond and, hearing a frog jump, intuitively perceive in that split second the nature of reality:

The old pond, ah!
A frog jumps in
The water's sound

Long uses the same simple geometrical shapes he creates in landscape, circles, crosses, lines, spirals, as containers for the materials he causes to form themselves into organic entities on the floor, or on the walls that mark the boundary of the work within doors. The original process of nature which created these materials seems enhanced by their placing; bark differs from willow sticks and driftwood as flint from slate or chalk. One can never forget the aspect of touching and its meaning; movement and time and physical activity are specific to every piece. Not only is placing a willow stick different from placing a block of slate, or the imprint of a muddy hand print different from the smack of a waterfall of River Avon mud from a bucket, each element of each sculpture has its own distinct character. In revealing by these simple means the nature of the work and the space these pieces inhabit, Richard Long seems to hand us back our kingdom polished for inspection in the poetic tradition.

It seems that Long applies a kind of human geometricisation to nature, partly as an aid to analysis and description, but also partly that the two things should exist side by side. Science, art and nature have traditionally been bedfellows, despite the recent separation of the shaman's original roles in modern society. These geometrical shapes are, in any case, as old as man. Although, as Long says, his work is 'abstract art laid down in the real spaces of the world', these forms have a certain reality as archetypes. They are simple, practical and adaptable. Like Long himself they act as a kind of organic ruler; they can measure more things than just space, and are the agency which creates, in visible or invisible form, a three-dimensional portrait of the places in which they are delineated or laid down. Such ideas and images may seem self-contained, as if made by magic, but they also express Long's total activity in their making. Nothing is fudged, the precision of what has been made is there to be seen in a way essentially no different from a portrait by Velázquez or Francis Bacon. We are brought up to believe that no action is so mean that it does not deserve our full attention, yet in art, whenever new frontiers are crossed, James Abbott McNeil Whistler, or Bacon or whoever, invariably gets misunderstood for throwing pots of paint in the public's face.

The simplicity of the reality which Long presents can at first sight be shocking because it is so straightforward. Miles are measured, photographs, real maps, printed words, muddy hand prints are used, entirely without artifice, to state facts about relationships in space and time. But it is precisely this objectivity and straightforwardness which enables us to experience Long's ideas. By expressing them through reality we are able, for the first time perhaps, to deal with the abstract in the same context as the real or natural, and we can also make the transition from small detail to huge vista, from visible to invisible, from past to present, from the artist to the work of art, and between the work of art and ourselves. Long has taken abstract art out of the space-frame, out of its previous pictorial reality, and into the real world of ideas, actions, time, space and movement. He has disentangled art from its stranglehold upon itself, and at a stroke solved the problem of the image's being itself and not a representation of it. Experience of emotion in the face of substance, colour, form or idea takes on a new aspect. We can now perceive all of it as part of the same reality. The exciting thing, following the opening up of this new pictorial world, is that the depths of that reality are still as hidden from us as they have always been.

There are other interesting aspects which concern the involvement of the viewer in the work. Although every part of an exhibition installation is considered by the artist, when it comes to the placing of the work in another context, in the home of a future owner, for instance, it is the owner who, given only the simplest instructions, may follow Long's example and set the work out for himself in the place of his choice. The idea which holds the work together is so strong, that although he may do it more or less precisely or appropriately, he cannot destroy it. As Sol LeWitt pointed out in his *Sentences on Conceptual Art* (1969), 'It is difficult to bungle a good idea.' This like many of Long's solutions is simple and practical, but it seems to me it is also a matter of trust, a way of not proceeding selfishly, of passing on the understanding of a vision.

The artist leaves the viewer alone with nature, as he himself has been. As DT Suzuki has pointed out, in the hurly-burly of life to be left alone, without human drama, just with the infinitely varied forms and colours of nature, can seem like no experience at all. But aloneness is part of contemplation. Like the wandering poet, the artist travels from one unknown to another, and the loneliness engendered by travelling, having nature as his only companion, leads him to reflect on the meaning of life. Solitariness is as important in Long's work as it is in the Japanese haiku or the Japanese tea ceremony. In fact there are relevant parallels between his art and the Japanese idea of the 'spirit

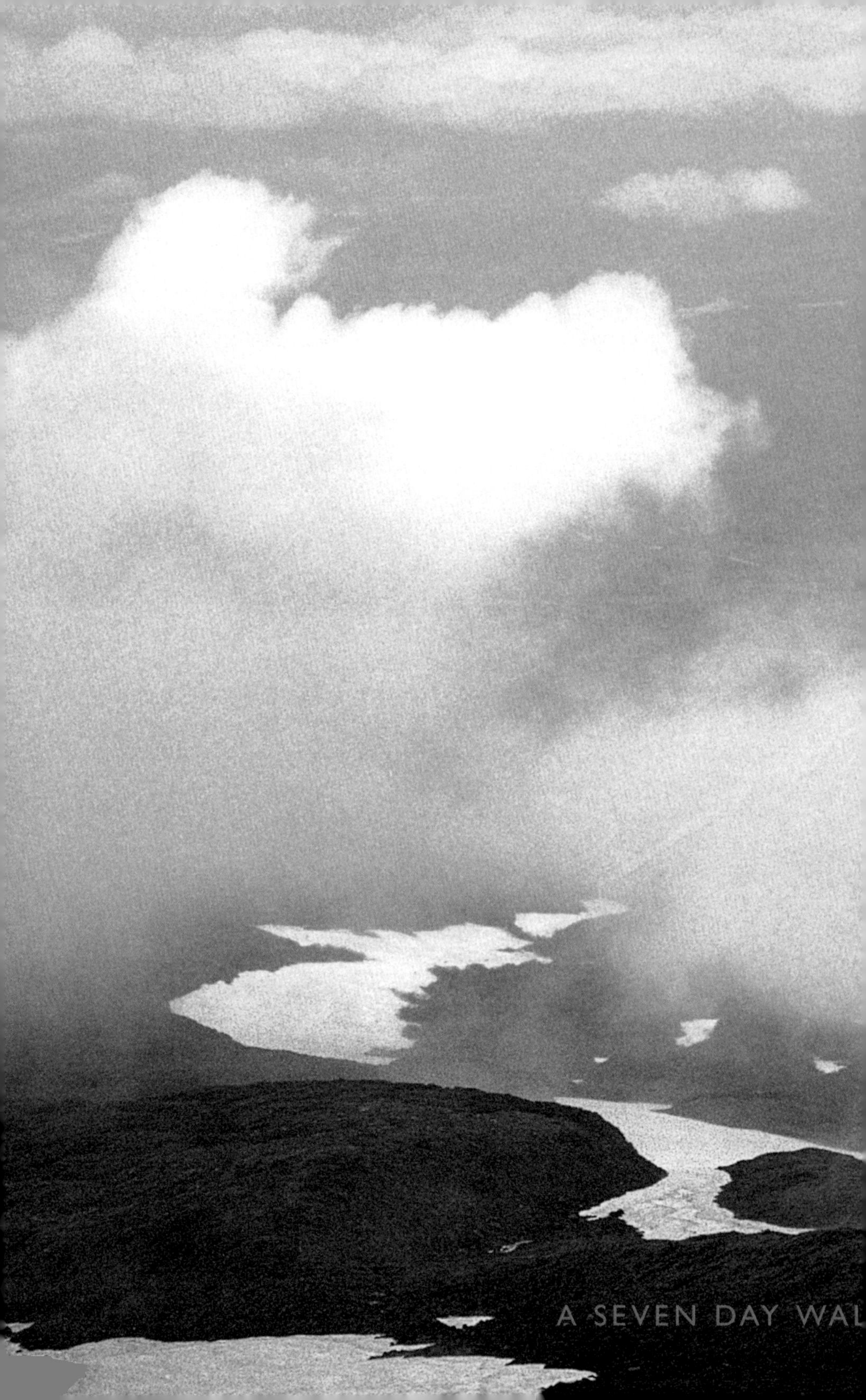
A SEVEN DAY

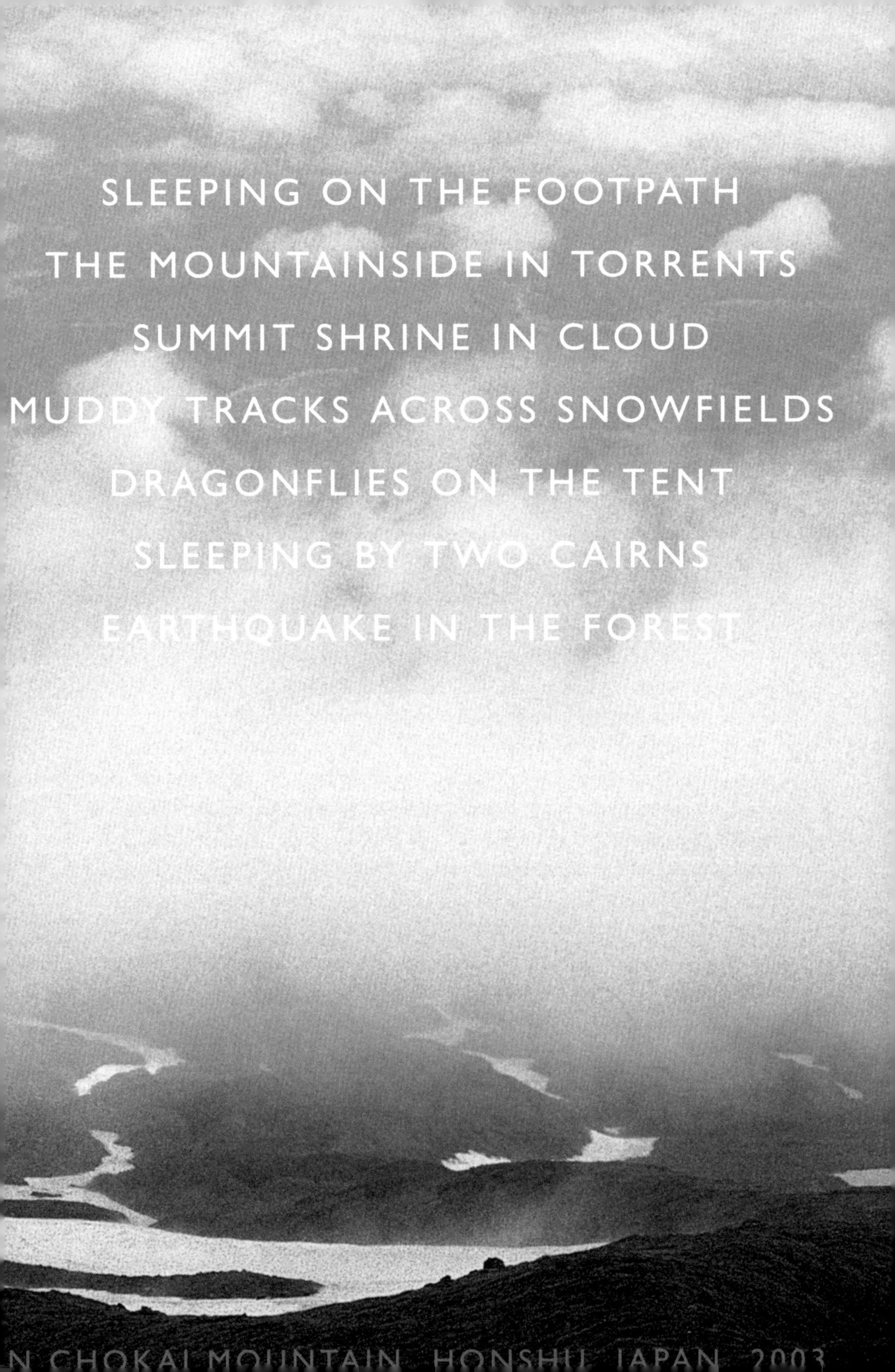

SLEEPING ON THE FOOTPATH
THE MOUNTAINSIDE IN TORRENTS
SUMMIT SHRINE IN CLOUD
MUDDY TRACKS ACROSS SNOWFIELDS
DRAGONFLIES ON THE TENT
SLEEPING BY TWO CAIRNS
EARTHQUAKE IN THE FOREST

N CHOKAI MOUNTAIN HONSHU JAPAN 2003

of tea', which also involves the appreciation of art and creativity, solitariness, poverty and the absence of ego.

The eleventh century Zen master Seccho described the tea man in his tea room as:

> Standing by himself between heaven and earth
> Facing infinitude of beings

Every artist is in a sense concerned to maintain the same kind of balance between people and solitude. In Richard Long's case his work may involve solitude and he enjoys wild places and being one-to-one with nature, but his art is very far from being conceived in isolation. His works and ideas are recorded in notebooks very much with other people in mind. He makes use of all the benefits of modern technology to move so swiftly round the world, and, in his capacity as all international artists, is a frequent visitor to its capital cities to create work there, as well as to its remote places. On his walks he is also aware of the presence of people, of past travellers, and he may make use of the tracks they have left, their fireplaces and shelters, and of the help they provide in giving directions as to how to find his way, food, water. He is always conscious of his role and life within the whole interdependent context of nature, which of course includes humanity.

The importance of the way the work of art is presented, and the artist's involvement and responsibility in this respect, has grown enormously during the century. There are some interesting parallels to be found in the Japanese art of tea. DT Suzuki has described how certain principles have been established to solve the problem of what happens when the tea room begins to fill up, violating its spirit of solitude, poverty and absolutism. These are named as Harmony and Reverence, representing social and ethical elements, Purity representing physical or psychological ones and Tranquillity representing the spiritual or metaphysical aspects. Zen Buddhism apparently comes into it under the latter heading, the tranquillity which emanates from our inner consciousness bringing the whole into relation with the larger sphere of reality. The tea room, somewhat like the art gallery, is the means through which the tea man expresses himself. The man and the room and its contents become one, and the whole is vibrant with his subjectivity, as all who enter are instantly aware. The 'Emptiness' and source of infinite possibilities, which the tea man seeks, is unobstructed concrete reality itself.

Although Richard Long's art must in many ways be regarded as 'abstract', it is also just as much part of reality on all levels, not least in the agency of ordinary objects and actions. Indeed this is one of the senses in which he makes art 'from nothing'. Long has written 'I am content with the vocabulary of universal and common means; walking, placing, stones, sticks, water, circles, lines, days, nights, roads.' He uses these real things – real stones, real water, real mud, real time, real space, real actions unshaped, unaltered, following their inner nature and nature's principle of economy of effort. Similarly Zen never leaves the world of facts and encourages getting to grips with them directly.

Long's work represents his personal choice, isolated and concentrated from the vast array of visual and social possibilities which life presents. What he does has meaning and resonance specifically for him. It may involve a lifetime of similar or repeated actions, but the very repetition brings understanding, accumulation of knowledge and meaning. He has said, 'Being an artist is having a point of view.' It also means having a deep belief in, and commitment to what he is doing.

To be completely sincere the artist or Zen master has to act in the same spirit of reality; he has to adopt a realism of behaviour, an unswerving attitude to truth in which there is no disguise or reserve. This is regarded as true sincerity, and the person who lives according to these principles is seen to become not only reality itself, but to become divine. The striving for truth and sincerity is constant in art, but this also raises the designation of the artist as shaman in contemporary art, and ties together the two apparently opposed elements of mysticism and reality which characterise it. Once again we come back to the idea that artist, art and real world are inseparable from one another. And thus by the same token we proceed to the notion that every man is an artist and that art should be for all. The Zen idea is that the Zen genius sleeps in everyone, and that it only needs to be awakened by penetrating the truth of reality to reveal the mystery and meaning of life.

The refusal of sincerity to separate itself from reality is also connected to the aesthetic of poverty, which lies behind the label 'Arte Povera' attached to certain art of the sixties and seventies because of its use of ordinary, even disregarded materials. The anti-materialism of this movement, which is also part of the direction of Conceptual art, is a relation of the Japanese notion of 'wabi' or 'sabi' which, deeply embedded in the cultural life of Japan, promotes an active aesthetic appreciation of the idea of 'poverty', the need to be satisfied with the spiritual contemplation of nature rather than material things, the need to feel at home in the world. Poverty is at the heart of the Japanese tea ceremony and Zen (like Christianity) inclines to poverty, advocating simplicity, frugality and straightforwardness, making it clear that while we are ruled by the idea of possession we can never be truly free. Richard Long has written, 'I like the idea of using the land without possessing it' and elsewhere, 'My work is simple and practical'. His preference is for the beauty of economy. His work is constructed from three basic raw materials: earth, water and time. He likes travelling light and has reduced the means for making his art to the simple essentials he carries with him in his rucksack – working gloves (for moving heavy stones), a piece of string (for marking the radius of a circle), a water bottle (for water drawings). As we have seen simplicity operates on all levels, his are simple ordinary activities, his achievement is pure sensibility without the encumbrance of technique.

Long believes that even reduced to the simplest means art can be the vehicle for new ideas. Just the act of walking can free the imagination. A simple unconscious activity like watching a river flow can heighten the senses. Natural rhythms such as walking, sleeping, walking, sleeping, can bring him greater understanding of the rhythms of life and nature. Zen demonstrates that the impulses of art are more primitive and more innate than those of morality. The latter can merely regulate and is imposed from without, but the former, which is creative, springs unbidden from within. It is only through such intuitive forces than we can learn about the real nature of things. Conceptual structures can reveal a certain level of truth but alone contain no creativeness. It is not accidental that the first line of Sol LeWitt's *Sentences on Conceptual Art* should qualify the misleading title thus: 'Conceptual artists are mystics rather than rationalists. They leap to conclusions which logic cannot reach.' The artists of the West have perhaps always been closer to the intuitive nature of the oriental mind than to the logical discursive approach and morality of the rest of their society.

The Japanese appreciate that the significance and mystery of life play an integral part in the composition of art, and in following this we are able to recognise in ourselves the presence of a mystery beyond intellectual analysis. Nowhere, perhaps, is this sense of mystery more clearly suggested today than in the work of Richard Long, in spite of, or more probably because of its factuality. It is manifest that those thin lines on Ordnance Survey maps, those circles of stone and muddy hand prints represent ideas of extraordinary grandeur. Part of their impact is because there is nothing but the simplest gesture on the part of the artist between the viewer and the reality experienced.

Long once described his work to me as 'magic and strong medicine'. He has also pointed out that sacred and totemic art is non-figurative. Paradoxically it is the shamanic reference in twentieth-century art which distinguishes it from that of previous times, even to the extent that in recent years the relatively shaman-like character of certain artists, in terms of the universality of their grasp of things (rather in the sense of the Zen master), has been used to characterise them as more remarkable than their fellows. Since the arenas of art and life were joined in earnest, artists have had to be more aware of their position again, of making sure that everything they do makes sense. They have to reconcile their roles as latter day Orpheuses and humble humans, part of a vast natural scheme. They have to accept the national accidents of their birth. Despite the international arena of art, despite the global presence of all these artists, every country seems still to have certain characteristics and interests, discrete from the quality of the work, which have built up over the years, and which the artists inherit and reflect and make part of their art.

When Long talks of magic he is involved with two kinds; on the one hand there is the traditional magic of the conjuror and the acrobat, who twirls the world and shows us things we have not seen before. On the other hand there is also the magic which comes from nowhere and which he can only partly control, the lightning flash, which crystallises the idea and burns and illuminates all round it, which comes intuitively and cannot at present be quantified by scientific methods. It is perhaps what Bashō felt when he heard the frog jump into the pond some time in the seventeenth century. It is the idea of a dynamic present, of a time both old and new, of a ripple which continues to resonate in the mind.

This revised text was originally published in *Il Luogo Buono*, exh. cat., Milan 1985.

Richard Long

Palacio de Cristal, Madrid, 28 January – 20 April 1986

Madrid Circle 1986 | *Segovia Slate Circles* 1986

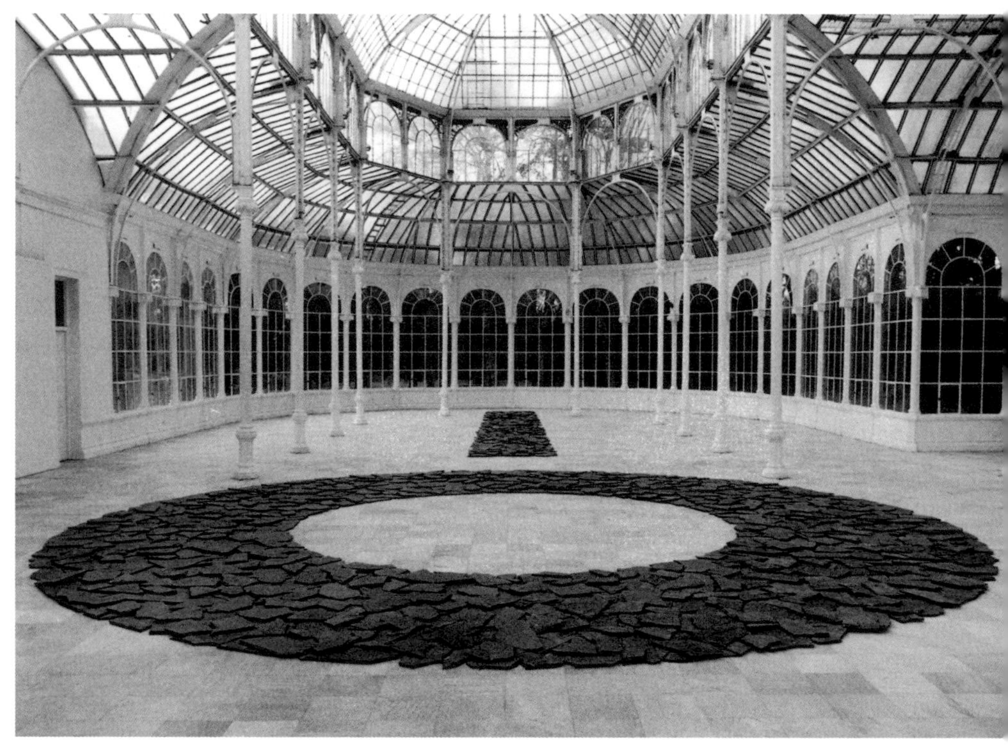

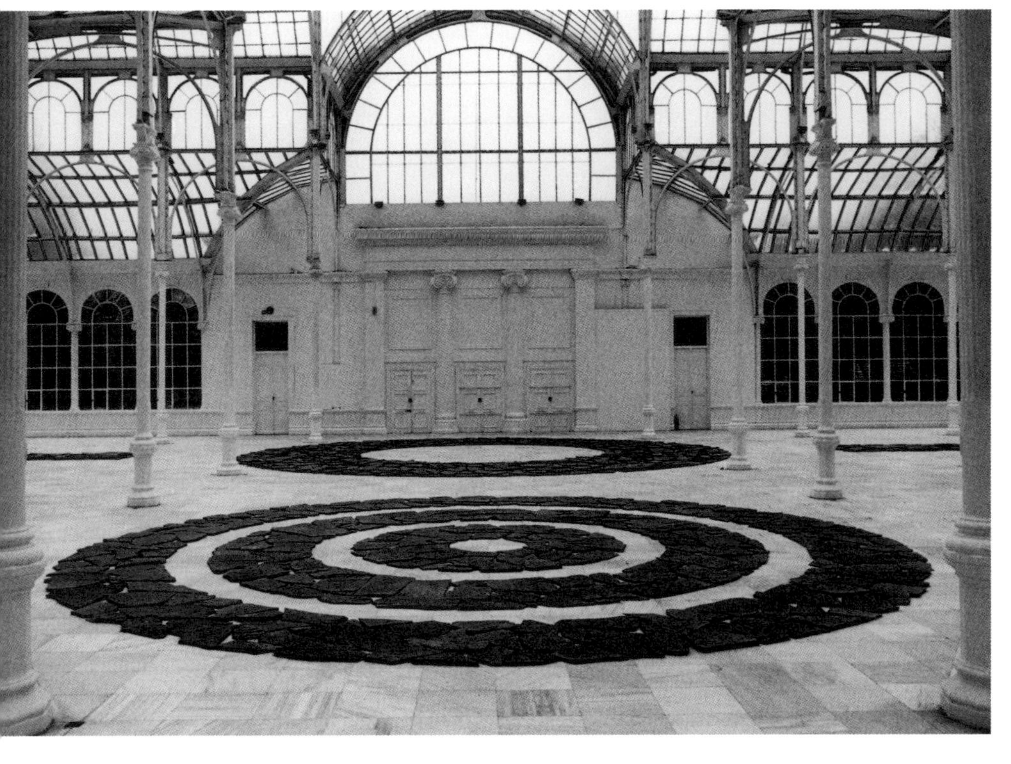

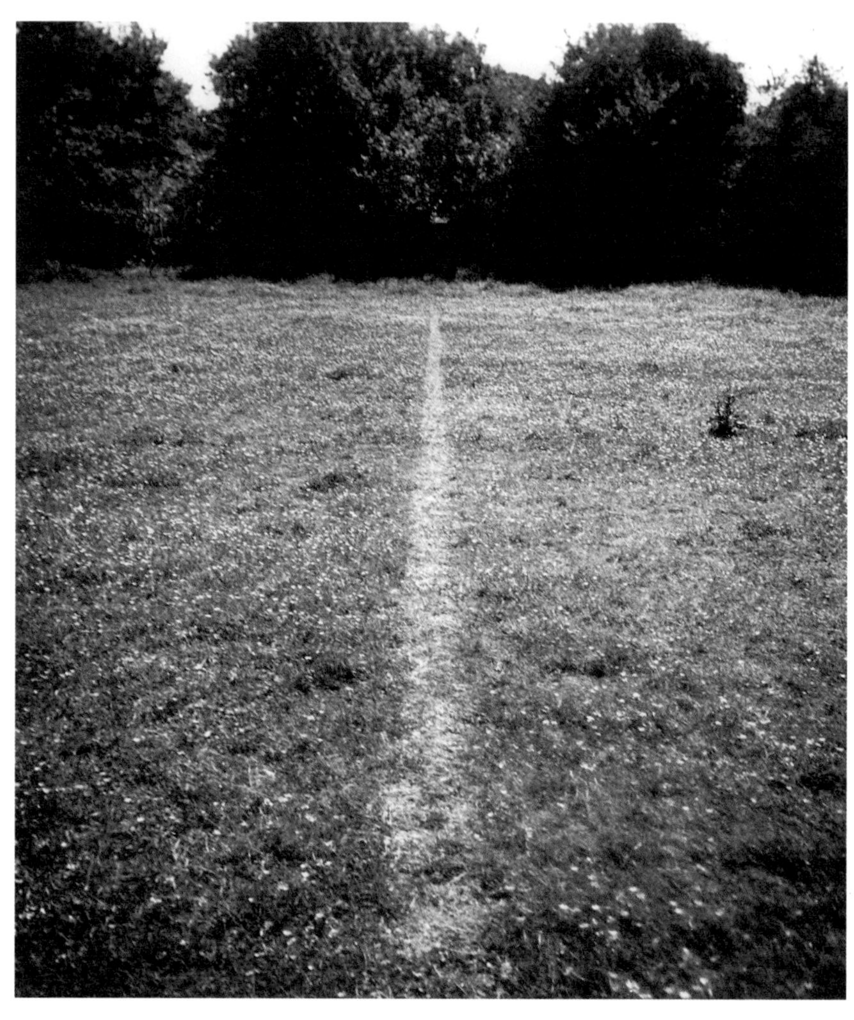

A LINE MADE BY WALKING
ENGLAND 1967

RH FUCHS

Walking the Line

He had, he said, always been attracted to the outdoor life, ever since he was a boy. He often liked being on his own. Now, he likes the ease and naturalness with which things come one after the other: walking, climbing, camping, gathering wood, lighting the fire, boiling water, packing up and walking again. Walking, he said to me, with its hardships and its pleasures, the surprise of discovery and growing experience, relaxation and concentration: walking is a good way to think. Steady rhythms. Your feet can take you anywhere in the world, except where there is no water or the water is too deep. When machines break down there are always your feet. A lot of ideas come while walking, or when sitting down to rest. The landscape puts them into your head.

He makes a work of art in the place he chooses, with the materials that are there, on the slope of a mountain, high under the sky – a line of stones if there are stones lying about, or if the place wants a circle, a circle. When there are no stones, he can walk up and down the footpath as often as necessary for a line to become visible, or with his boot he can scratch a mark in the soft earth, or he can make a line by pouring water from his flask. After a while the sun dries the line away; it may be gone when he moves on. There is no special reason, aesthetic or political, to make such works of art. The work is there because of the artist's desire to make it. The artist makes art because he is an artist.

The works are traces of staying and passing: each marks what was the centre of the world when he was there. The forms are forms of movement, like the straight line or the spiral, or forms of staying, like the circle and the cross. Many things come together in those forms. It is impossible to ascertain when and where a walk, moving lightly ahead, pauses for a while, curls up into a sculpture like a cat, and goes on its way again. In the end there is one giant work stretched out across the world, crossing and overlapping, an epic of art. I shall have to unravel something of the slow growth of this work: how the walk crosses over the sculpture like water passing underneath the bridge like the footpath going over the mountain like the valley rolling through the mountains like water slipping into the sea, walking slipping into sculpture like a cloud drifting in the wind.

There is a temptation, when one is writing about this extraordinary art and trying to understand it, to be romantic or poetic. The twentieth-century art world, the places where Richard Long's art is being seen, appreciated and evaluated, is urban and nervous – the total opposite, one would say, of the world in which the works are made. They have an other-worldliness, another sense of time, like things happening in a fairy tale. But one must take care not to present them as such. The idea of a natural landscape, even when wild and occasionally dangerous, as a landscape one can walk in, is profoundly different from that of a savage nature one has to live in – without the possible refuge of the city. Richard Long's landscape is, consequently, as modern (in feeling) as the city of Bristol from which he sets out for a walk. Modern life, modern equipment, modern means of transport – and modern ideas – have given him these landscapes.

He himself tends to see the choice of place in rather practical terms, playing down as much as he can the romantic, poetic connotations. The fact that the vast majority of people do not spend three weeks walking in the mountains of Ladakh, does not make it abnormal or eccentric to do so. To him Ladakh is as important as any cosmopolitan city, and maybe even more so; and the possibilities that it offers him for his work are different from those of any other place in the world.

The work he can do there, or in Lappland or East Africa or Alaska, may at times be formally very similar to works done near home, in the west of England; but it is different because the place is completely different in spirit and in scale. Even on Dartmoor, which is fairly wild ground, the heap of tinner's stones looks an almost intimate work compared to the vast and 'raw' circle of stones high in the Andes.

In some way we all know such feelings in relation to landscape: sitting by a narrow river, looking at the water, or standing on a high cliff in a roaring wind overlooking the grey, cold ocean. In Richard Long's work form and experience and memories and feelings come together, mysteriously and beyond the words of the prose-writer: so there is the intimation of poetry.

Obviously it is not quite so simple as that. The artist, even when he makes his first work, has a history behind him – his own history, the history of other art made before his time, and his perception of that history. In fact, the personal history of the artist, what makes him decide how to make his first work, in what formal language, is his perception of the history (and the presence) of other art. Then he makes his first work, and that first work, if it is any good, is already new and independent of previous history. There are always art-historical links and other aesthetic considerations to be pointed out, but they serve only to define the independence and the autonomy of the new work. Its present existence can never be deduced from what came before. The great *Black Square* (1915) of Kazimir Malevich was, in its stunning absoluteness, not announced in his previous work. In retrospect one can, maybe, understand that it was he who made that painting and not Picasso – because he was working within historical and aesthetic circumstances that permitted or fostered such radicalness more than the atmosphere of Picasso's Paris.

What then made Richard Long make his basic work, *A Line Made by Walk*ing (1967), right in the middle of the swinging sixties in London? There was very little in the atmosphere of the time to suggest the almost intolerable simplicity of that piece – a line made by walking up and down in a field until the flattened grass caught the sunlight from a different angle and became visible as a line. Thus the photograph which recorded the artwork was made.

His education, up to that point, did not simply lead him to walking that line. All that education can do is clarify the mind and clear things away. In 1967 he was still at St Martin's School of Art, in London, at that time famous for the 'New Sculpture' of welded painted metal practised by artists like Anthony Caro and Phillip King, the best-known teachers at the school. At St Martin's he had made artworks that used the floor or the flat roof of the school in conjunction with 'simple' materials like sand or water: works that resembled gently undulating landscapes, or dammed shapes of water within the rectangular ridges of the roof. Earlier pieces from 1965 were heaps of sand or heaps of blankets. Maybe it was the school's atmosphere of speculative innovation, its absence of doctrine, that encouraged a young artist to undertake such things. There were his contemporaries at the school too, Barry Flanagan and Gilbert & George and Hamish Fulton (each of them different and becoming artists in their own right); but there were, Richard Long recalls, no programmatic discussions among them about which course art, new art, should take. Artists talk and think about things directly at hand, how to get something right, and not so much about the distant future. Visual art, as Long's work shows, is the most concrete form of thought, because whatever you may invent in your head has to be actually made.

In any case, coming to London in September 1966 he had already brought a certain artistic formation, even a certain 'style', with him from his native Bristol, where he had been at the West of England College of Art from September 1962 to March 1965. In Bristol in 1966, he had made, among other works, a *Turf Circle* by cutting into the soil, first cutting the circle and then its segments and taking them out, removing an even layer of soil, then putting them back to make the sculpture a lowered, circular plane of ground. It looked like a bicycle wheel. In 1965 he had created a sculpture by digging out hollows, lines and holes in the grass and filling or lining some with white plaster. Like the *Turf Circle*, this was a work made by a young artist to test how to use materials and the idea of negative space. What is surprising is how close Richard Long, barely 20 years old, already was to what was to become his 'language'. The circle had appeared, the basic form, as well as the intention (almost a natural instinct) to treat his materials with gentleness, not wasting them. The turf was used and laid back, its tissue only momentarily severed; after a while the segments would grow back into the earth that produced them. In the plaster piece the white liquid, hardening while finding its way along the folds of the ground, marks a pattern which was already there: that too became a fundamental condition in his later work.

Concurrent with the plaster piece, he made two small 'models' of actual pieces of landscape, in plaster, carefully and realistically painted: *An Irish Harbour* (1966) (drawn on his first visit to Ireland) and *A Square of Ground* (1966) on the Bristol Downs. Even if here, too, the basic occupation is with ground, the idea is considered in a different way. The pieces are in a sense miniature copies; thus they are narrative – as was a work of 1965, environmental in character: an undulating, winding plaster path curving into the corner of the studio. It could be walked along. To indicate that idea, he placed a plaster figure of a walking man, with a hat, facing towards it. The work thus explored the idea of a walking viewer, moving, and a static walking sculpture. But its further development would have led Richard Long towards illustrative structures he did not want and away from the simple materials that, like the turf in the circle, stay simple. In the models and in the walking man the material was absorbed and hidden in the form, static and for ever.

In conversation Richard Long remarked that he liked many of his works to be impermanent. That way they were more human, their limited physical existence in the world resembling the impermanence and reality of human life; and he mentioned that already in the winter of 1964 he had made a ground-drawing by rolling and directing a snowball over the snow-covered plateau of the Bristol Downs. This, one of his very first artworks (of which only a casual photograph exists), is in retrospect an already rather perfect one: the meandering line is the path which the uneven ground forces the snowball to take as it gathers weight and slows down. The procedure of the work is beautifully circular, and is completed when the drawing melts away in the sun, leaving no trace at all. The piece is delicate as one's warm breath condensing against a cold window-pane and then evaporating. This principle of 'disappearance' was also taken up by *Turf Circle* and even more decidedly by *A Line Made by Walking*, in the spring of 1967.

Impermanence lies at the very heart of Richard Long's conviction as an artist. It has rendered possible the idea of walking as his comprehensive artform, containing all the other forms through which his art chooses to express itself. That the idea of physical impermanence was in his mind as early as 1964, when he was rolling a snowball over the grass, is an impressive fact of artistic conviction and of resistance, even if subconscious, against the dominant belief in most cultures that art is not only there to be used and enjoyed in the present but should also promote that present into an eternal future. It was a resistance borne out of instinct and practice. Even if Richard Long, young as he was, did not then know what precise direction his art should take, his instinct told him that the area he was entering had rich possibilities. He had somehow slipped into it by just doing what he liked to do without worrying about how art should look. (In one of the notes he sent me he observed how art carried the pleasures of childhood into adult life: damming streams, throwing stones or bouncing them across rivers, making sand castles – 'not so different in spirit from making my work'.)

One wonders, actually, whether an artist ever worries about the physical future of his work. The artist's business is I think always in the present: making a work leaves the previous work behind, while the next one is still beyond the horizon. His concern is to make the present work as powerful as he can. The beauty of art, the spiritual and visual density of the artwork, actually seems to derive from that absolute concentration on one moment – never, it seems, from an artist's direct, conscious involvement in history. Because when making a work (wherever he is, in a city or alone on a high mountain pass) the artist is momentarily absent from history: he is confronting history, intervening in order to change it. Thus, when he makes a work of art, it is precisely in that tense moment that art history is cancelled, denied its course – in a way denied its already shaky permanence. Nothing in history is permanent. The present modifies the past, most of the time by a slow, almost imperceptible process of erosion. Sometimes, however, changes are abrupt and dramatic, as when a major, irrevocable artwork appears in the world.

The *Black Square* of Malevich is a painting which cancelled previous art in one grand, abrupt statement of conviction – the conviction that something was over and that there was no need to hang on. The *Black Square* slapped the face of history, in order to wake it up. I believe Richard Long's *[A] Line Made by Walking* to be a work of equal importance. Like the *Black Square* it is a work with almost no formal characteristics, using the simplest form, the line. Thus, as it is hardly characterised by its form, it is overwhelmingly distinct in its passion and conviction. Its origin is a mystery. I have sketchily indicated Richard Long's involvement, from a very early moment in his career, with all the separate elements and aspects one again encounters in the *[A] Line Made by Walking*: ground, soil, nature, simple forms, common materials. But all the previous works did not by necessity lead up to that line. Such logic in art does not exist.

Only two years before (admittedly a long time for a young artist), he was hesitating, trying the miniature models and the walking man, circling as in other early works around something without quite touching it. One month before the *Line* he made his first travelling and walking piece. That work was made into a panel showing an outline drawing of Britain marked with six pairs of square photographs of the ground and the sky, each bearing the name of a day. The typewritten text reads: *April 1967. A journey, by hitch-hiking and walking, out and back, from London to the summit of Ben Nevis, Scotland – Two photographs taken at 11 A.M. each day at the position shown.* This piece is an invisible sculpture in space and time – in fact what excited Richard Long about it was its vast scale in time and distance. Still, one feels there is something congested about it; in relation to the *Line* it is, in structure and procedure as well as in presentation, overly complicated, as if several ideas were present in it without really joining. The same is true, I think, of a bicycling piece he made later that year: transporting and leaving 16 separate parts of a sculpture around an area of 2,401 square miles of central and eastern England. This was presented as an outline map and text, including the statement: 'No photographs'. The fact that the bicycle work was made after the *Line Made by Walking* shows how different ideas were germinating in his mind at the same time.

Although the *Line Made by Walking* does not in principle contradict these large-scale works, it has a different quality: it is very much about laying down a perfect, controlled and yet vibrant form, intimate but without real scale – not overwhelming like the Ben Nevis or bicycle works, which did, however, establish the possibility that pieces could encompass vast geographical areas. The *Line*, moreover, cleared up something about the lightness there could be in making art: it was made exclusively with the elements that were there and remained there, after the sculpture ended, without having been physically affected: the ground, the grass, the form of the line, the artist walking, the light of the sun. The *Line* is the result of the coming together, precisely in that place and moment, of these elements. Therefore, because there was nothing left out and nothing included that wasn't there before, this sculpture became somewhat of a prototype, or a matrix, a form so perfectly simple, open and resolved that it also became a clarification, even a revelation of how to make sculpture. Walking slipped into line, line slipped into form, form slipped into place, place slipped into image. It irrevocably cleared the air, just as the *Black Square* had once done, by suddenly, unaccountably, being there. The *Line Made by Walking* became classic the moment it was done; it made all the other early work look tentative and experimental, though surely it itself had started out as another experiment: an idea put to the test of practice.

In a note Richard Long commented that in making the *Line* he discovered that its visibility depended only on the quantity of walking. Walking once he left almost invisible footprints in the grass; walking up and down many times left a visible path. He realised that between the two 'states' there was no real 'conceptual' difference. It led him to think about visibility and permanence. Even the visible line would in the end disappear, only less quickly. Another idea that came to him was that, instead of going up and down a line, he could continue walking a line that would grow longer and longer, without changing form or identity (visible or not, that did not matter); that led to a new dimension of scale in execution. In that sense too, the *Line* was crucial because it indicated a way of encompassing the large scale indicated by the bicycle work or the hike to Ben Nevis. The *Line* revealed that the traditional, common means of walking could be used to make art.

The discovery of a new, expanded scale, in distance as well as time, was not just of formal importance in Richard Long's art. It is true that the *Line Made by Walking* looks like a carefully executed formal study, an essay in technique and procedure. But the fact that it used the real earth, without adding or subtracting other materials, hardly disturbing the ground that was walked on, opened up an enormous new range of content. In principle a walk could traverse different landscapes, at different times of day and night, in different conditions of weather and through different states of mind on the part of the walker – thereby making all these aspects of the real world part of the sculpture. The sculpture became part of the world, an articulation of it – not an addition, not a stable object. While being made, the sculpture was also moving along; it had a form but not an unalterable permanence of form – its form ultimately consisted in the direction of its movement and the shape of the land. A walk crosses over the surface of the earth which carries it with pleasure. The earth becomes the companion of the artwork, walking with it as the artwork takes pleasure in the world.

Around the time that the *Line Made by Walking* was executed, spring 1967, Richard Long made several other works which, without actually contradicting the principle of the *Line*, nevertheless took a slightly different direction, in practice as in spirit. One was a landscape piece, constructed on a stretch of parkland near Bristol. In the foreground he put up a thin vertical rectangular frame of wood, while much further away in the background, where the land sloped slightly upwards, he placed a flat circle of plywood, painted white. The idea was to make a work of three places (at the same time): the place of the circle, the place of the rectangle and the place of the viewer – and for the work to become 'complete' when the three were in alignment and the viewer could see (as in the photograph) the circle within the frame of the rectangle. But the work does more: it also demonstrates the character of the terrain. Its visibility is actually dependent on the fact that, beyond the trees, the land slopes upwards. Thus the construction offers, in its way, a picture of the place – more precise and articulated than if the photograph had been taken without it, because now perception has become literally pointed, structured and quite different from the 'roaming' glance practised in, for example,

Romantic landscape painting. The work then is more of a landscape than the *Line Made by Walking*, which concentrates on the line as form itself.

In a somewhat different manner, the conscious use of the character and condition of the terrain as an aspect of content and expression was explored in a work executed in various places in England and Ireland, using three concentric circles made of segments of plywood painted white. The *Line Made by Walking* had been walked on a non-descript piece of flat grassland – abstract and anonymous. That was what made it so uncompromisingly pure and simple and real. The construction in the park made the perception of landscape abstractly formal by projecting a precise viewpoint and line of vision. The concentric circles touched the ground. They were a transportable sculpture, to be laid out in various places and on various types of ground. The circles would fit snugly to the ground and visibly follow its uneven surface to the point of being interrupted by stones, as in the Irish version. Circles showed ground and ground showed circles, perfectly matched to the surface of the earth. They could be looked at from any point. The sculpture then demonstrated that no two places were alike, each place making the shape of the work each time. From here it was only a step to making circles in the landscape, tracing the earth's surface in a similar way, using the materials provided by the earth itself (stones, driftwood and so on) instead of carrying prefabricated circles to the place where the sculpture could be made. To come to that conclusion, which is simple only after the fact, a radical clarification was needed. That clarification, once again, was the *Line Made by Walking*. It presented a standard and a level of possibilities which other early pieces did not have.

Richard Long, exh. cat., Solomon R Guggenheim Museum, New York and Thames & Hudson, London 1986, pp.43–47.

ROBERT C MORGAN

Richard Long's Post-Structural Encounters

Solomon R Guggenheim Museum, New York,
12 September – 30 November 1986

In today's complex urban environment, taking a walk may involve a particular kind of tense alertness. Our sensory apparatus tends to shut down under stress unless, of course, we make a conscious effort to observe the visual spectacles around us or have the occasional luxury to take a stroll without the pressure of having to meet a schedule. For many, taking a walk is no more than an unconscious routine – like eating – a normal everyday activity, performed in a nearly automatic or involuntary manner. The typical urban/suburban dweller tends to bracket the visual environment in order to attend to the more expedient tasks of running an errand, crossing the street without getting hit by traffic, or avoiding potential hazards near parking lots, alleys, or construction sites. There is a distinctly detached attitude about routine walks taken amid a fabricated system of signs and buildings as compared with the experience of taking an isolated walk in a wilderness environment. It is this latter approach to walking which has been the source of Richard Long's art for two decades and the subject of his major exhibition at the Guggenheim Museum in New York last fall.

Unlike the contrasting sensory conditions found in cities, the experience of walking on the plains of Bolivia or in the mountains of Central Nepal – two examples of the artist's many walks, taken at various locations around the world – may be characterised as less detached and more internalised. In removing himself from the numbing congestion of urban signs, Richard Long has established a completely different basis of intentionality as an artist working in close proximity to nature.

Although structured according to specific sites, places, distances and durations, the walks and markings made by Long appeal not only to an essential experience of the sublime but to another kind of language system where meaning is immediately transcribed according to the subjective referent of one's own consciousness. In the wilderness, there is little necessity for mediation in that the mind is not imposed upon to deconstruct messages that intervene between the rhythmic flow of memory and the external and subliminal projection of ideological referents. The engagement of one's own physicality and sense of biological time with nature through the act of self-propulsion as an ambulating intelligence in upright form attends directly to the intentionality of consciousness. The language of meaning is not deflected into narcissism but expanded through memory.

Long's walking projects began in 1967 while still a student at St Martin's School of Art in London with a piece called *A Line Made by Walking* (1967). The work involved walking a straight line through a field of grass, thus marking the place of the walk in the process according to the traces of bent grass left by his footprints. While the structure of the walk was conceptually predetermined, the experience of the walk and the photo-documentary evidence which followed signified another type of subjective involvement with language other than a purely structural or scientific analysis of method and meaning. It was this post-Structural emphasis upon subjectivity in relation to the physical and perceptual experience of the site that implied the necessary means to transcend all bifurcated systems of language in favour of a direct involvement with time, distance and place.

As the recent Guggenheim retrospective has revealed, Long has maintained an indelible consistency in exploring these parameters of time, distance and place. In one sense, all of Long's museum and gallery installations, his inscribed maps, his inventive typographies, and sumptuously framed photographs – usually, but not always in black and white – add up to a single work, a continuum based on the first walk made in 1967 where he intentionally chose these parameters as his artistic medium. His works revive a sense of awareness in terms of what we sense in nature apart from the routine interruptions of the urban environment. It is as if Long is looking to regain some insight into those lost recesses of primordial consciousness as suggested by his ritualised circles and spirals, composed of stones, sticks, chalk, slate and driftwood, often arranged on location at the site of a particular walk using indigenous materials.

Long will give considerable attention to the natural forces present in the physical world and to the rhythms and observations he makes in reference to these phenomena as indicated in his more recent typographical notations, such as *A 118 Mile Walk Under the Sky* (1980), in which he concentrates on one aspect of the environment: the quality of light piercing through the clouds. In Long's photographs of site-markings, such as *Avon Gorge Water Drawing, Bristol* (1983), or an earlier piece entitled *A Circle in Alaska, Bering Strait Driftwood on the Arctic Circle* (1977), Long insists on presenting us with the evidence of having been there. In each of these works – two examples of many – there is evidence of an on-site representation, a signifying distillation of the experience that invites the outsider to arbitrarily participate in a place. The photographs then are metaphors of place as well as records of the artist's act of rearrangement and order given to the place in a very fundamental way.

In addition to the framed documents, word-works, and photographs, Long also reconstructs natural artefacts within the context of museums. He thereby translates a feeling for another place outside the domain of art within it, which gives the institutional space an aura of meditative transformation, an arena of contemplation that allows configurations of stones and sticks to be perceived as signs. This view of post-Structural reality does not attempt to reiterate the dialectical site/non-site juxtapositions of Robert Smithson. Rather, Long is attempting to establish within the institutional space a sense of subjective wholeness, an intentional reality of connectedness – that the physicality of self is commensurate with the physicality of nature. Along one section of the spiralling ramp at the Guggenheim, Long placed a line of red slate interrupted midway by a line of black slate. The impetus of the slate line spiralling down the ramp suggested walking – simply walking – as one observed the patterns of the slate in the course of the artist's reconstruction. There is a gestalt presence as the perceiving person clearly occupies the space of the work and thereby establishes a point of view that is in relation to the temporal act of perceiving. With Long, this act of perceiving through conscious ambulation has both epistemological and ontological dimensions. One might add that there is a teleological dimension as well. To walk is to become aware of one's consciousness in direct response to the natural environment, and by becoming aware of nature one may begin to de-acculturate signage and gradually to comprehend the real substance of design as the inner and outer relationship between those things that exist at the material foundation of culture.

This desire to transform is not located in the traditional romantic mode of perceiving; it is more about this artist's evolution through Structuralist philosophy toward a seemingly reduced post-Structural position. His documents and installations are not so much about a sensibility as they are about indexical connections with the sublime wilderness landscapes in which he walks. The markings, such as the series of *Avon River Mud Circles* (1984) which reveal the imprints of his own hand, are always induced according to the lexical presence of himself as a corporeal intelligence within nature as opposed to the radical transformations imposed upon nature in the tradition of classicism. Paradoxically, Long's work is wedged somewhere between Minimal and Conceptual art, for he gives us both the evidence and the idea.

Arts, vol.16, no.6, February 1987, pp.76–77.

RICHARD CORK AND RICHARD LONG

Interview

RC *Your exhibitions demonstrate that you know exactly how to handle gallery space with the spare lucidity which characterises your outdoor work. But of course remote country is a very different arena from a gallery. So how do you go about re-creating the outdoor experience indoors?*

RL In the way the photographs and maps feed the imagination. The sculptures you can see directly in the gallery feed the senses, and also the mudworks which are made directly on the wall. I like to present art in a very concrete way in a gallery, as well as presenting images from remote places. I think also the photographs have the function that I can make a piece of work, for example, in a canyon in Mexico, by pouring water down a rock face to make a water drawing, and then record that idea and bring it back into the world of art. Photographs are useful for recording a work which may only last for the time that the water drawing dries in the sunshine.

RC *Do you find it easier to work outdoors than in a gallery context?*

RL I enjoy both ways of working, and for me it is necessary to use both possibilities. I think if I only worked outdoors it could perhaps be seen as romantic escapism.

RC *Do you ever wish that the gallery visitor could actually see your work in the landscape?*

RL All the places where I make my work, such as the Highlands, or on Dartmoor, are free public places where anyone can go. So it is quite possible that people can go to the locations of my walks and often the information is provided, as in the mapworks. It is not my intention that they should actually repeat the walks, because not only do they belong to a certain place, but they also belong to a certain time. You can never repeat the time but certainly people can go to the places of my walks. Also, it is not true to think that my landscape sculptures are never seen. They are sometimes seen by local people in the country, occasionally as I make them, or discovered by chance by people who might not recognise them as art but who would nevertheless see them. I am sort of interested in all the different contexts that work can be put into the world and then also received back by different people in different circumstances.

RC *But it is surely significant that you would never, by choice, make your work outdoors with people looking on while you were doing it.*

RL No, it is never a performance. It is usually a very private, quiet activity. I am happy to make it in solitude. I think part of the energy in my work is that I have the opportunity to make art in amazing, beautiful landscapes which are very strong and powerful. Somehow part of the power and the energy comes from being alone in that place. The simplicity and feeling of being alone is actually part of the work. So it would be quite inappropriate to have a load of people visiting it at a particular site, as that would change the whole nature of the place. So I think that is another way my photographs work. They present the idea that art can be made in solitude or in very remote places, or lasts for very few minutes, or be seen by very few people, or be seen by people from a different culture.

RC *How much of the year on average do you spend walking, would you say?*

RL It is difficult to say. I have never measured it, but probably not more than half. I don't consider myself a nomad, and I am not a person who is endlessly wandering. I like to go to places for a certain reason, following a certain idea, and to do a piece of work which lasts for a certain amount of time. Then when I have finished that work I always like to come home. So it is a necessary part of my life to be quiet at home in Bristol. That is also part of the way I like to live. I think if I was travelling all the time I would not have the right type of energy to start making a big walk. It is necessary to have an appetite. Often a good walk comes after spending a month or so in Bristol, just answering letters and doing paperwork. Then I have a good appetite to go out into the landscape.

RC *Since you also spend a lot of time holding exhibitions all over the world, you must be a highly organised person.*

RL Well I think to be a professional full-time artist it is necessary to be very organised. I think, like a lot of artists, the most organised thing you see about me is my work. So probably the work is more organised than my life.

RC *How do you decide where to take the next walk?*

RL Oh, for a variety of reasons. I like the idea that it is possible to go around to the other side of the world almost on a hunch. I may have a feeling or an idea that some place might be interesting, or I may never have been there before, or know anything about it. That is a good enough reason to find out what that place is like.

RC *So you don't necessarily research a place before you go there?*

RL Well it depends. There are certain walks close to home, like a piece I did this summer in Scotland where I had a particular idea about making a walk in the Highlands. Because you can get good maps in Britain it was possible to plan the walk by looking at maps; I could know the place in advance. So then, it was just a question of going to the place and carrying out the walk. In other places, like the Hoggar Mountains in the Sahara where I went this year, it is not possible to get good maps. So you have a completely differently way of going about walking. The way I found my way in the Sahara was just by following the places where I could get water, without using a map. So some walks are with maps and some are without.

RC *Do you ever get lost?*

RL There are different ways of getting lost, but not fundamentally lost. Sometimes just for a couple of hours here and there in a mist. In the early days, when I used to make straight walks across Dartmoor, one of the nice things I used to like about walking in a straight line was that, apart from the intellectual beauty of a straight line, it is the most practical way to cross a moor. No matter what the weather is doing, and it can be a very thick mist, because I am following a compass line I can do that walk in any conditions and not get lost.

So walking by compass in straight lines, apart from anything else, is a very practical part of my work. I think basically all my work is very practical. The only reason I could do the walk in the Sahara was that I had the amazing good luck that before I went there, there happened to be some freak storms that left pools of water in the mountains. Those storms determined that I could walk there, and where I could find water determined the shape of the walk. So, in fact, how it turned out was that the walk lasted for six days. Each day the little pools of water were drying up and disappearing into the ground. So at the end of the six days the water had disappeared, and that is when the walk ended. So it had a nice kind of practical logic about it.

RC *What do you actually think about when you are on your own and walking, mile after mile, in often quite deserted territory?*

RL Well, you can think about everything. I think all I can say is that somehow having the rhythmic relaxation of walking many hours each day puts me into a state of mind which frees the imagination. Quite often I get ideas for new works by doing a walk. In other words one walk leads to another.

RC *So you never feel lonely?*

RL Oh, no. It never occurs to me to feel lonely. I just think I am very lucky to have these pockets of freedom and silence, escaping from the normal chaos of everyday life in the art world. It is like another dimension I can have in my life.

RC *Do you find some landscapes are more conducive to work than others?*

RL Oh, yes. I would say that for a start, the British landscape is interesting. It is my home landscape, and I find it very rich. Even the footpaths and lanes of the West Country, and then the moorlands and the Highlands. The moorlands in Britain are interesting – it is a very particular type of landscape. Ireland is another country which I feel very sympathetic to. I have very strong feelings about it because basically, in the west, it is my type of landscape, a sort of stony, wet desert, also with a lot of nice people and a lot of humour and beautiful music. So that is another interesting country. I would also say that Bolivia is again another big, stony desert. I think in a strange way that landscapes like the tundra, like Alaska for example – it's almost like being on Dartmoor but it is much bigger. So in a way I often feel at

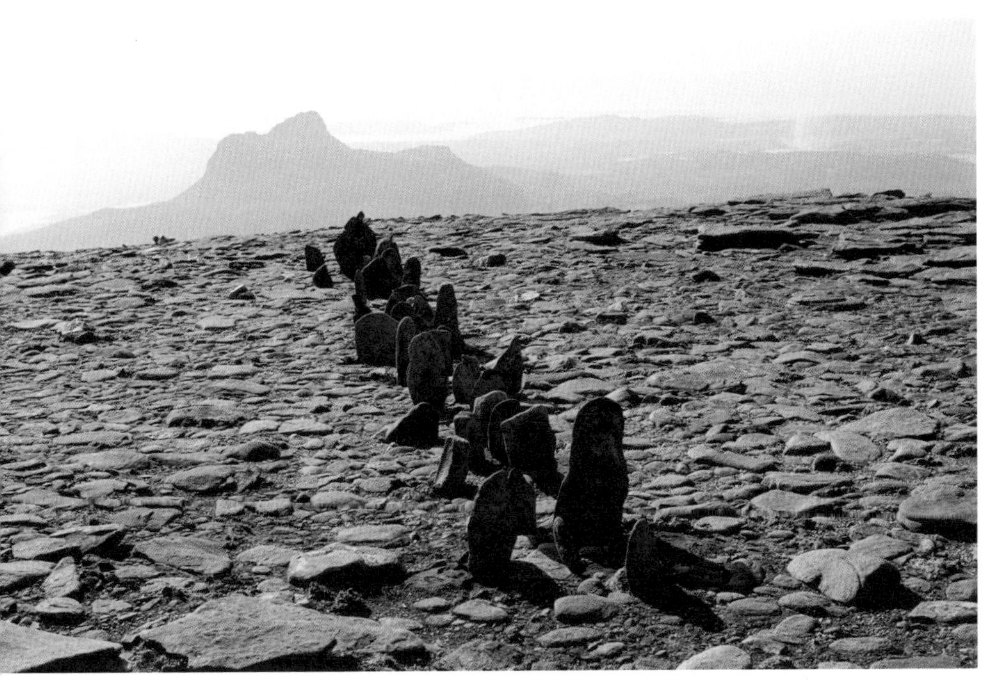

A LINE IN SCOTLAND
CUL MÓR 1981

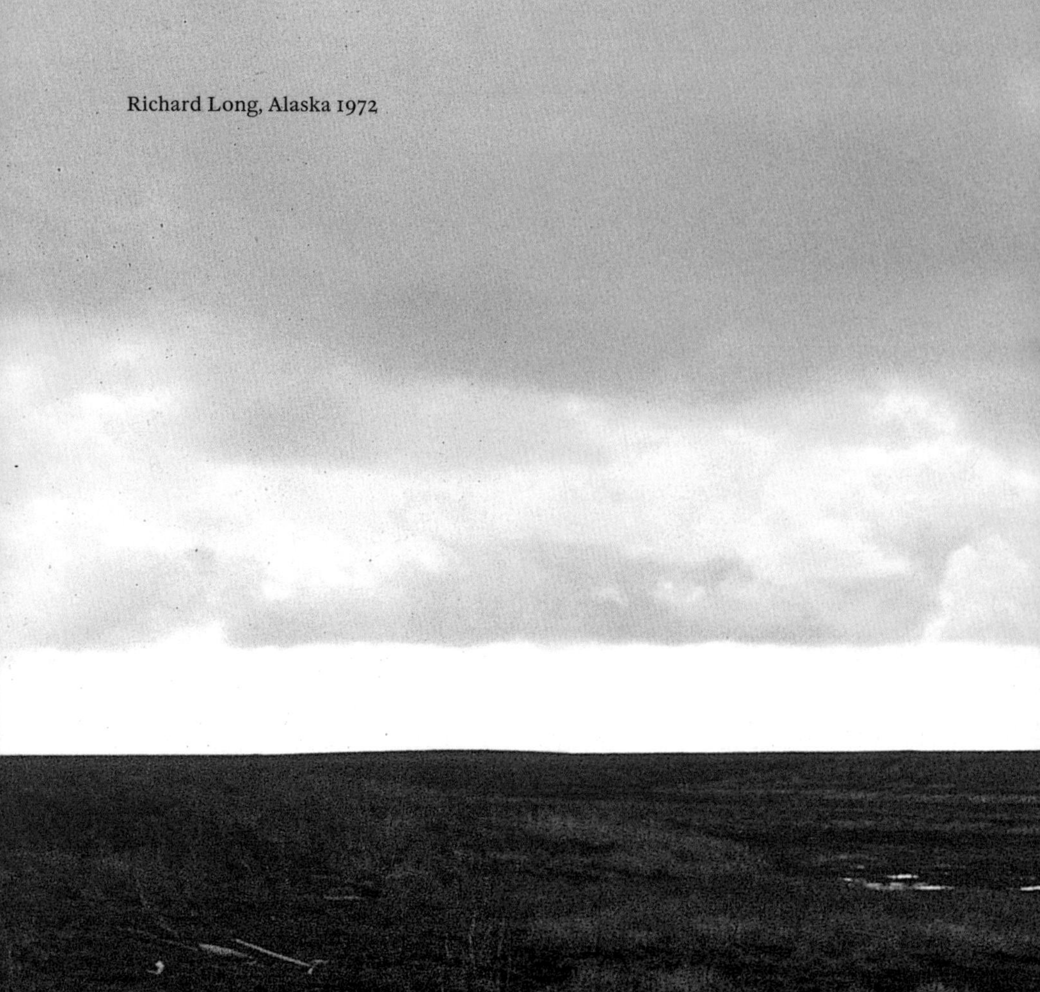

Richard Long, Alaska 1972

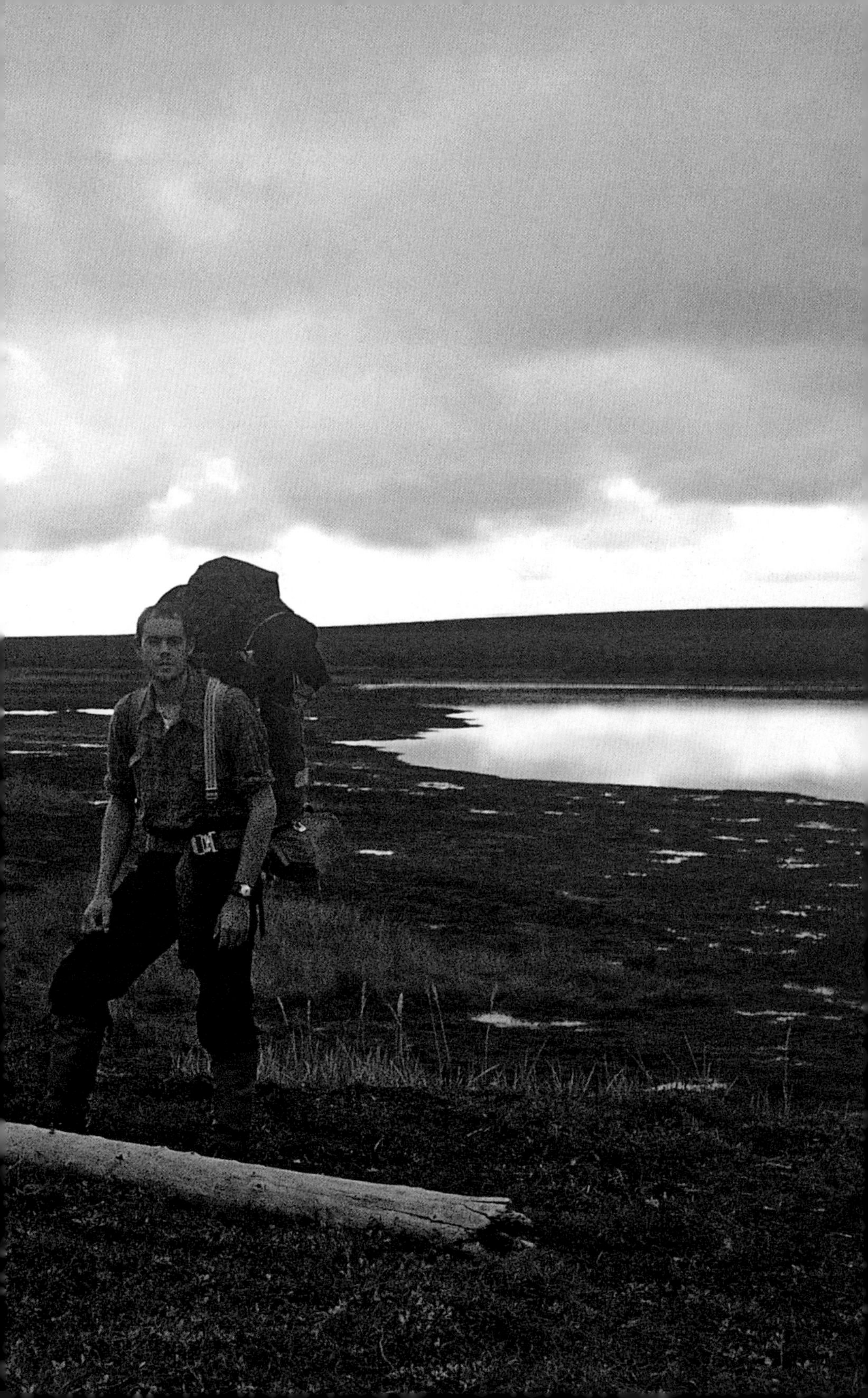

home in places like Lappland or Alaska because their boggy, windy, flattish kind of landscape is sort of familiar to me. I think there are certain things that are fairly universal. Footpaths interest me a lot, and you could almost say that the footpath going up Ben Nevis is more or less the same as all the great footpaths in Nepal. It is just that in Nepal the views on either side are bigger and higher and the precipices on each side are much bigger, but basically a footpath is a footpath and it is probably the same in China as in Scotland. It is just one stone after another. It is like a walk, just one footstep after another no matter where it is. So I am interested in homing in on the universal similarities between things, but also on the great differences between places, because each place on the earth is absolutely unique, and no stone is like another stone in that respect. I am all for using that as well.

RC *Do you mind bad weather, or extremes of heat or cold?*

RL Oh no. I think being a sort of typical British walker, being used to the pouring rain, I'm not bothered about getting wet, and I utterly love all the different types of weather. I just take the world as I find it really. I suppose that I would say that I have been in cold, wet temperate climates more than very hot climates. But that is more to do with the fact that to make walks alone and to be independent I always have to be near water. So, apart from this last strange occasion in the Sahara, I would not go to a place where it was so dry that I couldn't find water, as I cannot carry water with me.

RC *How do you decide when to stop walking and make a work?*

RL Well, when I come to an incredible place I don't have to make that decision. I have an instantaneous feeling that this is the place and here are the stones and I just get on with it.

RC *Then it is absolutely a question of taking your cue from the place that you find?*

RL Oh, yes. But that is not to say that certain sculptures can't be pre-planned. Again, it is a combination of things. For instance, in Ladakh, in the mountains of Kashmir, on the last trip I made there, by walking on the footpaths after a few days I had the idea to make actual walking lines on the footpath. That is an example of having an idea after a few days of being on the walk. The actual walking and the footpaths give me the idea to make the work. When I was by some strange circumstances in Alaska, I happened to find myself on the

Arctic Circle, and it seemed just the perfect opportunity and place for me to make a circle. Sometimes it might happen that I have the idea to make a circle or something and then the actual place will – like in Africa, I was going to make a circle of stones on a high mountain in Malawi and then, when I got there, I couldn't find any stones because there was no ice and snow to break the rock up. So I kept the idea of a circle and I changed the material to burnt cacti which were lying around, that had been burnt in lightning storms. That is just to show how I can keep one half of the idea and then change the other half because of the circumstances of the place. I am an opportunist; I just take advantage of the places and situations I find myself in.

RC *There is still a contrast, though, between what you describe as the opportunism of responding to a particular place that you didn't previously know about, and the unwavering constancy of the language that you always favour – the lines and the circles.*

RL Yes, it is always like a balance – a harmony of complementary ideas. You could say that my work is also a balance between the patterns of nature and the formalism of human, abstract ideas like lines and circles. It is where my human characteristics meet the natural forces and patterns of the world, and that is really the kind of subject of my work.

RC *Since they play such an important role in the form assumed by your work, can you say something more about why you favour lines and circles as such?*

RL Well, I have to say that the first time I used a circle I had no idea why I used it. It seemed like a good idea at the time, but having made it, it looked great and seemed a very strong and powerful image, and I have used it ever since. There are a lot of things theoretical and intellectual to say about lines and circles, but I think the very fact that they are images that don't belong to me and, in fact, are shared by everyone because they have existed throughout history, actually makes them more powerful than if I was inventing my own idiosyncratic, particular Richard Long-type images. I think it cuts out a lot of personal unwanted aesthetic paraphernalia.

RC *They give you freedom, in other words.*

RL Yes, that is right. In fact, they actually allow me to home in on other things, so the circles stay the same in the different places I make them around the world but the places change. It means that the viewer

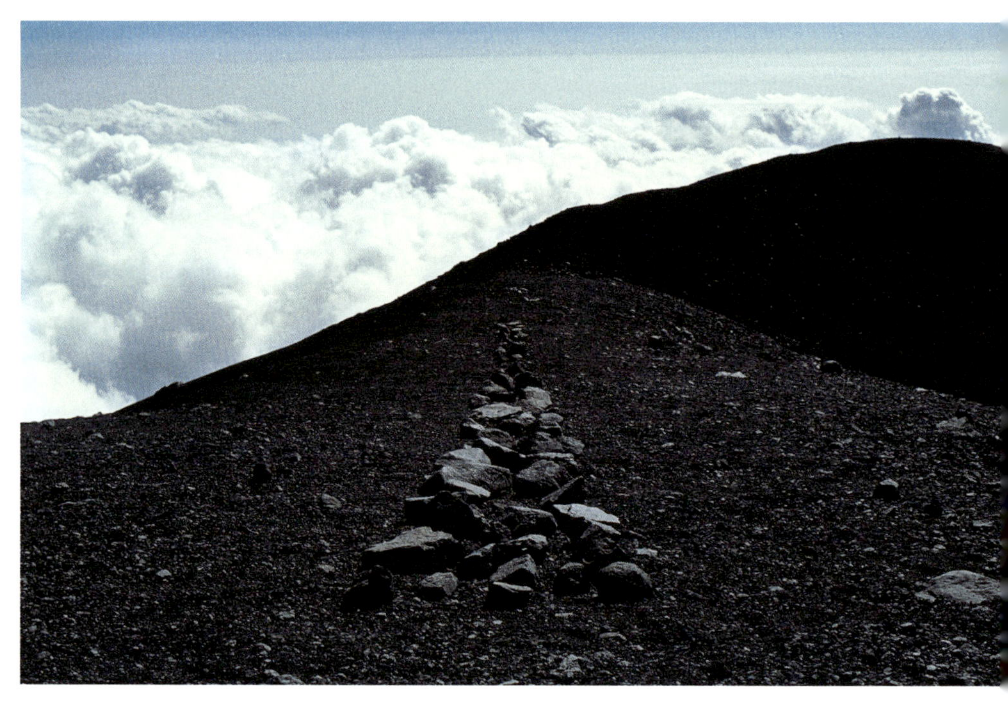

A LINE IN JAPAN
MOUNT FUJI 1979

of my work is noticing that there are circles, but he is also seeing that the places are changing and the materials are changing. I think, anyway, a circle is such an open system and that it can be a vehicle for perhaps any idea under the sun. It is a freedom, as you say. I can make a circle of words, I can make a circle of stones, I can make a circle of mud with my hands on a wall, I can walk in a circle for one hundred miles. It is a completely adaptable image and form and system.

RC *Yes, you can make full circles, empty circles, circles with upright stones, circles with horizontal stones.*

RL And it is also an image that everyone recognises. So people don't actually have to fathom out what they are looking at.

RC *You are aiming then, in essence, at universality.*

RL Yes, but I think nature is universal. It is no coincidence that there are parallels between my work and work from certain people of other cultures and societies, as nature, which is the source of my work, is universal. We all live in different cultures but we all share the same nature of the world. We all share the same air, the same water and everything.

RC *When I see lines in your work, they often remind me of the fact that duration is involved, that walking is fundamental and that a journey is being undertaken. You have always been strikingly preoccupied with movement, distance and time.*

RL Yes, time is the fourth dimension in my work, and I am interested in using it in a very particular way. So I have made walks about pace, walks about time only, and also certain geometries, for example, walking between a hundred tors on Dartmoor in a hundred hours, or walking a thousand miles in a thousand hours. So it is possible to use time almost in a very classical way, as a very formal, geometric thing.

RC *Why is walking so central a part of your work? Does the act of walking make you experience time more vividly than you would do in normal life?*

RL Yes, I think it does. Like art itself, it is like a focus. It gets rid of a lot of things and you can actually concentrate. So getting myself into these solitary days of repetitive walking or in empty landscapes is just a certain way of emptying out or simplifying my life, just for those few days or weeks, into a fairly simple but concentrated activity which, as you say, is really quite different from the way that people normally live their lives, which is very complicated. So my art is a simplification. Also, a walk is a great vehicle for very particular ideas, about colours, trees, time, anything I choose.

RC *Does time pass more slowly for you during a walk, or more quickly?*

RL Ah, well, it plays funny tricks doesn't it, time. It is both. I would say it is very curious that if I am doing a long walk, at the beginning the number of days ahead seem a lot, and it seems like a long way to the end of the walk! After about three-quarters of the way through, it seems that the completed days have just flashed by, so time is completely subjective, or relative. There is no real time.

RC *While you are making the work in the landscape, what state of mind do you like to be in, or do you find yourself in?*

RL Well, usually I am happy and relaxed. I would say that the way I make my work is from the things that give me pleasure and the materials that I like using – my work doesn't come from a kind of *angst* or discontent. A sculpture in a landscape, when it really happens well in a good way, is like a celebration of the place and my feelings of me being there and having the right idea at the right time and everything coming together in a good way. For me that is the perfect way to make a good work. But I can be happy like that in a gallery making a big mud work on a wall or something. Part of the pleasure actually comes from the physical side of things. It is very important for me to make my work, you know, the actual physical making – standing the stones up, the long walking, the physical toil, the sweating and the getting tired, or the getting covered in mud in a gallery throwing mud around in a circle. I would say that as well as my work being about ideas, it is also about that physical enjoyment.

RC *Do you think that in order perhaps to engage your mind and your imagination fully you have to involve the whole of your body as well?*

RL Oh, yes. The work is the expression of both the intellect and the body, they are absolutely complementary. It is no good just having a good idea, it is also necessary for me to make it, and also not have somebody else make it – for me to do it myself, because my work is in my own footsteps, it is only what I can do, so the hand prints in the gallery are my hands and the stones that I turn up on the mountainside are the stones that I can physically handle myself at that place. And I have found that place by walking to it. My work is a portrait of myself in the world, my own personal journey through it and the materials that I find along the way.

RC *Watching the film that Philip Haas recently made about your work [*Stones and Flies: Richard Long in the Sahara*, 1988], I was very struck by the amount of physical exertion – the amount of sheer hard work, if you like – involved in making some of these big stone pieces.*

RL Well, it is not hard work because I enjoy it, but anyway it is work.

RC *And you must feel fairly tired afterwards.*

RL Yes, but it is a nice kind of tiredness.

RC *And then you take a photograph of the work. How do you go about that?*

RL Well, normally I just step back and point the camera and try and get it in focus. Even though it is necessary to get a good photograph, the photographs should be as simple as possible so that when people look at the photograph they are not dazzled by wide-angled lenses or special effects. Because my art is very simple and straightforward, I think the photographs have got to be fairly simple and straightforward, so that the feeling of the work somehow accurately comes through. That is why most of the photographs are taken from my eye level. Usually, after I have made the work, I kind of walk around it and somehow find the best place to take the photograph. A line usually has the characteristic of pointing out of or beyond itself, maybe to the horizon, so often the alignment of the viewer, the line, and something a long way off is important. Circles are different, they are more enclosed, more of a stopping place.

RC *Let me end by asking probably the most important and difficult question which arises from your work. Why do you think that you do go out to these remote places again and again? Is it bound up with establishing and developing an increasingly close relationship with nature?*

RL I have no idea really. I have never had any ideology or fixed ideas. I think all that has happened is that my first landscape works were made in and around Bristol. My first turf works were actually made in my parents' front garden. As I have got older and I have had the wherewithal to extend my arena of making work, it has just got wider and wider, so that finally I have made works in different countries around the world.

RC *But I want to press you a bit further on this. What do you think you gain from this closeness with the natural world?*
RL I think it is just the choice that I have made for myself. I do the things that have a deep meaning for me. I have the most sublime or profound feelings when I am walking, or touching natural materials in natural places. That is what I've decided to do and that is what I am showing you in my art.

RC *Since so much of the finest art produced in this country has revolved around an intense response to landscape, do you feel close to any British tradition in this wish to commune with nature?*

RL No, not particularly. Just by being English, in my childhood, having my grandparents living on Dartmoor, in Devon, or going on cycling holidays with my father when I was boy. I think all those things were much more important than this so-called tradition of English landscape art. I realise there was a sort of Romantic movement as a result of the Industrial Revolution. I suppose if you have to put some historical or political slant on my work it does tie up in some ways with the Green philosophy, 'small is beautiful', and of seeing the world as one place, and using its raw materials with respect. I like to see art as being a return to the senses.

Broadcast in 'Third Ear', BBC Radio 3, Friday 28 October, 1988.

MARTIN GOLDING

Thoughts on Richard Long

The knowledge of my actions, in whatever form, is the art.
My art is the essence of my experience, not a representation of it.

Richard Long, *Words after the fact* 1982

Richard Long's *works* – the photographs and maps of his walks, and texts based on them, and the assemblages of stones and sticks, and marks of mud and chalk (often entitled with their place of origin –

Cornish slate, Avon mud etc.) – seem to present uncompromisingly modernist forms to the spectator. They are called 'sculptures'; but the materials which constitute them remain unequivocally what they seem to be. By this insistence, Long refuses the transformation of experience implicit in the idea of 'representation', which lies at the root of what we normally understand by art. 'My work', he emphasises, 'is real, not illusory or conceptual'. He hopes, on the other hand, that his works will 'resonate in the imagination': he says they form together 'a simple metaphor of life'. But if they are in any figurative relation to an original experience, it is metonymical – a literal part of what he has seen and touched, which stands for the whole. And it is as those things that he wishes them to be taken – as literally a circle in the mountains, a chalk line or slate ring in a gallery.

Long's 'text-works' operate in a similar way: the words or phrases almost never connect in sentences, but each stands alone as the literal referent of some object or thought which occurred to him in the course of a journey: put together, the assemblage offers a condensed equivalent to the experience. The juxtapositions imitate the sequences and conjunctions of what he has passed through, but imply no more than the things themselves. Although certain combinations may encourage a mild synaesthesia, the words usually remain discrete objects along the way – something close to a blunt sequence of sensations. Even when what each 'means' is explained, they cannot in themselves make up a world of experience.

This insistence on untransformed materials is characteristic of a certain view of modernist art, in which the elements which compose it become the subject matter, and claim thereby to be emancipated from the taint of 'imagery': Carl Andre comes to mind. But unlike Andre's objects, Long's more clearly derive from and depend on an anterior life: their materials are stones and sticks, but they recall the empty places from which they came, and the stone circles and lines made in passing as he walked in remote landscapes, preserved in photographs. Looking at Long's assemblages on gallery floors, one is not looking at 'sculpture', but at the precipitate of that originating activity, of an engagement with nature which is not seen but remembered, for it has already taken place – 'a figure walking down his road, making his mark'. And Long's commitment to walking in the wild, his building small vestiges of his passage in desolate places, is in fact, unavoidably, rich with romantic associations. His is a different line of descent from that commonly alleged – that from Henry Moore and Anthony Caro.

Both Long and his principal commentators, however, have always denied the presence of a 'romantic' element in his work, in order to maintain for it a distinctly modern and vanguard character. 'Richard Long's landscape is… as modern (in feeling) as the city of Bristol from which he sets out for a walk', writes RH Fuchs:[1] Long himself describes his work as 'the laying down of modern ideas in the only practical places to take them'. And certainly, his identification of the succession of his steps across the ground with the succession of stones which he places as a 'sculpture' has modernist analogies. In the course of this century's art, a primary misunderstanding of the character and intent of Paul Cézanne's brush-marks has developed, in a series of very loose derivations, through Abstract Expressionism, to the doctrine that the marks themselves constitute the subject matter: one of its outcomes is the art of materials of which both Andre and Long are, in different ways, practitioners. The stones, as undifferentiated as steps, gathered together, make up an ensemble which *may* strike us as more than their sum, but which in the first place simply faces us with the mass and weight of the material which, essentially untransformed, *are* the works – the lines, rings and circles of chalk, flint, slate, granite, marble, driftwood and sticks.

Words too may be like steps. Another modernist analogy is with a postwar American poetic, associated in different degrees with William Carlos Williams and Charles Olson, in which (very broadly) the line's energy is gathered into the breath and the syllable, *reculant pour mieux sauter* [stepping back for a better jump]. The movement out of these smallest units of expression is the dynamic which preempts an 'easy lateral sliding' (Williams) into the banalities of standard poetic rhythms and their banal poetic associations: the poet must, Olson puts it, 'keep moving'. Appositely, this latter-day attack on 'poetic diction' also drew on the American landscape: the recovery of 'the language of men' proceeded through an acutely registered engagement with the physical world of the continent – via (for example) the perambulations of the great American geographer CO Sauer ('Locomotion should be slow, the slower the better, and should be often interrupted by leisurely halts to sit on vantage points and stop at question marks') and classic journeys into the wilderness like those of Meriwether Lewis and William Clark, and JW Powell.

These are complex matters, broadly sketched. However, the analogy of syllable and brush-mark is not an historical accident; nor, therefore, the development from brush-mark to step. And it is not accidental either that this return to fundamentals may work through experiencing the primitive landscape. I think of Gary Snyder's first book, *Riprap* (1959), whose title means 'a cobble of stone laid on steep slick rock/to make a trail for horses in the mountains'; and whose title poem begins:

> Lay down these words
> Before your mind like rocks
>   placed solid, by hands
> In choice of place, set
> Before the body of the mind
>   in space and time:

The purging of poetic language pares down also the sense of human presence in an immemorial landscape· 'Sky over endless mountains./ All the junk that goes with being human/Drops away... (*Piute Creek*). Implicit in this version of modernism which, like Long's, identifies authenticity of utterance with a spare resilience of expression, is a version of the Romantic Sublime, reading like a colloquial expansion of Lucretius ('The person is torn away, the thing remains') which seems echoed in Long's 'Time passes, a place remains'. We should hold this in mind as we investigate further the 'anterior life' of Long's objects.

Behind the objects is Long's activity as a walker, and that activity is his primary subject: 'My work is about my senses, my instinct, my own scale and my own physical commitment'. The walker is also, usually, solitary. Though Long has walked with Hamish Fulton, most of his characteristic images – for example *A Circle in the Andes* (1972), *Mountain Lake Powder Snow* (1985) – suggest the solitary condition. They derive their suggestiveness from the contrast between the small and simple construction or mark and the huge landscape which surrounds it. Long has also collaborated in projects in which that defining solitude is brought into relief. Thus in Philip Haas's recent film *Stones and Flies: Richard Long in the Sahara* (1988) we are required to forget that the persuasive depiction of the single traveller could only have been made by an accompanying film crew. But this fiction of the Wanderer comes late on the scene: it derives from 20 years of real experience. That figure is balanced by an attitude to what is being made that seems self-effacing. His works are 'a few stones among millions'; 'A walk is just one more layer... laid upon the thousands of layers of human and geographic history on the surface of the land': he likes the sense that in some cases, having dismantled the arrangement before moving on, he will leave no trace.

In Long's statement that 'seen and unseen works have an equal importance' one is brought back to something inaccessible in the constructions themselves which compromises their apparently ruthless materiality. One remembers his description of what his work is 'about'. What it is 'about' is in fundamental respects sealed up: wholly inward sensations, visual experience which, since it cannot be 'represented', remains unknowable; a pleasure in spontaneous activity in the outdoors, often identified with childhood play. He frequently speaks of his childhood in and around Bristol, and of his love for the River Avon, whose mud he therefore uses extensively in his gallery work. There is a sense in which his whole walking activity simply recreates for himself that childhood world of sensation. Youthful ingenuousness, furthermore, marks some of his statements – as when he says to Martina Giezen, 'I could make a sculpture which surrounded an area of 2401 square miles. All I had to do to make that was just to cycle around the countryside and leave it as a sculpture'. However one imagines or conceives the status of such a work, it must be as opaque to a spectator as uncommunicated or incommunicable childhood memories. And this returns one, unavoidably, to the solitary Wanderer – not as anonymous, but as an intense focus of interest.

What is often forgotten in discussion of Richard Long is that the predominant outcome of his activity is photography. The landscapes showing his arrangements of stones and pathways made by his feet are, because he is a good photographer, often beautiful and evocative. But what they necessarily evoke as well as the majestic spaces shown in them is the activity of the photographer, an activity that always lies in the past. In conversation with Martina Giezen, Long described how he had quite recently recreated *A Line Made by Walking* (1967), one of his earliest works: he was exhilarated by being able to 'reuse' it. But the photograph of 1967 remains as the permanent deposit of a past action, overtaken by time – as do all his subsequent photographic works. It shares an inherent pathos with, for example, SI Witkiewicz's *Road Near Krzemieniec* (1904), whose faint path trodden out by successive wayfarers only more obviously appeals to our feeling for disappearing memories because it is further removed into the past. In effect, the photographs are the only accessible evidences of the walks and the works made on them (many ephemeral, subject to tide or sun, or dismantled by Long himself immediately afterwards). Indeed they now constitute the works in so far as they exist at all: they create a past for us of Long's outgoings which is inescapably romantic and personal. The photographs, as inescapably, bring the protagonist strongly before us. His spoor is historicised, recreated as a memory and infused with sentiment. The Lucretian adage, meshed with other records of exploration, stories of long-abandoned trails and campfires on other continents (TE Lawrence's, say) – becomes his own.

Some of the difficulties involved in seeing these works as modernist rhetoric means them to be seen emerge in photographs whose details do not record Long's own interventions. *Childhood Ground Abiding Places* (1983), for example, is a photograph of the 'Rock Slide' near Clifton Suspension Bridge, a steep limestone slope worn smooth by generations of children who have slid down it. Superimposed on it below the title is a list of places where Long and his friends played as children. The specific content of the photograph is known perhaps only to those who played there (I owe this knowledge myself to Long), but the associations summoned up by the place remain clear. Here is an explicit appeal to the past, the creation of an image which is powerfully sentimental. In a sense, the virtually secret identity of the place as far as most spectators would be concerned makes it even more so. From that point of view there is no difference in the appeal of that work of generations from that of Long's footsteps through the grass on Clifton Down. From both spring pathos and nostalgia.

Roisin Dubh (1974) (subtitled *A Slow Air*) is a beautiful colour photograph of The Burren, County Clare, taken at dusk. The title is superimposed against the purple sky and along the foot of the photograph in small type runs the statement: 'A thousand stones moved one step forward along a seventy four mile walk in County Clare'. Here two impulses seem to be in tension. The title is of a melancholy old Irish song (usually translated as 'Dark Rosaleen'), lamenting the sorrows of Ireland, for which the girl's name is code: 'A Slow Air' literally describes the measure. So in one sense the image is a tribute to Ireland itself; and 'A Slow Air' becomes also the slow light of evening, grainy and thick, slow to reach the eye and also the lens of the camera. But the implication of the necessary spectator, the walker, is curious: if the burden of the image is this evocation of ancient tribulation expressed through the intransigent presence of the rock at nightfall, what do the scurrying steps at its foot have to do with it? The annexation of the image to the walk is quite overbalanced by the former's evocativeness. Here again, the inherent qualities of the photograph preempt an ambition to give it a more active identity: it remains what it was, at that time and place, forever.

It does not disparage photographs to allege that they are sentimental; for that is also a quality of human memory, which enlarges our sanity by keeping our vulnerable past experiences from the designing animus of the present. Long's evocation of 'the tradition of the wayfarer', 'an idyllic way of life', even as he acknowledges how his walks, because they are not 'real' journeys, have the character of rituals, recognises the sentimental continuities which underlie his activities, and which must therefore affect the way his works resonate, if they do, in the viewer's imagination. The yearning for 'uncluttered empty spaces' has a long and powerful history, touching our deepest fears and wishes, and that recognition is an underpinning of the Romantic attitude. It draws on a fantasy at once natural, corporeal and heroic, necessarily more complex than the critical simplicities which turn landscape into a 'surface' for 'abstract art'. The poet John James's resonant tribute to Long sees farther:[2]

> I was a walker before I was proficient in learning
> catching the deep night & dawn divide
> the line of the curling wave on the extended shore.

One cannot deny the power of a sentimental projection on the sublime inseparable from the condition of a man deliberately alone and 'arm in arm with the earth in its infancy'.

An 'international modern artist' can of course come in many different guises, and Richard Long certainly seems to fulfil many of those somewhat attenuating requirements. To the extent that he does so, the emotions which his work is alleged to provoke often puzzle me: why for example, should the row of printed arrows which constitute *Wind Line* (1985) seem to RH Fuchs to be 'an *exciting* piece'; and why do many of the massed materials on gallery floors not exhaust the contemplative interest of their admirers as soon as they do mine? But it is often in the gaps allowed by confusion of purpose that insight and pleasure offers. For me it is the dimension of romance, which his commentators refuse in the interests of modernity, that draws me to the *idea* of his activity, and to the photographs which issue from it – notwithstanding the egregious pretension with which they are often described. Once again, the engagement with the American continent which predates its more recent poetic rhetoric suggests a guide.

At the beginning of his classic essay 'Walking' (1862), Henry David Thoreau speculated on the etymology of 'saunter' and settled happily for 'Sainte-Terre', which for him endowed the word with elevated associations, making each walker a crusader in the reconquest of a Holy Land and in effect a pilgrim. Later in the same essay he wrote:

> It is not indifferent to us which way we walk... We would fain take that walk, never yet taken by us, through this actual world, which is perfectly symbolical of the path which we love to travel in the interior and ideal world.

'It's a good step/that will continue to the end without arriving', as John James's poem testifies. Seeing Richard Long as a pilgrim towards the unreachable Sublime is less strange than it appears, for his work depends on an idea of nature which, though it is without transcendence, is dense with commitment and respect. The work does not however 'lay down modern ideas' in that medium so recalcitrant to human desires. Instead, it returns attention to the much older notion implicit in the figure of the Artist-Wanderer, his dry, spare appearance, his effort, his solitude and his integrity: the 'Egotistical' refracted, but still recognisable, as an attribute of the Sublime. It is this determined activity and its traces which save Long from the worst consequences of his fame. The photographs evoke, as he has described it, an 'idyllic life', infused with the pathos and romance of Man in Nature, the traces of which we always come on – as in all photographs – just too late.

Modern Painters, vol.3, no.1, spring 1990, pp.50–53.

1 RH Fuchs, *Richard Long*, exh. cat., Solomon R Guggenheim Museum, New York and Thames & Hudson, London, 1986, p.43.
2 John James, *Lines for Richard Long*, Silver Hounds/Ferry Press, Lewes/London, 1988. The final section was first published in Pat Adams (ed), *With a Poet's Eye*, Tate Gallery, London, 1986.

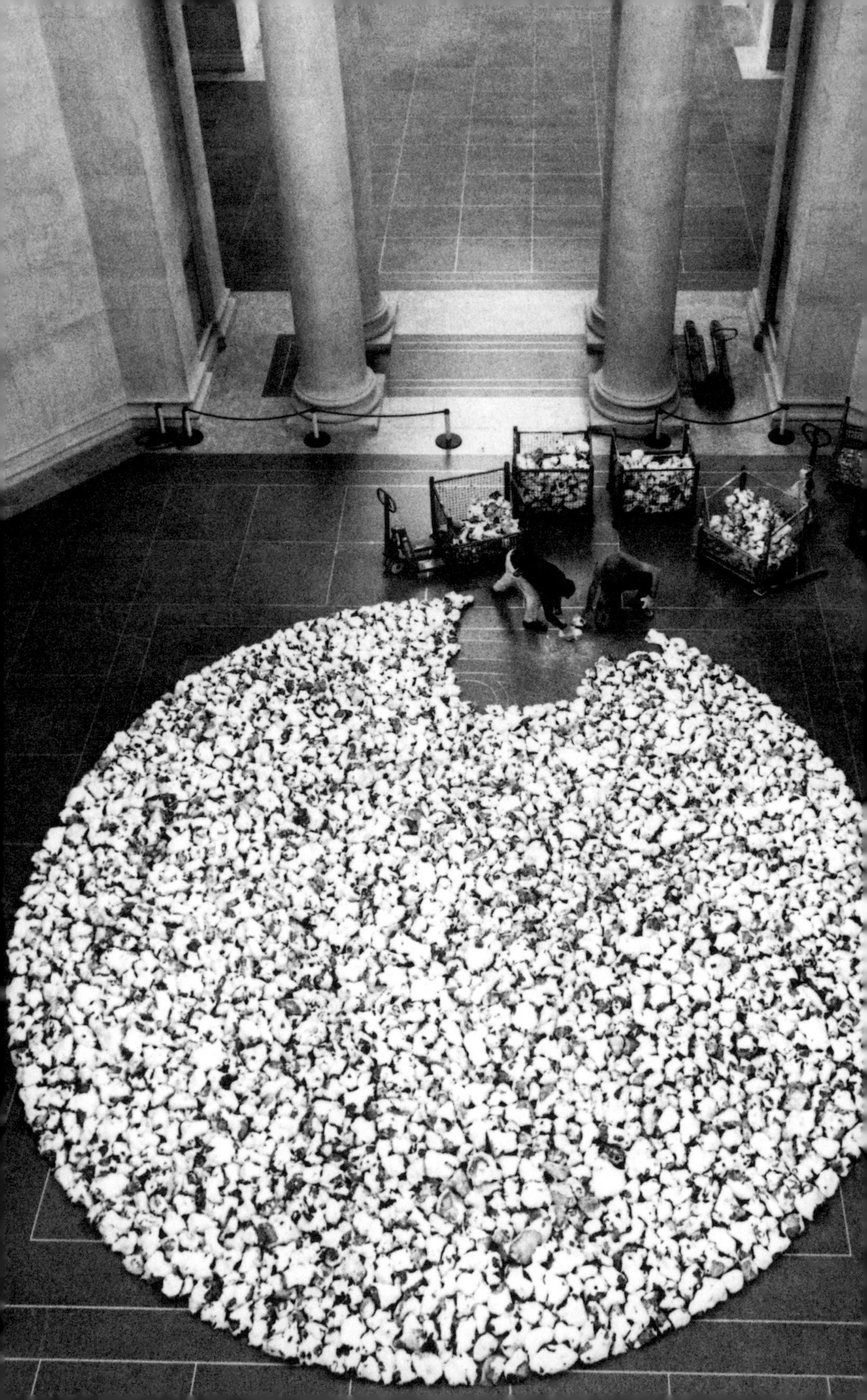

NICHOLAS SEROTA

Richard Long

In the art of our time Richard Long stands alone; single-minded, consistent, working to his own rhythm and at his own pace he is a still point in the turbulent waters of movements and fashion. Parallels for his work have been traced in the English landscape tradition of John Constable and Paul Nash, in the Taoist and Buddhist traditions of the Far East and in the signs and markings of so-called 'primitive' peoples, such as the ancient Nazca Indians of South America or the Aboriginals of Australia. However, we may also observe that like Nicolas Poussin, Paul Cézanne and Piet Mondrian his art is fundamentally rational, even classical, in its concern with the inner harmony of the natural order and with the place of man in the terrestrial realm.

Characteristically, his art takes the form of a walk recorded by means of a line on a map, by a text noting places, signs or sounds encountered en route, by a photograph of a significant location, or by a sculpture or mark made by the artist at a particular point on the journey. These records may be displayed as photographs or texts on the wall of a gallery or museum, or published in catalogues and books, as here.

In galleries he also makes sculptures, arranging natural materials, usually stones and wood but also sometimes in river mud or a solution of chalk, literally 'walking the line' on the floor or imprinting the hand on the wall. In these, as in his outdoor sculptures, he works with the most simple and deliberate marks known to man: the line, the cross, the circle and the spiral. In galleries he most commonly uses stones, taken from local quarries but never specially cut or sawn, simply off-cuts selected by a man who knows the properties of a particular stone, its density, its surface quality and the way it may reflect the light. Thus no two circles or lines are identical, since stones will be laid down according to different rules in order to take advantage of the character of the material.

Richard Long installing *Norfolk Flint Circle*, Tate Gallery, London 1990

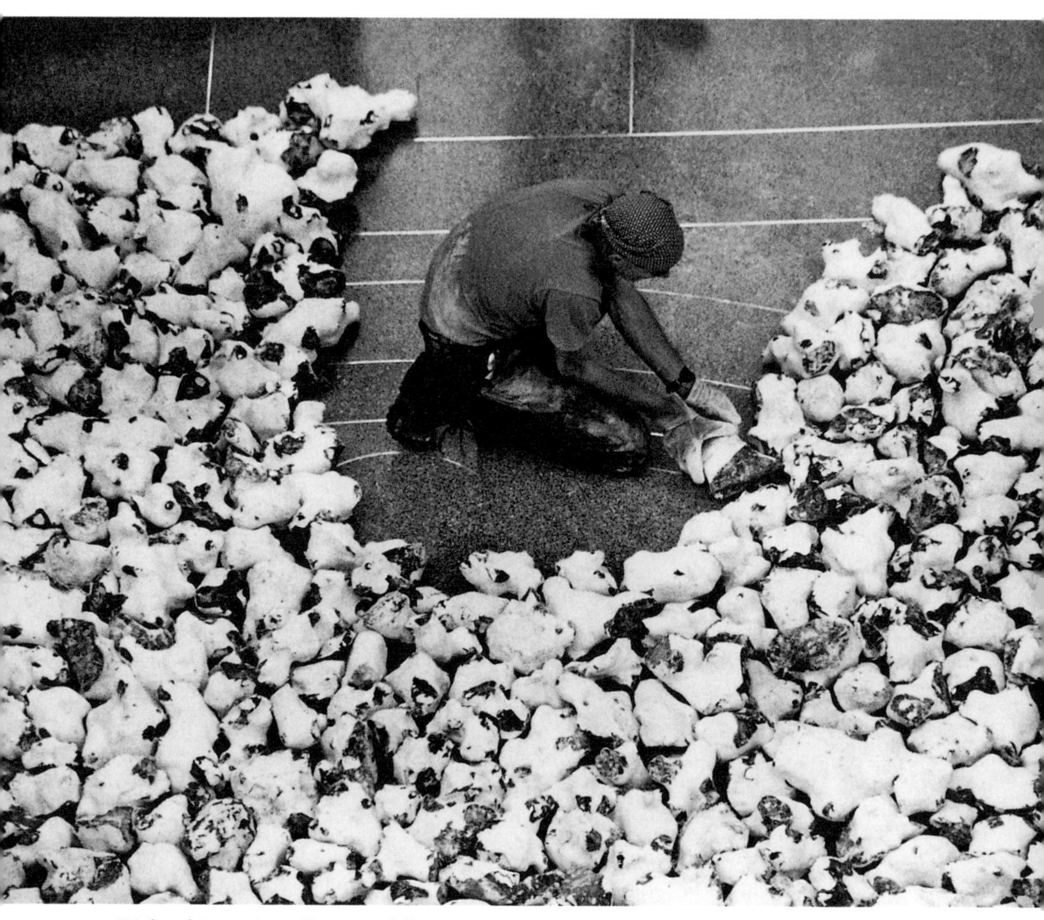

Richard Long installing *Norfolk Flint Circle*, Tate Gallery, London 1990

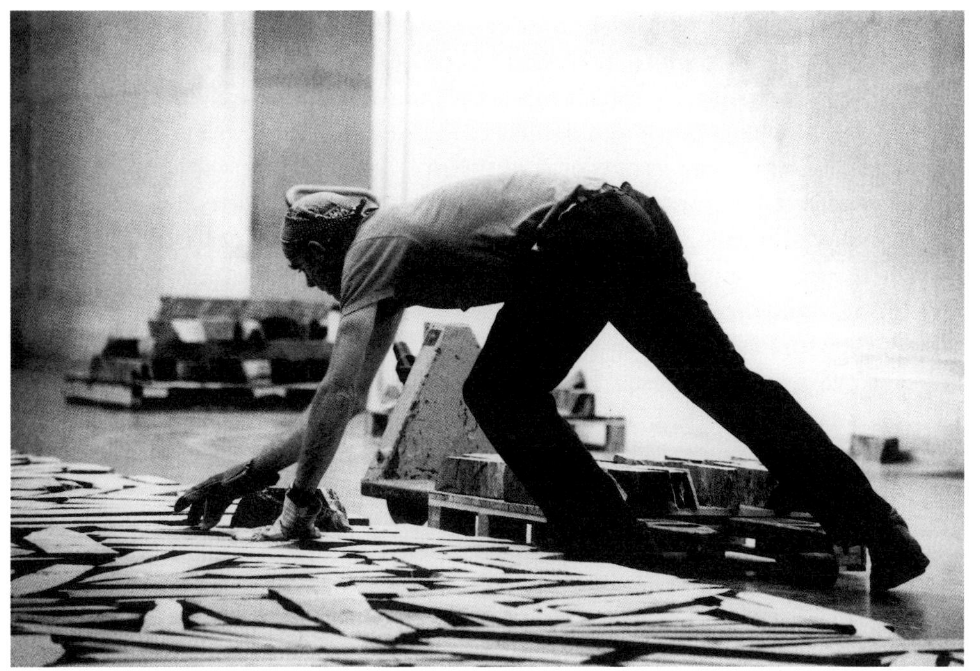

Richard Long installing *Cornish Slate Line*, Tate Gallery, London 1990

His journeys have taken him to all parts of the world, but most frequently to the remote and ancient parts of the earth where few have preceded him. He travels to the uplands of Europe, to the Arctic Circle, to the dust bowls and deserts of the Americas and Africa and to the mountain ranges of every continent.

In each of his works there is the simplicity of form achieved by an economy of means. 'Rigour' is the word which most aptly describes both the state of mind and the commitment involved in walking through wild terrain or in collecting stones. Though it is intimately bound with nature and natural rhythms, his art never describes, or even evokes nature as such, but serves to heighten our understanding of our own place within the universe. Long reminds us that we are not simply observers but, working with or against the grain, we are ourselves participants in the natural order.

Each work may be executed at a particular moment but it also carries echoes of man's place on the planet through the ages. His art makes us acutely aware of time; the time spent in its making, in the gathering of material, in the duration of a walk, in the evolution of the weather, or indeed the time which his mark may remain on the surface of the earth until it is obliterated by animals, natural growth or the elements.

But there is also the time which we must give to an art which only discloses the layers of its meaning in response to prolonged contemplation. Like all art which seeks to explore the order of the universe, Richard Long's work serves as a stone pitched into the centre of a calm pond. The spread of the ripple is limited only by the banks of our own imagination and by our ability first to still the surface so that the ripple may travel without impediment.

Richard Long, Tate Gallery 1990–91, exhibition pamphlet,
Tate Gallery Publications, London, 1990–91, n.p.

Richard Long installing *Cornish Slate Line*, Tate Gallery, London 1990

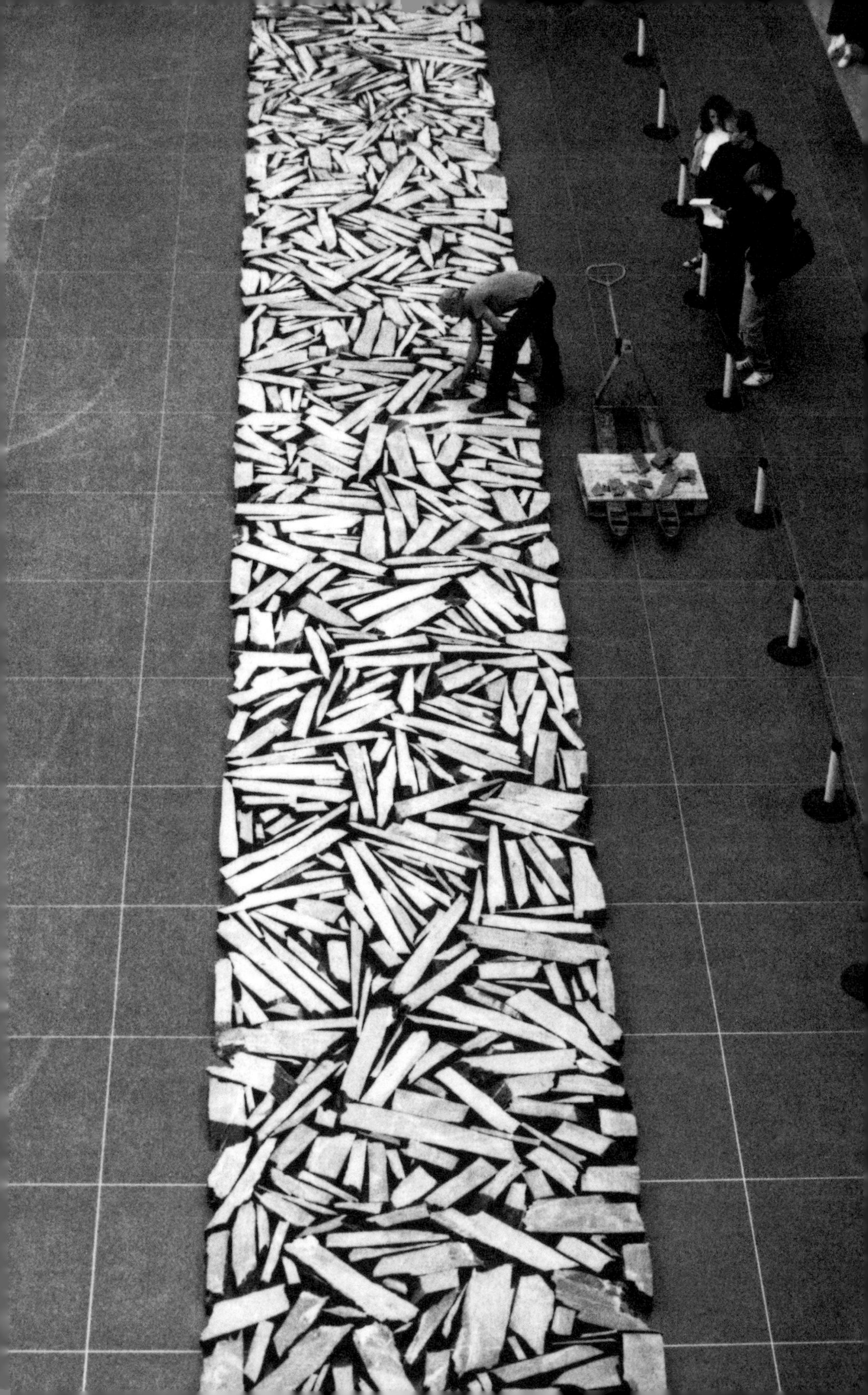

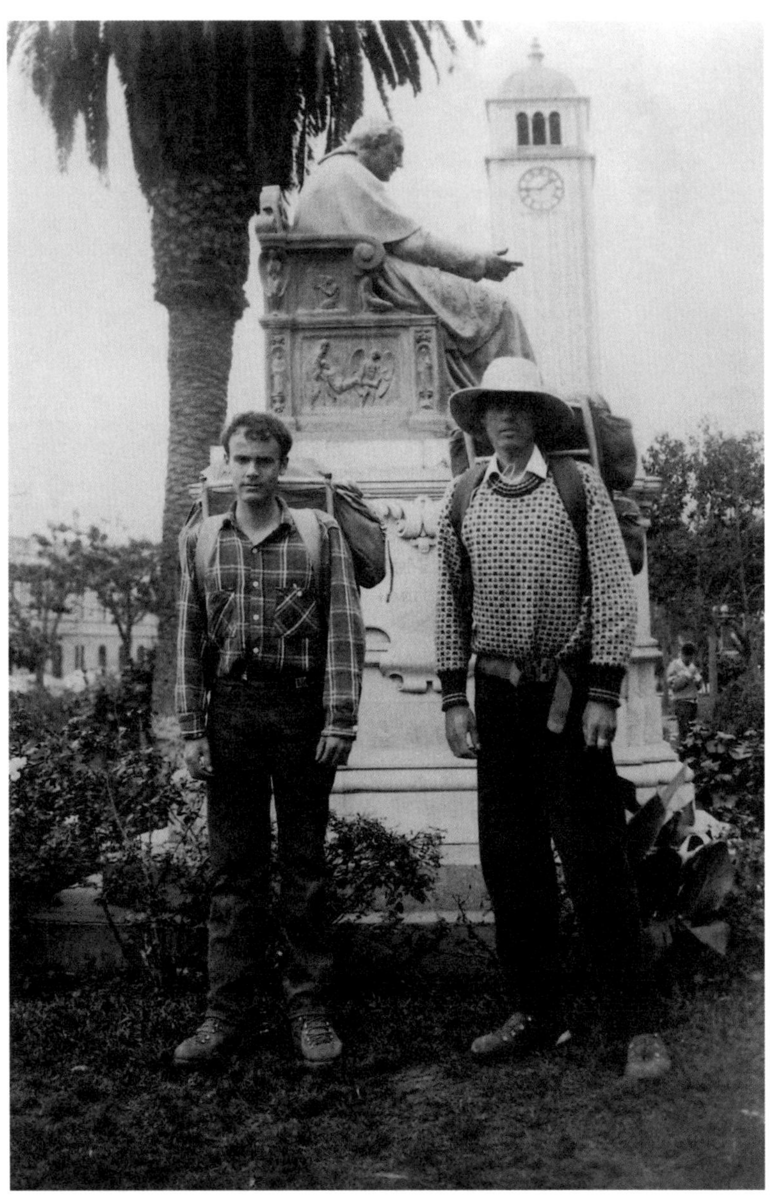

Hamish Fulton and Richard Long, Lima, Peru 1972

HAMISH FULTON

Old Muddy

WELL, THESE ARE THE STRAIGHT FACTS
BUT THEY DON'T COME IN A STRAIGHT LINE.

Roll over Beethoven 1956.
North Face Eiger Direct 1966.
'A LINE MADE BY WALKING ENGLAND 1967.'
First moon walk 1969.

One evening in June 1972, as I was preparing to sleep out for the night near Stonehenge, I saw another traveller arranging his sleeping bag beside a haystack. The following morning was the solstice. Some months later, after a conversation with Richard Long, I deduced he was the solitary figure I had seen, prior to his walk from Stonehenge to Glastonbury.

'ON MIDSUMMER'S DAY A WESTWARD WALK FROM
STONEHENGE AT SUNRISE TO GLASTONBURY BY SUNSET
FORTY FIVE MILES FOLLOWING THE DAY 1972.'

(Circumference of the earth – measurement of circles – steps of the sun.)

In November 1972, Richard Long and I made a visit to the prehistoric ground drawings in Peru, known as the Nazca Lines, located approximately 250 miles south of Lima.

By chance, we met Maria Reiche, the German mathematician who has devoted her life to the study and preservation of the drawings. Maria Reiche very generously gave us a copy of her booklet, *Mystery on the Desert* (1949) published in Lima. On page two, under the heading, 'How the designs were made', she writes: 'A reddish brown, almost black colour characterises the plains and mountains of this region, which is exceptionally rich in iron. Being produced by oxidation and the effects of thousands of years of daily morning dew followed by excessive heat, this colour does not reach deeper than one or two inches. The stones and gravel underneath are yellowish white. This contrast made it possible to use the level surfaces as immense blackboards on which white designs could be produced on a dark background by simply removing the upper-layer of black stones.'

(The line of sight.
'... make straight paths for your feet... ' Hebrews XII, 13.
Lines of energy – rings, spirals, and straight channels of magnetic current.)

In Tony Morrison's book, *Pathways to the Gods* (1978), he asks whether comparisons could be made between the animal drawings of Nazca and the Zodiac at Glastonbury.

(Dod Lane.)

'Over hill, over dale,
Thorough bush, thorough brier,
Over park, over pale,
Thorough flood, thorough fire... '

William Shakespeare, *A Midsummer Night's Dream*, 1590–97, Act Two, Scene One.

'A TEN MILE WALK ENGLAND 1968.'

(Unerringly straight line walked on ground – drawn straight line on map.)

(Dartmoor compass tacking.)

February 1981. Richard Long and I made an eleven-day walk on the Altiplano of western Bolivia. From General Perez train station by the Rio Mauri, we walked out to the Rio Achuta, and back to General Perez. From our turn-around point we could see a snow-capped volcano on the horizon. This was the 6,542 metre high Sajama. Back in England, looking through *Pathways to the Gods*, I read a description by Morrison who made a reconnaissance flight over Sajama. 'Lines led in every direction. All of those I could see were single paths and often led unerringly over hills and gullies. All were apparently clear, so either the vegetation had been reduced by recent clearings and walking, or it had never grown over since the paths were made.'

(Nothing hidden.)

On our 1981 visit we had no knowledge of any straight pathways across the Altiplano.

(We-speak-of-what-we-have-seen.)

'Why are you doing this?'
'To get to the other side.'
'Do you have a special diet?'
'No, just food and plenty of it.'

Bruce Tulloh, *Four Million Footsteps*, 1970. (A 64 day, 21 hour, 50 minute marathon run across the United States, Los Angeles to New York, 1969.)

'And what sense has the undertaking?'

'That I can't explain. But I am mad enough to contend that above all else the inexplicable gives meaning to life.'

Reinhold Messner, *The Crystal Horizon*, 1989. (The first solo ascent of Mount Everest without the use of artificial oxygen, 1980.)

'It's the going-for-ever-on-ness that I find the attraction.'

Sebastian Snow, *The Rucksack Man*, 1976. (Snow walked 8,700 miles from Tierra del Fuego to Panama City, 1973–74.)

'There are times in life, you can count them in minutes, when you experience an awareness far greater than you usually find in a year.'

FM Dostoevsky (quoted in *All 14 Eight Thousanders*, by Reinhold Messner, 1987).

'I noticed how Pete used to make copious entries into a diary, so many that I could not visualise how he could do or say anything without the awareness that he was going to record that action or word. I had found after Dunagiri the value of recording the days as they passed, in order to keep track of time, and I made one-line notes in the form of a diary.'

Joe Tasker, *Savage Arena*, 1982.

'Never write anything. You'll only regret it.'

Don Whillans, 1983 (as quoted in *Thin Air*, by Greg Child, 1988).

YAK-YAK-YAK-NAG-NAG-NAG-YAK-YAK-YAK

('A dog is not reckoned good because he barks well, and a man is not reckoned wise because he speaks skilfully.' Chuang-Tzu.)

Campfire friendship. River water, liquid fuel. Hot tea. Why make walks? To clear the mind, thoughts drifting effortlessly to the surface like tea leaves. Why walk? To make sculpture. Why walk in nature? To attempt a balance of influences. (Quantities of time.) Why walk? Partly to live in 'real time'. In 1975 I made a walk with Richard Long in Nepal. I remember becoming aware of 'foreign topics'. In a sense, the 'foreign topics' were like newspapers – they had nothing to do with the walk. On several of our walks we have had no map for part or all of the walk. No map – no tent – no stove. (No boots, no hair... Like a rolling stone.) In Nepal in 1983 we travelled for one week on paths without a map, simply asking the way. As our destination found us, I can say in retrospect that everybody we asked gave the appropriate instructions. We lived in 'real time', addicted to walking.

(Escapism – commitment.)

Hinterstoisser Traverse.

'The magic line.' It would be true to say that Richard Long has no real interest in mountain climbing as a sport, but I have chosen to introduce the topic because it is both physical and philosophical in ways that much contemporary sculpture is not.

Why visit Nepal? Jet time is not 'real time'. For the mountaineer it is clear – Wanda Rutkiewicz could not have climbed to 8,611 metres (K2 summit, Pakistan) in Poland. An artist is free to take up a different position, and only walk on her or his native country. My answer to why visit Nepal would have to be: spiritual influence. (Fly to the other side of the world on a 'hunch'.) To be influenced both by nature and people's lives (who live in nature). As a walking sculptor, Richard Long has been influenced by a wide range of landscapes: Dartmoor (Alaska), Ben Nevis (Kilimanjaro), Alaska (Lappland), riverbeds (riverbanks), Lappland (Dartmoor), Altiplano (Sahara), Silbury Hill (Mulanje Mountain). Any natural location of 'power' demands honesty.

(Twisted ankle and vice versa.)

'Please don't take away my highway shoes.' Bob Dylan

Boots. Wear them in. Wear them out. Put them on. Take them off. Put them on. (The wrong boots.) The right boots. *The dead boots*. The-boots-without-soul. (As the boots walk, so they stand still, momentarily, with each step.) 'One thing leads to another.' 'Here we go again.' 'So far, so good.' 'Win a few, lose a few.' Familiar phrases can have a new dimension on walks. Often the humour of a popular line has a sense of depth and irony the other Zen classics cannot reach. On a coast to coast road walk, TV's Magnus Magnusson says it all: 'I've started, so I'll finish.'

(Forest fires – unemployment time, employment time – wolves.)

Heathrow and the pre-walk tonsure.

Diary entry: 22 February 1987. Tarahumara, Sierra, Mexico. 'This morning while sitting round the campfire I related to Richard how, when I was a kid, with friends, we used to cook potatoes in my father's wheelbarrow. Gazing silently into the flames for some moments, Richard then said, "Meals on wheels." We laughed. He then continued, "Wheels on fire" (after the C+W song). Laughter. To which I replied: "This me-al will ex-plode."'

Neither overstated nor understated.

An *ordinary* location can be transformed by an *incredible* walk.

'He who knows does not speak, he who speaks does not know.' (Lao Tzu).

(Heavy as a rock, carrying food. Lighter, weaker.)

'Using a stone for a pillow, I drift towards the clouds.' (Santoka Taneda, Japanese haiku poet, walked 28,000 miles between 1926 and 1940.)

No matter what the length of a walk by Richard Long is, it is approximate to the art. A few straight muddy feet (*'Walking a Line in Bordeaux'* (1981)), a handful of miles (*Granite Stepping-Stone Circle A 5 Mile Circular Walk on Dartmoor Passing over 409 Rock Slabs and Boulders (1980)*), or a thousand mile spiral on England in 1974, kicking off at Bootle near Liverpool. 'Walk a thousand miles, and there is always a beyond... ' A short walk is not a short walk that should've been a long walk, not short because of a lack of stamina or an excess of alcohol. (The body determines thoughts.)

(British Rail regrets to announce the late arrival of...)

'I'm growing tired of the big city lights,
tired of the glamour and tired of the sights,
in all my dreams I am roaming once more,
back to my home on the old river shore... '

'Miss the Mississippi and you', as sung by Jimmie Rodgers the singing brake man.

(River Avon dreaming – clear mind, 'muddy waters'.)

SNAKES (CAPITALISM) WORMS (SOCIALISM) RATS (WEALTH) LICE (POVERTY) RAIN (HOMELESSNESS).

Diary entry: 9 July 1984. Ladakh, India. 'Set off at six walked up to the ravine, followed it up till it obviously was not the route. Back down to the main river then back downstream to a cairn and small track, no track up scree slope – this also no good. Back down to the main river then upstream arriving at correct river fork at 15.00 in the rain. Feeling slow on the path up towards the pass – but too wet and tired, back down again to the 15.00 stop. Now under a rock overhang. We have no idea how it will go, a problem to solve: time and distance, river conditions, rain, visibility. A cold damp night – mind uncertain.' HF

'Uncertain the journey's end, our destination; uncertain too, the place from whence we come.' (Noh play, Japan.)

Crossroads – river crossings. Rivers are roads that move.

Decisions, decisions. Walking is all about decisions, unfolding and (very carefully) folding the map. (Retracing, through the rain-soaked, disintegrating folds.) In the art of Richard Long there are two areas of interrelated decisions – the sculpture and the walk. (Walk works. I grew up in Newcastle, and of that city, Wilfred Pickles once commented, 'It's the only place where people work to wak, instead of wakin' to work.') When I see an exhibition of Richard Long's art I savour what I imagine were the decisions, some ideas even causing me to laugh, in appreciation. For instance, the 1980 150 mile walk home. ('Hello. I am a Dutch art student. Please may I make a plaster cast of your doorstep?') From Totnes to Bristol. First day walked ten miles, second day 20 miles, third day 30 miles, fourth day 40 miles, fifth day 50 miles. Strong idea followed by a strong walk – words after the fact. (Unlike the mountaineer who learns from her or his peer group, Richard Long has acquired his walking abilities alone.)

Event as object – distance no object.

Dusty Torma.

Where do you *construct* your art? In a *studio*? Where do you 'spend' most of your time? Twelve days on foot crossing 12 mountain passes in Ladakh… or touring the country for weeks on buses?

(Standing stones – a journey into stillness.)

'Adopt the pace of nature: her secret is patience.' RW Emerson.

Circling and drifting
la-te-ral thinking

Canyons of your mind –
and those circles in the corn.

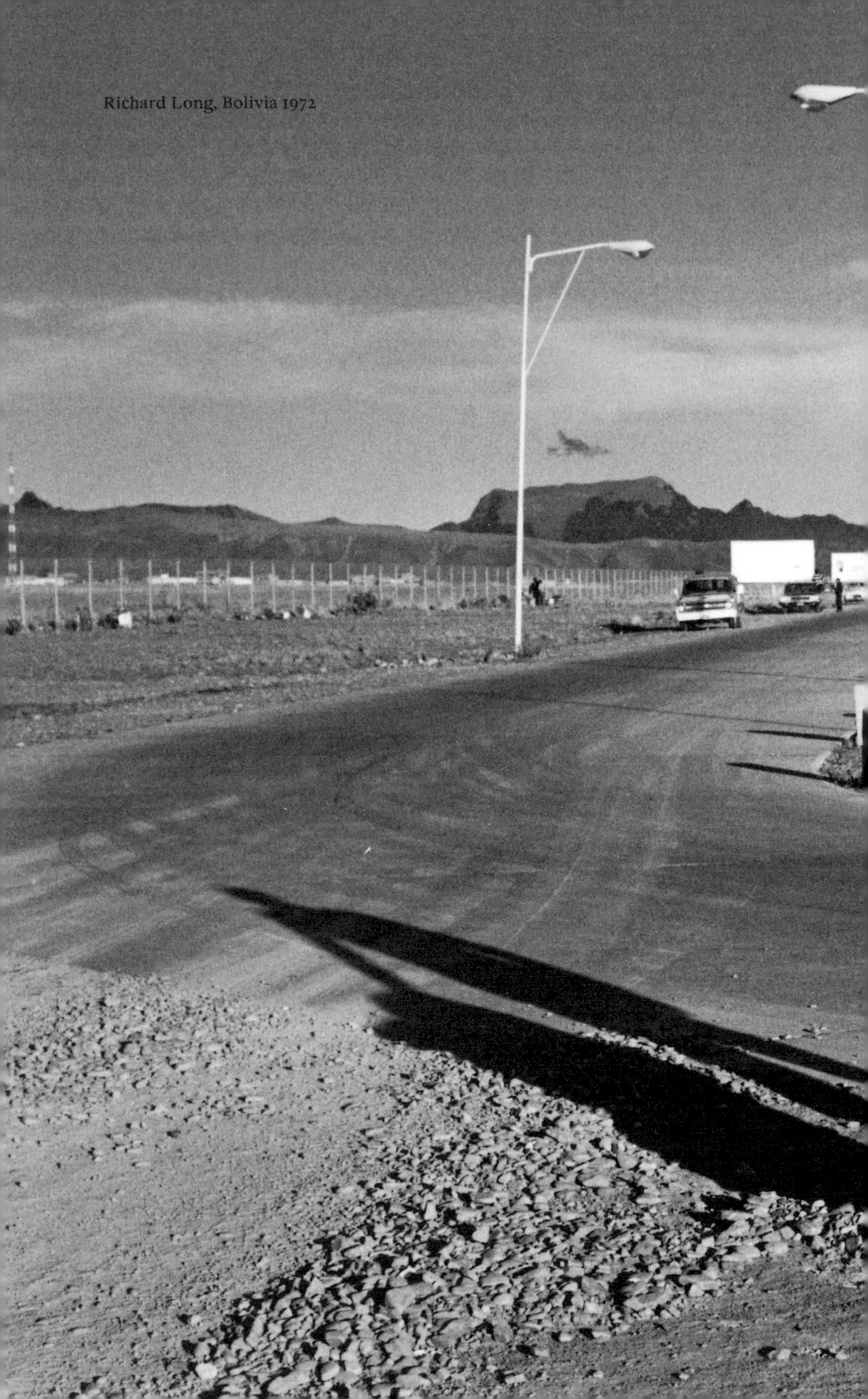

Richard Long, Bolivia 1972

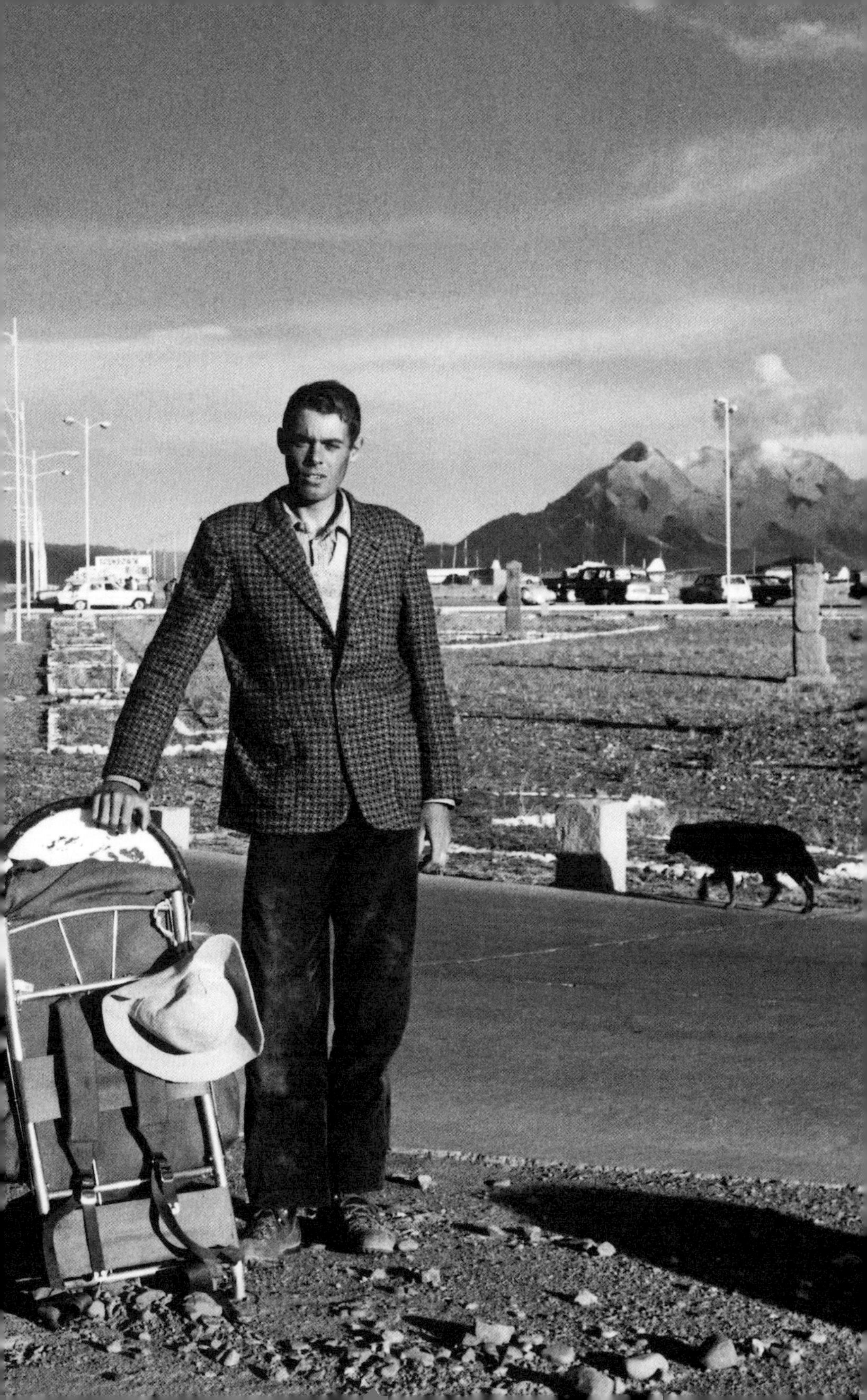

‘Our local shopping mall now has a club of people who go “mall-walking” every day. They circle the shopping centre *en masse* – Caldor to Sears to JC Penney, circuit after circuit, with an occasional break to shop.’

Bill McKibben, *The End of Nature*, 1990.

Belgium, July 1986. Georges Holtyzer walked 418.49 continuous miles in six days, ten hours and 58 minutes (452 laps of a 1.49 kilometre circuit). He kept moving for 98.78 per cent of the time (*Guinness Book of Records*).

Neutral wordless distance.

Corduroy Road.

Of the sculptures I have had the pleasure to see on walks, I remember two stunning ‘lines’. Wandering over a ridge on the Bolivian Altiplano (1981), I glimpsed, out of the corner of my eye, a line in the distance that flashed at right angles. Becoming unaligned, it was lost amongst the scattered stones and animal tracks. The second line was in Mexico, 1987. An Indian path. By pouring river water from a plastic bottle onto the existing path, Richard Long emphasised several feet of its inherent straightness. The wet, visible line eventually disappearing under a light flurry of snow, melting through momentarily. Walking away, looking back – swirling snow, rocks and pine trees – the line now existing only in my memory. Sweat on the boots.

‘Imagine,
No more sculpture
No more Henry Moore... ’

From the Roger Ackling version of *Imagine* by John Lennon.

‘Nothing is so precious that we cannot afford to throw it away.’
Jacks, *Religious Perplexities*.

The Strand ley line:
St Martin-in-the-Fields.
St Mary-le-Strand.

St Clement Danes.
St Dunstan-in-the-West.
Arnold Circus.

Sometime in the late 1960s, I remember walking through London's crowded streets with Richard Long. We discussed the possibility of seeing someone who had walked to Oxford Street (a figure in the crowd) from the port of Dover, having taken the ferry from Calais. The point of this story is that the hypothetical traveller had walked to Calais from Vladivostock in the eastern USSR.

(Corina Corina – mud on the tracks – blood on the socks.)

The early sculptures of Richard Long had a strong impact on me. Disarming simplicity – a whole new way of thinking (since childhood). Lightness – contemporary art with no history. This year (1990), I clapped eyes on a new work that immediately reminded me of the student days, the sixties' sculptures. In the small back room of a London gallery was a powerful work (*Dragon*), embodying that unique sense of risk – spirit – nature. A small zigzag line of white china clay splashed across the clean floor (go with the flow – earth's gravity).

(The wave: walk water sculpture sleep – walk water sculpture sleep – walk water sculpture sleep.)

STONED

No Monday Morning Blues. Today it might be easy to criticise Richard Long's success, but it must not be forgotten that after leaving St Martin's School of Art he did not look for a job. He made sculpture. ('Instead of earning a wage, you are earning mountain experience.' Dougal Haston, *In High Places*, 1972.)

'Crossing the Ohio at Louisville, I steered through the big city by compass without speaking a word to anyone.'

September 2nd 1867. John Muir, *A Thousand Mile Walk to the Gulf*.

About 100 years later Richard Long created *A Line Made by Walking* (1967), surely one of the most original works of twentieth-century

Western art. ('The longest journey begins with but a single step.') At the age of 23, Long combined two seemingly unrelated activities: sculpture (the line) and walking (the action). A line (made by) walking. In time, the sculpture will have disappeared, long before the commercialisation of the word 'green' … and those footprints on the moon.

'Leave no turd unstoned.'

Don Whillans, 1983, as quoted in *Thin Air*, by Greg Child, 1988.

As Britain's *premier* sculptor, Richard Long has not been tempted into making U-turns (except for his walk, crossing and recrossing England and Wales, *Crosssing Stones* (1987)). Fame and fortune have not caused him to employ bulldozers after a lifetime of 'placing' sticks. Long makes a variety of work – enough for four artists, but they are related, one to another. This variety is not so diverse as to be hypocritical. We are not confused as to his real concerns. Rain, snow, sleet and ice eventually form the same river.

Calumniare Fortiter,
Et Aliquid Adhaerebit.
(Throw dirt enough, and some will stick.)

(River mud – hand of the artist – life line – the all-meaning circle – Lascaux.)

Feng-shui (wind and water) Chernobyl.

Six months before 26 April 1986, Richard Long and I drank river water, flowing through the land of the Lapps. A 15-day walk of wind, rain, freezing rain, snow, blizzard and friendship.

(Shigechiyo Izumi. Japanese. Born 29 June 1865. Lived for 120 years and 237 days.)

Length of a stride – length of a life.

Spain, February 1989. Walking down a snaking road through pine trees, I was reminded of the *Tour de France* cycle race. Richard Long and I had set out to walk coast to coast across Portugal and Spain. For the record, the walking artist walks every step of the way, whereas in recent years the *Tour* cyclists have been flown between two stages, creating a gap in the chain of roads. Similarly, in 1974, the Scottish hill-walker, H Brown, made a walk billed as the first non-stop climb of all the 3,000 foot Scottish Munro peaks. On the road-links between the hills, Brown in fact travelled by bicycle. Inevitably, Richard Long and I began to talk of the English racer Tommy Simpson. We recalled the view on film of Simpson in the 1967 *Tour*, falling from his cycle, to die where he fell, on the road. Our short conversation then switched to the American, Greg LeMond, who at the time of our walk had won the 1986 *Tour*. After an incredible recovery following a shooting accident, LeMond went on to win a second *Tour* in July 1989. (Teaching by example.)

(On the road.)

In the late summer of 1989, I made a coast to coast road walk across France. From west to east, my route developed daily. One particular day I remember well. On the dawn of October 5th, while descending Mont Ventoux, by chance I came across the roadside memorial to Tommy Simpson. A plaque and a cairn of cyclists' caps.

(Dartmoor renewal.)

BASHOBECKETTBARTHES – LEMOND?

I do not mention the *Tour de France* to glorify a competitive way of life. The truth is, I find the three-time winner of the *Tour de France* an inspiration: LeMond has passed-through-the-eye-of-a-needle. These events are the landmarks of his life. This is magic.

Richard Long makes his marks… This is magic.

It has been my great privilege to make ten journeys with Richard Long, and I thank him.

Hamish Fulton Summer 1990

Footnote December 1990

Dream walk. Eleventh journey. This winter, Richard Long and I walked on 622 miles of roads from the north coast to the south coast of Spain – Ribadesella to Málaga, crossing our previous west to east route in the town of Villanueva. 'Whoso shall compel thee to go one mile, go with them twain.' DOS MAS. On the road to Las Hazuelas, the bottom line –

THE REALITY
OF THE LOCALITY

Walking in Circles, exh. cat., George Braziller, New York, and South Bank Centre, London, 1991, pp.241–46.

SEAN RAINBIRD

Crossing Place: Some Notes on the Work of Richard Long

Richard Long's art is simple and direct, based on the primacy of ideas and motivated by a purposeful, rigorous engagement with his chosen materials. It draws on the artist's experience of nature encountered through walking, at once continuing an English tradition of engagement with the landscape and immediately unique in its personal characteristics. His art embodies the essence of his experience, not a visual representation of it and signals a radical departure from the tradition of landscape depiction.

Richard Long's approach is pragmatic, unheroic and quiet: he uses simple marks and clearly records actions and emotions. Over the past 25 years, his basic artistic means and materials have expanded, yet they remain rooted in the practice he first developed in the mid-1960s when taking his art outdoors. Natural materials, often stones, are displaced close to where they are found along a walk, to make a sculpture which is recorded by a photograph and title. Alternatively, stones (usually quarried) are moved to domestic and gallery spaces and placed in straightforward, powerful shapes, mainly circles and lines, on the floor, while textual records of ideas, observations, sensations or measurements recorded along a walk are made into text works. These means form the basis of his art in conjunction with more recent works involving mud and water, a natural extension of his experiences outdoors.

The sculptural concerns of form, volume and structure within self-sufficient objects, the guiding philosophy behind the *New Generation* exhibition at the Whitechapel Gallery in 1965, had by the beginning of the 1970s, given way to a wide diversity of approaches to artistic questions and practices. Issues such as reinvestigating the intrinsic properties of natural materials, exploring art's links to the environment, redefining the spatial, perceptual and temporal exchange between the work of art, its display and its relationship to the spectator, all stood at the forefront of artistic debate. Richard Long's earliest works involved subtle and temporary adjustments to the landscape, through controlled and preordained actions by the artist, resulting in works of apparent simplicity and considerable conceptual daring.

Before enrolling on the St Martin's School of Art vocational course in 1966 Richard Long had already worked outdoors, responding to strong feelings that things like clouds, grass, water and natural places defined his attitude to art and his interest in the natural world. He felt that a larger reality was being left untouched in the art of his time. Early works, made using turf, snow and leaves, involved direct engagement with natural materials. The transience of these works was merely a by-product of the generating thought behind each one. That works such as his *Snowball Track* (1964) or *A Line Made by Walking* (1967) might later only be known through photographs was at that time a side issue. After 1967 walking became a way to bring great distances into a work of art, of engaging the real space and shape of the world through direct physical commitment.

The arena for Richard Long's chosen activity, initially centred around the West Country, in particular Dartmoor and the Avon Gorge in the immediate vicinity of his home and birthplace, now embraces many continents and some of the most remote regions on the earth. Traversing known and unknown tracks across the surface of the ground, with a special association for places where the land meets the water or where water has eroded channels down towards the sea, Richard Long adds his tracks to those made by others, or adds those never before made to the layers of paths marking human and animal progress across the land. On some walks, human histories, mapped, cultivated and named, are integrated into the artist's own plans or observations, intimating a layered archaeology of the human presence over the ages. On others, the lie of the land, the flow of its rivers, or the lack of adequate maps determines the artist's path across the ground. The walked line marked in *Fresh Water Salt Water Line Walk* (1980) exemplifies the artist's predetermined route yielding to the natural barriers of alternate fresh and salt water lochs and inlets which impeded his direct progress across the ground.

Long's way is fugitive, and his markings on the surface of the land ephemeral: photographic records of lines and circles in remote regions and notebook jottings are demonstrative moments of an unassuming presence. To make a record, he takes photographs, without artifice, from ground level and usually from the angle revealing the work at the point of greatest visual impact. Richard Long takes what he finds from his surroundings when he feels a work needs to be made. Unlike other artists working predominantly in wide open spaces, particularly the American Land artists, he neither excavates nor tries to stamp his presence on the land in other ways, preferring minimal to massive interventions and demonstrating his physical commitment to his art through the rigours of walking great distances. He moves with his bare hands or through kicking those stones which are closest by, aware sometimes that he is probably the first person to have ever disturbed them, or, that he has become simply one further human engaged in a ritual exchange with the land.

The physical traces of his interventions are frequently erased over time, washed away by water or shifted by the winds. The strong tidal flow in the Bristol Channel, near his home, has reinforced an intuitive awareness of the underlying forces of transformation and flux in nature. He has made many works with driftwood collected or dropped at the water's edge and, on occasion, has seen the natural processes of ebb and flow magically transform specific works. In conversation with Anne Seymour, he recalled a cross of stones – entitled *Half-Tide* (1971) – made in Bertraghboy Bay in Ireland at low tide:

> the tide was out, and there was this beautiful bed of wet, soggy, bubbly seaweed on this stony beach, and I made a cross of stones on the seaweed… When I woke up the next morning, the tide had come in, and instead of seeing my cross of stones, I actually saw the image of my work suspended on the surface of the water, because the stones were keeping the seaweed down… when the tide came up full, all the seaweed was completely under the water… You only saw the cross on the surface of the water at half-tide.

In recent years he has used mud, often from the River Avon, to make wall and floor works in gallery spaces, thus imposing on himself the challenge of working swiftly, without the possibility of correcting errors. The corollary of the risks involved in their making is the powerfully spontaneous impact of such works and their intimate

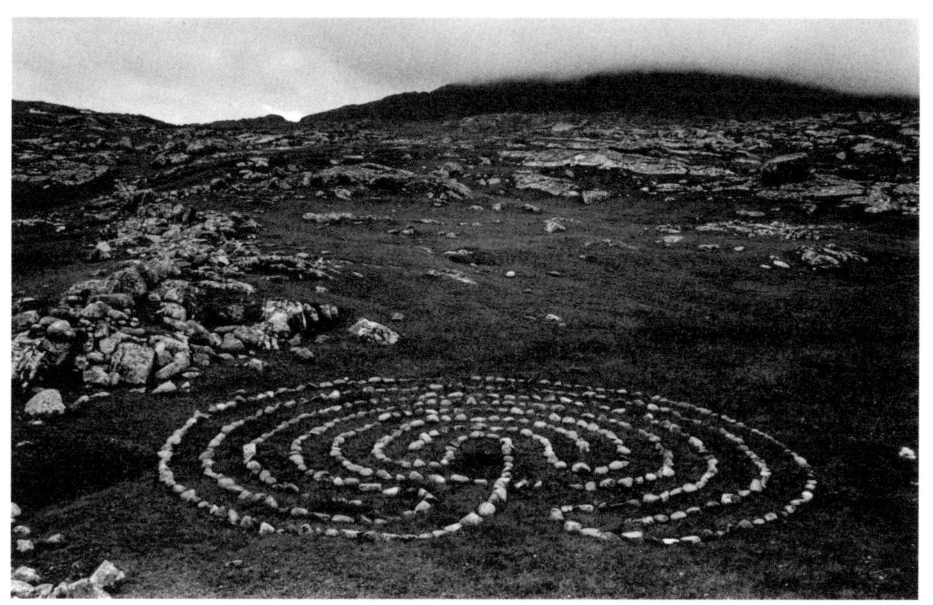

CONNEMARA SCULPTURE
IRELAND 1971

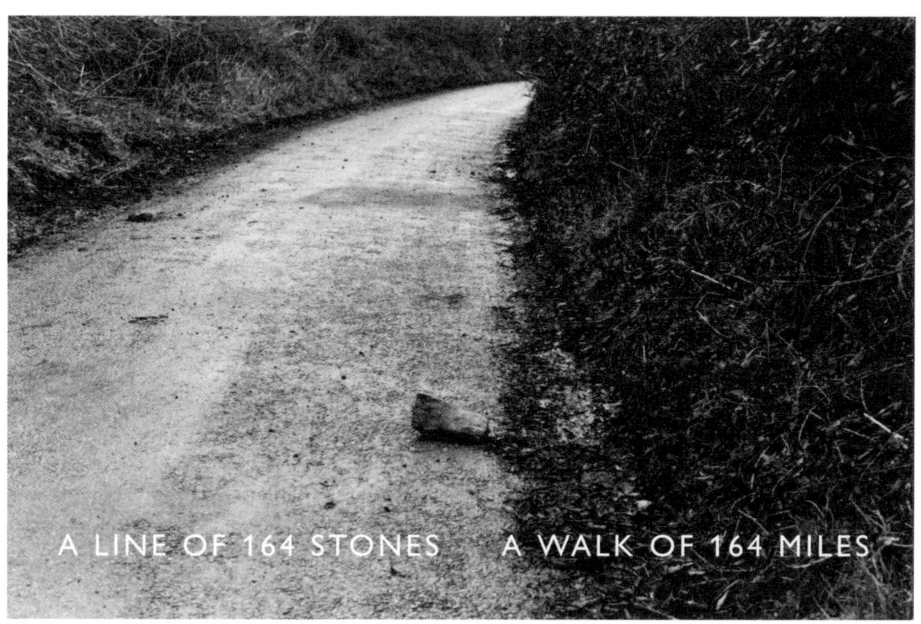

A WALK ACROSS IRELAND PLACING A NEARBY STONE ON THE ROAD AT EVERY MILE ALONG THE WAY

CLARE 49 STONES TIPPERARY 38 STONES KILKENNY 27 STONES LEIX 9 STONES CARLOW 20 STONES WICKLOW 21 STONES

1974

connection to the most ancient forms of human mark-making. As much about water as mud, they are the indoor equivalents for his pure water-marks in the landscape. In many other works, he acknowledges the implicit transformative power of water – reducing mountains to mud through erosion, and itself experienced in both fluid and solid states.

Through encoding, researching and recording his walks in photographs, maps and texts, and by bringing into interior spaces the materials he uses along the way or which are readily available in their most crudely extracted form, Richard Long has found a highly focused and formally pure way of bringing his work to public attention. His stone circles and lines, such as *Planet Circle* (1991), are first made with particular exhibitions and spaces in mind, frequently using quarried stone or materials found near the place of the exhibition. In recent years his text works contain an expanded set of references beyond places and visually perceived phenomena, and increasingly include records of the other senses – taste, smell and sound – as well as the interrelationships of each of the elements: fire, water, air and earth. *1449 Stones at 1449 Feet* (1979), along with similar works of the same year, underlines the symbiotic link between land and sea, not only in the natural world, but also in mankind's systematic calibration of it, relating each point on the map to sea level as a basic standard of cartographic measurement. Sound becomes the predominant expression within *Stone Water Sound*, a walk made across Wales in 1990.

Over the past 25 years Richard Long has simplified and purified the language in his text works. The more descriptive captions to his earliest photographic images, particularly those published in his extensive body of artist's books, have been supplanted by text works giving the barest factual information. The linguistic tautness of Long's texts has given his language a condensed quality, an equivalence perhaps to the language of poetry, where words, however common, acquire a specific rhythm and density and appear to resonate more powerfully than in everyday speech. For Richard Long, words are interchangeable with stones: 'I can make a sculpture using a line of stones. I can make a sculpture using a line of words. Stones and words are both the same.'

The evocation of fleeting and elusive experiences lies at the heart of his text works in particular, which become linguistic maps charting, fixing and joining the physical discontinuities created by his itinerant passage. The time lapse between sensations and perceptions recorded, the actual separation of physical objects – the essentially episodic nature of his actions and experiences – are all vital moments subsumed within the overall balance and unity of the walk. The properties of time (whether as duration or the agency of change), distance and place interrelate in his work, sometimes invoked deliberately as part of the strategy behind a given work, or admitted as part of the essential experience of human beings within the natural world.

His own presence, siting his tent, making tea, recalling the phrases of a song (*No Woman No Cry*), emptying his boots of grit or flopping down fatigued at the end of the day, is sometimes integrated as a biographical fragment, locating specific and personal moments within the wider experiences of walking. These serve, also, as an affirmation of the processes of artistic mediation, an essential part of the works' content. (One of the artist's favourite images is the photograph of two rucksacks belonging to himself and Hamish Fulton – with whom he has travelled on several occasions – propped against a wall in Mexico during a walk in 1979.)

Within the expanding body of works resulting from walks, Richard Long makes clear distinctions between guidelines he adopts for each particular walk and which give each a distinct character and emphasis. The familiar territory of Dartmoor and the many crossing points linking different walks from different times – the evolution of a personal history connected to a region – have become a recognised part of Long's work. A five-day walk in 1980, from Totnes to Bristol, was robust and precise: the artist set himself the discipline of walking ten miles on day one, increasing by multiples of ten until 50 miles were covered on day five. The geometry of days to miles and the shifting balance between ease and difficulty was the main subject of the walk. Pace itself, within preset limits of time and distance, determined his progress in *A Thousand Miles A Thousand Hours* (1974), while variations in speed and pace lie at the heart of *A Walk of Four Hours and Four Circles* (1972). Here, Richard Long planned a walk round four evenly spaced, concentric circles drawn on a map of Dartmoor: different distances to be covered in the same unit of time. Richard Long often sets parameters for his walks in advance – the distance to be covered, the pace to be set, the direction of the walk, whether the walk should follow a fixed compass point – while at other times the actual route is left to chance and the necessity of circumventing obstacles. The *Cerne Abbas Walk* (1975), centred on the landmark of the Cerne Abbas Giant, records a particular kind of walk, that is, a walk within and over a complete area (a circle) using all roads and tracks, as opposed to a linear or journeying walk from one 'end' to another.

Over the years, the range of Richard Long's work has become more diverse and the works' presentation more refined, allowing different facets of the artist's experience along the way, such as the changing wind (in works such as *Wind Stones* of 1985), or the observation of particular colours, to be evoked for the spectator with great formal simplicity. All his works, motivated by a clear, central idea, exemplify a core quality in Richard Long's art and its ability to transcend the private sphere of the artist and communicate on a wider level. In one of his statements, he has written, 'a walk expresses space and freedom and the knowledge of it can live in the imagination of anyone and that is another space too.' The power of Richard Long's art rests in its ability to invoke an imaginative response in the viewer; to share publicly the stream of private fragments and thoughts that form a delicate thread closing the full circle of the artist's engagement with the natural order of things. His art, unmistakable and consistent, achieves an almost classical poise between movement and stillness, activity and contemplation, nothingness and substance, as reflected in his comment, 'a good work is the right thing in the right place at the right time. A crossing place.'

Published as a pamphlet to accompany the exhibition *Walking in Circles*, Hayward Gallery, The South Bank Centre, London 1991, n.p.

COLIN KIRKPATRICK AND RICHARD LONG

Richard Long: No Where

> Genghis Khan he could not keep
> All his kings supplied with sleep
> We'll climb that hill
> No matter haw steep
> But we still
> Ain't going nowhere
>
> Bob Dylan, *You Ain't Going Nowhere*, 1967

CK *In 1967 you made* A Line Made by Walking.

RL That was in my first year at St Martin's.

CK *What made you make that piece and did you realise at the time it was going to be a fundamental starting point for you?*

RL No. I didn't realise it then, but I definitely had a sense that what I was doing was really important and I had a terrific conviction and belief that it was interesting.

CK *Just for that one piece?*

RL Well, not only for that one piece, that didn't seem like the crucial work at the time, but just in general, like digging lines in my parents' garden or making works which were paced out across a hillside. I think possibly the *Line Made by Walking* was… maybe I began to notice, after walking between parts of sculptures in fields, that I had left a track. I had a very strong feeling that art could embrace so many more things than it was at the time, that it could be about things like grass and clouds and water, natural phenomena, rather than just the slightly sterile academic, almost mannerism of welding bits of metal together, or using plaster, or the general kind of studio work at that time.

CK *Was it important to you that your fellow students could see what you were trying to do?*

RL Oh yes, we were all interested in each other's work – we were all fans of each other so it was a great time to be a student in London.

CK *The swinging sixties…*

RL It was the spirit of the time that was innovative and imaginative. One big influential moment was a lecture by John Cage, in a concert he gave at a theatre near St Martin's. It was all about chance and eccentric, lateral thinking – sort of Cage ideas which were new to me then, and later there was a taped lecture by him called *Indeterminacy* (1959), where he told 60 stories. Each story was a minute long, so if it was a very long story he had to speak very fast to get it in and if it was a short story he would speak very slowly, so it was about pace and time, rhythm and humour and formal ideas about time, and so from many points of view it was really interesting.

CK *That sounds a bit like some of the time pieces you do yourself – the word pieces.*

RL Oh absolutely, and also it had connections with Eastern philosophy and thought – Zen – so all these ideas were floating around at the time – sort of radical, avant-garde, imaginative.

CK *A lot of people would like to tie your work into a Zen way of thinking, but you don't have any strong beliefs in that yourself?*

RL Well, I believe in the coincidences that exist between all really profound ideas and thought. I think there are some things in human life and history which are quite universal, that's not saying that I am a practising Zen Buddhist, but I do feel very close to the spirit of many of their points of view. Zen is quite pure and philosophical, it's close to art, and the Japanese religion, Shinto, is based on nature, and nature is universal. Nature belongs to every culture. I am a Western artist, part of the avant-garde Western tradition, but nevertheless, in a century where cultures can go round the world very easily, you can have access to the thought and philosophy of other countries.

CK *The nature of the places you go to might mean you wouldn't meet many folk.*

RL That's true – for preference I'm attracted to the empty wilderness places, but often to get to those places I travel on public transport and meet all sorts of people. There is some comment on the lack of people in my work, but it is just a question of choice, the subject of my work is walking, or making sculpture in empty landscapes. The form of the work is a particularly chosen aspect of each journey. Through choice I'm not an urban artist – my work is about being in the natural world. Most of the world's surface is still open landscapes. I feel like I'm a realist working in the real spaces of the world.

CK *Though often in the word pieces you are moving through rural or urban areas.*

RL The map works and also many of the road walks take me through towns and villages because that is where I can buy food, or find a bed-and-breakfast, find shops. If you really pay attention to the work you realise that I use many aspects of the world – it is just that I don't make park sculpture in the middle of big cities.

CK *Have you ever been asked to?*

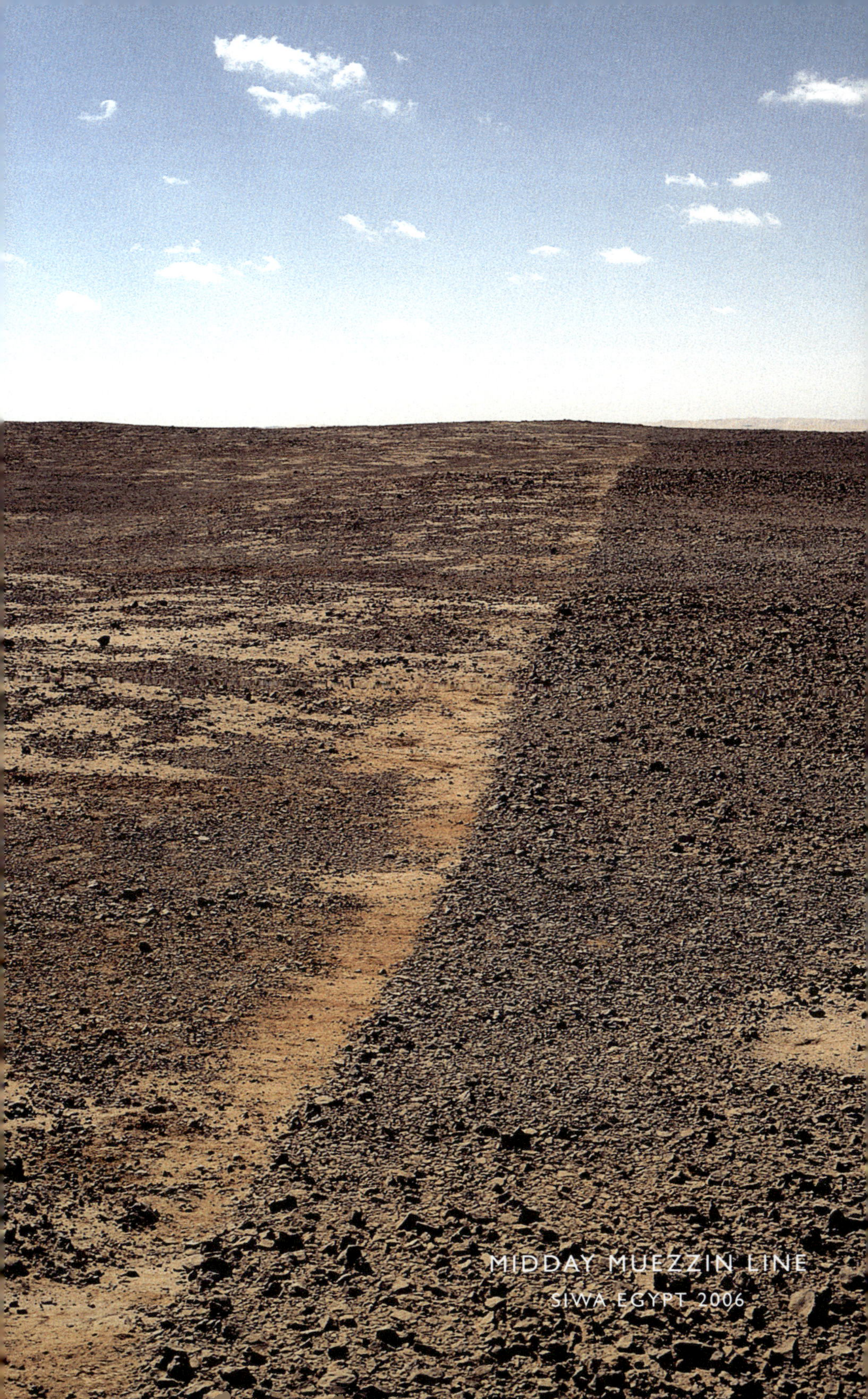

MIDDAY MUEZZIN LINE

SIWA EGYPT 2006

RL Yes, and I always say that since I have won a kind of freedom to make work in remote places all over the world, I would choose to do that rather than have to go and plonk a sculpture down in the middle of a park in a city – it is just my choice, that's all.

CK *When you take your stones into a gallery space they are usually stones you have got from some urban area, or quarry.*

RL That's right. It is a different procedure, it's a different rationale. The stones I make sculptures with in the landscape are just the stones of that place – I leave them there – like the stones on Hoy. And you are right in saying the gallery sculptures are taken from quarries.

CK *Do you feel as happy making work in the gallery space?*

RL I do, but it's different, it's complementary. I feel happy making all the different aspects of my work, whether the mud walls in the gallery or making the walks. I am interested in showing real sculpture in galleries and museums as well as just photographs. I have often said before that the maps and the texts and the photos feed the imagination, and the sculptures in the gallery feed the senses. Both aspects for me are important.

CK *Do you feel that the maps and photographs take the gallery spectators in their mind out into the landscape, and make them think as they would in the landscape?*

RL Yes, I suppose the point to that idea is that art can be somewhere else, that even though it is a work of art in its own right in the gallery, it also makes that imaginative leap, that the actual work also happens somewhere else, in time and places maybe thousands of miles away. So in a way my work demonstrates that art can be made any time, anywhere – it could be a walk which lasts three weeks or it could be in a place that no one else has been to, or it could be a work that disappears in two or three minutes in the sunshine. So in a way the photos and the maps and the words all demonstrate that kind of freedom. They are the simplest way for me to distil the space and time of the world into a form of art, but they are not meant to copy the experience of it.

CK *I often think that in the gallery installations you are making your outdoor art in the landscape of the gallery – you make them on the gallery surface.*

RL I suppose another way to look at it is that whether I am out in the landscape or making a show in the gallery, it is always the same person, the same sensitivity, it is just a slightly different way of doing it, and in a different place. Often the materials are the same – I could use water in the landscape, but if I use water in the gallery, then it makes sense to mix it with mud, because otherwise you would not see it, it would just disappear. So if you think of water as one of the main themes of my work, the mudworks in the gallery are really about water – the splashes, the mud prints, the wateriness of the mud, it is just another way of using water. It's the equivalent of the outdoor works.

CK *You often see in your books and exhibition catalogues, 'Mississippi' or 'River Avon mud drawings'. Do you collect mud as raw material from these places?*

RL Sometimes I do. Because I was born in Bristol, I grew up playing along the riverbanks, so the River Avon is a big influence, the huge tide and the mud banks. In the early days if I was doing a mud circle in New York, I would take a plastic bag of mud from the Avon. One part of my work is the practical aspect – it is possible to take a big handful of mud from the Avon on the plane to New York, mix it with a bucket of water when I get there and make a huge work in New York with my River Avon mud. On the other hand if I want to make a huge sculpture of many tons of stones, then it doesn't make sense to take stones across, so then the stones would always come from near that gallery.

CK *The piece you did at Jesus College Cambridge,* Orcadian Stone Circle (1992), *would be an example of this.*

RL That title came about from another route – I had just got back from Orkney, where my good friend Colin Renfrew, the Master of Jesus College, has done a lot of work – he's an archaeologist – so it was a sort of sentimental token.

CK *Early on, you made some work in Kerry and Cornwall where you used the tide – you were working between the edge of the land and the sea.*

RL Yes, the idea of those works was that between two tides I made my own pattern, which would be dispersed by the next tide. So even though the work was extremely temporary, it pointed to the idea that the tides leave a new pattern of seaweed on the same beach every day and have done for millions of years.

CK *They are almost like an intermediate point between your water drawings and your more solid pieces in the open landscape, your water drawings are away in a matter of seconds and the tide pieces lasted six hours or whatever.*

RL That's right. I suppose coming from Bristol I was often on West Country beaches, in my childhood, watching the surf for hours, and being interested by the tides in the Avon, with the huge lock gates on the harbour.

CK *Have you done any more pieces relating to the tide?*

RL Recently, in the past couple of years, I did specific tide walks, for example from the high tide in Plymouth to the low tide in Weston-super-Mare, a continuous walk of about 104 miles or something – then I bought this really interesting book that gave for a whole year all the tables of the tides around the coast. It's like the breathing of the sea. So yes, I did specific works particularly about tides. Normally, my walks have been measured by days, which is the sun going round the world, and if I make a work about the tides it is like using a lunar clock instead.

CK *When you first came up to Orkney what made you decide to go to Hoy?*

RL I think it was the combination of a great place, really mountainous, it's probably the most wilderness place in Orkney.

CK *Looking at the map piece,* Walking a Circle on Hoy *(1992), where you chose to draw your circle implies something about your use of maps. Your route and the line intersect the 'H' and the 'Y' of the word 'Hoy' on the map.*

RL Yes, that's no coincidence. Often, I think I'm a classical artist – if you can line something up, line it up. It really was just that the lettering was exactly in the middle of the island and so therefore the circle could also be centred visually in the middle of the island.

CK *So it was an aesthetic decision?*

RL Oh yes. I study the maps very carefully to see that the places I am walking, whether it's following lines or circles, have no features like a cliff or a lake in the way of my route – all those considerations are very important in making both the drawing and the walk. With the map pieces I will actually make the drawing on the map first because you have to do it that way round. First of all I have the idea. Whether it is a circle walk, or walking inside a circle, and then I'll think of the area that's most appropriate, that's most practical to realise such an idea, and carry out that walk, then I'll buy the map and look at it and figure out exactly where that circle should be.

CK *Do you ever decide on a piece, go to a place, and find that there is something not shown on the map which inhibits what you do?*

RL Occasionally, not often. A few years ago I did a straight 12-hour walk across the Highlands – the idea was to walk exactly a straight line, but there was one little cliff that was marked on the map, almost unnotice- ably, but in reality it was a huge cliff. If you look closely at the artwork you will notice a kink in the line where I had to go round the cliff.

CK *Was that the landscape reminding you who was in control?*

RL Yes – it always does.

CK *Have you ever been interrupted on a walk whereby you can't complete it?*

RL Yes, sometimes a walk has to change because of unforeseen circumstances. For example, Hamish Fulton and I planned to walk around the Annapurna Massif in Nepal and just before we were due to go over the main pass the monsoons came and blocked us off with deep snow, so we had to go on to Plan B and completely re-route ourselves back another way. So it can happen.

CK *When you go on a journey with Hamish Fulton, you come back with separate works. Have you ever collaborated on a piece?*

RL No, but we once did a show together in Madrid. We are very good friends, we have a great deal of respect for each other's work and get on well together. We are old friends and have the same sense of humour. In many ways we are very similar – we are both artists, both like walking and camping, but having said that, we are very different artists. When we are on a walk we are both making completely individual work along the way – the collaboration is the walking.

CK *How easy is it to adhere to circles when you are walking? Do you have a technique you use?*

RL Yes, obviously it is much easier when I have visibility, then I can align myself visually by looking at the map and the topography. But what really makes it easiest in the first place is choosing – looking very carefully at the map and avoiding deep rivers and bogs or cliffs, any features that would stop me walking a circle. So with that particular line of the circle on Hoy, it is actually possible to follow that route, quite easily, if you pay attention.

CK *Relating to maps, are you ever attracted to features other than the landscape, and the aesthetics of the map – are you attracted to place names?*

RL Of course, yes. You can tell from many of my works, especially the textworks, that place names play a really important part. I think the way places are named affects the way we know places. It's like language, how we talk about things is part of our understanding of the world.

CK *Referring back to Hoy and looking back through your catalogues, you haven't made a lot of other work on small islands.*

RL But I really like islands.

CK *You feel drawn to islands?*

RL Oh yes. In fact back in the early seventies I had this idea to make straight hundred mile walks along straight lines in different landscapes. I did one in the classical boggy temperate landscape of Ireland and then I did one on the prairies of Canada so that the idea was that the hundred mile walk was always the same but the landscape had changed. I did another one in the bamboo forest in Japan, and another in the red Australian outback. One idea that I had at the time that I never carried out was to make a hundred mile walk on a straight line on a very small island, like in the middle of the Pacific somewhere, so it would be straight up and down many times on a really small atoll. So maybe that's an idea I will go back to, one day.

CK *You told me you lived in the Aran Islands for a period of time.*

RL Well, I spent a summer on Inishmore. I have a whole history of going to Ireland. It is one of the great countries in the world, I think. I first went there in 1964 just after I'd been thrown out of Bristol art school. I think it is really my kind of country. Of course another aspect of Ireland is that in the west, in County Clare, there are the stony deserts, the Burren, so it is a combination of being my kind of landscape, wet and temperate and balmy, but it's also full of wonderful people, full of humour. I also love the music.

CK *Is music important to your work?*

RL Obviously not a direct influence as I'm not a musician, but imaginatively, inspirationally, music is really important. I couldn't imagine life without music. I think it is a really fantastically emotional feel-good kind of artform.

I used to give slide shows for art students where I would play one track of my favourite music accompanied by just one slide, so that students would have to look at just one slide for the duration of one whole piece of music, with no art talk. I did that show with slides of different combinations of places, different audiences. But the one piece of music that always got the most rapt attention, where you could almost hear a pin drop, was *Roisin Dubh*, the slow air played on a tin whistle, with people looking at the circle in Ireland. That was always the most moving piece in the slide show.

CK *Why did you choose the Bob Dylan quote to go on the private view card of the Hoy piece?*

RL There's no real reason, except that it has gone through my head like a mantra, that particular verse, occasionally.

CK *I just wondered, because when you start looking for those musical whispers…*

RL I think you're one of the first people to interview me that has picked that up, but I'm glad you have, for I'm very conscious of it always being there.

CK *I know that for one person the Tennessee stream piece, with the Johnny Cash quote, was the key into your work.*

RL I honestly believe my work is accessible, if people open their minds – you have to go with it, like music. It's not my intention to be obscure or elitist.

CK *If you had been at work four thousand years ago in the Orkney landscape, there would have been no problem whatsoever with your art. Are you ever conscious that you are treading the footpath of ancient man –*

not necessarily in what you make, but in the materials you are using and the places that you go?

RL Yes, it's literally the same stones and the same surfaces of the world that people have always walked over and used. All the place names are like layers of history and different cultures. My work is just another layer on the surface of the world that has been shared by all these different generations, so it's really about continuity. But it's also about new ideas about time and space and walking. Also, I'm of the first generation where as an artist I could use the world as one arena, as it's possible now to fly almost anywhere completely normally and cheaply. So my work is connected to both old and new ideas.

CK *Have you ever come across the remains of the indigenous culture in the wilderness in a place that you're in?*

RL Yes, from Dartmoor, to Orkney, to South America – the famous Nazca plateau in Peru. Everyone knows the famous lines and images of Nazca but if you go off into the mountains away from the plateau, you can find your own lines. You can find little notches that line one ridge to another so it seems those lines are limitless.

CK *That Peruvian line* [Walking a Line in Peru *(1972)*] *– did you make that line or was it an existing line?*

RL That's a good question. There was no line existing but I actually made it by aligning two notches on the horizon and keeping them in line, as I walked the line, so it is really a combination of me making the line, but also using the existing site lines so there could well have been a line there before – I just reactivated it – I like to think that actually.

CK *What sort of distance was that line?*

RL About three hundred yards, roughly.

CK *It looks like it could be 20 miles.*

RL No, if you look very closely in the foreground you can actually see the footprints.

CK *It seems very compressed but at the same time it seems vast.*

RL Sometimes things seem more compressed because I photograph them end on. They open out if you get a side view.

CK *What do you take with you when you make a journey?*

RL Apart from the normal camping stuff, the equipment I take to make my art is leather gloves, just ordinary work gloves, a big collapsible water bottle which I can use as a tool to make water drawings, and also a piece of string, and I think on one trip I had a length of climbing rope – it was actually more useful for laying out a straight line for a sculpture – so these are the only things I take for making work.

CK *You travel as light as you can?*

RL Yes, with a stove and camping gas, then to conserve fuel I make campfires sometimes, when it's possible to. But on the really long road walks, I travel with no food at all, as it is possible to buy food on the way. So for road walks I would have different boots and a lighter rucksack with less stuff in it. Each walk is completely different. For wilderness walks I would have much heavier boots, bigger rucksack, carry all my food, carry fuel and stove, walk slower because the load is heavier, so each walk is different for these reasons.

CK *When you travel on your own, are you ever lonely?*

RL Never, no. I think it is a big luxury to be alone, because a lot of the art world is really social and tiring and complicated, so it is a real luxury and relaxation to go off on my own and do a long walk.

CK *Do you have places you would like to go back to?*

RL Oh, absolutely. That is why I keep going back to Ireland and why I have been coming to Scotland since 1967. I find really powerful places like Ireland – the west coast of Ireland – and I keep going back to them. Or even Dartmoor, or the South West of England. I have done so many walks in England – it is really my landscape, my home turf. I think accumulated experience is really great, and that too becomes part of the art.

CK *Do you get cabin fever when you get back from a trip?*

RL Occasionally, but I'm not a nomad. I don't have this desire to be always travelling, always on the road. It is really necessary to come back to Bristol to see my family, or do some gardening or just to go shopping, and to regenerate. I think another important thing to say is that if I go on a trip or a walk, I really have to have an appetite to do it, and if I was doing it all the time, probably the appetite would be dulled. Sometimes it is really good to have a month in Bristol doing other things. For example this spring I have been far too busy making exhibitions in different places – so I've been in the art world too long, so that recently, when I made my first walk after all this urban time, I had a fantastic energy, which was good for my work.

CK *Is adventure quite an important part of what you do? Do you look forward to it?*

RL Yes, I do. There is a real edge of excitement. I'm not like a professional mountaineer, but once in a while there is an element of danger, working out crossing boulders or gorges or going over log bridges, over ravines. Quite a lot of the walks are adventurous without being dangerous. It's all part of the life of walking in the wilderness. I also like the day-to-day ritual of camping every night in a new place, getting firewood or sleeping under the stars; having amazing dreams, eating quite little food, but really enjoying it. All that's a great pleasure, which is what my work is all about. The sculptures along the way are just another part of that daily ritual.

Orkney Arts Review, no.6, February 1995, pp.4–8.

This interview was arranged by the Pier Arts Centre, Orkney and took place during an exhibition of Richard Long's work held there in summer 1994.

JOHN HALDANE

Points Along the Road

Richard Long is a distinctive and important figure in the history of postwar British art. His first solo exhibition was in 1968 at the Konrad Fischer Galerie in Dusseldorf. The following year he showed again at Fischer's gallery and had four other exhibitions in New York, Krefeld, Paris and Milan. Interest in his work grew rapidly, and through the 1970s he developed a reputation as the most interesting of the new British artists. Not only was international appreciation fast in arriving, it came very early in Long's career. At the time of the first Dusseldorf exhibition he was 23. By the end of the next decade he had had some 60 solo exhibitions in ten countries, including shows at national galleries in Australia, Holland and Scotland; and in 1976, aged 31,

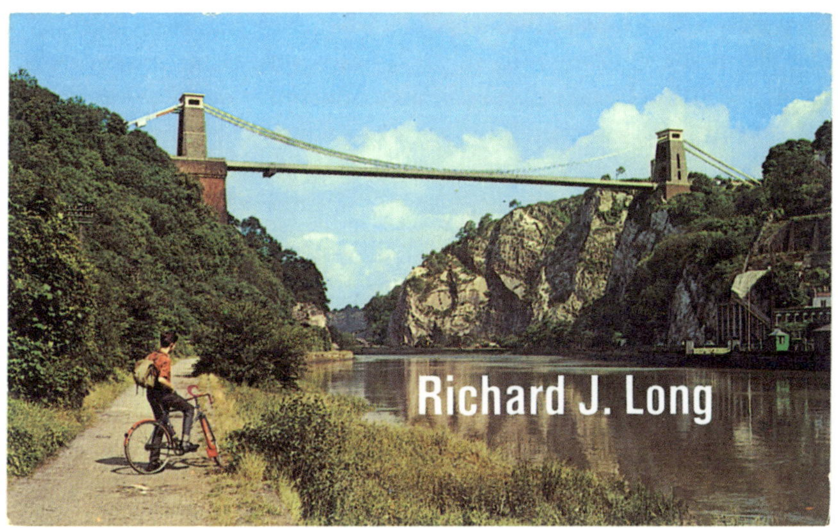

Exhibition invitation card, Konrad Fischer Galerie 1968

he represented Britain at the Venice Biennale. The next decade brought further recognition. In 1986 he had a major exhibition at the Guggenheim in New York which was also the occasion of Rudi Fuchs's book, *Richard Long* (1986). Two years later he was awarded the Kunstpreis Aachen by the Neue Galerie and in 1989 he won the Turner Prize at the Tate. The following year he was named *Chevalier dans l'Ordre des Arts et des Lettres* by the Government of France, and in 1991 the entire Hayward Gallery on the South Bank of the Thames was given over to the retrospective exhibition: *Walking in Circles* (1991).

To date there have been over 150 solo shows of Long's work, with perhaps a similar number of occasions on which he has been shown as part of a group exhibition. For all that, the present modest exhibition in St Andrews and this small catalogue which accompanies it can each claim to be unique.

The title *A Road From the Past to the Future: Work by Richard Long* from the Haldane Collection was suggested by Long as capturing the defining feature of the exhibition, namely that it represents a long-standing and continuing relationship between the artist and a friend and his family. Herein lies the first point of uniqueness: this is the first showing of work by Long drawn from a single private collection. The special claim of the catalogue is that it shows two very early works never previously published. The collection has been formed over 25 years largely by gift from the artist. It consists mostly of printed material: bookworks, catalogues, cards, posters and editioned prints; however, there are also a number of drawings and sculptures. [...] There are three generations of recipients: my mother, myself (and my wife), and my children. To explain how this came about I need to go back to my own youth.

In the summer of 1972 I was living with my parents in Kent and looking forward to starting a degree course in Fine Art (Painting) at Wimbledon School of Art. I had left school in Scotland the previous year and my experience of art and art making were highly conventional. The appeal of Wimbledon was that then, as now, it was a small, independently minded school that enjoyed a good reputation; my impression from visiting in the spring was that it was also fairly traditional. Excited at the prospect of the start of a term that was then only a few weeks away, I went up to London to see an exhibition at the Hayward Gallery entitled *The New Art* (1972). I had no idea of what was on show, though I suppose I may have expected abstract and Minimalist paintings and sculptures. There were few if any of these – Keith Milow's process paintings might just have qualified. Instead, I found rooms with tape recorders in them, displays of mirrors, boxes and shelves, documents and photographs, pseudo-philosophical texts, lengths of rope and sacks of sand. Everything was strange and little made sense. However, there were two sets of works that deeply impressed me. The artists were Hamish Fulton and Richard Long, and their subject matter was landscape.

From early childhood I had been familiar with the different landscapes of Scotland and Kent: the one mountainous and dramatically composed, the other wooded and gently undulating. Both may have featured in the exhibits; certainly between them Fulton and Long had by then made works (walks) in each environment. I might have assumed from his name that Fulton was a Scot but later I discovered that he had been raised in Newcastle and lived close by in Kent. As well as various photographs, texts, and maps documenting walks, the Hayward exhibition contained a very large stone circle by Long. As best as I can remember I was not much interested in the work of the other artists, nor have I been since, but although I did not know quite what to make of it I was sure that I had seen something new and special in the work of Fulton and Long.

Back in the train to Kent with the *New Art* catalogue. In the coming days my appetite and curiosity grew. I wanted to see more of the work that had caught my imagination. Neither artist had provided or permitted descriptive material for the catalogue, but from the bare details I discovered that there was a publication by Long produced by the Lisson Gallery. I went back up to London and found the address – the first of many visits to Bell Street. Within minutes I had my first work by Richard Long, the simple but beautiful booklet *Two sheepdogs cross in and out of the passing shadows The clouds drift over the hill with a storm* (1971). My interest has been constant ever since and I still regard that bookwork with special delight. I believe it remains one of Long's best. Then, or shortly after, perhaps at the Whitechapel Gallery where Long had exhibited the previous year, I acquired another bookwork, *From Along a Riverbank* (1971).

The start of term at Wimbledon was then a week or two away. I was ever more certain that I wanted to be an art student but circumstances had changed very radically. I was set to go to a traditional painting school where I assumed the emphasis would be on figurative work or gentle abstraction, yet the only contemporary work I knew of, and with which I felt immense sympathy, seemed to represent an abandonment of traditional painting and sculpture. My situation could be likened to that of a student about to begin scholastic theology at the Gregorian in Rome who has just discovered and fallen in love with Quaker spirituality. Both circumstances might seem set for tension and tragedy.

That was not at all how it turned out, however. First of all – and this is true of the theological example also – there was not a deep opposition between the 'classical' and the 'new'. In fact, as I was to discover, those artists and critics who are most antagonistic to Long's work are generally modernists preoccupied with certain formalist concerns or ideologues whose aesthetic sensibilities and imagination have been dried out by theorising. There is a sense in which Long is a deeply traditional artist: he is not concerned to reject the art of the past but to recover its ancient animating spirit. Second, however, life at Wimbledon turned out to be full of pleasant surprises. In my first year I worked through the various standard drawing classes and other exercises but I also talked about the work of Long. This brought me into friendship with two people there: a tutor, Roger Ackling; and a student two years ahead of me, Tony Cragg. Both shared my enthusiasm and, *mirabile dictu*, Ackling knew Long from their student days at St Martin's School of Art and promised to introduce me to him.

By the start of my second year I was sharing a flat with Ackling and Cragg in the Fulham Road. Cragg had started at the Royal College of Art and was already producing the sort of work that has made him famous. Long would come over when he visited London from Bristol and there were other regular visitors, including Bill Woodrow who had recently completed studies at Chelsea Art School. It may be hard for those who do not know the world of recent British sculpture to get a sense of what this means. Suffice it to say that at the age of 19 I was regularly in the company of four remarkably inventive artists, two of whom were to become Turner Prize winners. Long was unquestionably the inspiring genius, but I want to add for the record that Roger Ackling was a wonderful impresario. We all owe him a debt of gratitude for his generosity and enthusiasm.

The Fulham Road commune came to an end and we went our separate ways. From our first meeting, however, Long and I remained in touch by correspondence and occasional meetings, usually exhibition openings. Over the years he has been generous with his work and straightforward in expressing his ideas. He is by nature a quiet and solitary figure. Though keeping himself informed about the art world, especially artists he admires, Long is rarely seen, other than when exhibiting work. He lives quietly not far from the Clifton Suspension Bridge and the River Avon, which feature in the image incorporated in the cover of this catalogue. These are like beacons marking the traveller's route home. Richard Long has walked thousands of miles throughout Europe, in North and South America, in Africa, in Asia, and in Australia. But he is not a rootless traveller; he goes away but he always returns to the place of his childhood. In connection with this exhibition organised by students on the University's Museum/Gallery Studies course, Long came to St Andrews to discuss various aspects of the show and brought with him more works, including the two early photographs reproduced here. We talked at a length greater than ever before about the nature of his work, its development and his views of some contemporaries. I hope I can soon incorporate this material in an extended essay. For now, however, I can only offer a brief commentary on the art of Richard Long.

Long is not an artist of technique. He is not concerned to develop skills of draughtsmanship, carving, modelling or construction. His art is about ideas, but unlike others who emerged in the same period he is not a conceptualist (though he admires the work of Lawrence Weiner). While he shares a sensibility with Hamish Fulton and they have made walks together, Long does not refrain from rearranging the landscape and is not reluctant to mix his labour with earth, fire and water to make art out of nature. Yet although his images are spare, often simple geometrical figures, he is not in the tradition of Minimalist sculpture. One fascinating aspect of Long's life and art is the fact that he began activities continuous with his present ones while still a teenager and without any apparent art historical influences. It is a waste of time looking to British and American art of the mid 1960s to try to find the sources of Richard Long's simple mark-making. He is that rare human being: a working artist who represents a fresh start in his subject.

Later in the 1970s the main focus of my own interest moved from art to philosophy. This informed my thinking about Long's work but in an unexpected way. As I learned about the earliest philosophers, the pre-Socratic cosmologists, I began to think of Long as someone also possessed of a basic urge to relate his activities to the frame of the universe: to measure space and time by marking the earth; to work the elements in search of the mystery of nature. There is in Long's art a conviction that nature transcends matter, and that human making adds a further level of intelligibility to the patterns of time and change. The study of philosophy also introduced me to another enigmatic figure of our century, Ludwig Wittgenstein. They both manage to combine a relaxed naturalism with a sense of the transcendent. They both seem childlike in their conviction that the world is an enchanted place; and it is difficult to imagine either in any field but that which they chose. It is well for the rest of us that such examples of benign creativity exist in a century in which denial has been more common than affirmation. Yet each defers to the primacy of something external. Wittgenstein writes, 'I believe that my originality (if that is the right word) is an originality belonging to the soil rather than to the seed' (*Culture and Value*, (1977) and Long observes, 'My art is in the nature of things'. We did not make the world; what matters is our response to it. Long's response is original, simple and strong.

A Road From the Past to the Future: Work by Richard Long From the Haldane Collection, exh. cat., Crawford Art Centre, St Andrews, 1997, n.p.

Richard Long

Spazio Zero, Cantieri Culturali alla Zisa, Palermo,
1 November 1997 – 15 January 1998

Mud Circle 1997 | *Circle of Life* 1997

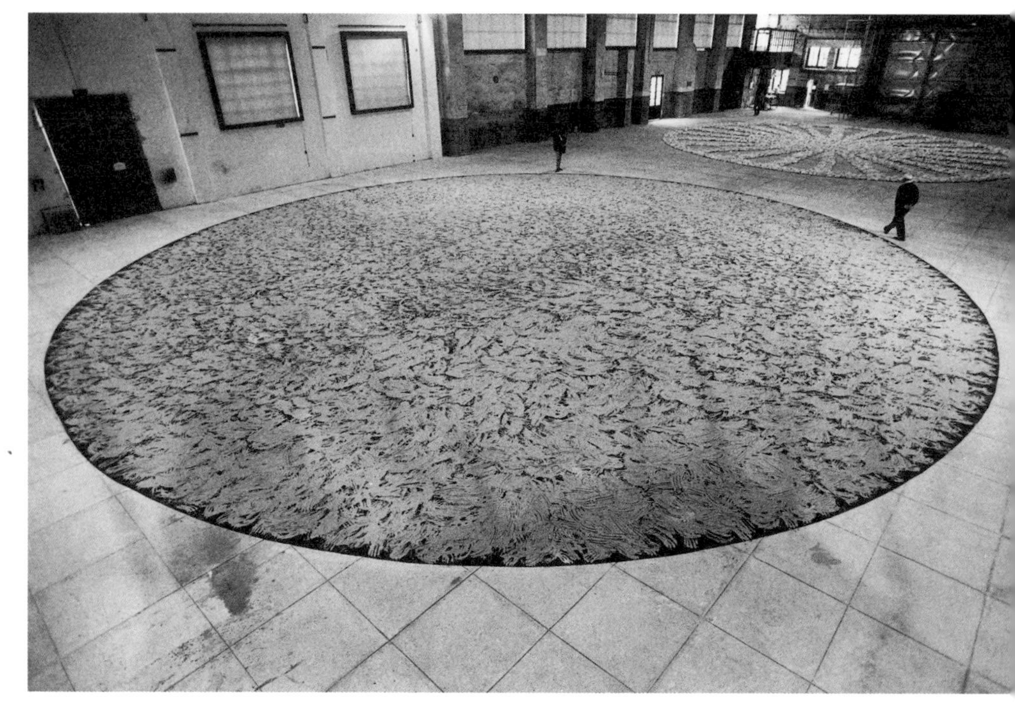

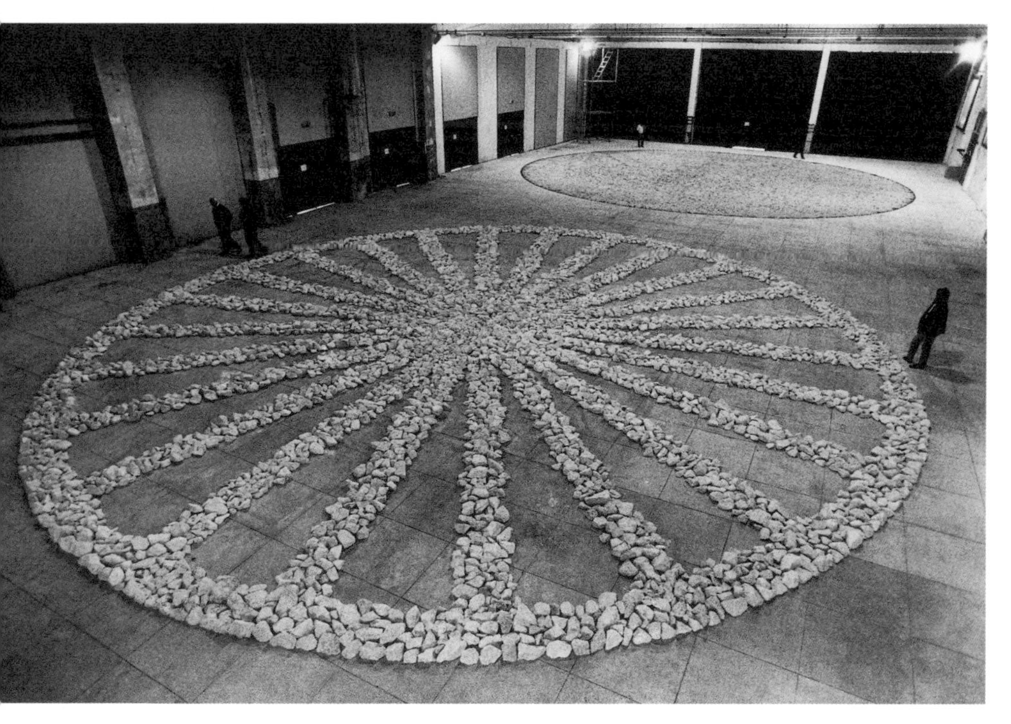

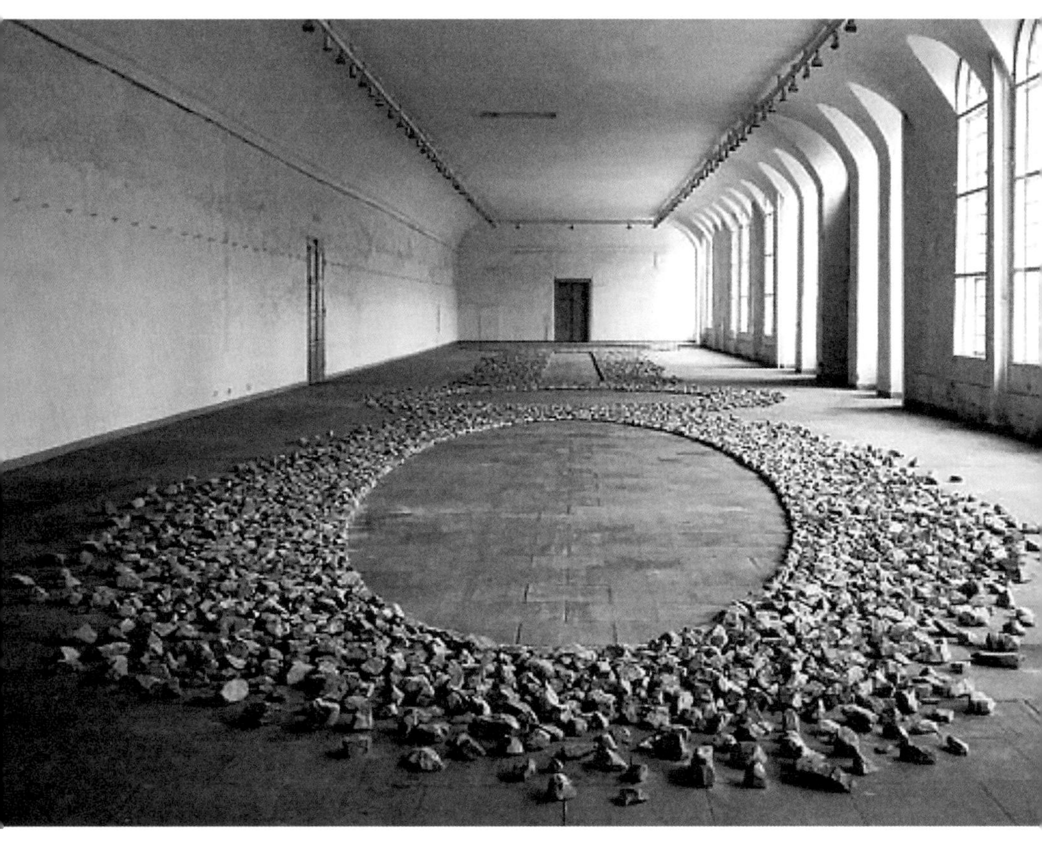

Periphery Stones 1999

ECKHARD SCHNEIDER

Richard Long, Kunstverein Hannover

The idea is as inspired as it is simple. The artist declares that the world is his studio. Freed from all traditional bonds, left entirely to his own devices, he travels the world and makes it his workshop: it becomes his material, his working and living space, his archive, his chronometer, his research field and his dwelling. The world defines and governs his rhythm, his radius of operations and the rules of his daily existence; it makes available to him its potential of memory and stored time.

The artist becomes the earth's daily travelling companion, and in return he is able to garner its fantastic wealth of real images, undistorted and unbeautified. Across all political, social and ideological boundaries, the continents of the earth offer themselves as inexhaustible quarries of ideas for his work. Richard Long defines the earth as the locus of the self, but with no power-crazed aspiration to ownership, no false explanations, no sentimental narcissism and no pantheistic inflation.

Stones, water, sky, mountains, light: everything is as it is. The works no longer present themselves as Richard Long's. For Long, this is the artistic crux. His works, in all their laconic simplicity, convey the impression of a power and urgency that is generated, as it were, from within themselves. This is entirely the consequence of the rigorous artistic rules that Richard Long has set for his own work: walking and action related to his own person, in the real space of landscape; scale; closeness to materials; temporal and spatial relation to Nature; reduction to elementary forms; striving for objectivity.

Richard Long thus eliminates from his work both the Romantic apotheosis of nature and all misconceived attempts to equate art with nature. His sculptures, photographs, texts and wall pieces are works of art: they are neither substitutes for nature nor affirmative metaphors for it. His works are real stones, real time, real walking: so real that they can be understood anywhere on earth, irrespective of all differences of language, culture, socialisation or intellect. Perhaps this is where their particular significance lies. Beyond all art-historical evaluation, they turn the earth, potentially, into a single, equal place of sensory and mental wealth for every human being.

Translated from the German by David Britt, *Every Grain of Sand*, exh. cat., Kunstverein Hannover, 1999.

IAN TROMP

From Walk to Text: On Richard Long

Rudi Fuchs treats *A Line Made by Walking* (1967) as Richard Long's prototypical work. He compares it to Kazimir Malevich's *Black Square* (1915), arguing that both of these works 'canceled previous art in one grand abrupt statement of conviction.'[1] But *A Line Made by Walking* articulated ideas and methods that had been initiated as early as 1964, when Long made a 'drawing' in fallen snow on the Bristol Downs by rolling and steering a snowball. This earlier work described four important themes, all of which have been developed and extended throughout Long's career: movement in space, marking the earth's surface, laying out paths across the ground, and his photograph of the 'drawing' as documentation or text-making. *A Line Made by Walking* itself demonstrates these four themes: the act of walking the line for movement through space; the path walked; the mark on the surface of the earth; and the artist's photograph as a document of his actions and their outcome.

In fact, each of these themes could head a category within Long's oeuvre. Under 'movement in space' would be the walks that are the foundation of his practice as an artist. 'Marking the earth's surface' and 'laying out paths across the ground' might be combined, as in *A Line Made by Walking*, or counted separately. They would contain, respectively, the 'objects' Long has made – the lines of stone, the circles of blackened wood, the splashes of mud and water – and the paths he has followed from maps, the tracks he has walked into dust and grass. 'Text-making' takes place on at least three levels: first, there is the immediate fact of photographing many of the objects; at one remove, there are the texts with photographs, words and maps; and there are the many books that Long has made over the years since 1970.

In what follows, I distinguish between walks, works and texts. While the first of these categories is probably clear, the second two might require some explication. The distinction is derived from Roland Barthes's seminal essay, 'From Work to Text,' (1977). Barthes suggested that whereas a work is 'a fragment of substance', a text is 'a methodological field'; while 'the work is held in the hand, the text is held in language'.[2] In relation to Richard Long's oeuvre: whereas the texts – with photographs, maps, words – form a 'field', a significant system capable of being decoded, of being 'read', the works themselves – of stone, wood, earth – are solid, weighty fragments of the real.

Long's walks emerged from the culture of dematerialisation of art objects during the late 1960s.[3] For him, they expanded the range of possibility in art, removing it from the white cube of the gallery space and literally extending the boundaries of sculpture.

He has summarised the development of his working methods in the late 1960s as follows: 'I progressed from using natural materials, from a snowball drawing in 1964, to a line made by walking across a field in 1967, to making just walking itself the medium of an artwork, by walking ten straight miles across a moor in 1968 (*A Ten Mile Walk*). This enabled me to bring time and a great increase in scale and potential space into a work of art.'

This genealogy does not indicate the prehistory of Long's methods, the temperamental and perhaps cultural determination of his walking. It does not tell us, importantly, that as a child he enjoyed walking and cycling holidays with his family, There is a certain mould of an English outdoorsman into which Richard Long fits – of course, he is in many ways quite unlike this cultural type, but recognising in him a characteristic set of attitudes to landscape and place can be helpful in understanding the motivation of his work.

In speaking of *A Ten Mile Walk*, he describes the 'physical pleasure in actually just doing the walk, spending a day walking across the moors following the compass point… which is a very enjoyable way to spend the day'. But then he goes on to say, 'It was also enjoyable because of the fact that I knew that I was making a very original, a unique and dynamic work of art which had a new scale to it, which was a sculpture which was invisible and in many other ways was interesting as art.'[4] To every one of Long's walks there are at least these two aspects, the physical and the conceptual.

The walks bring together physical endurance and principles of order, action and idea. These two elements are well illustrated in the walks recorded in the text *Hours Miles* (1996). The idea for the walks is a simple inversion, a transposition of distance and duration, of time and space. Clearly, the physical commitment required to walk 82 miles in 24 hours is extraordinary; when we met in Bristol in 1997, Long spoke of this first of the two walks as 'serious walking, with bloodied, blistered feet at the end.'

Long walks in different ways, and different kinds of walk are often embedded within longer journeys. He has referred to 'ritualised' walking, explaining that 'when I use the word ritual… I mean that I am walking, but the purpose of the walk is not to make a journey.'[5] In this practice of walking without destination, the walker's passage is marked by criteria other than arrival.

A few examples of these criteria: *Alternatives and Equivalents* (1996), a four-day walk on Dartmoor, involved four different kinds of walking: 'slow walking / or meandering walking / or straight walking / or fast walking'. *From Uncertainty to Certainty* (1998) is described as 'a walk carrying a bag of pebbles with a word written on each.' The random withdrawal of a pebble from the bag directs the walker's pace, direction, or manner: 'Up down fast slow north south east west straight meandering.' The movement from uncertainty to certainty is implicit in the diminishing range of possibilities as the number of pebbles in the bag is reduced – when Long withdraws the first pebble, ten actions are possible, then he takes the second, ninth, and so on, until the message of the tenth pebble is certain.

Other walks may be governed by ideas other than changing the actual way of walking. *Dartmoor Riverbed Stones* (1991), for instance, is a circular walk beginning and ending at the River Bovey on Dartmoor, England. A stone from each riverbed met is carried to the next river, so: 'A stone from the river Bovey carried to the river Webburn / a stone from the river Webburn carried to the river Dart / a stone from the river Dart carried to Holy Brook.' The walker moves stones from one location to another, articulating one of the fundamental tropes of Long's oeuvre, the transposition of place. This theme was played out elsewhere in *Mud Walk* (1987), 'a 184-mile walk from the mouth of the river Avon / to a source of the river Mersey / casting a handful of river Avon tidal mud / into each of the rivers Thames Severn Trent and Mersey / along the way.'

Mud Walk and *Dartmoor Riverbed Stones* allow an easy transition from passage to place, from consideration of Long's walks to speaking of his works. In an illuminating statement, *Five, six, pick up sticks Seven, eight, lay them straight* (1980), he wrote: 'My outdoor sculptures are places. The material and the idea are of the place; sculpture and place are one and the same. The place is as far as the eye can see from the sculpture.'[6]

The works made on walks are of 'common materials, whatever is to hand, but especially stones'.[7] By contrast, when Long makes works for exhibition or on commission, he usually uses quarried stone: 'I go to the quarry and find the stones I like and order them, but without making the work, and then I have to make a guess. Those stones are delivered to the gallery and I make the work for the first time in the gallery.'[8]

On walks or in galleries, Long's sculptures most commonly take the form of circles or lines, with occasional crosses, spirals, squares and heaps. A sculpture's form is decided by its location. Long says: 'I have the idea by just being in the place.'[9] In the case of gallery works or commissions, the materials are sourced from other locations – so they are not of the place in the same way the stones are in a sculpture made on a walk. But the sculpture's form is still made in response to the environment, to the place of the gallery. One could say, paraphrasing Long, that while the material is not of the place, the idea is.[10]

The effects of these different ways of working with materials are quite marked. Because he works with 'whatever is to hand' on his walks, the range of formal possibilities is proscribed. And yet, paradoxically, because he works with whatever he finds in a place, in a sense these works are open to great variation.

Though the material and formal premises of his sculptures are simple and limited, Long has in the course of his career produced remarkably varied work. Sometimes an outdoor sculpture will involve making something, sometimes it will require removal; sometimes a sculpture calls for moving stones or sticks from around the place into a pattern, sometimes it will mean Long walking back and forth in a straight line to flatten grass or smudge dust. Within the range of circles and lines it is possible to observe several distinctions: there are, first of all, those made by placing stones or sticks and those made by removing them; there are those in which stones are laid flat, those in which they stand upright; there are works in which the materials are tightly bunched together, overlap, or touch, and others in which they are widely spaced; works in which the parts are aligned along an axis, works in which the eye follows swirls and patterns of stone, and others in which the placement of materials seems entirely haphazard. Each of these distinctions stands equally for works in stone and wood and earth.

Comparing a few circles clearly demonstrates the range of Long's approaches. In *Norfolk Flint Circle* (1990) and *Rome Circle* (1984), the stones are packed close together, forming an impenetrably dense visual field. By contrast, *Circle for Konrad* (1997) contains more space, its long slivers of stone disposed in graceful patterns, its edges defined and contained by stones placed side-on to the circle's perimeter. And then, finally, in *Circle of Memory Sticks* (1996), sticks of varying length are placed with staccato regularity to define an open, still space within the circle.

Long has sometimes disassembled outdoor sculptures – he might make a circle of stones, photograph it, and then take the circle apart. Other times he leaves sculptures behind when he continues walking. In the text *Dartmoor Time* (1995), he records: 'Passing a pile of stones placed 16 years ago.' It is in the nature of some of the works that they will quickly change or disappear. *Along a four day walk in Norway* (1973), for instance, is printed with a text reading: 'the stones / sink slowly / with the melting snow / of summer.' Likewise, the line walked into burnt heather in *West East Line* (1991) will begin to lose its sharpness as the wind blows and eventually be obliterated by new growth.

Long has made several lines of poured water on earth and rocks and walls *Shadows and Watermarks* (1983), all of which very quickly evaporate and disappear. In galleries, he has often worked with mud on floors and walls. These works have ranged from lines walked in River Avon mud to hand prints and thumb prints, enormous circles and arcs and long lines, as in *Muddy Water Line*, made for a 1996 exhibition at the Guggenheim Museum in New York. Again, within the mudworks it is possible to distinguish quite different inflections: some have been made slowly, so that each hand print is visible *White Mud Hand Circle* (1996), others are made with fast, broad gestures, so that mud is splashed and sprayed widely, creating a nimbus around the form *White Water Circle* (1994). In floor works, the mud tends to be contained within the line or circle; on walls it runs towards the ground. But look closely at one of the wall works and the carefully pencilled perimeter becomes clear through the splash marks, revealing the contained energy of these works.

When a work is meant to last, as in gallery pieces and commissions, Long prepares a certificate giving instructions for its remaking should the work need to be dismantled. He says, 'If the procedure says that this stone must be placed here and that stone there, or if it just says that stones can be chosen at random to make an equal density, then they should follow that. Each certificate is very precise for that particular work. If the procedure is followed correctly, each time every stone will

WALKING WITH THE RIVER'S ROAR

GREAT HIMALAYAN TIME   A LINE OF MOMENTS

MY FATHER   STARLIT SNOW

HUMAN TIME   FROZEN BOOTS

BREAKING TRAIL   CIRCLES OF A GREAT BIRD

COUNTLESS STONES   HAPPY ALERT BALANCED

PATHS OF SHARED FOOTMARKS   ATOMIC SILENCE

SLEEPING BY THE RIVER'S ROAR

A TWENTY ONE DAY FOOTPATH WALK NEPAL 1983

be in a different place within the work, but nevertheless each time the work will look the same.'[11] The certificates function as a kind of document: they describe and prescribe the manner of a sculpture's making, so that it can be made again. They are texts existing alongside the work, both recording the form in its initial making and defining the sculpture.

The bulk of Long's texts have a memorialising function, recording the walks and outdoor works. In a 1982 artist's statement, *Words after the fact*, Long described his photographs as, 'facts which bring the appropriate accessibility to the spirit of... remote or otherwise unrecognisable works'.[12] Of course, this leaves out those photographs of works which are not remote but are inaccessible, either because they are privately owned or because they are records of sculptures that have disappeared.

It is useful to distinguish some of the ways in which Long uses photography. There are images that apparently simply record an action – as in the photograph by which *A Line Made by Walking* is known. Such images are obviously focused upon a work; they record both work and place, 'as far as the eye can see from the sculpture.' Another example is the photograph of *Along a four day walk in Norway* (1973). Photographs in this first mode I will refer to as recording images. Then there are images showing the landscape in which a walk is made. The photograph in *Throwing a Stone Around MacGillycuddy's Reeks* (1977) does not show the thrown stone or the path of the walk; rather, it records a view of the landscape in which the walk takes place. I will refer to photographs in this second mode as establishing images, following the cinematographic convention for a shot providing a key view of a landscape, person, or scene. Extending his use of establishing images, Long sometimes presents a series of photographs, often begun with a titled page, as in *Walking with the River's Roar*, a sequence in *Every Grain of Sand*, the book published in 1999 by Kunstverein Hannover, or – more comprehensively – in *Countless Stones* (1983) and *A Walk Across England* (1997), both books recording single walks.

These two quite different modes of photography are combined in *Mirage*, a book published in 1998. A text titled *A Walk in a Green Forest*, described as 'eight days walking in the Shirakami Mountains / Aomori Japan 1997,' is printed on the left-hand page of a double spread. On the facing page is a photograph of a tent pitched within lush forest. The following three pages show photographs – in the first mode – of works made in the course of the walk (*Shirakami Line*, *Shirakami Circle* and *Early Summer Circle*, all 1997). The first image functions as an establishing image, recording a scene from the landscape in which Long walked. But then one notices in the centre-background a circle too deliberate to be natural – Long has included in this second-mode photograph a view of *Early Summer Circle*.

This insetting of a recording image within an establishing image demonstrates something of the different expectations of each mode of photography. The recording images seem presented as transparent – we look *through* them to see the sculptural works they represent. By contrast we look *at* the establishing images – from them we learn about the atmosphere and landscape of a place rather than the particularity of a work. In this instance, once one recognises *Early Summer Circle*, a tension is set up in the image, and the eye shifts between these ways of looking.

In a conversation with Martina Giezen, Long says: 'taking a photograph does a certain type of job, records one moment, makes an image. And words do a different job. They can usually record the whole idea of a walk, maybe much better, more.'[13] Whereas the photographs can represent just one image at a time from a walk, words are able to evoke many different aspects simultaneously.

One can, at least provisionally, transpose the terms from the above discussion to speaking of the texts with words, distinguishing between recording and establishing texts. The recording texts usually recount a walk or the idea for a walk – an example is *Mud Walk*, cited earlier, as is *Hours Miles* (1996); another is *Granite Line* (1980), which reads: 'scattered along a straight 9 mile line / 223 stones placed on Dartmoor / England 1980.' As in cinematography, establishing texts provide a more diffuse view, in which the observer is presented with a range of information rather than a specific focus, as in *On the Road* (1990) and *Rain Drumming on the Tent* (1997), which records, among other information, 'the wild flapping of the tent in the wind / a gurgling stream / abbey bells.'

While the recording texts are more closely tied to the idea of the walks, the establishing texts relate the experience thereof, restating the two fundamental aspects of any walk, the conceptual and the physical. It is the establishing texts that are able, as Long says, to 'record the whole idea of a walk, maybe much better'.

GRANITE LINE

SCATTERED ALONG A STRAIGHT 9 MILE LINE
223 STONES PLACED ON DARTMOOR

ENGLAND 1980

A FIVE DAY WALK

FIRST DAY TEN MILES
SECOND DAY TWENTY MILES
THIRD DAY THIRTY MILES
FOURTH DAY FORTY MILES
FIFTH DAY FIFTY MILES

TOTNES TO BRISTOL BY ROADS AND LANES
ENGLAND 1980

On first glance, *Early Morning Senses Tropical Island Walk* (1989) is composed simply of five descending columns of words. The title, however, directs one to the key to reading the text: each column corresponds to one of the five basic senses. Thus the first column lists a number of sights: 'bougainvillea', 'white birds', 'lilac flowers', 'goats'. The second catalogues objects touched and sensations felt: 'damp dust', 'mosquito bite', 'Coco de Mer bowl'. The third lists a number of sounds the walker hears: 'cooing', 'rustling', 'bonjour'. The fourth lists smells: 'orange', 'turtle droppings'. And the final column is a list of tastes: 'coco plum', 'rainwater', 'cinnamon bark'. *Early Morning Senses Tropical Island Walk* forms a dense matrix of words, recording all aspects of the walker's physical, sensible experience of his walk.

Another good example is *A 118 Mile Walk Under the Sky* (1980). This piece records climatic conditions and the appearance of the sky during the walk. It is printed to form a bank of words, 11 lines with seven phrases each. The words soon lose meaning as one reads, devolving to simple sounds and appearances. This effect is heightened by the lack of specificity in the walk's description and locale. As one reads, the words become confused; one's eyes get lost in their mass, scanning forward and slipping backward. The effect is similar to that of reading concrete poetry. One senses that the best response might be simply to take in the bank of words as such, without attempting to read each word, as one looks up at the sky without discerning the margins of each cloud, and yet seeing everything. The words are abstract in that they give no indication of the walk, except its season and its length. One does not know if each of the 11 lines of words and the seven descriptions of the sky given in each line records a single day's observation of the sky, or if they just represent an appropriate way of organising the information for display. In his 1997 book, *Time After Time*, Long heightens the sense of this text's abstraction by printing it in Japanese – texts are sometimes translated for overseas exhibitions, but the decision to print this text in Japanese in a book otherwise in English, printed in Germany, demonstrates an intentional distancing. As the title suggests, this is a walk 'under the sky' rather than over the earth – and so the phrases describing the appearance of the sky operate as a kind of map of that perpetually changing locale.

Although many and diverse artists have made use of maps – from Johannes Vermeer to Joseph Cornell and Robert Smithson – few have used them as literally as has Richard Long. It is obvious that an artist who, in a career of more than 30 years duration, has worked primarily by walking across the earth, must have need of maps. He first began working with maps toward the end of the 1960s, in such works as *A Ten Mile Walk* (1968) and *Wiltshire* (1969). Like most of his map texts, these early texts employed maps produced by the Ordnance Survey. Since then he has used many different methods to plot his journeys; speaking very broadly, these various approaches to the map can be divided into two tendencies, which I will discuss as literal and as rhetorical usages.

The older, more literal map texts have in general included actual fragments of maps used to plot a passage through the landscape. More recently, Long has removed the information on the maps, to join words with certain aspects of the landscape, for instance, altitude, outline, or contour (*Wood to Stone*, 1991). It is this tendency to remove the actual, literal map from the completed text that I refer to as rhetorical modes of mapping. Again, one might suggest that the older, more literal maps were made primarily in recording mode, whereas the rhetorical map texts have more of an establishing function.

In 1990, Long combined a circle of words with an Ordnance Survey Map to make *Sound Circle*. He pencilled a circle onto a map of Dartmoor Forest, touching its northern extremity, and cut and pasted 120 words around the circle's perimeter. The words, stuck to the map's surface, each record a sound, be it natural ('wind', 'pattering rain', 'stream'), animal ('bleat', 'hoof thump'), human ('not too bad a day'), or mechanical ('aeroplane'). Thus Long plots the aural experience of his walk on a more traditional representation of the countryside, transposing personal and impersonal indices of landscape. The circle becomes a secondary mapping, an account of the walker's experience meshed with the objective facts of altitude, distance and place.

Long says, 'Some walks are with maps and some without.' Speaking to Richard Cork, he related that when he walked in the Haggar Mountains in the Sahara, it was not possible to get good maps, which necessitated an entirely different approach to the walk. 'The way I found my way in the Sahara was just by following the places where I could get water, without using a map.'[14] Of course, the plan to walk from source to source of water is itself the basis of a kind of map. Similarly, in *Water Way Walk* (1989), Long used water sources to map a 152-mile southward walk in Wales and England. Long has also used his experience of wind as a means to record his passage. In his *Wind*

Line Across England (1986), he used the wind as a measure of distance travelled. If one reads from left to right across the line of arrows (and in so doing reads from west to east), the first arrow – pointing eastward – would represent the Irish Sea coast's onshore winds, which are soon met a little inland by an offshore breeze. Here, the landscape is mapped entirely abstractly, with no explicit reference to the landforms the walker traverses.

Richard Long's books have not yet received the attention they are due. Like the recording images and texts, they are usually seen as a transparent medium, a means of knowing his works and walks. On one level this is what they are, but they are very deliberately constructed, and I believe they can be seen as an artform in their own right.

Long suggests that they are a secondary form to the walks and the works, and by extension to the various kinds of text which they anthologise:

> I always say that my task as an artist is to put a stone on the ground, to walk a straight line across a mountainside, to put my hand on the wall with some mud. That really is the making of my art. Making a book is a completely different procedure. I don't deny that part of my work as an artist is making books, but it is very clear to me that there is a fantastic distinction between the art of walking across a mountain and the craft and aesthetics of making a book. And I only made the books because I walked across the mountainside.[15]

Different books are conceived with quite different intentions. I have already mentioned *Countless Stones* and *A Walk Across England*, two books recording single journeys. Long has also designed the two major retrospective volumes, Fuchs's *Richard Long* (published for a show at the Guggenheim Museum in New York) and the book accompanying his 1991 Hayward Gallery retrospective, *Walking in Circles*. Both of these books give exhaustive overviews of his oeuvre. This is one obvious way in which Long uses the book as a form. But there is a wide range of other objectives and structuring principles among the books and pamphlets Long has published.

Long begins planning his books by working with individual images, testing different combinations and conjunctions, and then making miniature mock-ups with quick drawings of each page. This allows him to have an overview of the entire book, thereby to establish and direct continuities of place and image, combine individual texts into sequences and passages, and to play with conventions of the book.

Falling roughly within the category of books produced to record single walks are pamphlets such as *Prom Around a Lake* (1973). This booklet has no words other than the title and the artist's name printed in black ink on the front cover and the colophon on the back outside cover. Within are 19 close-up photographs of leaves, presumably collected 'from around a lake' in the course of a walk, printed in colour (green) on pure white pages. The specific conjunction of facing pages seems to have been decided visually, since in most cases facing pages exhibit similarities of form; or perhaps the leaflet records a narrative continuity; for example, the leaves are presented in the order in which they were found. The spareness of the layout and the elegant vertical lines of the leaves harmonise to give the pamphlet a restrained beauty.

Different books can have quite distinct moods. For instance, *From Time To Time* (1997) seems more intimate than many of the other books, and even feels slightly nostalgic. Several of the texts in it are concerned in some way with time and the passing of time. It begins with *Dartmoor Time*, a text to which I have already alluded, which evokes time in several different ways, from the precise record of 'One and a half hours of early morning mist' to the geologic time of 'climbing over granite 350 million years old on Great Mis Tor' and the historical 'skirting the Bronze Age Grimspound'. Further on is *Ten Stones*, which brings together two walks separated by the passage of 20 years. Described as taking place on 'a long slope of lava dust on a flank of the volcano Hekla' in Iceland, the text reads: 'a line of five stones sent rolling down it in 1974 / a line of five stones sent rolling down it in 1994.'[16] Later, one finds two texts in direct dialogue, the more recent walk erasing the earlier. *Granite Line* (1980) and *Granite Line Removed* (1995) are printed on facing pages, the earlier text in a single colour, as Long was wont to produce his texts in the past; the more recent text in black and red. The earlier reads: 'scattered along a straight 9 mile line / 223 stones placed on Dartmoor / England 1980'; the later: 'along a straight 9 mile walk on Dartmoor / 223 stones thrown off and scattered away from the walking line / ENGLAND 1995.'[17]

The variousness of Richard Long's career, the tremendous diversity within the self-established boundaries of his formal vocabulary, makes it very hard to write concisely and yet do him justice. I have here attempted to provide a comprehensive overview of his work, but fear I have managed only to draw the faintest perimeter.

'All the works... flow in and out of each other.'[18] As he continues to walk, to make his sculptures and his texts, this flow becomes ever more complexly articulated. But his work remains intensely simple in its conception. In *Five, six, pick up sticks Seven, eight, lay them straight* he wrote: 'I like common means given the simple twist of art.' For all its nuanced variation, his oeuvre is yet fundamentally about walking, about real stones and simple geometries, about keeping a record.

Sculpture, March 2000, pp.26–35.

1 RH Fuchs, *Richard Long*, exh. cat., Solomon R Guggenheim Museum, New York and Thames & Hudson, London, 1986, pp.44–47.
2 Roland Barthes, 'From Work to Text' in *The Rustle of Language*, Basil Blackwell, London, 1986. p.57.
3 This period is well documented in Lucy Lippard, *Six Years: The dematerialization of the art object from 1966 to 1972*, Studio Vista, London, 1973.
4 *Ibid.*, p.16.
5 *Ibid.*, p.6.
6 Reprinted in Fuchs, *op.cit.*, p.236.
7 *Ibid.*
8 Richard Long and Martina Giezen, *Richard Long in Conversation: Bristol 19.11.1985*, MW Press, Noordwijk, 1985, p.8.
9 *Ibid.*, p.1.
10 An interesting point is that Long maintains an aspect of working with 'whatever is to hand' by the fact that he never has stones especially cut. He told Martina Giezen: 'The stones I choose are always the stones that I just find in the quarry. Sometimes they may be cut for certain uses... maybe for people to build walls, or maybe they are just thrown away, offcuts.' *Ibid.*, p.9.
11 *Ibid.*, p.8.
12 Reprinted in Fuchs, *op.cit.*, p.236.
13 Long and Giezen, *op.cit.*, p.7.
14 Richard Long, *Walking in Circles*, exh. cat., George Braziller, New York and South Bank Centre, London, 1991, p.249.
15 Long and Giezen, *op.cit.*, p.19.
16 The first of these lines of five stones is recorded in the photograph titled *Five Stones* (1974).
17 Though Long assures me it was accidental, it is worth remarking that in *Mountains and Waters, Halfway Stone*, which includes the text 'in the middle of the road / in the middle of the walk,' appears in the book's centre pages – so also 'in the middle of the book.'
18 Richard Long and Martina Giezen, *Richard Long in Conversation: Part Two*, MW Press, Noordwijk, 1986, p.15.

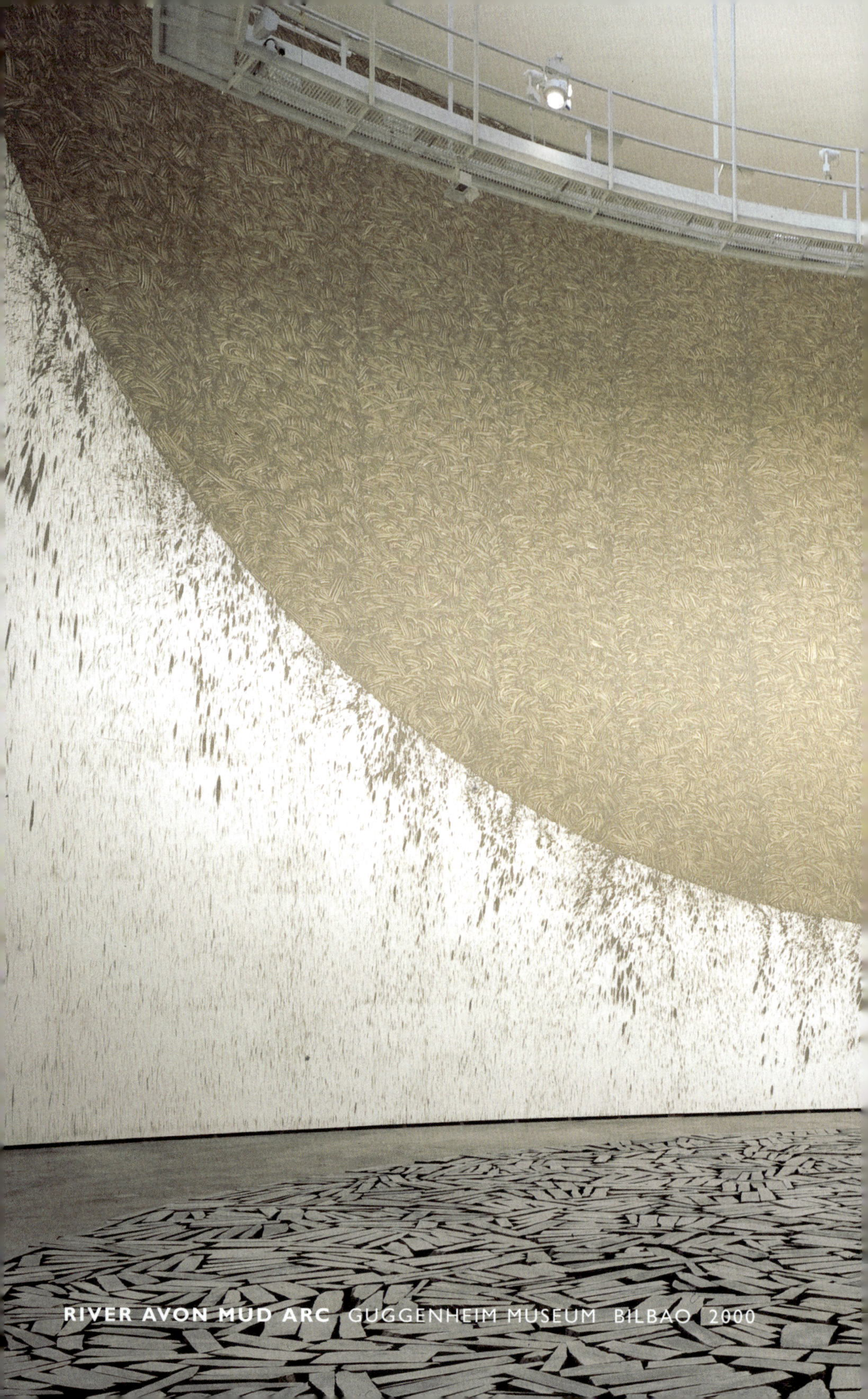

RIVER AVON MUD ARC GUGGENHEIM MUSEUM BILBAO 2000

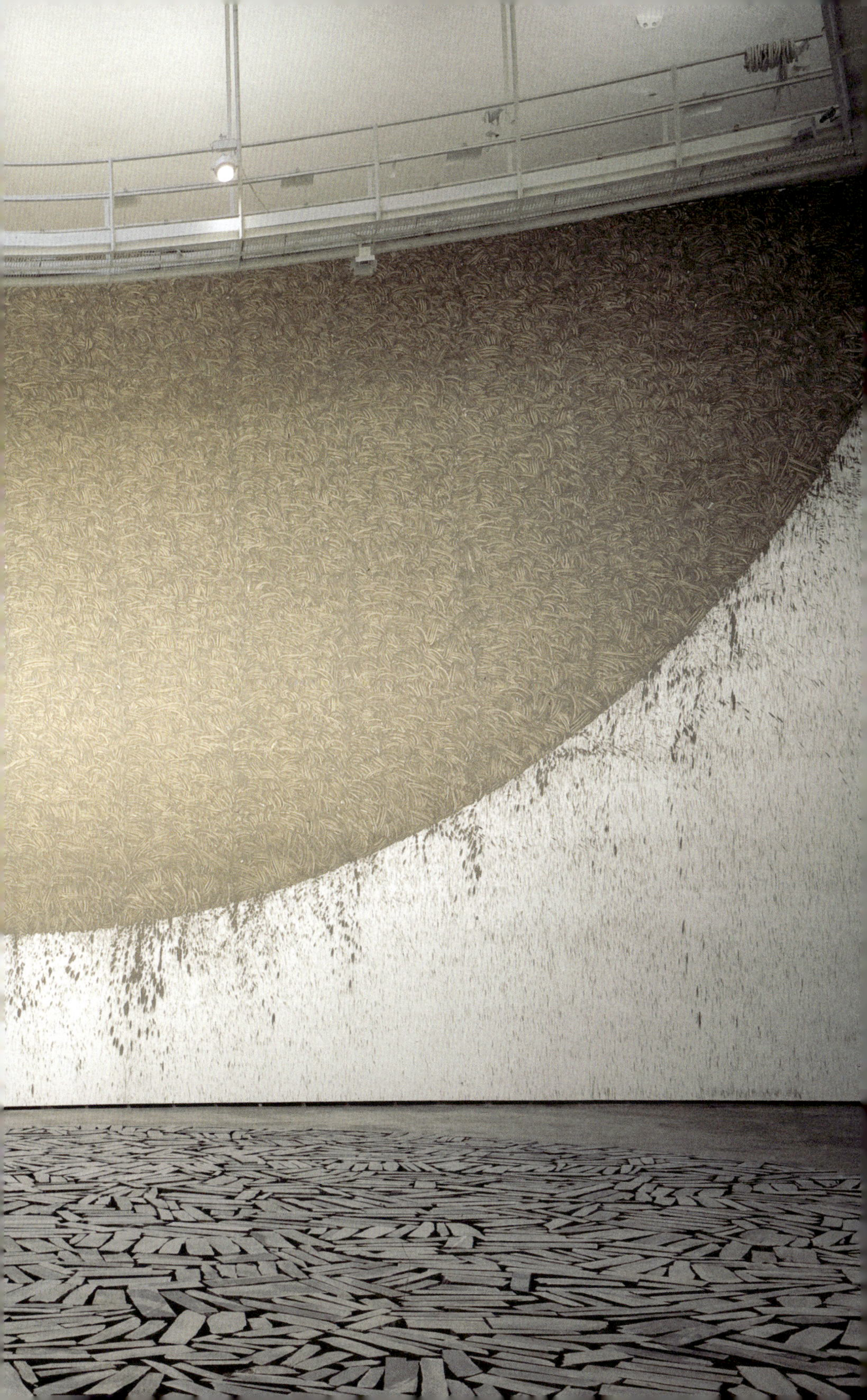

PAUL MOORHOUSE

The Intricacy of the Skein, The Complexity of the Web – Richard Long's Art

> Always think of the universe as one living organism, with a single substance and a single soul; and observe how all things are submitted to the single perceptivity of this one whole, all are moved by its single impulse, and all play their part in the causation of every event that happens. Remark the intricacy of the skein, the complexity of the web.
>
> Marcus Aurelius, *Meditations,* AD170–180 [1]

In 1987 Richard Long made a work of art involving two stones. The size, shape and colour of these objects is not recorded but undoubtedly they were small enough to be held in the hand and light enough to be carried. At a certain, unspecified moment in that particular year, Long stood on the beach at Aldeburgh on the English east coast and, from the millions of similar pebbles there, he selected the first stone. He then set out on a journey, carrying this modest, natural relic of the Suffolk landscape.

His destination was the beach at Aberystwyth on the Welsh west coast. He walked all the way, covering a distance of over 300 miles in around ten days. We are not told what he saw and felt during his journey. It appears, however, that when he reached his destination he placed the stone he had been carrying in these new surroundings. He then picked up a different stone and reversed the process, taking it with him as he commenced the walk back to Aldeburgh. Whether he used the same route is not divulged. On his arrival at the east coast, 20 days after he last stood there, he placed the stone he had carried from Aberystwyth on the beach at Aldeburgh. Some time after the completion of this walk he then made a framed text work – *Crossing Stones* (1987) – which provides a succinct description of this activity.

It is now 15 years since Long carried out this walk and almost certainly the two stones are no longer exactly where he left them. The weather, the tides, and endless natural movement in the landscape will have ensured that nothing at either place will have remained the same. In placing the stones Long created a fragile structure which has presumably disappeared; or, rather, it has simply returned to nature. Nevertheless, somewhere at Aldeburgh and Aberystwyth, these two stones are almost certainly still there: transplanted and assimilated; endlessly buried, exposed and covered over again by the elements; each moving imperceptibly in the orbit of their radically altered situation. For what *is* certain, is the significance that Long's intervention has had for the natural order of things.

Plucked from their former situation, the stones remain physically remote. Now, however, they are also intimately *connected* by the bonds of their shared condition. Both stones have made a unique crossing and the resulting connection between them exists in the context of the work of art which created this situation. A particular relationship between certain landscape elements has been defined by the power of an idea and its *actual* execution: nature touched lightly, yet articulated at the deepest levels. In the fertile interaction of these apparent opposites – a living human presence and the inert matter of the natural world – the intangible essence of Long's art may be glimpsed.

A MOVING WORLD

In a career that now spans more than 35 years, Long has created a substantial and varied body of work in which the relationship between man and nature is a central, unifying concern. Taking nature both as his subject and as the source of his materials, Long's artistic ethos has always been one of direct, dynamic, physical involvement with landscape. This is evident in his earliest works, notably when in 1964 he made a drawing on the ground on the Bristol Downs simply by rolling a snowball across the snow-covered grass. The notion of impermanence entailed by this work has been an abiding principle in his subsequent interactions with nature. It was, however, the decision he took in 1967 to make sculpture out of walking which established the principal defining characteristic of Long's art and the course it has followed to the present day.

Long's first walking piece, *Ben Nevis Hitchhike* (1967) comprised a six-day walking and hitchhiking journey from London to the summit of Ben Nevis and back. As shown in the related map work which provides a record of Long's route and itinerary, during the course of this trip a photograph was taken at each of six locations, each unnamed location being specified on an outline map of Britain by the day the photograph was taken. Even today, in a visual culture long accustomed to art being made from any material whatsoever, including pre-existing objects, there is something about a sculpture being made out of a *walk* which still challenges some deeply held assumptions. Mostly firmly rooted among these is, perhaps, the sense that – no matter what it is made of – a sculpture should at least have a physical form or attributes that can be perceived. From the outset, walking as art confounded such expectations. Since then, Long's innovations have been widely embraced as a radical redefining of the boundaries of sculpture. But, even so, it is still pertinent – and illuminating – to ask: in what sense *can* a walk be a sculpture? Indeed, how does a walk function as a work of art at all?

Part of the difficulty of accounting for such developments is that they cannot easily be accommodated within recognised art historical theories and categories. Marcel Duchamp's designation of pre-fabricated objects as works of art is the source of a major tributary running through modernism. It has, however, limited relevance to an appreciation of Long's designation of walking as art. Duchamp's innovation – bold as it was – rests on the perception of one or more physical objects. In contrast, Long took sculpture into the domain of the immaterial: the walk comprises the movement of a body through time and space and, as such, has no permanent physical attributes. Nor can the walk as artwork be understood by reference to avant-garde art movements such as Conceptual art whose emergence formed the backdrop to Long's own artistic development. The premium placed by conceptual artists on ideas – to the extent that their actual realisation is secondary – is completely antithetical to Long. As in the example of *Crossing Stones*, the walk itself may have no lasting physical attributes but the work could not exist if the walk had not happened.

Other approaches to these questions are needed and Long himself has provided insights. He has observed: 'Walking itself has a cultural history, from Pilgrims to the wandering Japanese poets, the English Romantics and contemporary long-distance walkers.'[2] Walking is a fundamental, universal activity, the basis of locomotion through the world for human beings. But as well as being essentially practical, as Long implies it is also closely bound up with the cultures of different races throughout the ages. Though its principal function is movement, people do not only walk to get from one place to another. Walking is a way of engaging and interacting with the world, providing the means of exposing oneself to new, changing perceptions and experiences and of acquiring an expanded awareness of our surroundings. Through such experiences, and through a deeper understanding of the places we occupy, we acquire a better understanding of our own position in the world.

Such considerations are germane to an understanding of the importance of walking in Long's art. For example, the subject of *Walking in a Moving World* (2001), the textwork that commences the present exhibition, is relativity. It describes a five-day walk undertaken by Long in Powys in 2001. It does so in terms of the artist's different physical relationships with various natural phenomena as he moves across the landscape. The text is arranged by listing these phenomena in order of the speeds at which *they* are moving, from fastest to slowest – from fleeting cloud shadows to an imperceptibly slow glacial boulder moving at geological speed. The impression conveyed is of a world in movement, never still. There is a vivid sense of *relation* between the walker's movements and his changing surroundings through the use of particular phrases – *between, into, across, through, under and over* – words which only have meaning in relative terms. In these ways, the underlying subject of the work is revealed: through walking the intimate connection between man and nature is revealed.

In Long's art, the walk is thus the most direct, immediate and practical way of interacting with nature. It would however be wrong to assume that this universal activity has, in an unqualified way, simply been redesignated as art. As *Crossing Stones* and *Walking in a Moving World* both demonstrate, Long's walks are considered and structured. They have a sense of purpose and a definite character. Each walk is structured, so that different elements become connected and drawn into perceivable relationships. Sometime these connections are relatively simple. In an early work such as *A Ten Mile Walk* (1968), for example, Long walked for ten miles in a straight line. As a result, distance and direction were linked. In turn, from the relationship drawn between those two properties, two specific places – the start and finish of the walk – became connected, as did all the unnamed points traversed during the walk. The walk has a structure which the related mapwork makes explicit and which the viewer can experience imaginatively.

Other walks are more complex, making subtle connections between abstract properties of time, distance, speed of walking and perception in addition to the linking of particular geographical points. These developments are evident in a walk made on Dartmoor in 1970: 'For six consecutive nights I walked by compass, from east to west, the line drawn on the map. The time taken was recorded at the end of each walk.' Walking in darkness, Long paced out precisely the same route on six nights in succession. Using a compass to determine his direction, he timed himself on each occasion, noting that overall his walking time became shorter as his familiarity with the landscape at night grew and his speed increased. The walk is structured in terms of the relationships created between the artist's body, his experiences, aspects of the landscapes – and time. That the walk defines certain relationships locates it within the language used in speaking of sculpture. That these relationships do not have a material form shows Long's achievement in taking the definition of sculpture beyond the making of objects.

FOLLOWING AN IDEA

The relationship between the idea for a walk, the walk itself, and the physical evidence of the walk, is a fundamental issue in Long's art. While it is possible to identify these different components singly, it is the interaction of these components that provides the fabric of his work. It is for this reason that, as already seen, Long's art falls outside the definition of Conceptual art. The idea is vital in that it defines the structure for a walk. But the walk is equally important in that it realises the idea, actualising the structure as physical movement through time and space, so that the work of art has a *real* – if transient – existence.

The walk's lack of permanence is intimately bound up with its subject. Nature is synonymous with movement and change. In providing a vehicle for exploring these issues, it is appropriate that the walk should be in harmony with them, providing a way of making art that is also impermanent. Nevertheless, nature also shows some evidence of the changes which galvanise it, even if some of these changes are recognisable only through a microscope. It is clear, therefore, that from the beginning, Long considered how the focus of his work – the walk – might leave a trace on the surface of the land.

His first such work was *A Line Made by Walking* (1967). In keeping with his ethos of using means which are direct, immediate and practical, this took the form of a straight line running across a grass field: the result of repeating his steps. He then photographed the work. Simple to make and easy to describe, the implications of this piece were nevertheless profound. Essentially, its subject is the interaction of man and nature. Yet the way the work conveys this is economical, pure and appropriate. Without describing nature or adding anything superfluous, the work takes its place, temporarily, in nature – its subject and its means brought into perfect alignment. The principle of making a work of art about the meeting of man and nature by leaving a sign of that interaction is encapsulated in this work and in Long's subsequent development of that approach.

Since making *A Line Made by Walking*, Long has made numerous other works which exist as impermanent traces of his walks, and of his physical presence in the landscape, at a range of sites and in various countries around the globe. In some cases, the connection between a walk and its physical consequences is overt. In *A Line of 164 Stones A Walk of 164 Miles* (1974), for example, Long walked across Ireland. During the course of his journey he stopped after every mile and placed a nearby stone on whichever road he was walking along. The resulting sculpture thus comprised 164 separate stones and spanned a distance of 164 miles – a sinuous, skein-like structure, from coast to coast, which tracked his movement across the landscape. In other works the connection with the walk is less obvious. Using stones, sticks, dust, mud, water – whatever is locally available – Long has made sculptures at certain points during the course of particular walks. These constructions belong to a restricted vocabulary of elemental shapes: lines, circles, spirals, crosses and ellipses. Sometimes they are formed by drawing together individual elements so that they form a shape. On other occasions, Long has removed elements – for example by kicking stones aside – to expose a shape on the surface of the ground.

Much has been made by commentators about the significance of these shapes. Allusions have been made to the way they echo forms in nature and also to their universal qualities in the way they cut across different cultures and periods. Such interpretations can certainly be accommodated within the broader context of Long's work. Arguably, however, the principal significance of these sculptures lies elsewhere. For example, in a work such as *1449 Stones at 1449 Feet* (1979), a sculpture made on Dartmoor in 1979, there is little sense of any shape in particular. Instead, the stones are piled amorphously and it is their number and location that are important. As the title implies, the structure makes a connection between the precise number of stones that comprise the work and the exact height at which it is situated.

What this work has in common with those which are formally more pure – such as the circles or lines – is the way that both provide evidence of the artist's presence in a particular place. As with the walks, there is an inescapable sense of structure. This structure can exist in terms of the relationships drawn between invisible qualities of measurement, as in *1449 Stones at 1449 Feet*. Alternatively, the connections made can be physical and primarily visual, as in the grouping of stones in one of the circles. In both cases, what is preeminently significant is the fact of *arrangement*: the connecting of different elements. In Long's work, arrangement arises from the meeting of human characteristics with the natural materials of the world. As such it is an index – a trace – of the relation between man and nature.

The sculptures in the landscape are therefore a vital aspect of Long's art, making visible the relationship that is its central subject. To a large extent, however, these works are not seen by anyone apart from the artist and others who happen to come upon them. Not only are they temporary sculptures which begin the process of their assimilation back into nature as soon as the artist leaves them, they are also frequently in remote locations. In seeking to record the walks and sculptures, and to make them more widely visible, Long has adopted other strategies – in the form of maps, photographs and text – which can also be seen in terms of following, or providing the trace of, an idea.

Such strategies are apparent in Long's work almost from the beginning. For example, the track left by the snowball on Bristol Downs in 1964 was short-lived but the related photograph preserves a trace of this work's brief existence. Three years later – in *Ben Nevis Hitchhike* (1967) – the walk was documented by photographs, a map and words used in combination. Long continued to use these elements in his subsequent work, sometimes independently, sometimes in different combinations. In Long's work, maps, photographs and words relate to a walk or sculpture as a footprint does to a foot. As signs, they are partial, revealing aspects of the experience that caused them; but they also provide – in their different ways – sufficient information for the viewer to *imagine* the circumstances which led to their creation.

This is most evident in the text works. Since 1977, Long has used words less as factual or descriptive annotations to photographs or maps and more as a discrete way of working in its own right. As the selection of text works in the present exhibition demonstrates, their role is to tell the story of individual walks. However, they take the form of words or phrases – notably observations, feelings, experiences, place-names, measurements of time, duration, number and distance – drawn into arrangements whose structure is rarely a narrative one. Neither poetry nor straightforward prose, the structure of such texts is closer to sculpture than to literature, arising from the connection and interrelation of words, ideas and experiences. For example, *Walking to a Solar Eclipse* (1999), traces a walk in which destination, duration and distance are aligned with a certain momentary relationship between the sun, the moon and the earth. *Sunrise Circle* (1998) also evokes in words the meeting of a human gesture with certain natural forces: in this case the fleeting connection made between the rising of the sun and a hand drawing of a circle in snow on a mountain top in Ecuador.

In this way, the textworks – like the photographs and maps – 'feed the imagination',[3] as Long puts it. They follow an idea, evoking its realisation as a walk or as a sculpture made during a walk. In the absence of these phenomena, words, cartographic symbols and images made with a camera are the traces that remain.

EARTH

The primary purpose of texts, maps and photographs is to document works which occur in the landscape, evoking that which is formless or remote. If their character is that of feeding the imagination, the works that Long makes specifically for display in a gallery space feed the senses. They have an immediate, tangible physical presence. The mudworks are executed directly on a wall; the indoor sculptures use natural materials obtained locally. Both ways of working mirror Long's activities in the landscape. In the case of the sculpture, the connection between outdoor and indoor work is explicit. The mud-works have no obvious counterpart in the landscape. This said, the use of mud connects directly with the works, using water alone, that Long makes in a natural setting. In a gallery space, mud makes the action of water and the rhythms of hand gestures visible and lasting. Mud is a natural bridge between water and stone, like fluid earth. Viewed in that light, a mudwork–made rapidly and spontaneously – suggests a stone sculpture executed at lightning speed.

One of the mudworks made for the present exhibition extends Long's engagement with ideas derived from Zen Buddhism and also his recent use of Chinese hexagrams as the basis for works using mud. This new work is based on the I-Ching symbol for 'Earth'. As such, the medium for the work of art is aligned with its meaning. Taken from the earth, the mudwork now refers back to it. Echoing Chinese ideas about the reconciliation of opposites, it exists as a record of impermanence: energy made visible, order imposed on chaos, a trace of the artist's direct involvement with his materials.

As suggested by their splashes, drips and hand marks, such works are made freely and gesturally. They are nevertheless underpinned by principles of arrangement and order. Like the stones and sticks used in the sculptures, inert matter is drawn into a complex pattern or system. A mudwork by Long is a *constructed* thing: its cumulative hand marks echoing the individual steps in a walk or the separate stones that comprise a sculpture made in a landscape. The relationships between constituent parts are vital in each of these activities. But as *Earth* (2002) suggests, in Long's work medium and meaning are closely interrelated. Beyond its formal characteristics, there lies a deeper significance.

Fundamental though the principle of arrangement is in Long's art, it is the singular character of the relationships created that carries meaning. In particular, the sense of *unity* expressed by these relationships is important. In the text work *River to River* (2001), displayed near the end of the present exhibition, a linking thread is drawn between three natural features – river, wood and tor – as the result of a walk on Dartmoor. The walk and the resulting text have imposed a pattern on these disparate elements. In another way, however, the work suggests that these natural features are *already* joined as part of an invisible and infinitely complex natural web. As such, the work of art is not just about imposing connections and order. Rather, there is a sense that it *reveals* a system of relationships: that it discloses a unity that already exists.

The idea of unified nature has antecedents in earlier art and philosophy. In the nineteenth century, the notion of the natural world – including man – as a single entity was a mainstay of Romantic thought. In *The Philosophy of Nature* (1797), the influential German philosopher Friedrich Schelling advanced the idea of nature evolving from matter into living things: plants, animals and humans. According to this view, everything is interrelated. The Romantic idea of the organic relation between man and nature has a resonance in Long's work. It would, however, be mistaken to over-emphasise the affinity with Romanticism. Long's art does not foreground emotion or indulge in flights of the imagination. It is grounded instead in the direct experience of the real world. Also, whereas the Romantics stressed the primacy of the individual in perceiving and interpreting nature, Long's work draws man and nature into balance, proportion and equilibrium.

Rather, the sense of order, unity and harmony in Long's work is the product of an approach that is essentially rationalist. While its innovatory means of expression are embedded in the art of the late twentieth century, its roots, if anything, are classical. In the ancient world, the relationship between man and nature was an abiding concern and the idea of order a passion. In Stoic philosophy, for example, human beings and nature were seen as the unified manifestation of the universal Mind. Consequently, the individual expressed his relationship with nature through the exercise of reason, which is a part of the universal Reason. As the Roman Emperor Marcus Aurelius, who was versed in Stoic philosophy, observed: 'an act that accords with nature is an act that accords with reason.'[4]

These principles find eloquent confirmation in Richard Long's art. Founded on a sense of deep accord with nature, his work expresses the beauty and fragility of this relationship. Involving direct interaction with nature and natural materials, its central means are rational and empirical. In the modern world, with a vastly expanded capacity for destruction, the relation of man and nature is as pressing and relevant as ever. For that reason, Long's art has a significance that is both timeless and universal.

Richard Long: A Moving World, exh. cat., Tate Publishing, 2002, pp.9–27.

1 Book Four, 40, trans. Maxwell Staniforth, London 1964, p.73.
2 Artist's statement, 2000 (see p. 304).
3 *Ibid.*
4 *Meditations*. Book Seven, 11, *op.cit.*, p.107.

DENISE HOOKER

Warli Days

Journey's end came after the heart-stopping game of dodgems that was the main Mumbai to Ahmedabad highway, clogged with garlanded and tinselled lorries. Upturned vehicles marooned like insects on their backs littered the sides of the road. It was, Richard Long said, 'the drive from hell'.

We branched off into another world, looping through tree-lined country roads past small clusters of low Warli huts dotted among lush green paddy fields. It was Sari Day in the local schools, and the painted and bejewelled young girls with flowers in their hair parading like Bollywood film stars made Gauguins of Richard and Hervé Perdriolle, the French curator. A winding dust path led to Jivya Soma Mashe's family compound. His substantial brick house dominated the horizon, facing the Sacred Mountain which rose opposite like a finger pointing heavenwards.

Jivya's son Sadashiv, a compact, stocky man, welcomed us on to the veranda, and in one step we entered the world of Warli art. The wall of the house was covered with paintings, alive with figures. He took us into a dark interior room full of big sealed wicker jars of rice and proudly showed us the traditional wall painting of the goddess Palaghata done for his son's wedding. Jivya appeared noiselessly, a dignified, charismatic man in shorts and a white kurta top, with a confident though modest demeanour. Richard presented him with some postcards of his work, which he held at an oblique angle and looked at sideways, sometimes upside down, appearing uncertain how to read them.

Jivya and Sadashiv took us first to see the red painted stone altar to the tiger god near the house. We strode along like giants beside them over the patchwork of small, irregularly shaped, dried-up paddy fields, where cows grazed. Jivya pointed out the clay pots hanging from the tops of palm trees to collect the foaming sap oozing from the cut trunks, which would be fermented and made into alcohol. We watched two young girls balancing barefoot like gymnasts or dancers on the edge of a deep stone well as they let down tin cans on long ropes to scoop up water, pouring it into metal pots which they stacked on their heads before swaying gracefully away in the golden late afternoon light.

That first glimpse of Warli life left us with mixed feelings. I felt uncomfortable about taking photographs, intrusive, a voyeur; but everywhere we went children and adults played up to the camera, seemed to invite it. Richard was uneasy too, unsure if Jivya had understood about the exhibition or what he was doing there, uncertain what work he could make. After the mayhem of Mumbai we were still on city time. We needed to slow right down, learn to share silence.

The next morning we sat on the veranda with Jivya going through albums of photographs of his trips to Japan, Canada and Russia, and postcards from his visit to London. Then he unrolled two large paintings wrapped around a bamboo pole depicting intricate scenes of every aspect of village life – from sowing to harvesting the paddy, worshipping the tiger god and the ancestors, and a marriage ceremony. The gods were above the mountains, the humans below. All of Warli life was embodied in those two paintings, a world where the realms of gods, men and nature, the rhythm of the seasons and the cycles of life coexist, the modern (trains, buses, auto-rickshaws) alongside age-old religious rituals and rites of passage.

When I pointed to a motif I did not recognise, Jivya replied by taking us inside into a room with a big wooden bed to see the metal-lined rice hole bored into the smooth, swept floor. He picked up a long heavy wooden stick and began to show us how it was used, when his diminutive wife came in and sat on the ground to demonstrate, rhythmically pounding grains of rice, which she then tossed in a broad, flat, wicker winnowing fan.

Preparation for lunch had begun and Richard was chafing to get on. I said, 'You have to go with the flow'. 'Yes', he replied, 'but I have to go with my flow too' and disappeared, leaving me with the women as they ground the rice into flour under a heavy circular stone. It was slow hard work needing muscles and energy; and the phrases 'a hard grind', 'the daily grind', 'grinding poverty' took on a new meaning. All of daily life was in these regular, repetitive tasks. I sat on the floor of the small dark kitchen while Sadashiv's wife made the chapatis over a wood fire. Rays of light from a high window gleamed on the brightly polished metal pots stacked on a shelf. Everything was pared to the minimum; form and function perfectly matched in the few simple, traditional utensils.

Richard appeared in time for lunch looking pleased with himself, his hands white with ash. As a guest I was treated as an honorary male and sat with the men on a bright pink patterned mat while Jivya's wife brought round a pitcher of water for us to wash our hands. She then served him first with rice and placed dishes of dhal and bamboo shoots on the floor in front of us.

After lunch Richard went off alone to walk around Jivya's land, to make a map drawing of the shapes of his fields. Hervé took me, Jivya and Sadashiv to see the work he had done earlier: an ash circle of radiating lines on the parched, cracked earth. Richard said it was just a shape – but it also looked like a sun in one of Jivya's paintings or a child's drawing in its elemental simplicity. It was modern yet timeless, abstract yet suggestive. Jivya and Sadashiv spent some time looking at it then laughed, Jivya pointing up at the sun.

It is volcanic country, and there were great piles of basalt collected from the fields near the house that looked like an obvious choice of material for Richard; but he thought it was a delicate matter for a Western artist to come in and make something on the land of a tribal artist. He wanted to do something non-intrusive, which would return to its original state after his intervention. And over the next few days he produced a series of evanescent works responsive to the place with great lightness of touch, using minimal means.

He made several brushed lines in the landscape by briskly sweeping over existing paths with a traditional reed brush, then going over them again so the earth was a deeper brown where it was freshly turned. He welcomed the fact that even as he was doing it, the path was blowing over in the hot wind. 'Nice the way it disappears', he said. Jivya came in the gate from his field when Richard was making *Brushed Path – A Line for Jivya* (2003), but he carried on walking into his house without appearing to take any notice. I wondered if maybe Jivya thought Richard was doing women's work with his sweeping; but Jivya too had developed a traditionally female art form in his painting.

Before the paddy is planted, the earth is spread with cow dung, leaves and twigs, and set on fire. *A Walking and Running Circle* (2003) was made by placing a tent peg attached to string in the centre of a large rectangle of ash, and tracing a circle with a stick tied to the other end. A group of barefoot children watched silently as Richard tread it round again with rapid shuffling, stamping steps, raising clouds of ash as he kicked in the circle with a rhythmic movement. 'A Richard Long dance', he quipped, clowning, when he finished. The earth was tamped down smooth on the circular path where his footprints were visible.

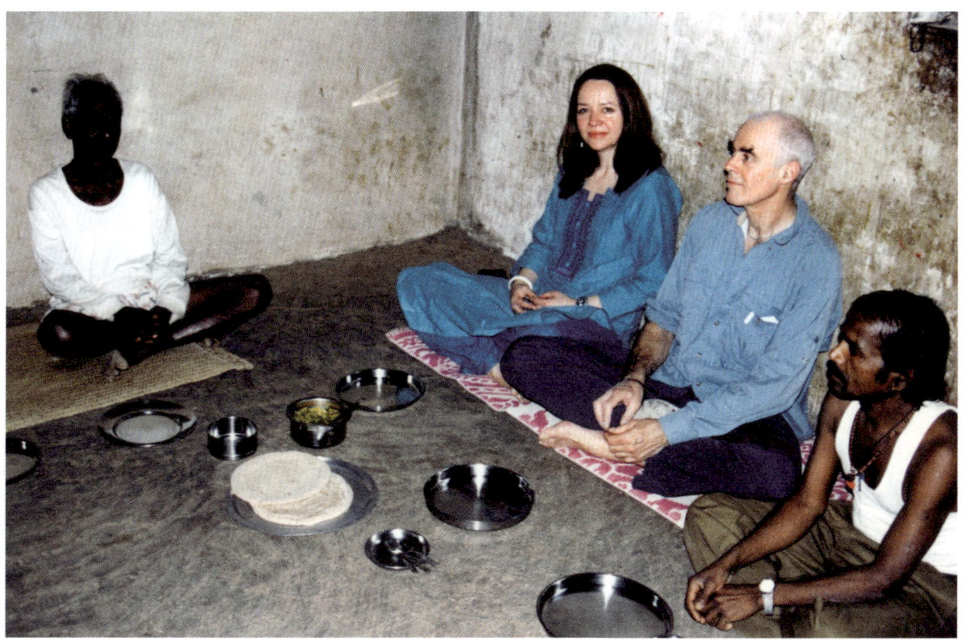

Jivya Soma Mashe, Denise Hooker, Richard Long and Sadashiv Mashe at a meal in Jivya's home, Kalambipada 2003

There was just the crisp sound of dry leaves rolling along the ground, cocks crowing, children's distant voices, the high reedy notes of birdsong, and the loud grunting of cows. Four brown and black goats gambolling across the field stopped to stare. Then one bold boy, carrying his baby brother on his hip, approached the circle and ventured inside, followed by a whole flock of girls. They imitated Richard's shuffling, stamping step, then laughing ran freely, wildly round and round. Richard smiled, delighted: 'It's a Warli painting come to life. Fantastic, fantastic! Children can play with a drawing.' The circle was full of life and laughter now the children had run in it. Their feet had erased the tread of Richard's boots, and the neat edges of the circle were already blurring. 'It looks better now', he said. Once again Jivya had crossed the corner of the field with a smile and a pleased look while Richard was working, but had not come to watch.

Near the circle I found some rich orange-coloured palm leaves with a grainy, papery texture. Richard sat on the ground with legs outstretched in front of Sadashiv's house putting white acrylic paint dots and fingerprints on the palm leaves, watched attentively by

Sadashiv and Hervé. Just as he had finished, Jivya appeared at six o'clock in a heavy woollen sweater with a reindeer motif on the front, a souvenir of his visit to Russia, reminding us it was winter here. Sadashiv explained the drawings to him and they talked among themselves about them, but made no comment to us. Did they look childlike, unskilled to Jivya? His young great-granddaughter was already making detailed paintings on paper. It was impossible to read his response.

The day before Jivya left for Delhi, Richard made *Paddy-field Chaff Circle* (2003) in the field behind his house. He measured out a circle and moved a brick attached to a central string in rays two hands' breadth apart, rapidly sprinkling fistfuls of chaff from a wicker basket on one side of the line. Jivya walked by barechested in shorts, his head wrapped in a Juventus football scarf, a shirt over his shoulder, carrying a bucket on his way to wash his clothes at his large modern well. He glanced in Richard's direction but did not stop. As ever he had an air of apartness, self-containment, gravitas, even when performing the humblest task. He often sat alone silently staring out over his fields. When he returned from the well, Richard was photographing his work. I pointed to the chaff circle and then at my eyes, inviting him to come and look. He smiled, said 'Painting' if I heard him right, but did not pause and continued on to his house, where he crouched in the courtyard rinsing his canvas and rubber shoes with water from a little pail.

Other sculptures Richard did took the form of the subtlest, most ephemeral adjustments and alignments in burnt paddy fields. In *Ash Arc* (2003) he scooped up the edge of dark ash to make a more precise arc. In *Leopard* (2003) he stamped on the white ash almost like an animal pawing the ground to reveal the sandy-brown earth underneath, in a pattern which reminded me of leopard skin, and led to Richard adopting his uncharacteristically figurative title. In *Smoky Arc* (2003) he brushed the semicircular edge of a still smoking field until it resembled the curved arc of the moon, the wind blowing the smoke first one way then another.

Even more transient were the poured water lines made by the river, which exist only in the moment of their making, drying to a different shape immediately afterwards as some parts evaporate quicker than others, before disappearing altogether. Most magical were the colour lines in the river. Richard mixed up a small amount of orange paste from chilli powder and yellow paste from turmeric. He dipped his hand in the paste and put it in the water, the colour streaming from his palm on the swift current like a bolt of silk unravelling or a sari laid out to dry.

It was hard to avoid asking the old question: 'Would it still be art if I did it or one of the herdsmen?' 'No', he said, 'because I know how to tilt the bucket, the pace, the height, where to go. I choose the direction, the speed of flow.' 'Joseph Beuys would say everyone was an artist.' 'I know what he means, but I also believe only artists make art – the fact that you might do it would be because I've done it. You could copy anything. One definition of an artist is the person who makes it first, puts down a marker as their language.' 'So you take a Duchampian rather than a Beuysian view? It's art because you do it.' 'You'd also have to say that my work looks completely different from Duchamp… It's the twin rivers of the twentieth century: Duchamp and Picasso, intellectualism and expressionism. There's a lot of expressionism in my work. Picasso represents the line of beauty, expression, colour, dynamic mark making, which can go on for many years. Duchamp is the intellectual line, reinforced by postmodernism. It's almost impossible now to make art with a readymade, it has to be really good to get away with it.'

Because Richard usually makes his works in the landscape alone with just a photograph for record, I had not been so aware before of the performance element in his art (in the sense of it being an action that is performed) and how much it is predicated on a Western audience, or one with a sophisticated knowledge of Western art. I had been used to thinking of his simple forms, particularly the circle, as universal, somehow comprehensible in all cultures; but I was learning that did not mean they were necessarily understood as art. Indeed, perhaps only those well versed in the language of contemporary art would understand them as such anywhere. Richard said he could understand Jivya's work, but Jivya did not understand his: it was a different language; in the end Jivya was a figurative artist.

Hervé took the view that all that mattered was good art and bad art; there was not just one truth in art, but different truths. I agreed, but this cultural relativism is a modern Western concept – 'Or post-modern', Richard added – the end of grand narratives. Maybe for the Warli there is only one truth. 'Artists have to believe in their own truth to make art', Richard said. 'I'm in the modernist avant-garde tradition as well as a "primitive".' All art depends on other art. Jivya too works in his tradition, but goes beyond it, has his own personal style and subject matter.

Throughout our visit Jivya remained friendly, polite, ultimately enigmatic. Nothing as grandiose as a meeting of cultures took place, but it was a meeting of individuals. If Jivya appeared not really to engage with Richard's art, he had been welcoming, patient, tolerant of our intrusiveness; allowing us to move freely where we wished on his land. There had been no direct communication with Jivya as we had no common language, but Sadashiv spoke English and I spoke French, and there are many ways to communicate beyond the verbal. There had been an exchange of energy, fellow feeling, and mutual respect. The experience of Warli life explained their art, with its all-embracing vision and interweaving of the mythic and the everyday, perhaps as well as any words or abstract theorising.

I often felt an intense sense of well-being in the peace and beauty of the Warli landscape and way of life. Things were not revealed at once. It was not until the last day that Jivya showed us the bulk of his work. I learnt that it was only by slowing to the pace of India, sitting still and allowing life to take place around me, that I really began to see anything. And if we were staring at the Other, they were staring right back, often only a foot away.

It is, however, all too easy to idealise the traditional rural lifestyle when we have the privilege of choice and the freedom to come and go. At first glance I found it encouraging that in this age of globalisation and homogeneity, cultures could stay separate, strongly rooted in their own traditions. But it would be disingenuous to ignore the other factors that were in play. The meeting was not entirely innocent or disinterested on either side. We all had our different agendas. When the Indian Handicraft and Handlooms Board first gave the Warli paper and paint to use, in what was essentially the Western mode, their art moved away from being primarily a ritual, religious activity and became commodified, acquired an exchange value and entered the global market. Our visit, one of a trickle of people from around the world, with our purchase of work and offer of an exhibition, was part of that process bringing Warli art – and ultimately society – into the global system, for good and bad. However, although Jivya Soma Mashe is a substantial, influential man in his community, with an international artistic reputation, the disparity between the price of his work and that of Richard Long speaks volumes, not just about market forces, but the distribution of power and wealth in the world.

Dialog: Richard Long/Jivya Soma Mashe, exh. cat., Verlag der Buchhandlung Walther Konig, Koln, 2003, pp.100–107.

COLM TÓIBÍN

Richard Long

In Book Four of *The Faerie Queen* (1590) Edmund Spenser lists 18 famous rivers of the world, 'which doe the earth enrich and beautifie'. He includes 'the fertile Nile' and the 'Faire Ister' – which we know as the Danube – 'flowing from the mountains high', the 'long Rhodanus, whose sourse springs from the skie', and the 'Swift Rhene' and the 'Tygris fierce, whose streames of none may be withstood.' He goes on to mention the 'Great Ganges' and the 'immortal Euphrates' and the rivers recently found and named by some of his more adventurous colleagues: the rich 'Oranochy, though but known late, / And that huge Riuer, which doth beare his name/ Of warlike Amazons, which doe possess the same.'

He then names 40 English rivers, before moving closer to home, or further away from it, depending perhaps on whether he is asleep or awake, or in a state of reverie, or looking at a map, or staring from his window. He lists 18 Irish rivers, 'sith no lesse famous than the rest they bee.' He lists the Liffy and: 'the sandy Slane' – which must be the Slaney – and 'the pleasant Boyne' and 'the fishy fruitfull Ban' and 'the gentle Shure that making way/ By sweet Clonmell, adornes rich Waterford'. He lists 'the pleasunt Bandon' and 'the spreading Lee'.

Then he moves into his own territory, the land he looks at every day and knows by heart, the land he walks and sees, that he has mapped with his eyes and feet. He names the 'swift Awniduff, which of the English man/ Is cal'de Blacke water'. He names his own river, the Awbeg, which flows through his estate at Kilcolman on its way to the Blackwater, but he has another name for it, not the name on the map, but the name by which it is locally known, the Mulla. 'And Mulla mine', he writes, 'whose waves I whilom taught to weep.' Later in the poem he mentions this river again, 'Mulla, faire and bright', and Galtymore, the highest peak of a range of hills near his castle, which he calls Arlo-hill, transferring to the hill the name of the valley below, Aherlow. He asks rhetorically in parenthesis: 'Who knowes not Arlo-hill?'

By naming it in his great poem he is making it known, giving it the same weight and importance as anywhere else in the known world.

As we read Spenser working so seductively with his cadences and his rhymes, we have to allow him to move outside history. By the beauty of his song he forces us to forget that his landscape has been newly mapped by colonists, to put aside the danger he himself will be in, or the trouble he will cause, or the tragedy which will befall the country around him and its people. We have to allow poets their lyrics, even if the lyrics come as part of a long poem and a more elaborate design.

We have to allow too the memory which the landscape holds, however ironically, that the world was once undisturbed. A world before archaeology, before maps, before human sounds and shapes. A time when there was pure geology; when there were bird sounds and loose stones and forest and water, when history came in the form of clouds and rain, and social change came from a clear sky and the beginnings of a twisted pathway.

I remember a summer day in the Catalan Pyrenees coming to the top of a pass and being faced with what looked like a catastrophe of boulders, running for miles down a valley. We could have turned back. This was going to be hard, climbing down, jumping from one rock to another. In the distance was the disc of the sun and some of the greatest mountain peaks in the world. Each boulder was different, each step we took distinct. The human presence did not matter in that place. I was awestruck at the idea that the place was indifferent to the fact there had ever been people in the world. Or that we were there now. The boulders had been tossed down by forces more brazen and elemental and fierce than the ones which allowed skin and bone, human memory, the careful eye, the wary step, the soul.

Richard Long's art has gently accepted the intense majesty and dark persistence of the world. He has asked merely for the small mercy of the light or hard step and for the camera's eager and unhurting intervention. He plays a game then, as though survival depended on it, between our mysterious need to make shapes and to create forms in the world and the possibility that we may in the end leave only vague traces of ourselves behind.

We have to imagine what it would be like to walk in his wake; a day later, a week, a year, a century. The tracks he leaves can exist purely in the imagination for miles on end, he has made something by an act of will and witness, by simply being here, by announcing later that he has passed. He can also work with the natural elements in ways which belong to culture's most essential shapes – circles, lines, spirals, crosses,

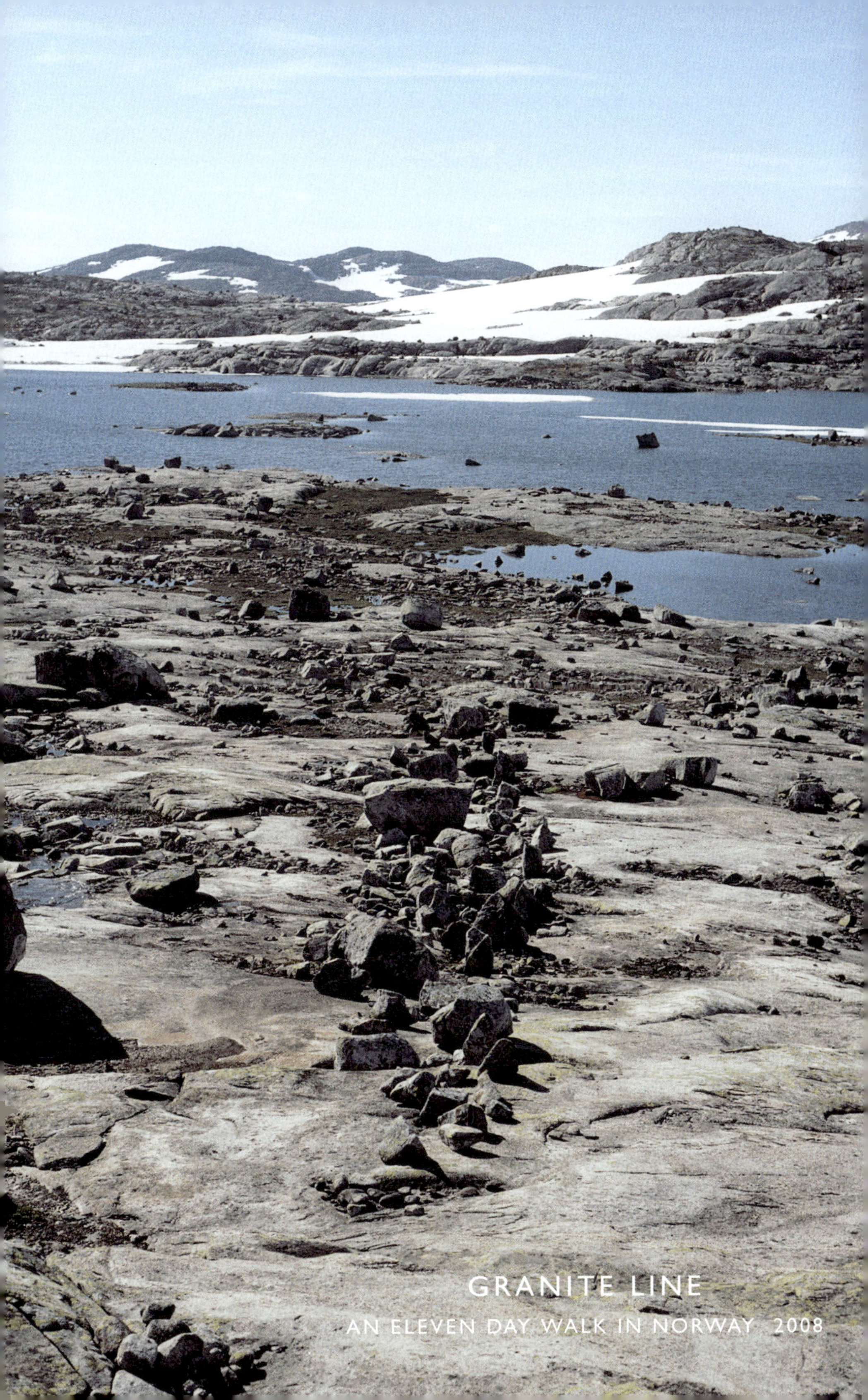
GRANITE LINE
AN ELEVEN DAY WALK IN NORWAY 2008

forms using whatever comes to hand, such as wood and stone and mud and snow and water. He can bathe iconic forms in the mysterious liquid of ambiguity, the style deliberate and intense, but allowing always for the easy and generous fact that what is left on the surface of the earth can be easily overgrown or kicked aside.

If the world is nature, then the guiding compass is culture, as are the breath and the word and the shaping hand. There remains something heroic now, as ever, in making an art out of solitary splendour, the simple fact of being alone. The eye itself is intrusion, intervention. I love the decisions made in Long's art, the watching and waiting, the play between the jagged and the symmetrical, the tension between the random footfall and the deliberate planning of a journey by foot, the counting and the countless. I love his ability to leave things alone, to allow the subtle harmonies of silence and stillness their full weight and measure, and then his urge to play God in arranging and re-arranging nature, insisting that the will and the imagination and the shaping spirit themselves are as natural as moss on stone or the coldness of the snow.

Without this urge the world itself is dulled, doomed, but it is never as simple as that. Richard Long wants context and text, a world untouched except by pathways and rights of way, so that he can move freely and plan freely and imagine at his ease, and then with the same zeal he also wants magic, sacred space which he is willing to create should the need arise in a place of his choosing. He wants the world as it is made and he wants to make the world.

He wishes to displace the self and the world and settle them both at the same time. He needs to choose and decide, put order in things, aware of the strange and futile beauty of such desires against the vast randomness of the place where we have been sent to live. It is the same as the urge to name a river or a hill, as though that impulse alone, which Edmund Spenser felt so deeply and celebrated so richly, will rescue and redeem the water and the soil from their fierce and elemental urge to escape us. The world remains itself. It is fixed in its being all the more radically and sweetly by our need to dream that it might not always be so.

Richard Long, exh. cat., Lismore Castle Arts, Lismore 2006, pp.11–14.

ANDREW WILSON

From Page to Page: An Introduction to Richard Long's Books

Left hand; left-hand page. Right hand; right-hand page. A heavy card sheet bearing the mud imprints of Richard Long's hands is folded and bound into covers, with tissue additionally bound in to protect the mud prints and separate the two pages. This form emphasises a comparison of one page to another, and between one image to the other. Each example of *Mud Hand Prints* (1984) is different and unique – a real work and not a reproduced print.

For Long, as for many artists of his generation, the book form provides a portable, relatively cheap, democratic and easily circulated means of distributing his work. Designed and conceived by Long, these books are made out of the same materials as his gallery work – text, photograph, mud – but take many formats, from what might appear at first to be fairly orthodox exhibition catalogues to books which are exemplary artist bookworks in their own right, carrying within their pages work that can exist in no other form. Where some books adopt aspects of the mass-market paperback or hardback, a book such as *Mud Hand Prints* – hand printed and hand bound in an edition of 100 – adopts a very different form. Loose, within each copy of the book is a small printed slip of paper that concisely sets out Long's rationale for using the book form:

> Books put the ideas and images of my work into the public domain in an interesting, accessible and cheap way. For me, all the different forms of my work are useful and complementary. Because I make photo works and text works the book form becomes appropriate. Also a hand print can be the same size as a book, actual size.

For many artists of Long's generation who make works that have an ephemeral or dematerialised presence, the book offered a clear form of presenting such work as information or documentation. The availability of such work in a, more-often-than-not, inexpensive book form allowed for a more inclusive exchange between the artist and the viewer or reader to take place. Long's bookworks exist categorically within such a framework where an attention to distribution and ownership of a work of art finds definition within the book as a mass-produced form that indicates an availability to all. Early in his career he formulated the notion of categories of work that might have what he termed a 'public freehold' – certain sculptures and photographic works that no one person could own but that existed within the public domain and so within a common field of experience, as itself a kind of ownership that could have no exchange value. The way in which Long approaches his work produced as books equates directly with this idea of public freehold. This is not just in respect of the wide distribution that a work – as a book – can have, but that ownership of a copy of one of his books can be understood as an opportunity to experience a work with actual ownership not being an issue – with any number of people having the possibility of holding the same book, turning those same pages and directly experiencing the work.

In 1968, while a student at St Martin's School of Art in London, the Dutch artist Ger van Elk showed Long a postcard that he had made from one of his black-and-white photographs and which he had had cheaply printed in one colour. For Long this was a revelation of how a photograph could be used, and that anyone in the world could receive such a work through the post and hold it in their hands virtually simultaneously – providing a clear model for a democratic and inclusive distribution of art. Over the 40 years since, Long has produced cards and other works to be sent by mail, these cards have both employed works that already exist (such as that for John Weber Gallery in 1974 – *A Line of 164 Stones A Walk of 164 Miles* (1974)) or offered a new work. However, with both approaches the card provides a commentary to the exhibition and to Long's activity as an artist. The terms of such works were set early with those cards produced for his first exhibitions at Konrad Fischer Galerie in 1968, 1969 and 1970. The first and the last of these used commercially available postcards – of Clifton Suspension Bridge over the Avon Gorge and a view of St Kilda – that were then overprinted with exhibition details as a means of providing an introduction, as a kind of overture, for his work (and in the knowledge that many who received the cards may not necessarily see the exhibition). The announcement cards produced for his 1970 exhibition at the Dwan Gallery in New York give a good example of how this works. These two cards, mailed together, show three uncaptioned works (*England 1968* (1968), *A Sculpture Left by the Tide* (1970) and *Valley*

(1969)) alongside a photograph of Silbury Hill, under which has been printed the legend of the hill's origin. In his exhibition at Dwan, Long presented a spiral of boot prints (echoing the spiral that occurs in *A Sculpture Left by the Tide*) as *A Line the Length of a Straight Walk from the Bottom to the Top of Silbury Hill* (1970), condensing and collapsing an English hill into a New York gallery. The Dwan cards set this work in the context of other sculptures (and the Neolithic earthwork of Silbury Hill) that are traces in the landscape: the cards providing the conditions for a viewing of sculpture as a form of walk not in the landscape but in the gallery. The similarities and differences of these different traces is thus made explicit.

In a similar manner, Long's attention to the content of his books can be explained in terms of his understanding of the book format as a way of making books that are works in their own right, and as such have the potential for a much wider distribution than orthodox gallery-based wall works. The seven Art & Project Bulletins that he made between 1971 and 1983,[1] present photographic works of which only two related to his exhibitions at the gallery, received as a form of gift through the post. Many other publications that serve as exhibition catalogues – for instance *John Barleycorn* (1974), published on the occasion of an exhibition at the Stedelijk Museum, Amsterdam; *The North Woods* (1977), published for his exhibition at the Whitechapel Gallery, London; or *Twelve Works* (1981) and *Sixteen Works* (1984), both published by the Anthony d'Offay Gallery, London – might not illustrate in any identifiable way these particular exhibitions but instead offer a markedly different presentation when compared to what hangs in the gallery. It might just be that the particular pacing and narrative that unfolds between the pages is wholly different to our experience of a group of works hanging in a gallery, or it could be that the work within the book serves as an alternative or parallel text or introduction to what actually appears in the exhibition (as is the case with the majority of his cards). This latter is especially so for those publications accompanying many of his different survey exhibitions, such as that for his first museum exhibition *Richard Long Skulptures* (1970) at the Städtisches Museum Mönchengladbach or *Inca Rock Campfire Ash* (1974) for the Scottish National Gallery of Modern Art in Edinburgh. These books bring together work from different times and made in different places to suggest a lexicon of form and a narrative of approaches that Long has to making his sculptures.

Pacing and rhythm are at the heart of experiencing a book – turning a page is an intrinsic part of reading. Pacing, rhythm, measurement and duration are similarly key elements that establish many of the parameters for Long's work; they are materials through which particular content can be fashioned and this is one other clear way in which the book form can be identified as occupying an important and quite distinctive place in Long's art. Take, for instance, the 1977 book *A Hundred Stones*, made for the Kunsthalle Bern. Though produced at the time of an exhibition, it is in no way a catalogue. It is, in production qualities, akin to any mass-produced publication. It is a work that can have no other form than the book. Its content is uncompromising. Each page reproduces a black-and-white photograph, bled to the edges and with no caption. Each photograph is of a stone, centred on the page, among other stones. The book carries no text other than what appears on the book's title page: 'A Hundred Stones: One Mile Between First and Last: Cornwall England 1977'. It is a record of a short journey paced or counted by the choice of particular stones along the route taken. We know nothing of the journey other than what the book presents; that it is in Cornwall, that it is a mile long and that, by the evidence of the photographs, the terrain slightly changes; seaweed can sometimes be seen among the stones, in other photographs, later in the book, grasses appear. It is one record of a short walk along a stony beach. The photographs are matter-of-fact and dispassionate, yet one intention of the book was to convey the 'cosmic variety' of the similar-looking stones or pebbles he had chosen to photograph; that every stone in the world is as unique and different as every hand print is also unique and different. The cumulative feeling from reading the book is meditative and reflects a state of private ritual; counting, is observing, is pacing, is walking, is being in the world.

Richard Long's introduction to the idea of artist's books was while staying with Konrad Fischer in 1968 and seeing the books of Ed Ruscha. *A Hundred Stones* is one of the handful of books by Long – *Labyrinth* (1991), for the Städtische Galerie im Städel Frankfurt am Main would be another – that adopts Ruscha's strategies so closely. The books that Ruscha published in the early 1960s mark a sea change from those books produced by artists as 'livres de luxe' – largely limited edition, luxuriously printed illustrated books – to an era of artists' books that adopt the feel of commercial mass-produced illustrated booklets.

Ruscha's first book, like Long's *A Hundred Stones*, had no text other than the title page and colophon, and consisted solely of pages bearing black-and-white photographs. This book, *Twentysix Gasoline Stations* (1963), has been well described by artists' book historian Clive Phillpot: 'Rather than illustrating a text by another person, Ruscha constructed a linear sequence of nondescript photographic images to document the gas stations that punctuated US Route 40 between Los Angeles, where he lived, and Oklahoma City, where he grew up. These images are like 26 letters of a personal alphabet that are structured by the form of the book.'[2] The gas stations, like Long's stones, when taken individually as photographs give no clue to their position within the work's narrative, which can only be provided within the context of the book and its position within the sequence of pages. Beyond the centring in the page of each stone that is the focus of attention for each image, there is the sense that Long does not pursue usual photographic effects of lighting, composition or print quality. Instead he intends a degree of truth to his subject matter within the constructions of his images: 'the work itself is simple and straightforward and I hope that the photographs of the work are also simple and straightforward. So, it is a factual record of that place.'[3]

Long's matter-of-fact assessment of his work, however, diverts attention from the complexities that this simple book form can unlock. *Countless Stones* (1983), published in connection with an exhibition at the Stedelijk Van Abbemuseum in Eindhoven, is a good example of how this occurs. The book records a walk in Nepal – but rather than the walk in Cornwall of *A Hundred Stones*, here the book concentrates on pathways made out of stone. The journey that the book relates is a walk where the rough terrain required Long to pay particular attention to the ground where he walked; that on precipitous trails such as these the walker has to look at every step and at every stone (literally these are 'stepping-stones'). The title page states that this is 'A 21 Day Footpath Walk' and that the book is made up of 'Views Looking Forward in Sequence'. Though this might suggest a sequential reading of the photographs, the book instead unlocks an experience of the work in other ways. The snow on this walk in Nepal obscured a section of the footpaths, so two photographs in the book show snow appearing around a path and then the book's narrative jumps. It is relevant here that he chose not to photograph the snow-covered footpath as that would have introduced another level of intervention and complexity that would have disrupted the book's narrative of 'countless stones'.[4] There is also a clear bunching where some stretches of the walk are documented in the book with a greater intensity than others – just as in any walk certain stretches of a path can capture the imagination in ways that do not reveal themselves in other sections of the walk.

Another way of pacing a path can be realised by what one finds, takes away and preserves – not unlike the ways in which pressed flowers and grasses can suggest particular memories and experiences that for the gatherer can adopt a private, diaristic and talismanic force; or that for a botanist or scientist exist as 'specimens'. Long's small pamphlet books *From Along a Riverbank* (1971) and *From Around a Lake* (1973) engage with such a private exchange with a place, and make it accessible and transformative for anyone holding one of these books and turning their pages. In each case, one in colour and the other in black and white, photographs of individual or paired leaves and grasses are laid out on each page as if pressed – each page providing evidence of the punctuation of a walk by picking up the grasses or leaves and holding them, and then ultimately presenting them in the pages of the two books as the parameters of an experience privately remembered but publicly made available for access.

Another small pamphlet publication, *Two sheepdogs cross in and out of the passing shadows The clouds drift over the hill with a storm* (1971), provides a similar narrative of experience but in a markedly different way. Each page carries a photograph from a walk on Dartmoor, captioned by a text that describes the photograph and the walk as a type of experience that can be felt and projected within the land itself that Long passes through. Here Long does not present the work through material collected during his walk, but instead reads in a narrative that connects the experience of the walk to the sites themselves quite directly. For instance, a rocky outcrop has the words, 'From in here the buzzard in the sky and I can watch each other' printed under it, bringing it alive – the buzzard not appearing in the photograph itself, but the sight of which forms a tangible part of the walk connected with that place, in such a way that we have to ask if it is Long and the buzzard watching each other, or the tor watching the buzzard. Another photograph shows Long crouching by a stream with his hand in the water, with the caption: 'The stream says I can touch you as I pass by'. Each caption gives identity and a living character to places and their situations – the brook and the clapper bridge that 'are old friends', or the hilltop that 'can see the sea on a fair day'. These suggest another type of relationship or dialogue between the places of a locality and a person passing through them. *South America 1972*, published in 1973, also does this, but with text and with images that are drawn notational references rather than photographs. Each double-page spread depicts a different way of making a work in the changing landscapes and circumstances encountered by Long on a journey through Bolivia, Peru and Chile. This is one of Long's most personal and particular books, recording those ephemeral marks or ritualised actions that punctuated his journey: '"Moon Drawn With My Hand On The Surface Of Lake Titicaca At Night", "Sun A Circle Made From Gold Particles Panned From A Stream On The Cuzco-Lima Road" ... "Spiral Two Walks Made Slowly Along An Ancient Peruvian Ground Drawing Near Nazca" ... "Condor A Drawing In The Snow At 20,000 Feet On Mount Illampu in Bolivia. As I Sat On A Rock Near The Drawing A Condor Suddenly Glided Straight Overhead. It Flew So Close I Could Hear The Air Whistle In Its Feathers."' This book is the embodiment of Long's statement that 'I like to see art as being a return to the senses.'[5]

Dartmoor is a place that Long has returned to time and again since his childhood, and his recent book *Dartmoor* (2005) relates an eight-day walk by playing with those perceptions of time and space that are implicit in turning the pages of this particular book. Portrait in orientation, it consists of colour photographs taken in sequence along the walk, one view of the moor on each right-hand page. But like a children's book he once had, each page is cut into three equal lateral sections, delineating foreground, middle ground, and background horizon line and sky. So the book becomes an object where the holder has multiple options and choices to turn pages or parts of images, to upset or syncopate the rhythm of the walk, to mix up places, foregrounds and horizons, and time, backwards and forwards. From the 78 pages there are 474,552 potential combinations of different images. An earlier book, *Dartmoor Stones*, from 1987, weaves photographs of rocks isolated in the moorland through the pages of a diary – the counting of the granite slabs and the walking from one to another intimating the passage of time. Another variation of Long's use of the book form specifically to represent time is *Walking and Sleeping* (2003). This book presents the concurrent days of seven walks simultaneously as lines of text on each page. Each walk was of a different duration, and is printed in a different colour, one line from each day of each walk on each page. The different ideas, objectives or sensations of each walk can thus be read at a glance, simultaneously, day by day, so that time collapses on the page only to run out at the end of the book. As each walk ends, its place on the page becomes empty, until only the longest walk, in Spain, is left. The book also shows photographs of a selection of the camping places from along some of his walks. Sleeping is the complementary activity to the walking, the stopping time in the movement, the 'out-takes', the parallel back-story which enables the walking.

The card for Richard Long's second exhibition at Konrad Fischer in 1969 is a photograph of Long with his bicycle crossing the River Avon on the Pill Ferry. The Avon in Bristol is at the core of his work, it is where he grew up and where he lives. The river describes a flow, the passage of which can be measured by the tide – the quarried limestone sides of the gorge and the river's mud have both provided Long with materials. The mud has been used for floor and wall works as well as books – *Mud Hand Prints* being one, *River Avon Book* (1979) being another. In holding this book you literally hold the river. The book is made up of paper that has been dipped in mud from the river and then bound to make the book; the pace of the turning pages akin to the shifting currents. Each page of each book is thus a unique and real image and each book is different from another as is each page, one from another. For *River Avon Mud Book* (1981), the paper is not dipped into the mud but made of it, mud having been mixed with the paper pulp. This process was repeated for *Nile: Papers of River Muds* (1990), each page having been made out of the mud of different world rivers – the Jordan, the Amazon, the Mississippi, the Avon, the Indragoodby, for example – with the name of each different river printed in letterpress on each page. Despite these books, Long is not especially in thrall with the idea of the handmade. The nature of these books encapsulates their idea – that the flow of a river as well as its materiality could be locked in its pages. Similarly, the newsprint production of *Muddy Water Marks* (1985) in a mass-produced edition more than ten times the size of Nile attains a different meaning and degree of distribution for its images of mud splashes. Whether small or large edition, handmade or machine-made, Long's books have remained consistent to his view that, 'A sculpture, a map, a text, a photograph: all the forms of my work are equal and complementary. The knowledge of my actions, in whatever form, is the art. My art is the essence of my experience, not a representation of it.'[6]

Heaven and Earth, exh. cat., Tate Publishing, London, 2009, pp.194–99.

1 The Art & Project Bulletins were a folded single-sheet publication produced by the Amsterdam gallery Art & Project and were mailed regularly between 1968 and 1989. With an unchanging cover design, the inside page spread was effectively a blank page open to each artist's intention, to the degree that each Bulletin was effectively an alternative form of exhibition space to that provided by the gallery itself. Every Bulletin was a stand-alone work of art.
2 Clive Phillpot, 'Books by Artists and Books as Art', in Cornelia Lauf and Clive Phillpot, *Artist/Author Contemporary Artists' Books*, Distributed Art Publishers and American Federation of Arts, New York, 1998, p.33.
3 Richard Long, 'Interview with Martina Giezen (1985–1986)', reprinted in Ben Tufnell (ed), *Richard Long: Selected Statements and Interviews*, Haunch of Venison, London, 2007, p.65.
4 Long has described this event thus: 'The strange thing is that when we came to the place which was blocked by snow, you don't see that in the book because I could not see the stones. That part of the walk is not in the book because the idea of the work was to record the stones I touched. Like here, there is a gap of maybe five or six days where the snow was. In this section you can see that the photographs are taken very close together ... Quite a nice thing about these photographs is, sometimes you cannot tell if they are going up or down. There is absolutely nothing flat.' *Ibid.*, p.83.
5 Richard Cork, 'An Interview with Richard Long' in *Walking in Circles*, exh. cat., George Braziller, New York and South Bank Centre, London, 1991, p.252.
6 Richard Long, cited in *Richard Long: Books, Prints, Printed Matter*, exh. cat., The New York Public Library, New York, 1994, n.p.

EAST DART RIVER	INTO A LOW SUN
LONGFORD TOR	GLISTENING FROST
LITTAFORD TOR	FOX TRACKS
CROCKERN TOR	BETWEEN THE GRANITE
WEST DART RIVER	DOWN FAST GROUND
ROYAL HILL	OVER A DRY WALL
STRANE RIVER	BOGGY AND SLOW
RIVER SWINCOMBE	ACROSS STEPPING STONES
FOXTOR MIRES	LEAPING
GREAT GNATS HEAD	FLOATING GROUND
BROAD ROCK	SUN SETTING
LANGCOMBE HEAD	CREAKING ICE
YEALM HEAD	FULL MOON RISING
DENDLES WASTE	DARKNESS

TWO STRAIGHT TWELVE MILE WALKS ON DARTMOOR

PARALLEL   ¼ MILE APART   OUT AND BACK   ONE DAY

ENGLAND   1980

ROBERT MACFARLANE

Five, six, pick up sticks

In 1980 Richard Long exhibited at the newly opened Anthony d'Offay Gallery in Dering Street, London. The show was mixed-media: maps and photographs recorded a *Water Circle Walk* (1980) made between four lochs in the Scottish Highlands; terse text notes detailed *Two Straight Twelve Mile Walks on Dartmoor, England* (1980); and across the floor of the gallery stretched *Somerset Willow Line* (1980), hundreds of barkless willow batons laid out in the form of a section of path, 16½ metres long and two metres wide. An allusion, in part, to the Sweet Track – the causeway of bound coppice poles that was built around 3800 BC in order to give safe passage across the swampy Somerset Levels.

Unexpectedly, the d'Offay show was accompanied by a 'Statement' from Long. Unexpectedly – because Long had previously kept silent on the subject of his own work, preferring to exhibit it unglossed. Printed at the Curwen Press, it appeared on a single sheet of card, folded into three panels. Its title was *Five, six, pick up sticks Seven, eight, lay them straight* (1980), and the text consisted of 44 sentences, laid out on the page almost as the stanzas of a poem. The simplicity and repetitions of his language (as seen in the fragments below), combined with the *mise en page*, gave the document a peculiar atmosphere: part Ten Commandments, part nursery rhyme –

> I like the simplicity of walking,
> the simplicity of stones.
> I like common means given
> the simple twist of art.
> I choose lines and circles because they do the job.
> My art is about working in the wide world,
> wherever, on the surface of the earth.
> My work is not urban, nor is it romantic.
> It is the laying down of modern ideas
> in the only practical places to take them.

You might be able to hear the rasp of annoyance in that last section. For Long had been provoked to issue his statement out of irritation – irritation at the persistent mischaracterisation of his work as 'romantic', and irritation at finding himself repeatedly placed in a tradition of reverie-minded walker-philosophers that started with

Henri Rousseau and marched through William Wordsworth, Samuel Taylor Coleridge, George Borrow and Henry David Thoreau. This was an attempt to clarify his methods and his ambitions.

Long's impatience seems to me quite understandable: romantic walking is so clearly a false genealogy for his art. The British version of this tradition is filled with pedestrians (William Hazlitt, Robert Louis Stevenson, Edward Thomas) who wish to stride back into a true sense of themselves. They foot forwards into the metaphysical wind of the world, letting it scour away the sour accretions of life – and they end their walks stripped back to their ideal natures. By contrast, American romantic roadsters (Henry David Thoreau, Ralph Waldo Emerson, John Muir) are more anticipatory: they imagine the walk as a way to find a new self, rather than to retrieve a lost one. British walkers recover, American walkers discover – and both traditions celebrate a self-consciousness on the part of the walker. They cherish the walker as thinker, and the walker as talker.

Either way, these walkers have very little in common with Long, who has always been far less interested in reflection than in motion, and less in mind than in body. His art practises, in fact, an almost immodest discretion with regard to the ego. The marks he has left behind in landscapes – rock-rows, snow-drawings, trails of crushed grass, circles of slate-blades – appear to be the scrupulously anonymised traces of an unspecific human body moving through space and time. That said, to describe his work as egoless isn't to declare it devoid of personal content. And one of the most intriguing aspects of his art is how subtly it registers and re-expresses aspects of his childhood. Michael Craig-Martin, reviewing the d'Offay show for *The Burlington Magazine*, noticed this: 'The art is rooted in his home territory and his childhood experience'. Long later confirmed Craig-Martin's intuition. 'I feel I carry my childhood with me in lots of aspects of my work', he remarked. 'Why stop skimming stones when you grow up?'

Why indeed? It's a lovely question – innocently seen and innocently phrased. And Long has never stopped skimming stones, artistically speaking. His hundreds of circles – made around the world in stone, sand, wood, grass and footprints – can be imagined as the ripples of these skimmed stones. To my mind, his work is best understood as a set of persistently childish acts: the outcomes of a brilliantly unadulterated being-in-the-world. The word kindergarten was coined in 1840 by the German educationalist Friedrich Froebel. Kindergarten, literally 'a children's garden: a school or space for early learning.' Froebel (less remembered now than Maria Montessori or Rudolf Steiner, for he didn't lend his name to his method) wanted to create an environment in which children could be childish in the best sense of that word. Banished from his kindergartens was the Gradgrindian sense of the infant as a vessel to be filled with facts. Instead, he fostered an ideal of the child as micronaut – an explorer of the world's textures, laws and frontiers, who should be left to make his or her own discoveries through unstructured play. Froebel wanted children to 'reach out and take the world by the hand, and palpate its natural materials and laws', as Marina Warner observes in a fine essay on play, 'to discover gravity and grace, pliancy and rigidity, to sense harmonies and experience limits'.[1]

A nature-lover and walker from an early age, Froebel had a passion for the patterns of phenomena, and in particular for what he called 'the deeper lying unity of natural objects'. It was for this reason that the early Froebelian kindergartens had few figurative toys. Instead of trains, dolls and knights, there were wooden cubes and spheres, coloured squares and circles, pebbles, shells and pick-up-sticks. Children spent their days singing songs and playing games, arranging the pebbles in spirals and circles, balancing blocks and picking up sticks. This open play was, as Froebel imagined it, the means by which 'the child became aware of itself, and its place within the universe'.

Long is a childish artist in the Froebelian sense, and the wild world is his kindergarten. When Clarrie Wallis, curator of the new Tate exhibition, observes that his work is about his 'own physical engagement, exploring the order of the universe and nature's elemental forces... about measuring the world against ourselves',[2] she could be describing the Froebelian method. For more than 40 years Long has been using his moving body to explore limits, sense harmonies and apprehend balance and scale. His materials and his vocabulary have always been uncomplicated and childish. 'I am content with the vocabulary of universal and common means', he wrote quietly in 1982, 'walking, placing, stones, sticks, water, circles, lines, days, nights, roads.' Again in 1985: 'My pleasure is in walking, lifting, placing, carrying, throwing, marking.' In 1968 he showed a sculpture of sticks cut from trees along the Avon and laid end to end in lines on the gallery floor. Five, six, pick up sticks Seven, eight, lay them straight.

'A walk', wrote Long in 1980, 'is just one more layer, a mark.' Children, like Long, are passionate mark-makers. As any parent knows, a child is happiest when playing with surfaces that record its passage or presence. Ice-lidded puddles that smash like mirrors or crockery. Leaf-drifts that scuff and kick into clouds. A crayon scrawled along a white wall (a line taken for a walk). A stick dragged along railings, leaving its steam engine sound-trail behind it. Dirty shoes tracking footprints across a kitchen floor. Long's first landscape work, *Snowball Track* (1964), occurred when he rolled up a snowball, and then photographed the wobbly dark path of revealed grass left by it. In 1970 at the Dwan Gallery he wore muddy boots and stomped a spiral of smeared dirt on to the floor, the uncoiled length of which corresponded to a straight climb that he had previously made from the bottom to the top of Silbury Hill in Wiltshire. This was among the first of Long's many daub-works from the 1970s, which he made by using his feet or hands to wipe, smudge, blotch and spread mud and soil on to the floor. Seeing black-and-white images of these works now, they resemble evolved versions of the hand prints left by the Lascaux Cave artists around 17,000 years ago – or of a child's first prints in mud or paint. Ontogeny recapitulating phylogeny.

When he was growing up, Long was lucky enough to be indulged in his compulsive mark-making. His parents let him draw all over his bedroom walls, creating a mural-in-progress. At the age of five he negotiated with his primary school headmistress over whether he could miss morning service if he spent the hour painting instead (his negotiations were successful). In 1966, while still an art student, he persuaded his neighbour to allow him to incise a work called *Turf Circle* (1966) into his manicured back lawn.

The lines of continuity from Long's childhood into his adult work are multiple and clear. 'My father used to take us down to see the spring tides [of the River Avon]', he recalled. 'I grew up playing on the tow-path ... when I was a child I just used to find the River Avon a great place. And children are no intellectuals. They just play in the places which are nice to be in. So all my fascination with water, the roots of my art, developed in my childhood.' The puddle splash, the muddy stick, the two-footed jump, fingers drawing pictures in the dust – how strongly those early river days have leaked into his later art. In the 1980s he extended his repertoire of daub-works, transferring them from floor to wall, and exploring new patterns and forms. He began to use his right hand as the brush: dipping it in a bucket of mud, then wiping the mud on to the wall to create splash paintings, then allowing the silt to drain down and disperse its alluvial deposits, forming arbitrary fans and deltas. The mud that Long uses most often for this work comes from the Avon, which he claims produces the most artistically helpful mud in the world, in terms of its adhesiveness and texture.

Lynne Cooke, in a 1983 essay that stung Long sharply,[3] described his textworks as 'wilfully precious', and compared his photographs with colonial 'trophies'. His art, she wrote, exerts a 'powerful hegemony' (this at a time when the word hegemony was thrown around rather more often in art criticism than it is today). Long 'attempts to order the world', she wrote, 'he... imposes order on nature'. But Cooke got Long wrong. He's no hegemonist, nor an imposer of order. Rather, he is a discoverer of order, an experimenter in limit and form. A *homo ludens*, to borrow the title of Johann Huizinga's synoptic 1938 study of the play-impulse, which so influentially connected play and art.[4]

Long the solemn child, then, whose work recalls Melanie Klein's definition of play as 'a serious form of meaning-making – often compulsive, repetitive and anxious'. And, in this respect, he can usefully be connected with those artists who have seen the walk as play (which is quite different from seeing the walk as comedy). He can be placed in the company of, say, Bruce Nauman, whose video performance piece *Walking in an Exaggerated Manner Around the Perimeter of a Square* (1967–68) shows Nauman placing his feet – with the amplified care of a tightrope walker teetering leagues above a city street – along the edge of a taped square in a room. And he can, perhaps, share at least imaginative space with Watt, the eponymous character of Samuel Beckett's third novel, whose 'way of advancing due east' (wrote Beckett with playful seriousness in or around 1942) 'was to turn his bust as far as possible towards the north and at the same time to fling out his right leg as far as possible towards the south, and then to turn his bust as far as possible towards the south and at the same time to fling out his left leg as far as possible towards the north'.[5]

Tate Etc., Issue 16, summer 2009, pp.54–59.

1 Marina Warner, 'Self-Portrait in a Rear-View Mirror', in Marina Warner (ed), *Only Make Believe*, Compton Verney House Trust, Compton Verney, 2005, pp.4–19.
2 Clarrie Wallis, 'Making Tracks', in Clarrie Wallis (ed), *Heaven and Earth*, exh. cat., Tate Publishing, London, 2009, pp.33–59.
3 Lynne Cooke, 'Richard Long', *Art Monthly*, no.66, May 1983, pp.8–9.
4 Johan Huizinga, *Homo Ludens*, Wolters-Noordhoff cop., Groningen, 1938.
5 Samuel Beckett, *Watt*, Olympia Press, France, 1953.

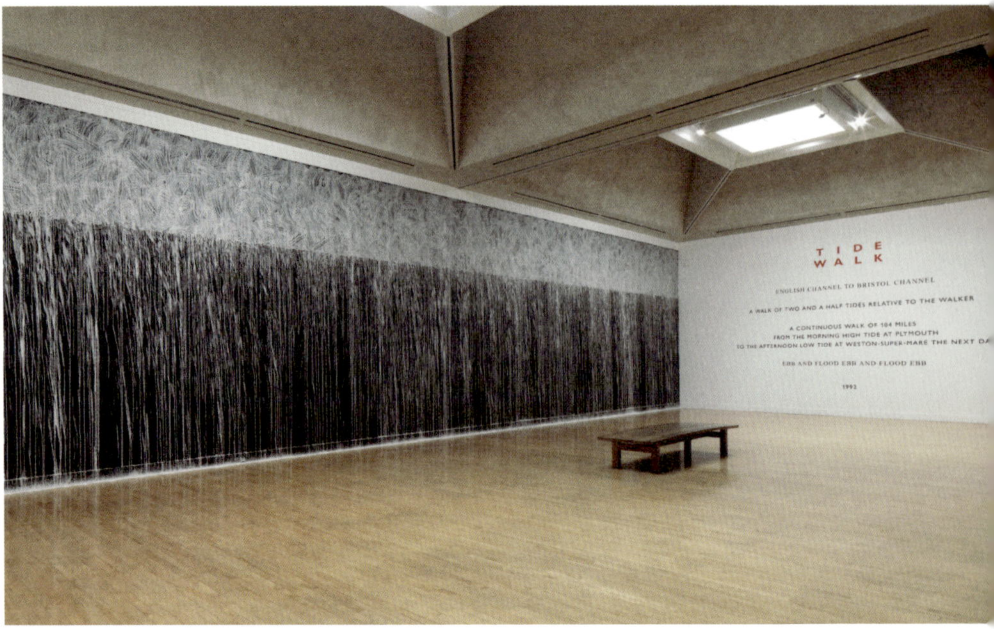

White Water Line (detail) 2009 and *Tide Walk* 1992

Archive room, installation view

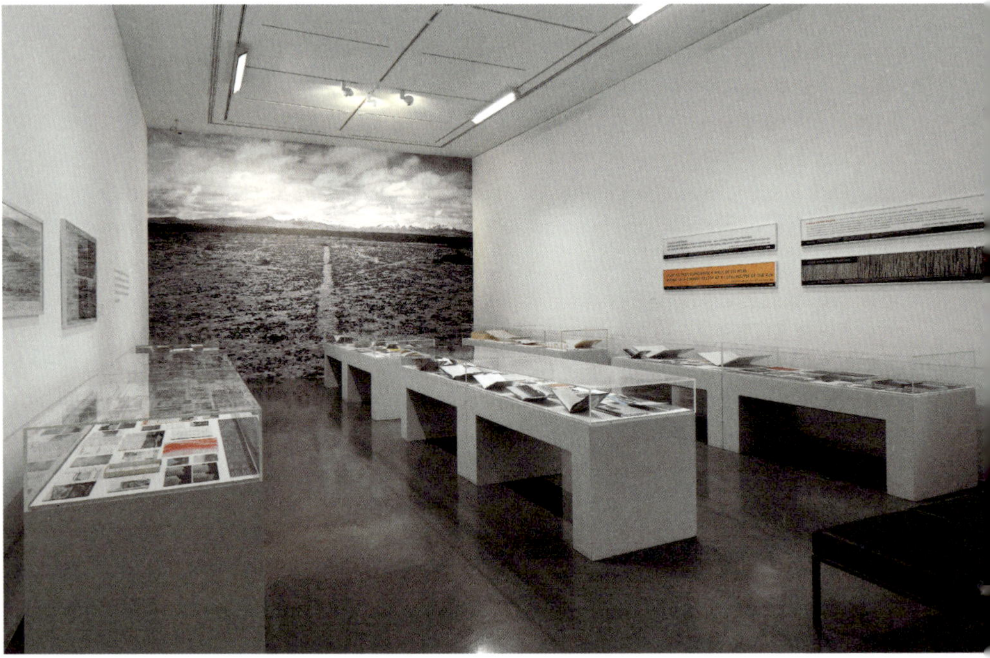

MARINA VAIZEY

Heaven and Earth

Tate Britain, London, 3 June – 6 September 2009

One of Shakespeare's most often quoted lines, from Hamlet, simply asserts that 'There are more things in heaven and earth, Horatio, than are dreamt of in our philosophy'. The current retrospective at Tate Britain of the art of Richard Long, the first in London since the Arts Council's Hayward Gallery show in 1991, has been titled *Heaven and Earth* by Long himself, a phrase he had earlier used for specific works of art. The phrase, implying complementary opposites, has been suggested by the I-Ching, that ancient Chinese text which for millennia has guided explorations of change and stability, order and chaos, the seemingly random and the discovery of pattern. The sophisticated yet simple concepts behind the I-Ching may well be an inspiration for three of the largest works on view: the great wall painting in Vallauris clay [*From Beginning to End* (2009)] and the first room with its two huge wall paintings in River Avon mud [*Heaven* (2009) and *Earth* (2009)], exploiting almost endless variations in density of tone and hue, dominated by light and dark ochres and browns so dark as to be almost black, shaped by the primordial forms of cross and line. The tidal Avon is Long's home river; he was born in Bristol, where he still lives, in 1945.

Long was part of the gifted generation at St Martin's School of Art which included those anarchic sculptors Gilbert & George, in a department whose faculty was led by Anthony Caro. Long is on record, however, as saying that, as might be expected, the students taught each other; and Long, uncannily precocious, is perhaps the most original of all the postwar generation of British artists.

Physicists tell us that even the most solid appearing object is actually continually in flux, that all matter is always on the move. Long's unusual gift is to make this visible, just as in the earliest part of the last century Wassily Kandinsky and later Paul Klee made the rhythms of music consciously visible. In part, originality does obviously consist in making others look and think in different ways and the surprising, even archaic simplicity of Long's strategies have done just that. He takes us with him on his seemingly solitary journeys which underline, usually in black-and-white photographs, very occasionally in colour, and printed or handwritten prose poems, the emotive beauties of everything from a scruffy English meadow to the Australian outback, from the Himalayas to the high Peruvian plains. We too can have a dream of self-reliance, of the enjoyment of solitude, of wilderness both near and far: nothing man-made is visible except for Long's own interventions which only use the found and natural materials to hand.

The first iconic piece in the exhibition, deceptively simple, was given by its creator its literal title: *A Line Made by Walking* (1967) was just that: from a train window Long spied a promising meadow, and finding it, made a line through the rough grass by walking up and down and up and down, wearing a path (as animals and humans have done for millennia). He photographed the surprisingly serene result, ensuring through the lens an almost complete symmetry, the wildflower meadow divided in half by the path, the path itself disappearing into a boundary which consisted, with a fairy-tale resonance, of a dark wood.

In 1968 Long had his first one-man exhibition, with Konrad Fischer in Dusseldorf, with whom he has shown ever since. The city was home to the Kunstakademie Dusseldorf, perhaps at that point the most innovative teaching institution anywhere – the prodigiously gifted photographers and teachers Bernd and Hilla Becher were among the faculty, not to mention Joseph Beuys, whose title was Professor of Monumental Sculpture. Dusseldorf was then the self-styled City of Artists, the city publishing a book by that name, and hosted, among others, the young Klaus Rinke who was throwing water into the Rhine as a piece of performance. From the very beginning, whether willed or not, Long has been at the heart of things. In London, his first commercial exhibitions throughout the 1970s were at the Lisson Gallery, which pioneered the exhibition of a remarkable range of young British sculptors (Tony Cragg, Richard Deacon, Anish Kapoor, Julian Opie) and, to the astonishment of the influential few who then visited, the leading American Conceptualists and Minimalists. By the 1980s Long was showing with Anthony d'Offay and indeed the Anthony d'Offay Artist Rooms includes one devoted to Long.

In the more than four decades since that first show Long has had hundreds of solo and group exhibitions, published countless cards and other ephemera, and been involved in scores of major publications, from such seminal group catalogues as *When Attitudes Become Form* (1969), to catalogues and monographs of his own work.

Long has made art of his own journeys, performance on the grandest scale, dominated and characterised by invented rituals, even at times by the repetitive actions which we may sometimes associate with captive animals pacing in cages, or routines which shore up human fragility by an external framework of ritualistic activity. He has made art of the most childlike activities, the playing with sticks and stones – a 1980 publication has on its title page *Five, six, pick up sticks Seven, eight, lay them straight* – mud and wood. Rather than sandcastles though, Long uses a free hand and intuitive geometry, no line exactly straight, each characterised by the individual physiognomy, so to speak, of a flint, a twig, a rock. For an art that can seem so austere, there is at times a surprising flamboyance; and, in several interviews over the years, Long has indicated the intense enjoyment his hard walking ways have provided for him.

Long's radical art is about the outside, the outside world of nature itself, seemingly untouched by human hand or intervention – except of course for the artist's – but in order to appreciate it, to make it visible, we, his audience, and his work have to be inside, in the confines of the classic white room, the gallery space, and often, in the case of the large sculptures made of permanent materials such as pieces of slate, rocks, flints or driftwood, in the cultivated garden, an outdoor room confined and defined by human design. The wilderness is domesticated, and the emotions landscape evokes are made clear; we cannot look at 'nature' and not anthropomorphise what we see. Do these hills know they are providing a view, these clouds know they are drifting, the buzzard know he is watching the artist?

The work at Tate Britain is arranged in a rough chronology, but the show opens with the two site-specific new wall paintings of *Heaven* and *Earth*, and then proceeds, again roughly chronologically. All but one of the galleries are filled with wall-hanging texts or text-and-photo pieces or wall paintings, but this intelligently and spaciously arranged spectrum of work from the 1960s onwards is punctuated at the centre of the exhibition by a room of six floor sculptures covering 20 years (1980–2000) – circles, a line and an ellipse, deploying slate, basalt and flint. *Black White Blue Purple Circle* (1998) is surprisingly Baroque, almost florid in its use of coloured Swiss stones, some upended. Two rooms further on there is another wall painting, an enormous *White Water Line* (2009) of cascades and waterfalls of Cornish china clay, made in situ, belying its title. Mostly there are hanging textworks, descriptions of walks, amplified by words or phrases indicating things seen, things felt, sounds heard. A text piece called *Circle of Autumn Winds* (1994) is a scatter of arrows framed in a circle, captioned as 'Reading the Wind Reading the Compass A Walk of 46 miles' inside an imaginary circle on Dartmoor, England, 1994. The text pieces are both

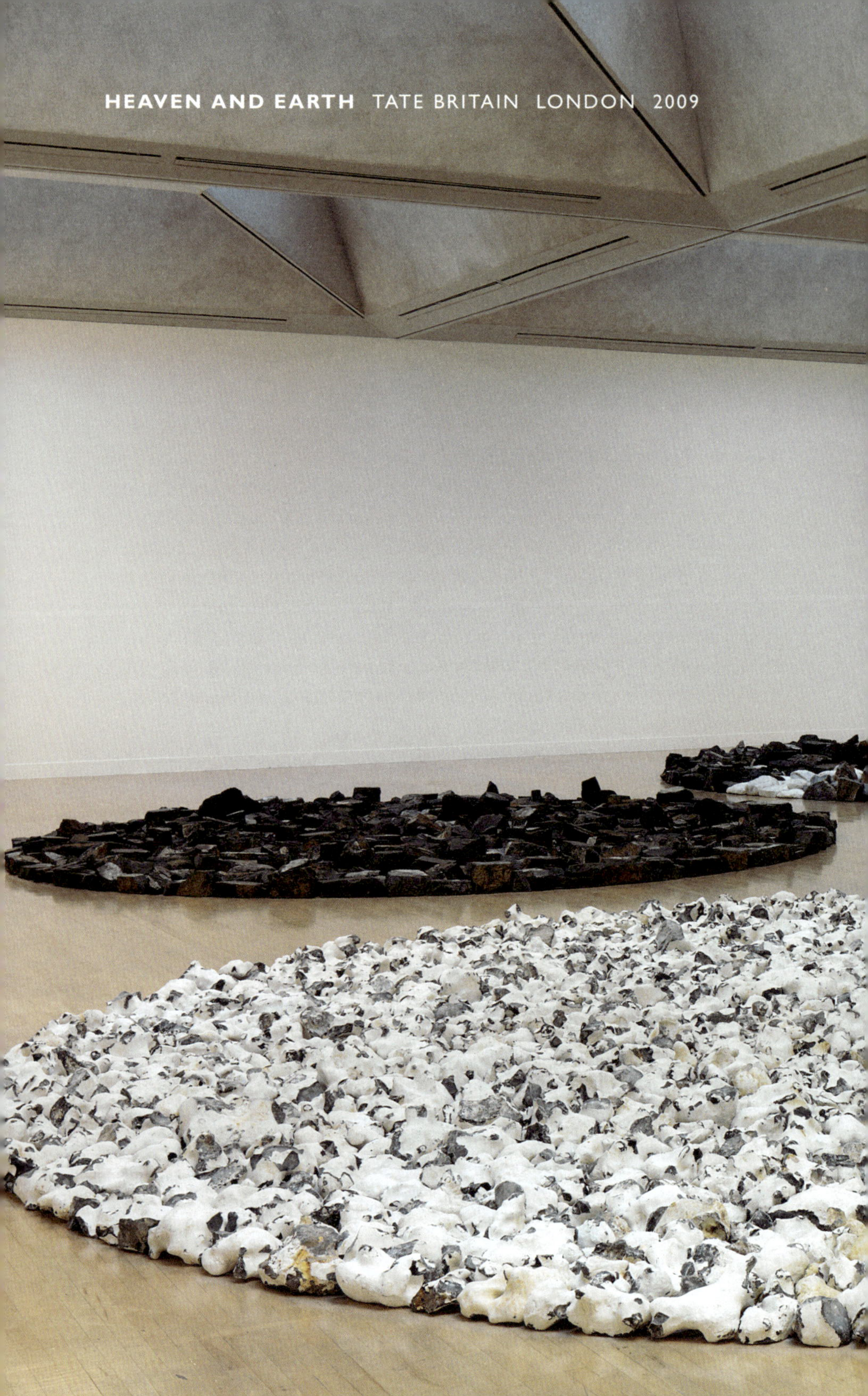
HEAVEN AND EARTH TATE BRITAIN LONDON 2009

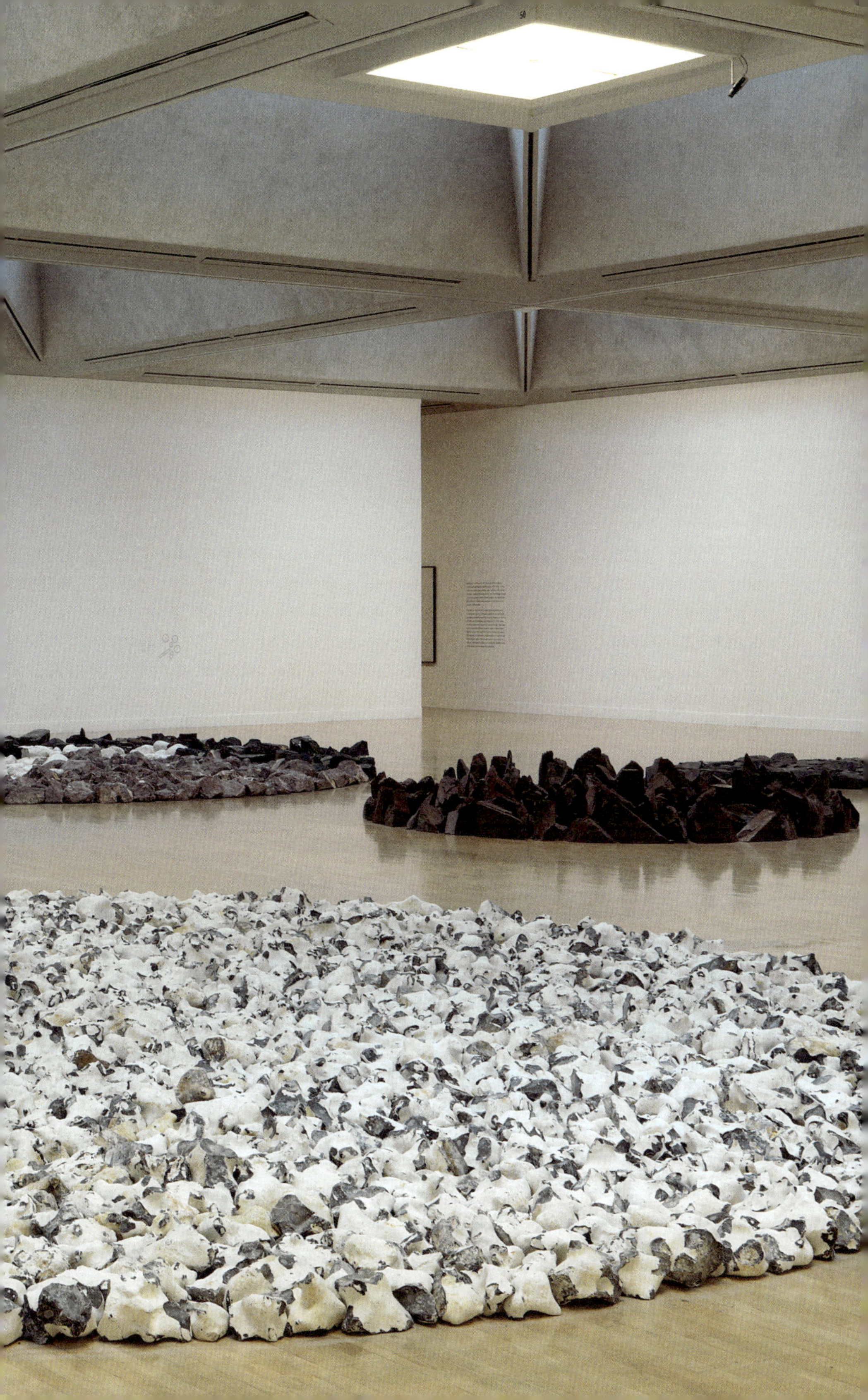

spare and informative. They work as formal arrangements of symbols, maps and words. Other pieces are photographs, each a moment in time with the text describing the walk, the sculpture or intervention, as well as time. The occasional use of colour is curiously jarring, the more typical use of black-and-white photography (no technical details are given) silvery in tone and peculiarly soothing.

One thing leads to another Everything is connected (2007) is a photograph of the Cairngorm Mountains overlaid with a written description of a sequence of things, from rainclouds to rainbow. This particular image and text is not at Tate but is published as a double spread in the catalogue which contains a significant number of works not on view, and does not include the site-specific wall pieces or the installations of the sculptures.[1] The catalogue shows work from 1966 to 2008, the exhibition to 2009. A separate gallery is devoted to a specialist exhibition of Long publications, from invitation cards to posters and books by (not on) the artist.

All this exemplifies one of the fascinating paradoxes of Long's oeuvre. An original text piece, a captioned photograph and, certainly, a large sculpture can probably only be afforded by major institutions and rich private collectors. The big pieces have to be seen in reality to be appreciated, for their relation to human scale, their textures and physicality being sometimes overwhelming. The highly legible yet rather touchingly quirky handwriting of the earliest pieces also needs to be seen. Yet many of the printed text pieces and captioned photographs are readily enjoyed in a myriad publications and are often available at modest cost. This means much of his work is accessible in book or pamphlet form, easily enjoyed domestically. He is the most democratic of artists, permitting us to be armchair travellers in a new definition of the relationship of the viewer to art.

Richard Long has vehemently denied being a romantic, suggesting if anything he might be a classicist. He has referred to path-making and mark-leaving as ancient activities, and although he has been labelled a Conceptual artist and has been included in anthologies of Land art, in most respects he is none of these. People do not make pilgrimages to see his work in situ; rather it comes to us, in publications often at low cost, and in exhibitions and public collections, in the heart of cities. His practice has many provocative contradictions. But above all else his work not only makes us think but is visually captivating, in both word and image.

The Burlington Magazine, vol.CLI, no.1277, August 2009, pp.557–58.

1 Clarrie Wallis (ed), *Heaven and Earth*, exh. cat., Tate Publishing, London, 2009.

A CLOUDLESS WALK

AN EASTWARD WALK OF 121 MILES IN 3½ DAYS
FROM THE MOUTH OF THE LOIRE TO THE FIRST CLOUD

FRANCE 1995

BEN TUFNELL

Foot Steps/Full Circle

When we die, the wind blows away our footprints,
and that is the end of us.

Richard Long first came to Africa in July 1969, coincidentally flying to Nairobi on the night of the first moon landing. He travelled there with his girlfriend Denise Johnston, intending to get married on the equator, each of them standing in a different hemisphere, and to make 'the highest sculpture in the world' on the summit of Kilimanjaro.

Long climbed the mountain and made his work, a cross on the summit stones made from black fabric, carried up in the manner of a prayer flag. He took a grainy photograph of it that was printed as a postcard work by the Konrad Fischer Galerie in Dusseldorf later that year. He subsequently also made a photowork, *Climbing Kilimanjaro 1969* (1969) which juxtaposed an aerial image of an ancient English hill figure, the Long Man of Wilmington, with a photograph of the artist taken during the ascent, thereby connecting distant times, places and cultures. While walking to Loitokitok, the town at the foot of the mountain, Long made *Two Lines Walked Through Dust-Covered Grass By The Roadside* (1969) while waiting two days for some lions to move on ahead of him. He also made a number of other works in the region of the Rift Valley, including *Line Dance* (1969) on the equator, boot-heel lines on the salt margins of Lake Naivasha, and a sculpture of concentric triangles inscribed into a dusty plain near Lake Turkana (documentation of which is now in the Museum Abteiberg in Mönchengladbach).

It is interesting that Long chose Kenya and Tanzania as the destination of his first big overseas trip. He was only 23 and while he had exhibited in Germany, Switzerland, Italy and in New York in the previous two years, he would not travel further afield, outside of the so-called Western world, to South America, until the following year. No doubt, Kilimanjaro, the highest mountain in Africa but relatively easy to walk up, was a powerful lure, but so too perhaps was the irreducible idea of Africa: the vast landscapes, the nomadic peoples, the rich culture of the Masai, and the epic wildlife. Long would later say the land sometimes seemed 'a vision of pre-human history' and the local people 'at one with nature'.

In the following years Long made many walks and works throughout the continent, visiting Malawi and Zambia in 1978, the Atlas Mountains in Morocco in 1979, the Haggar Desert in the Sahara in 1988 and Egypt and Niger in 2006, amongst other places. Much of the continent is ideal working territory for Long for it is empty, flat, stony terrain that he covets–open landscapes with clear, distant vistas, where one might walk unimpeded in a straight line. Deserts, then, above all else. In 2004 Long received an invitation to South Africa from Lex Petousis, who offered him time and access on and around his property in the region of Guarrie Berg in the Karoo, a vast semi-desert that was once home to the Khoi and the Bushmen, the last of the southern African Stone Age peoples. Long made a 15-day overlapping and meandering walk (as opposed to a linear walk from one place to another) centred on a borehole from where he was able to get water. He worked opportunistically, making improvised works in response to the landscape and natural phenomena such as a flash flood (which covered the plain on which he was walking to the depth of his knees), standing a group of stones upright under a clear sky (*Stones and Stars*, (2004)), and marking out sculptures in stones on the earth or along a path (*Karoo Crossing* and *Karoo Line*, (both 2004)).

In early 2011 Long returned to South Africa to spend an extended period at the Nirox Foundation in Gauteng Province, in the World Heritage region known as the Cradle of Humankind. The Cradle, an expanse of highveld grassland and mixed woodland, currently occupies 47,000 hectares and contains a complex of limestone caves, including the Sterkfontein Caves, where the 2.3-million-year-old fossil Australopithecus Africanus (nicknamed 'Mrs Ples') was found in 1947. It is an area of enormous scientific import. The name Cradle of Humankind reflects the fact that the site has produced a large number of, as well as some of the oldest, hominid fossils ever found, some dating back as far as 3.5 million years ago. It is a location associated with man's first faltering steps as a biped, the possible site of the giant evolutionary leap that produced man the walker.

At Nirox, Long had use of a studio space and was able to complete two stone sculptures, *Humankind Circle* (2011) and *Lightning Stones Line* (2011), using materials identified on his walks, as well as *Standing Stone Circle* (2011), which remains as a permanent installation in the landscape. The historic nature of the site and the particular character of the terrain were to influence the work Long would make there.

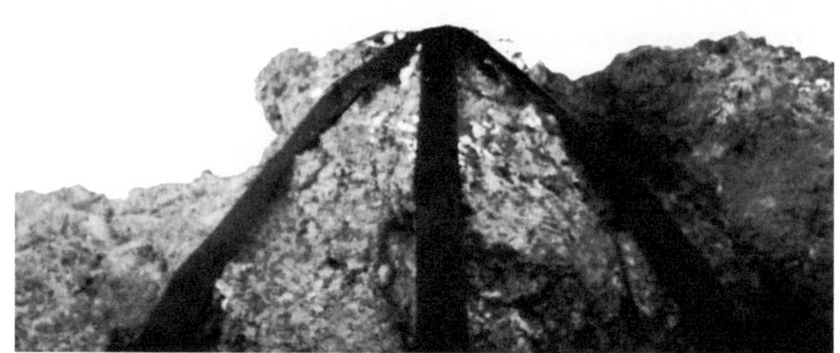

Sculpture on Mount Kilimanjaro 19,340 FT (5895 M) 1969

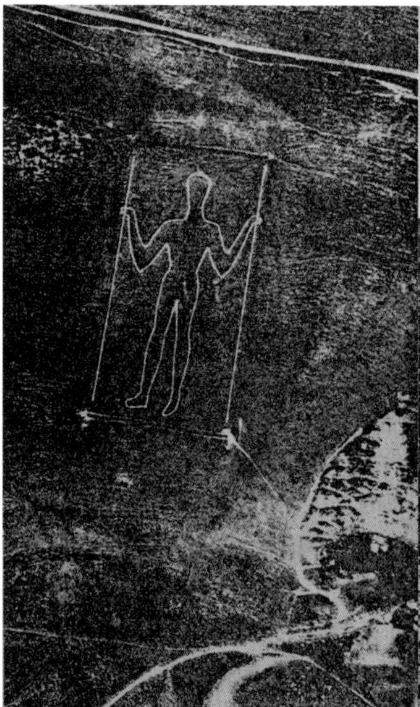

HILL FIGURE ENGLAND 600

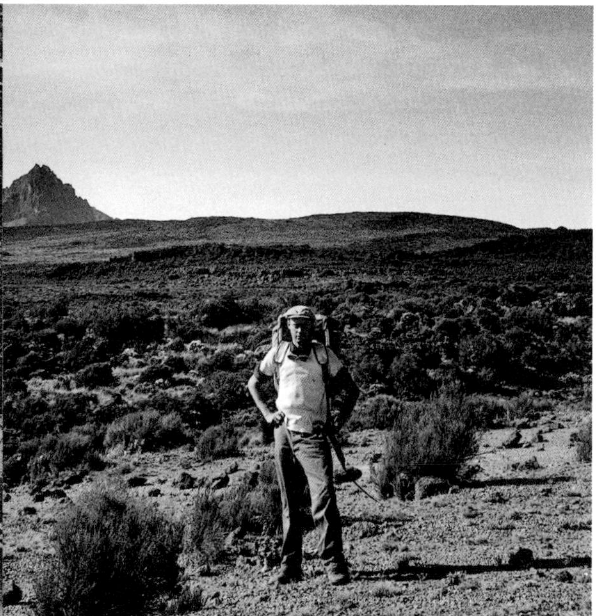

CLIMBING MT. KILIMANJARO AFRICA 1969

Here the landscape – open highveld, divided up into large private estates – meant that he was unable to make an extended walk. Instead, he made a series of 60 short walks, radiating out from a spring on the Foundation like the spokes of a wheel. On each walk he made a single footprint in mud or dirt, *Humankind Footprint Dispersal* (2011). He was also able to visit, with the paleontologist Professor Lee Berger, the site of his most important fossil find – of a nearly complete early hominid – in a rocky depression that he had named Malapa.

Long's works on the highveld engage with the (pre)history that distinguishes this particular landscape. They are based on an extended meditation on the meaning and implication of that place, its profound human significance. They use Long's characteristic means – observation, marking, measuring – and his pared down methodology of walk, gesture, sculpture, text and photograph – to relate profound and distant evolutionary developments to the here and now.

Footprints have been a recurring motif in Long's works since the late 1960s. In fact, footprints have often been his medium. Long's indexical and iconic work, *A Line Made by Walking* (1967), is a piece in which the work is made by footsteps but in which the individual prints are not visible, rather flattening the grass to reflect the sunlight, to make a line marked on the landscape. However, two key early works use actual footprints. In *A Line the Length of a Straight Walk from the Bottom to the Top of Silbury Hill* (1970), and *A Line the Length of a Straight Walk from the Bottom to the Top of Glastonbury Tor* (1973), a line of muddy footprints inscribes a spiral onto the floor of the gallery.

Long returned to the theme in the 1980s, making the print *Africa Footprints* (1986) for a charity project to aid African famine victims. In this piece Long's muddy footprints mark out the shape of the continent. The print evokes the fact that walking is still the principal means of travel in much of Africa, and mud a ubiquitous building material. Yet it also points towards the paleo-anthropological theories addressed in the Nirox works, the notion that this is the place from where the first humans dispersed on foot to populate the world.

The footprint is the basic unit of human measurement. The basic measure of locomotion. But it is also a symbol of connectivity, of rootedness: as in, 'to have one's feet planted firmly on the ground'. We are firm-footed. Fleet of foot. We put our best foot forward. Footsure, we become footsore. Sometimes we put our foot in it. The footprint also evokes the idea of physical contact which is central to Long's work, in the sense that his work addresses the idea of an artist 'touching the earth'.

But above all, a footprint is an archetypal symbol of human presence. In Daniel Defoe's *Robinson Crusoe* (1719), it is a footprint in the sand that shows the castaway that he is not alone. The footprint is a message from the past to the present that declares, a human being passed this way.

Richard Long: Karoo Highveld – Works from South Africa, exh. cat., Iziko South African National Gallery, Cape Town and Haunch of Venison, London, 2011, n.p.

ALISTAIR RIDER

The 'Curve Over the Crest of the Hill': Carl Andre and Richard Long

It might appear counterintuitive nowadays to pair the American Minimalist sculptor Carl Andre with the British Land artist Richard Long, since their differing nationalities have meant that they have come to be discussed within significantly distinct contexts and agendas. Yet that was not always the case, and there was a period, at least during the 1970s, when it was possible to envisage both artists as guided by shared interests and common themes.

The most explicit pairing of Andre and Long is to be found in Lucy R Lippard's 1983 publication, *Overlay*, in which she emphasises that both are artists who remain inspired by the prehistoric landscape of south-west England.[1] The basis of her argument is very much in accordance with the themes of her book. In her introduction Lippard explains that the catalyst for *Overlay* had been a year spent 'on an isolated farm in southern England' in which she had lived in proximity to numerous prehistoric sites. These places had provoked her to explore the deep associations between contemporary art and the archaic; as she puts it, it was 'an overlay of my concern with new art on my fascination with these very ancient sites'.[2] A layering of the contemporary with the ancient is further corroborated by the book's illustrations, which intersperse reproductions of work by current artists with evocative photographs of prehistoric monuments, the majority of which are situated within the British Isles. Thus, by the time readers approach the chapter in which she describes the work of Andre and Long, they are more than sufficiently primed to embrace the predominantly pastoral and agrarian presentation of Andre's sculpture, and to accede that this is work that is decidedly attuned to qualities of the English countryside. Andre's major artistic contribution, we learn, was to produce a kind of low-lying, segmented sculpture, often produced directly in a landscape, which provoked viewers to walk along its length, just as they might pass along a road.[3] From here, it is only a small step for Lippard to point out that unlike North America's spaces, the English countryside is eminently conducive to walking, and that it is this quality that defines the ethos of Richard Long's art. Lippard describes how Long's 'breakthrough' had been to present photographic documentation of a walk he had undertaken in 1969 across Dartmoor in Devon as a sculpture in its own right.[4] Furthermore, Lippard emphasises the extent to which Long's work is attuned to the ancientness of landscape. 'A walk is just one layer', Long is quoted as saying, 'laid upon thousands of other layers of human and geographic history on the surface of the land.'[5]

The tangle of cultural and national assumptions that surround the terms *walking*, *ancientness* and *landscape*, invoked in this context, clearly deserve to be negotiated carefully. Moreover, we may wish to question the degree to which Lippard's pairing of Andre and Long, elegant and provocative though it is, overemphasises the premodern orientation of their work at the expense of considering how much their outlook might be shaped by shared, late twentieth-century perspectives. Undoubtedly, both artists do share a fascination with the prehistoric, and Lippard's reading is a timely reminder of this point. In this case, how might we attend to their shared interests without ignoring the fact that their outlook is also decidedly modern and clearly attuned to the larger preoccupations of the transatlantic art world of the late 1960s and 1970s?

Posing this question will invariably raise issues relating to the ways in which national identity is figured in relation to both artists' work, but this is not the primary focus of my account here. Instead, I am interested in exploring the ways in which both artists invoke prehistory in order to define their sculpture, and how these references can help cast new light on some of the ambiguities and internal tensions within their respective practices. To examine some of these issues, I shall be contrasting Long's and Andre's investment in ancient sites in England with those of an earlier generation of British sculptors.

Andre met Long in 1968; they have remained in contact ever since, and have spoken openly of their mutual respect for one another's work. Of course, it should be emphasised that their compliments are truly complementary, in that their art has always remained sufficiently different for them to feel that their work does not encroach too fiercely on the other's territory. Long, for instance, once claimed that he admires Andre's sculpture yet would hate to work with prefabricated, industrial materials, while Andre has said that he envies Long's 'genius at ordering nooks and crannies of the natural world into works of art', but also stresses that he prefers to work with materials shaped largely by humans. 'You might say', he adds, 'I am the Richard Long of the vacant lot and the scrap heap.'[6]

What both Long and Andre might be said to recognise in one another's work is a shared investment in the principle of sculpture as 'placement'. Lippard is right to emphasise that Andre's major contribution to the development of sculpture in the 1960s was to appreciate that three-dimensional art could be made simply by setting units of similarly shaped materials directly on the floor.[7] This way of working releases the artist from having to be concerned with shaping or cutting, or, for that matter, even with assembling things. Instead, the selected particles simply lie where they are positioned and follow the plane of the ground.

Since Long's art is much more oriented towards a notion of landscape than is Andre's, there are of course differences in their art that need to be acknowledged. Long has created considerably more works than has Andre for sites outside museums and exhibition galleries, many of which are ephemeral and emerge, seemingly spontaneously, from his walks. These have largely taken the form of simple marks left on the land, such as a straight line generated by walking up and down repeatedly until a narrow track forms, or an arrangement of stones that are aligned into a small circle, a row, or a cross. Records of these sculptures only exist as photographs exhibited subsequently in galleries, or as reproductions in specially designed publications. However, he has also made sculptures to be shown exclusively indoors, and, like Andre, he too positions separable units – such as stones or pieces of wood – into elementary configurations directly on the ground.

Both artists have also emphasised how important a notion of 'place' is to their art. Long has often spoken, for instance, of the extent to which his art has been generated from specific places and observes that a good work 'is the right thing in the right place at the right time'.[8] Famously, Andre also asserted that a place 'is an area within an environment which has been altered in such a way as to make the general environment more conspicuous'. He understood place to be related 'to both the general qualities of the environment and the particular qualities of the work', such that, to see an artwork from the perspective of place is to recognise how an artist's intervention and the artwork's context are mutually determining.[9] Phrased in these terms, Andre's description is highly abstract, as though a place could be literally anywhere. Yet even by the late 1960s he began to explain what he meant by place by invoking very particular locations, which tended to be decidedly premodern. In 1968, for instance, he told his interviewer that he associated his understanding of place with the Indian burial mounds of Ohio, and shortly afterwards he was aligning his sculpture with Japanese rock gardens.[10] Place also had a profoundly 'Neolithic' quality, he explained to Phyllis Tuchman in an interview from 1970, and on this occasion his principal example was Stonehenge.[11] In the case of Long, however, it seems fair to infer that place is more a resting point on a longer journey. And while Andre's notion of place embraces prehistoric sites only in a generic and holistic way, Long's references to these locations have tended to be considerably more direct, with specific locations being named in titles, and particular features and attributes becoming the focal point for individual works.

Their different approach partly reflects their nationalities and the circumstances in which both artists became familiar with southern England. For Long, born and brought up in Bristol, the Neolithic and Bronze Age sites of Wiltshire, Devon and Dorset were familiar landmarks. He would later tell critics how he would often pass Silbury Hill on the Marlborough Road, while hitchhiking to London.[12] Silbury Hill is the largest Neolithic site in Europe; it is a man-made mound of blocks of chalk and turf, roughly 120 feet tall and 4,500 years old. For Long, places such as these were recognisable objects in a well-known landscape. In fact, Stonehenge itself seems to have felt almost too familiar and well known for him, and he has only referenced it by name in just two works.[13]

Andre, however, was born in Quincy, outside Boston, and first went to England to visit family relations in 1954, at 19. During his stay, his uncle and aunt took him to see a selection of their favourite places in Wales and England, including Salisbury Cathedral and Stonehenge.

The scraped-clean Gothic interior of the cathedral made little impact, but Stonehenge left a lasting impression.[14] I am not certain whether Andre has ever returned, although even if he has, he has never spoken openly of any subsequent trip. So, while Long could invoke these prehistoric sites in the context of his art with a casualness born of familiarity, Andre has tended to summon the name 'Stonehenge' – and with it all the other prehistoric landscapes of southern England – with a fervour that attests mainly to the vividness of a teenager's memory.

What would Andre have seen at Stonehenge in 1954? Certainly in those days the site would have felt markedly more remote than it does today. Passing vehicles were infrequent, and there were no visitors' facilities. Sightseers were free to meander among the stones and seek out the surrounding ditches, burrows and burial sites as much as they liked. It is also important to mention that during the mid-1950s Stonehenge was subjected to extensive excavation and restoration, so the stone circle would have been filled with substantial quantities of archaeologists' paraphernalia. In 1954, the investigation had focused on the inner circle. That year they dug up a number of stones that had become buried beneath the turf, and four years following Andre's visit, they straightened a number of the larger outer 'sarsen' sandstones, and reerected one of the giant trilithons that had collapsed in 1899.[15]

Clearly this was a high-profile undertaking, and it stimulated a renewal of public interest in the monument. Yet it is revealing to contrast the general image of Stonehenge that was generated by these excavations with the memories Andre would later retain from his visit. Consider, for instance, the evocative terms used by RJC Atkinson in his well-known book on the monument from 1956; Atkinson had been one of the principal archaeologists on the project, and his text was widely considered exemplary for the accessibility of its presentation of the archaeology of the site. In his introduction, he writes:

> Of the stones themselves no words of mine can properly describe the subtle varieties of texture and colour, or the uncountable effects of shifting light and shade… At a nearer view, each stone takes on its own individual pattern of colour and texture. Some are almost white… and so hard that even 35 centuries of weathering has not dimmed the irregular patches of polishing executed so laboriously by the original builders. Others are a dull matt grey, streaked and lined… like the grain of some vast stump of a petrified tree; and

> others again are soft, buff or even pink in colour, and deeply eroded into hollows and overhangs in which a man may crouch, the compact curves of his limbs and the rounded thrust of shoulder and hip matching the time-smoothed protuberances of the stone around him.[16]

What is noteworthy about Atkinson's somewhat high-flown description is just how naturally his metaphors help to anthropomorphise the stones. His concern is with the give-and-take between physical weathering and human shaping; his focus glides seamlessly between the rocks' mineralogical texture and their figurative appearance.

It might also be conjectured that Atkinson's approach to the stones is much more in keeping with the terms in which an earlier generation of modernist sculptors embraced the Neolithic past. The preoccupations in this passage are not entirely removed, we might feel, from Henry Moore's *Three Piece Reclining Figure* from the late 1960s, in which the human form seems to be petrified into folds of weathered rock. Or consider Moore's suite of 15 lithographs of Stonehenge from 1972–73, where his depiction of the imposing 22-foot-high sarsen trilithon is titled *Cyclops*, while a detail of a lintel hole is called *Arm and Body*. In a similar vein, we might also be reminded of the sculptures of Barbara Hepworth, whose works have long been affiliated with standing stones, albeit more with Cornwall than Wiltshire. Take, for instance, her *Two Figures, Menhirs* (1964) or *Rock Form (Porthcurno)* (1964), both of which adopt a decidedly anthropomorphised silhouette.[17]

For Moore and Hepworth, along with other artists of their generation, we might speculate that part of the allure of the weathered forms of these Neolithic stones is that they can be approached as shapes that are already abstracted; they are forms void of explicit meanings. They have been shaped by age, yet still can be regarded as suffused with evidence of human intention. Work of this nature plays into the assumption that a stone set into the ground and standing upright is an archetypal form of mark-making. Furthermore, invoking the historicity of ancient, standing stones is also a means of relaying attention from the vicissitudes of making sculpture in contemporary times. A work such as Hepworth's bronze *Figure for Landscape* (1959–60) contains its own base, which means that in practical terms there is no reason for it to be site specific. Potentially, it could be set down anywhere – in a gallery, or in a museum's sculpture garden, or even atop a hill. Yet the form and title of the sculpture encourage viewers to recognise in the proportions the monumentality of a monolith, and thus to conjure into existence the idea of an environing and complementary landscape, and this in spite of its modern-day placelessness. In other words, the sculpture projects an impression of magnitude and location that is essentially metaphorical.

It goes without saying that not all emerging artists in the 1960s were drawn to Neolithic sites for the same reasons. For one, the upright form of the human figure ceased to be the defining point of reference for sculptors, on both sides of the Atlantic. As many critics have emphasised, there is in Andre's work in particular a clear shift away from the vertical to the horizontal plane. In the case of his metal ground-based sculptures, for instance, the works may indeed possess distinct boundaries, yet because they remain at the level of the viewers' feet, they never come across as obstacles. The edges of these sculptures function more as thresholds, designed to articulate the movements of the viewer, rather than to act as barriers to confine and restrict.

This shift in orientation is reflected in the way Andre (and Long, for that matter) approached prehistoric locations. For both of them there was a clear concern with the larger topographies, and the extent to which monuments such as Stonehenge form an integral component of a much larger series of interlocking points and vistas that incorporate an entire landscape. A small booklet by Long from 1978 explicitly illustrates this shift in focus; it is titled *A Hundred Stones* (1977). Long photographed the various monoliths he passed en route, but it is the journey between them that is the focus of the work, not the stones themselves. Others of their generation were similarly not interested in the monoliths themselves. In an unpublished essay from 1966 or 1967, Robert Smithson commented, for instance, that when Robert Morris had visited Stonehenge, he had not been drawn to the huge trilithons at the centre of the monument, but to 'the mound-like fringes'.[18]

At a symposium in the United States in February 1969 Long famously articulated his interest in the wider landscape, explaining that: 'England is covered in huge mounds and converted hills... most of England has had its shape changed – practically the whole place, because it has been ploughed over the centuries – rounded off.'[19] Andre made a similar statement in an interview in December 1968, when he confessed that: 'one of the great influences on the course of my own development was the English countryside... which is one vast earthwork.'[20] The ramifications of their shared willingness to regard the entire topography of southern England as a single sculpture should not be underestimated. In fact, Andre was nothing but explicit about this: 'England in 1954 presented me with a countryside that was in fact a collective sculpture worked on over more than 3000 years.'[21]

This reorientation of sculpture from the vertical to the horizontal, and the concomitant interest in larger topographies that we see in artists emerging in the 1960s, clearly attests to a changed sense of scale. A shape representative of an upright figure registers either as monumental or miniature, depending on the relationship of its proportions to its surroundings, and to the size of the viewer. Yet a sculpture that is horizontally oriented is not necessarily bounded by such categories. In fact, it was partly for this reason that Clement Greenberg found Andre's work unsatisfactory. He pointed out that because Andre's sculptures are made up of separable units, he could not see how they had any sense of proportion.[22] Indeed, Andre's sculptures do certainly have the potential to continue extensively, or to be extremely short, and such decisions are frequently determined by purely practical factors, such as the amount of available material or the size of the space in which he is working. Andre has always been open about this. More to the point, no sculpture of his is intended to project a scale distinct from what it is, however large or small it might be.

The same is also true of many of Long's pieces. His *Walking a Line in Peru*, a work from 1972, consists of an almost perfectly straight path formed by the artist across a flat valley floor. From the photograph, which now stands as representative of the sculpture, the trajectory produced by Long's footprints appears to extend for several miles, and were it not for the elevated perspective and the good visibility, the line could never be depicted within a single frame at all. Yet the visible evidence of Long's movements cannot be described as either monumental or minute because the line simply has no scale. It is merely a literal dimension, just as the mountains in the distance and shallow streams in the foreground have measurable lengths and specific proportions.

However, one or two of Long's very early works have a rather more complicated relationship to scale. This is partly to do with the fact that he seemed concerned with the question of how a substantial terrain, such as an entire landscape, might be apprehended and represented within a single sculpture. Interestingly, the issue comes to the fore as soon as he invokes prehistoric sites in relation to his work. This first occurs in 1969 with an outdoor sculpture that he made in conjunction with his exhibition in Manhattan at John Gibson Gallery. Long dug up a small rectangle of turf in Battery Park, scooping out the earth and heaping it up into a slight mound.[23] Later it formed a grassy hump. In terms of its dimensions, it was only a few feet long, but this small intervention was intended to invoke the memory of a site vastly more substantial. The announcement card for the exhibition featured an aerial photograph of the grassy ramparts of the Bronze Age fort of Maiden Castle in Dorset, and it is clear that the young artist wanted visitors to draw an analogy between this site and his own earthwork. But the physical size of the ancient site literally dwarfs the actual dimensions of Long's small work; with its three tiers of ditches and rings, Maiden Castle is the largest hill fortification in Europe. Here, Long invokes a prehistoric site in quite a different way from an artist such as Hepworth. He establishes his association through synecdoche; he is claiming that the material he is using links him to this ancient site. Yet the difference between the extremely large and the disproportionately small is hard to overlook and seems to attest to a certain awkwardness regarding the matter of scale. It is almost as though there is no manageably sized, clear middle ground that Long feels his sculptures can happily occupy.

Simon Dell has pointed out recently just how many artists were openly exploring uncertainties of scale toward the end of the 1960s.[24] Robert Smithson is perhaps exemplary in this regard, and Dell notes that Smithson was never one to accede to the pre-given dimensions of an object. For him, scale was a means of undoing preconceptions about the actualities of perception, a theme he explored to great effect in his 'Non-Sites' from 1968.[25] Dell reads Smithson's preoccupation with scale in relation to Jack Burnham's extensive discussion of the subject in his 1968 publication, *Beyond Modern Sculpture*.[26] Burnham's argument was that formalist approaches to works of art had come under such pressure in recent years because artists were increasingly responding to new advances in science. As a result of technical innovations in new media, communication and perception often took place below the threshold of the visible, such that visual comprehension could no longer be said to operate always in self-evident or transparent ways.[27] Burnham also felt that 'continued technological exploitation of materials', both organic and inorganic, meant that ultimately 'no

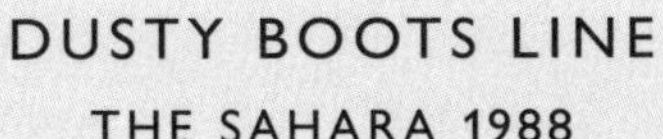

DUSTY BOOTS LINE

THE SAHARA 1988

scale is within range'. In his mind, the 'present fluctuations between miniaturisation and giantism' exemplified by much contemporary sculpture 'seems to reflect that apprehension'.[28] This may well be little more than provocative speculation on Burnham's part, yet it strikes me that the subject is far from irrelevant when it comes to evaluating some of the early works by Richard Long.

My point is that when artists such as Long and Andre invoke the prehistoric in relation to their art, we need to remain vigilant to the ways in which their perspective might also be informed by other contemporary agendas. In fact, we might suggest that what remains so distinctive about their practices is the degree to which a thoroughly modernist idiom rubs up against prehistoric and premodern references. Neither Andre nor Long draws attention to the potential divergences this may cause, yet arguably both their practices are premised on conflicting orientations.

There are a number of ways in which we might theorise this disjuncture, yet I want to do so here by invoking a short prose essay by the British modernist poet JH Prynne. I do not want to infer that there was any particular connection between his writings and the 1960s British art world; however, Prynne's 1968 essay 'A Note on Metal' could be considered a particularly helpful resource for speculating about how Neolithic sites come to signify in the ways they do for both Long and Andre.[29]

Let me provide a swift, abbreviated account of Prynne's argument. In four pages, plus notes, he provides a sketch of what is at stake when a prehistoric society moves from an investment in stone to one that values and esteems metal. A culture invested in stone, Prynne suggests, attests primarily to an economy of physical power. The bluestones in the inner circle at Stonehenge, which were quarried from the Preseli Mountains in Wales 125 miles away, along with the sarsen sandstones from the Marlborough plains 20 miles distant, had to be dragged to this spot using immeasurable quantities of physical exertion. This is why the stones invoke importance and status. Their significance is synonymous with their physical weight, and their embeddedness at this particular site.

Yet with the advent of metal, Prynne explains, weight and substance are displaced by other qualities that are more portable, such as brightness, hardness, or the sharpness of a cutting edge. Indeed, it is thanks to the discovery of metals that notions of abstract and hierarchical values can be developed. Gradually, significance becomes extractable from weight, and can be carried about in metonymic units; metallurgy, in other words, enables a notion to be advanced that value is 'essential'. Slowly, Prynne notes, this leads to the emergence for the first time of a metal currency. Eventually even metallic substance can be displaced entirely by the principle of mere numerical quanta, as it is in subsequent societies.

However, this is only half of the argument, because Prynne is equally insistent that this trajectory does not simply proceed uniformly. It is the seeming insubstantiality of modern, numerical economies that makes the reassuring solidity and weight of stone appear as an alternative source of value, enabling it to affirm, for instance, distinct memorialising responsibilities.

We need to appreciate, of course, that Prynne's essay is no more intended as archaeological history than 'Totem and Taboo' is meant to be a piece of academically researched anthropology. Literary professionals have tended to regard Prynne's essay as a philological note on terms that remain central to political or moral critique, a text that is secreted – typically for Prynne – in an exacting and very particular diction.[30]

However, Prynne's account is particularly productive for approaching the kind of mixed economy of stone and metal invoked in the work of Carl Andre, for instance. It keeps us alert to the competing terms in which his sculptures generate significance. From around 1967 onward, Andre became increasingly preoccupied with metals, yet he uses this material in a fashion that runs counter to the value it typically assumes within the larger economy. For his exhibition at the Dwan Gallery in December 1967, for example, Andre laid out over the floor of the gallery three sculptures, each made up from 144 plates of metal, a quarter of an inch thick and a foot square. In their dimensions they were identical, but they were each made from one of three different metals – aluminium, steel and zinc. The arrangement invariably encouraged viewers to compare the metals' qualities – to recognise the difference between the white sheen of the zinc and the soft, silvery qualities of the aluminium, and so on.

Yet Andre was also keen to emphasise that the distinctions between the three sculptures extended far beyond the merely perceptual. The announcement poster for the exhibition consisted of a periodic table of the elements, drawn up in the artist's neat hand, with the three metals highlighted in slightly thicker pen. We might suggest that the visual differences in appearance between the works are further consolidated and rendered absolute by this chart of atomic differences. As such, these metals become samples; they are ambassadors for pure, abstracted qualities that are best represented in the guise of a grid of compartmentalised numerical values. Essentially, that is why Andre was able to deploy steel plates in place of the element iron, as he does in *144 Steel Square* (1967). By the 1960s, iron had long since become obsolete as a manufacturing material and was barely available as a commodity. It had been replaced by the alloy steel. In that sense, steel serves as a stand-in for iron, just as the silver alloy used for the minting of 25-cent coins in the United States was replaced in 1964 with the much cheaper metal, cupronickel.

In claiming that Andre's metals act as samples of elements, we might be encouraged to assume that one set of, say, zinc plates is as good as any other, just as two ten-cent coins are of precisely equal worth. Or, we might be led to believe that the sculpture would still remain the sculpture were the metal units to be arranged in a completely different order, or merely heaped in the corner. Yet that is not the case. For Andre, sculpture is never merely conceptual; it has to be arranged in the designated formation, and the materials are not replaceable. Everything about his work may well imply that the units might be exchanged, or that the sculptures might be replicated effortlessly, but Andre has never embraced such working practices. Indeed, we might suggest that one of the means by which he has emphasised the fixedness of his selected arrangements is by invoking a notion of 'place', and of sculpture as 'place-generating'.

In 1968, Andre compared his work very provocatively to that of the artist Michael Heizer, who at the time was positioning multi-tonne boulders in crisply cut rectangular trenches in desert locations in the south-west. Andre believed that what Heizer was doing was essentially extending a modernist sensibility into a non-modernist context; he, in his words, was taking a 'nonmodernist sensibility, the archaic, earth-working sensibility and [bringing] it into the modernist context'.[31] Such a claim might appear to make little sense; after all, his squares of symmetrically cut metal, laid out on the gallery floor, are hard to envisage as having anything to do with an earthworking, archaic sensibility. Yet his statement does help reorient a viewer's attention away from the otherwise eminently modern, gridlike and rectilinear format of the presentation. It allows us to attend instead to a phenomenology of placement, and to the way the work is attuned to its surroundings. We might suggest that placing industrially sourced metal sheets flat down on the floor is partly a means of naturalising them, of invoking a sense that they always have been there, just as Stonehenge has stood on the Wiltshire plains for as long as there has been historical memory.

Very little attention has been given to the ways in which Andre successfully mobilises his interest in metals, metallurgy and the periodic table, with what we might call a more archaic, stone-age affinity for placement, such that many of his sculptures appear to equivocate between an orientation towards the present and a leaning into the far distant past. In 1975, for instance, Andre laid a sheet of aluminium on a stream bed beneath a bridge, allowing the rippling water to cake it in moss and turn its shiny surface to a furry, milk-white oxide.[32] Even better known is a work Andre made in 1969 consisting of a square arrangement of six different metals, which is intended to lie open to the elements and corrode gracefully. It is titled *Weathering Piece* (1970).[33]

Long's early works could also be said to generate meaning in potentially conflicting ways. To indicate how, I want to return to the issue of the strange, very distinctive dimensions he adopts in his works. Take, for instance, his exhibition at the Dwan Gallery in 1970. The elongated invitation card for the exhibition featured two black-and-white photographs set adjacent to one another. On the right-hand side there is a close-up of what appears to be the gentle grassy undulations of a ditch that might easily be read as some form of archaeological remain: a trace of prehistory in a modern-day field. Certainly, this would tie in with the image on the left, which is a snapshot of Silbury Hill. Beneath this picture is a short text – a piece of local folklore, or a mythological explanation as to why the hill ended up just here, and nowhere else:

> The townsfolk of Marlborough and Devizes were always at loggerheads. Marlborough sought revenge by using the services of the devil, who offered to wipe out Devizes by dropping a hill on the town. This threat was heard by St John who in due course warned Devizes, the townsfolk of which sent the biggest liar… to put the devil off. With a sack filled with old clothes and shoes he met the devil near Beckhampton, and there asked him the time. Old Nick

> was tired of carrying the hill, and asked… how far to Devizes. The old man said that he would never get there that night… as he had left Devizes as a young man and had indeed worn out the clothes and boots he was carrying. Old Nick was incredulous, but the old man stuck to his story, and fooled the devil into believing it. Flinging the hill down from his shoulders the devil departed in a flash of lightning. Devizes is still there, the hill at Silbury is for all to see, so the tale must be true.

Long may have included this little tale for a variety of reasons, not least for the piquant local colour it provides. However, we might also regard this as an account of place, distance and scale becoming truly confounded. Moreover, this is also a narrative that contends with the seemingly superhuman exertions that brought Silbury Hill into being. The devil truly is in the details, for this ancient hill has significance for us in our present times largely because of its uniqueness. Its substantiality and placement are synonymous with what it is. Yet this is precisely what Long undoes; he brings the dimensions of Silbury Hill with him to New York's West Fifty-seventh Street and paces out in muddy footprints over the brown carpet a work he calls *A Line the Length of a Straight Walk from the Bottom to the Top of Silbury Hill* (1970). Weight and scale are not represented in the sculpture itself; in fact, there is little that is graspable and tangible here, other than the precise distance, present through the indexical trace of Long's footprints, stamping out their course, round and round in a windowless New York gallery. With the course curled up in this way, it becomes increasingly difficult for a viewer to evaluate the proportions. The sculpture provokes viewers to envisage the artist, traipsing up the steep banks of an artificial hill on a different continent, counting off his steps. We might think of this work, then, as an attempt by Long to retain a hold on the nonsymbolic signifying power of materiality and place, yet he is only able to accomplish this through their displacement.

My aim has been to highlight some of the contradictory ways in which meaning is conveyed in the work of Long and Andre, as a way of indicating how the modern and prehistoric investments in both artists do not necessarily complement one another as might be assumed from reading Lippard's account in *Overlay*. That said, we might approach Lippard's own book as a publication in which the effort to draw ancient sites into present life only ultimately accentuates the disconnected, displaced nature of contemporary living. As mentioned earlier, the catalyst for *Overlay* had been a year spent on a farm in rural Devon, but as she explains on the opening page, the impetus for her thinking had been more precise than that. It had occurred one day when she was out walking the dog on the moors near the farm. She had been near the upper reaches of the River Plym, on Dartmoor, when she stumbled over the edge of a set of prehistoric stones known locally as the Trowlesworthy Group. New to the site, she had looked back, she writes, and had seen these ancient markers disappearing in 'a curve over the crest of the hill'.[34] For her, there was something in the trajectory of the line that had reminded her of a contemporary sculpture she had seen and reviewed just months earlier in Upstate New York. The work, we learn later in the book, was Carl Andre's *Secant* from 1977, which had been installed in the grounds of Nassau County Art Museum.[35]

Invariably, if we compare illustrations of *Secant* and the Trowlesworthy Group, then the differences look rather more substantial than their similarities. Yet Lippard, along with Andre, and arguably Long as well, partook of a mind-set in which it was possible to conflate a concatenation of machine-cut lumber hugging the incline of a grassy slope with an avenue of prehistoric stones on Dartmoor. Geographic specificity melts and blurs. What replaces it, however, is not similitude, but a distinctively particular and generic sensibility – which we might describe as a 'neolithic' sensitivity towards place. We might speculate that part of the allure of Andre's sculpture was that it appears to summon a sense of a distinct location, and in so doing provides a certain touchstone for a viewer. The sculpture, we might infer, renders the small grassy dell in which it was installed rather more precious and necessary than it otherwise might have seemed. Construed in these terms, 'place' may well be a decidedly modern phenomenon, yet, as with all good myths, its allure largely stems from the conviction that it is as old as the hills.

Anglo-American Exchange in Postwar Sculpture, 1945–1975, Getty Publications, Los Angeles, 2011, pp.113–147.

1 Lucy R Lippard, *Overlay: Contemporary Art and the Art of Prehistory*, Pantheon Books, New York, 1983.

2 *Ibid.*, p.1.

3 *Ibid.*, p.125. Lippard quotes Andre from his interview with Phyllis Tuchman in 1970: 'My idea of a piece of sculpture is a road', he explains. 'That is, a road doesn't reveal itself at any particular point or from any particular point. Roads appear and disappear... We don't have a single point of view for a road at all, except a moving one, moving along it.' See Phyllis Tuchman, 'An Interview with Carl Andre,' *Artforum* 8, no.10, June 1970, p.57.

4 Lippard, *op.cit.*, p.126. Lippard is possibly referring here to the series of photographs and documents which had been included in the catalogue *Fernsehausstellung Land Art*, edited by Gerry Schum and Ursula Schum-Wevers, Fernsehgalerie, Hannover, 1969. Initially, however, Long had conceived the documentation for the walk, which was titled *Walking a Straight 10 Mile Line Forward and Back Shooting Every Half Mile. (Dartmoor England, January 1969)* (1969) as a short television film, commissioned by Gerry Schum (16mm film, 6:03 min). For an account of this work, see Ulrike Groos, Barbara Hess and Ursula Wevers (eds), *Ready to Shoot: Fernsehgalerie Gerry Schum*, exhibition catalogue, Kunsthalle Dusseldorf, Dusseldorf, 2004, pp.74–77 and 140–41.

5 Lippard, *op.cit.*, p.129.

6 Richard Long, 'Interview with Martina Giezen (1985–86)', in Ben Tufnell (ed), *Richard Long: Selected Statements and Interviews*, Haunch of Venison, London, 2007, p.90. Carl Andre, 'Interview with Tim Marlow,' *Tate Magazine*, summer 1996, p.38.

7 Lippard, *op.cit.*, p.125.

8 Richard Long, *Five, six, pick up sticks Seven, eight, lay them straight* in RH Fuchs, *Richard Long*, exh. cat., Solomon R Guggenheim Museum, New York, and Thames & Hudson, London, 1986, p.236.

9 Carl Andre, 'Symposium at Windham College,' in Lucy Lippard, *Six Years: The Dematerialization of the Art Object*, University of California Press, Berkeley, Los Angeles and London, 1997, p.47.

10 Willoughby Sharp, 'Carl Andre,' *Avalanche*, no.1, fall 1970, p.20. The interview took place on 10 December, 1968. See also 'Taped Interview with Carl Andre, May 15', 1970, in James Meyer (ed), Carl Andre, *Cuts: Texts 1959–2004*, The MIT Press, Cambridge, MA., 2005, p.116.

11 Tuchman, 'Interview with Carl Andre,' p.20.

12 See, for instance, Fuchs, *Richard Long*, p.71.

13 Long began walks that started at Stonehenge in 1972 and 1999. The first he described in a short text: 'On a Midsummer's Day / A Westward Walk / From Stonehenge at Sunrise / To Glastonbury by Sunset / Forty Five Miles Following the Day.' The second he described thus: 'Walking to a Solar Eclipse / Starting from Stonehenge / A Walk of 235 Miles / Ending on a Cornish Hilltop / At a Total Eclipse of the Sun.'

14 See the television documentary on Carl Andre, Mark James (dir), Raymond Baxter (ed), *Upholding the Bricks*, Mark James Productions, Channel 4, 2 April 1991.

15 See KE Walker, 'Previous Work and Methods', in Rosamund MJ Cleal, R Montague and KE Walker (eds), *Stonehenge in its Landscape: Twentieth-century excavations*, English Heritage, London, 1995, pp.15–17.

16 RJC Atkinson, *Stonehenge*, Hamish Hamilton, London, 1956, pp.2–3.

17 For a discussion of Hepworth's interest in prehistoric sires, see Andrew Causey, 'Barbara Hepworth, Prehistory and the Cornish Landscape,' *Sculpture Journal* 17, no.2, 2008, pp.9–22.
18 Robert Morris, quoted by Robert Smithson, in 'The Artist as Site-Seer; or, A Dimorphic Essay' (1966–67), in Jack Flam (ed), *Robert Smithson: The Collected Writings*, University of California Press, Berkeley, 1996, p.340.
19 Richard Long, 'Earth: Symposium at White Museum, Cornell University', February 1969, *ibid.*, p.182.
20 Andre added that, in contrast, 'in America there has been a lot of slash and burn, slash and cut, there have been a lot of scars but very little cultivation'. See Sharp, 'Carl Andre,' *Avalanche*, no.1, fall 1970, p.20.
21 Carl Andre, interview with Tim Marlow, *Tate Magazine*, summer 1996, p.38.
22 Clement Greenberg, interview with James Faure Walker, *Artscribe*, no.10, January 1978, p.16.
23 Long's exhibition at the John Gibson Gallery ran from February 22 to March 14, 1969.
24 Simon Dell, 'The Dialectics of Place: The Non-Sites and the Limits of Modernism,' in *On Location: Siting Robert Smithson and His Contemporaries*, Black Dog, London, 2008, pp.12–69.
25 *Ibid.*, pp.28 and 48.
26 Jack Burnham, *Beyond Modern Sculpture: The Effects of Science and Technology on the Sculpture of this Century*, Allen Lane, London, 1968.
27 Dell, *op.cit.*, p.41.
28 Burnham, *op.cit.*, p.153.
29 JH Prynne, 'A Note on Metal' (1968), in *Poems*, Agneau 2, Edinburgh, 1982, pp.125–30.
30 See Ian Patterson, '"the medium itself, rabbit by proxy": Some Thoughts about Reading JH Prynne,' in Denise Riley (ed), *Poets on Writing: Britain, 1970–1991*, Macmillan, Basingstoke and London, 1992, p.235. See also the reading of the essay in CD Blanton, 'Nominal Devolutions: Poetic Substance and the Critique of Political Economy,' *The Yale Journal of Criticism* 13, no.1, 2000, pp.129–57.
31 Sharp, 'Carl Andre,' *Avalanche*, no.1, fall 1970, p.23.
32 The work, called *B-Void*, was temporarily retitled *Water-Void*, and was shown at the group exhibition *Projects in Nature*, at the Merriewold West Farm, Far Hills, New Jersey. The exhibition ran from September to October 1975. For an account of this work, see Jonathan Crary's review, 'Projects in Nature,' *Arts Magazine* 50, no.4, December 1975, p.52.
33 This particular 36-unit sculpture is made up of plates of aluminium, copper, steel, magnesium, lead and zinc, and is now housed in the Kröller-Müller Museum, Otterlo.
34 Lippard, *op.cit.*, p.1.
35 *Ibid.*, p.125. Andre's *Secant* (1977) was part of a group exhibition called *Wood*, which ran at the Nassau County Museum of Fine Arts from May to July 1977. Lippard's review of this work, 'Wood at the Nassau County Museum,' is in *Art in America* 65, no.6, November–December 1977, pp.136–37.

COLIN RENFREW

A 'Lecture' by Richard Long

I very clearly remember the first occasion I encountered Richard Long. It was in the University of Southampton, some years after I went there to follow Barry Cunliffe as Professor of Archaeology in September 1972.

At that time the University of Southampton had an enlightened programme for an Artist in Residence. The artist was Ray Smith, a very talented painter (and sculptor), who later did a wonderful series of portraits of all our family and became a lifelong friend – but that is another story. He had arranged a series of evening lectures by a number of young British sculptors, and it was through his initiative that Jane and I first met and admired the work of several artists, including David Nash, Barry Flanagan and Richard Long.

Richard's 'lecture' was unusual since he did not speak at all, indeed did not initially appear. He was in the projection box at the back of the lecture room, from which was displayed a series of slides of his work. As a background there was a soundtrack, mainly country music, not at high volume, but giving a sense of movement, a pace, to the display of images. I remember specifically the music of Johnny Cash.

He simply showed the sequence of his slides of his work, for about an hour. He didn't say anything at all, so the art was speaking, the work was speaking in a sequence, and it was absolutely breathtaking. Initially, I'd found his work, as I often do with all abstract art, slightly enigmatic. By the end of that slide presentation, it was enigmatic no more. That was a wonderful experience. I have been a great admirer of his work ever since.

Published in 'Colin Renfrew: a Conversation', in *Art and Archaeology: Collaborations, Conversations, Criticisms* edited by I.A. Russell and A. Cochrane, New York, 2014, pp.9–19 and reworked for this publication.

EDMUND DE WAAL

For Richard Long

The mind, says Rebecca Solnit, works at three miles an hour. This is walking pace, the humane pace.

We are here to celebrate the pace of Richard Long.

After a century of walking in the city, the *flâneur* on the grey pavements of Paris, Berlin, Vienna, Richard took us back to land, to the earth.

He made a line made by walking.

He makes a life made by walking. One foot after another, pacing the world.

He makes records. He makes scores and poems to mark where he has been.

Stones, footprints and words. Flints and pebbles. Shards and hand prints.

His text works are like John Cage's scores. They are markers and glyphs. We feel the silences as much as the sounds.

Words are placed on a white page like stones on a cairn. Hand prints are placed as in the cave.

Richard Long has done the rarest of things. He has altered our sense of the spaces of the world.

This text was originally a speech, delivered by Edmund de Waal to mark Richard Long's acceptance of the Whitechapel Gallery Art Icon award on 19 March 2015. It was adapted by the author for this publication.

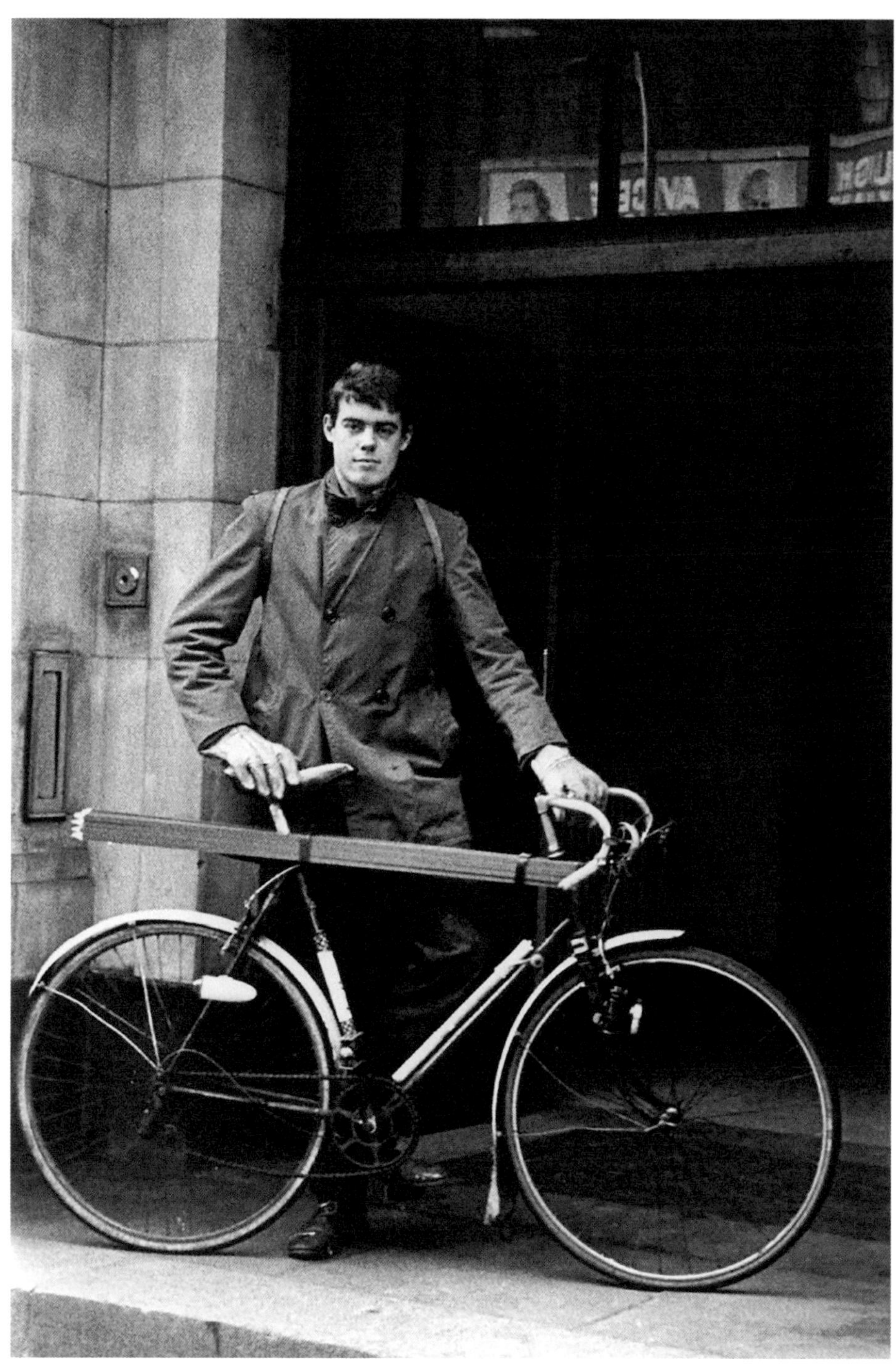

Richard Long outside St Martin's School of Art, London,
at the start of *Cycling Sculpture, 1–3 December 1967*

JON DAY

Off the Map

Almost fifty years ago, while he was still a student at St Martin's School of Art, the artist Richard Long embarked on a different kind of mapping: a bicycle ride from WC1 to Cambridgeshire. A photo of him about to set off shows a young, steely-eyed man carrying a rucksack and standing beside his road bike, a simple six-speed machine with mud guards and dropped handlebars. To the top tube of his road bike were tied a bundle of sticks he would use to mark out his way and record his journey.

Long's ride took him three days of largely non-stop cycling. He pedalled out of London, through Ely, Tring and Cambridge. He cycled along A-roads and canal towpaths, along country tracks and across muddy fields. At sixteen locations along his route he drove one of his stakes into the ground. 'Starting from the entrance of St Martin's in London', he later recalled:

> and carrying the components of the sculpture strapped to my bicycle, I commenced a more-or-less continuous day-night-day-night cycle ride around the counties to the north of London, ending back at my flat in the East End. At random places and times along the way I left one part of the work at each place. Each consisted of a yellow-painted vertical piece of wood stuck into the ground, with a blue horizontal crosspiece at the top. They were left in gardens, on verges or village greens, in fields etc.[1]

Near the location of each stake Long attached a notice which his mother had typed for him on her typewriter. The notice read:

> THIS IS ONE PART OF A PIECE OF SCULPTURE WHICH SURROUNDS AN AREA OF 2,401 SQ. MILES THERE ARE FIFTEEN OTHER SIMILAR PARTS, PLACED IRREGULARLY.

With this simple yet radical act Long broke free from the confines of the gallery, and from the constraints of traditional sculpture. He marked his progress and recorded his route on a map, which is all that's left of the work.

Originally Long's map was part of a triptych, locating the local journey he'd made in progressively more abstract space: first in relation to an Ordnance Survey map of the area, then in relation to the country itself, and finally in the context of a map of the world. Much of Long's art is about reclamation. A few months before he made his cycling sculpture Long had hitchhiked from St Martin's back to his home in Bristol, stopping somewhere in the Wiltshire countryside before finding a field and walked up and down in the damp grass. He took a photograph of the resulting track, which he called *A Line Made by Walking*. He has been walking ever since – on moors, up mountains, over deserts and across the frozen glaciers of Antarctica – and you can tell. At sixty-nine, Long is lithe and energetic, a looming presence with the slightly weathered air of a country vet.

For most of his career Long has used natural materials to make his works, stones arranged on the floors of galleries or mud applied directly to the walls. In the 1970s he began making sculptures using River Avon mud – still his favoured material – and he's since become something of 'a mud expert'. With his walking works he reclaims the act of movement itself as a form of artistic activity. With his mud works he reclaims an elemental material. His cycling sculptures, which he's made several of over the years, reclaim the map as something in its own right: not as a reference to the world but as an abstract shape with some intrinsic beauty, suggesting but not describing the journey it portrays. His work evokes the poetry of travel rather than its prose. Much of his art is about the space in between stopping points, about bodies and measurements, about moving through time and spaces and leaving traces of this movement only in faintly algebraic commemorations of the routes taken or the work done.

His subsequent work has occupied that fertile territory between an idea and its actualisation, between the act and its record. Often he documents his walking sculptures as maps, prints and photographs, narrating the story of them rather than reproducing the journeys themselves. Many of his walks are recorded only as text works, haiku-like prose poems, and talking to Long is a bit like encountering one of these enigmatic pieces. Underneath it all is an understanding that ideas can be beautiful in and of themselves. Long's *Cycling Sculpture, 1–3 December 1967* now only exists – perhaps only ever did exist – in map form. The shape marked out by the points he traced doesn't resolve into anything else. As a map it is vague, stripped of place-names, roads and topographical features. It is the record of a dreamt or unreal journey.

When I discovered Long's map I saw it as a challenge. I wanted to ride the route myself, to recreate the event of Long's journey, to see if

I could experience what it might be like to turn a bicycle ride into a work of art. But I didn't quite know what the route the map described should be. When he made his sculpture the road system provided Long with his basic structure. The rest was inspired by what he described in a letter to me as a process of 'randon attractiveness'.[2] There was no forward planning. He was moved only by the environments he encountered to mark his arbitrary points on the map. 'I did not draw it or plan it first', he wrote:

> or even mark it afterwards, only the 'sculpture' points. I remember (in particular) empty fen roads, Ely Cathedral & also passing by chance! Henry Moore's studio/village – Much Haddon? And the fire engines at the crash.
>
> The sculpture points were also 'random' but chosen for ease, practicality and to be fairly even spaced, one from another. They were always near or adjacent to the road.

Long's map was only half the story.

'The audacity of Long's early work', writes the author Robert Macfarlane, 'lay in freeing sculpture from the constraints of scale. He dispersed his art into the landscape, busting it not just out of the gallery, but out of almost all spatial limits.'[3] The mock-terse note on the signs he erected as part of *Cycling Sculpture, 1–3 December 1967* is a testament to this: 'No Photographs', a simple statement of fact. This was a sculpture it would be impossible to photograph, impossible to see, unless you went on your own journey around it. This was Long's great artistic realisation. 'I could make a piece of art which was ten miles long,' he recalled in 1986, 'I could also make a sculpture which surrounded an area of 2,401 square miles [. . .] by almost doing nothing, just walking and cycling.'[4] The action formed the map but the artwork itself existed nowhere, somewhere in between the ride and its record.

Many of his works are secret, unacknowledged, hidden. 'I like the idea,' he once told an interviewer, 'of making art almost from nothing or by doing almost nothing. It doesn't take a lot to turn ordinary things into art. It is enough to use stones as stones, for what they are.'[5] Anonymity is key to much of what he does, but because of this subtlety his work re-enchants the world, making you read it in a new way. After exposure to Long's work you never quite know if that stone by the side of the road was left deliberately or is there by random chance. In a sense it doesn't really matter. 'I love that', he has said,

'I love the idea that people might see a work of mine in the landscape, and that they might recognise it as a human mark but not necessarily as a work of art. Let alone a work made by me. So often people find a circle of stones and think it might be a Richard Long. Other people can make my work for me.'[6]

I wanted to leave London and follow Long's map, a map of empty space, a series of ghostly way points scattered across the landscape. It was October, the weather was warm and looked like it would hold for a last few days before the winter came. I thought I'd get a journey out of it–a structure emerging from the ride, connecting the dots. I wanted to leave the rutted runs of the courier-circuit behind. Long's project was too tempting to ignore: sixteen points making no reference to cities, to pick-ups and drop-offs, or to the landscape itself. The gravitational sling of London throwing you out before drawing you back in. Emptiness and the road.

I wondered if there would be any connection between my discoveries as a courier and Long's sense of the bicycle journey as art. I liked too, the idea of a journey made not according to the dictates of controllers and clients, nor according to the tyranny of the *A–Z*, but within the looser confines of Long's map. And so I decided to emulate Long, to recreate *Cycling Sculpture, 1–3 December 1967*, to go on a circuit that would take a few days to complete and wouldn't end back where I began.

I overlaid the route over a map of Britain and plotted the rough course: out through Hertfordshire, through Aylesbury, Buckingham and Towcester. Then north through Cambridgeshire, bypassing Peterborough and Huntingdon, before heading north to Ely, marooned in its island in the fens, before turning south again for Cambridge, Newmarket and then down to Bishop's Stortford. It would be a long ride, quite different from the day job, giving me time to lose myself on the road. I'd do nothing else.

Before I set off, however, I wanted to speak to Long about his journey, to find out what he had to say about the bicycle ride not just as experience, but as art. So I sought him out. We met in the Magdala pub in Hampstead, famous as the place where Ruth Ellis shot her lover David Blakely in 1955, subsequently becoming the last woman to be hanged in Britain. You can still make out the bullet holes in the wall outside – faint traces, like Long's work, of historical events scored subtly into the surface of the world.

Though nearing seventy, Long is tall and lithe, with the enthusiastic, boyish air of a Scout Leader. He was wearing a nondescript anorak and sturdy walking boots. His eyebrows are the only unruly thing about him, sprouting up over his forehead and giving his face a permanent expression of surprise.

Long said he couldn't remember much of the route of this, his first cycling sculpture, or of the journey itself. He remembered riding through Tring, and recalled passing Ely Cathedral in the dark during the small hours of the second morning of his ride. He remembered sleeping for a few hours in a shed by the side of the road, lying on piles of mangelwurzels and being woken by hundreds of rats that had emerged from the woodwork to nibble on them. He said he had received a single enquiry about his signs from a man on whose lawn he'd placed one of his sculpture. He couldn't remember what the man had asked him.

On the way back home through East London he remembered passing the smouldering aftermath of a car crash, with firemen cutting someone out of their car with acetone torches. 'The smell was unbelievable', he recalled, 'burning rubber, thick black smoke. I think there was blood on the road, and I just whizzed by on my bike.'[7]

The idea of the piece, he told me, was to create a sculpture bigger than any other: to create a sculpture that could not be viewed all in one go, couldn't be consumed from one single vantage point, that resisted the tyranny of the gaze. The idea of the work was to be bigger than the reality. The piece was part of a body of work that played with scale. Long had once erected a sculpture on the top of Kilimanjaro, telling the papers that he'd created the world's highest sculpture. 'For some reason they didn't consider it newsworthy', he told me. 'Really it's the shape itself that was important', he said of *Cycling Sculpture, 1–3 December 1967*, 'you could do the same ride anywhere, move the markers, place it over a map of London. The actual landscape I travelled over is unimportant'.[8]

Long's art is founded on the traces left by the body in motion, but in its making it is also about the enjoyment of the body, and this he associates with his own childhood pursuits and interests. The joy of bodily exertion I'd discovered as a courier he'd applied to the making of art. 'Lots of people make art out of anguish', he says, 'I make mine out of pleasure'.[9] As a boy he'd always been a walker and a cyclist. His parents met because they were both members of a rambling club, and at school he was the captain of the cross-country running-club.

He's often misread as a romantic artist, or as a political radical of some kind. I asked him if there was anything of the activist about his work – suggesting as it does ideas of right-to-roam and open access – but he told me he was an 'art animal, not a political animal'. He does, however, draw a distinction between his work and that of the American land artists, who use bulldozers and earthmovers to shape their environments to their will. His work isn't interventionist in quite that way. 'I'm not interested in imposing myself on the world',[10] he said.

Stories do seem central to his practice: the story of his own body moving through space and time, the story of the marks he makes as he goes, but he resists over-investing in the idea of art as a form of

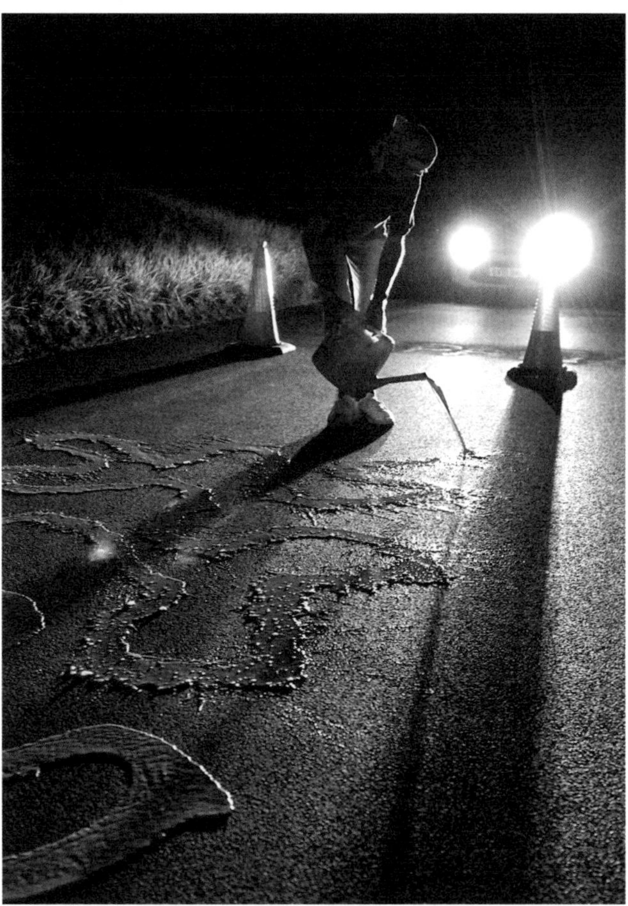

Richard Long making *Box Hill Road River* 2012

narrative. 'I don't have any great grand theories of walking, or of making art into a journey', he told me later, 'they just seemed like good ideas at the time'.[11] Though the backdrops to his journeys–mountains, forests and deserts – are often beautiful, they are largely irrelevant, or, if not irrelevant, a happy outcome of the pieces he makes. Instead he talks enthusiastically about technicalities and practicalities. Of the making of *Box Hill Road River* (2012), a meandering line of paint he dripped onto the tarmac of Box Hill in Surrey, to be ridden over by the road cyclists during the 2012 London Olympics, he said, 'we had to use biodegradable paint. And we had to do it overnight, and the paint would dry very quickly'. He's interested in what he has done rather than in why he has done it.

Outside the pub, as we were leaving, he examined my bicycle. 'A track bike?' he asked. 'That's a strange choice'. He asked me who I thought would win the Tour. 'Chris Froome's looking good', I said.

'He is', said Long. 'Well, never meet your heroes', he said, as he smiled and stalked away back up the hill. I left the next day, at first light. London fell away gradually and I never really knew when I'd moved beyond it. After a while the city gave way to suburbia, to the monolithic headquarters of medium-sized companies, to traffic depots and mysterious sidings by the motorway, to increasing rural paranoia. There were signs on fences reading 'Country Watch operates here'. The roads altered too, out here, roughing themselves up, clad in a firmer asphalt covering the better to resist the trials of winter.

Cyclogeography: Journeys of a London Bicycle Courier, Notting Hill Editions, April 2015, pp.119–131.

1 Clarrie Wallis, 'Making Tracks', in Clarrie Wallis (ed.), *Richard Long Heaven and Earth*, exh. cat., London, Tate, 2009, p.43.
2 Letter to author from Richard Long, 9 May 2014.
3 Robert Macfarlane, 'Walk the Line', *The Guardian*, 23 May 2009, p.16.
4 Richard Long and Martina Giezen, *Richard Long in Conversation: Bristol 19.11.1985*, MW Press, Noordwijk, 1986.
5 'Richard Long', in David Sylvester, *About Modern Art: Critical Essays 1948–1996*, Chatto & Windus, London, 1996, p.310.
6 Jon Day, 'Richard Long: The Last Amateur', *Apollo*, vol.CLXXXI, no.629, 18 March 2015, p.137.
7 Richard Long in conversation with author, September 2013.
8 *Ibid.*
9 *Ibid.*
10 *Ibid.*
11 *Ibid.*

NICHOLAS LOGSDAIL

Good Morning

One day in the late 1960s I found a beautiful postcard nestled among a pile of bills and letters with a message that was confidently inscribed in pencil: 'Good Morning. Richard Long.' When we met, we were both in our early twenties, but through the revolutionary nature of his work, Richard was already becoming a legendary figure. I didn't ask him to make an exhibition at the gallery right away but I was increasingly interested in making artist's books, especially encouraged by Dan Graham and Sol LeWitt, in order to get to know artists and their work better. So Richard and I embarked on a small publishing project called *Two Sheepdogs cross in and out of the passing shadows The clouds drift over the hill with a storm* (1971). This was the first artist's book the gallery had made and was printed locally on a letterpress.

As I got to know Richard, I also came to understand the significance of his work far more profoundly. The thought-provoking nature of what he was doing began to occupy my mind and when that happens you know you have an authentic and empathetic connection with an artist. Having also been brought up in the countryside I realised that the landscapes of my childhood had been manipulated by human needs over thousands of years, as much as they were formed by nature. This is an allegory of what Richard does with his work and describes the relationship he has with his surroundings.

Everything Richard makes comes from the world and remains within it – he neither adds nor takes away from what already exists. Although he is one of Britain's most significant artists, in many ways his art is concerned with reality – with real sticks, real stones, real walks. The idea of making a sculpture with only those materials at hand and then taking a photograph of it, before leaving the work behind at peace with nature is revealing in its beauty and simplicity. Unlike much of the large-scale American Land art, Richard's work requires no mechanical means. Compare, for example, the 200-tonne industrial Corten steel sculptures by Richard Serra or the enormous earth displacements of Michael Heizer that used industrial excavation equipment with Richard's gentle, spontaneous art. I'm sure many of those stone works he produced on his walks still survive today; as Richard might say, they are seen by few in the wild, but known by many through the photographs.

Richard has always walked his own line. Imagine him walking continuously around the earth, if that were indeed possible, until he created not only a 24,859-mile straight line, but also a circle and the circumference of the largest sculpture imaginable as well. On his many walks across all five continents, he has already done the mileage and more.

He's happiest when alone outdoors with a rucksack on his back, anticipating the challenge of the work ahead. Being outside the studio has to be more interesting for him than being inside. Whether he is walking the desert in Peru, or over man-made landscape, the process is the same. Throughout his 50-year career, Richard has been making each work as if it were his first, with the consistency and clarity of vision that characterised his first walks.

Walking in the upright position is how we all got here, we all walked out of Africa. For this reason, I don't just admire or like the work of Richard Long, I have a deep affinity with its sentiments and its sediments. There is not only joy and serenity there, but an intelligence and consciousness that creates a link back to the very beginning of consciousness. To have such a connection also suggests that if we cannot walk into the future, we will have a big human problem.

Walking, observing and decision-making are fundamental to the core of man's spirit and origins. Richard reminds us that life can be more straightforward than our modern existence would have us believe. For any of us who like to walk – and walking is the best way to clear your mind and have new and organised thoughts – we know instinctively that it is a deeply human and fundamental component of our very being. There is a little bit of all of us in Richard's work. This, in my view, makes him a modest, but influential giant among artists.

Richard Long: Time and Space, exh. cat., Arnolfini and Verlag der Buchhandlung Walther Koenig, Bristol and Koln, 2015, pp.4–5.

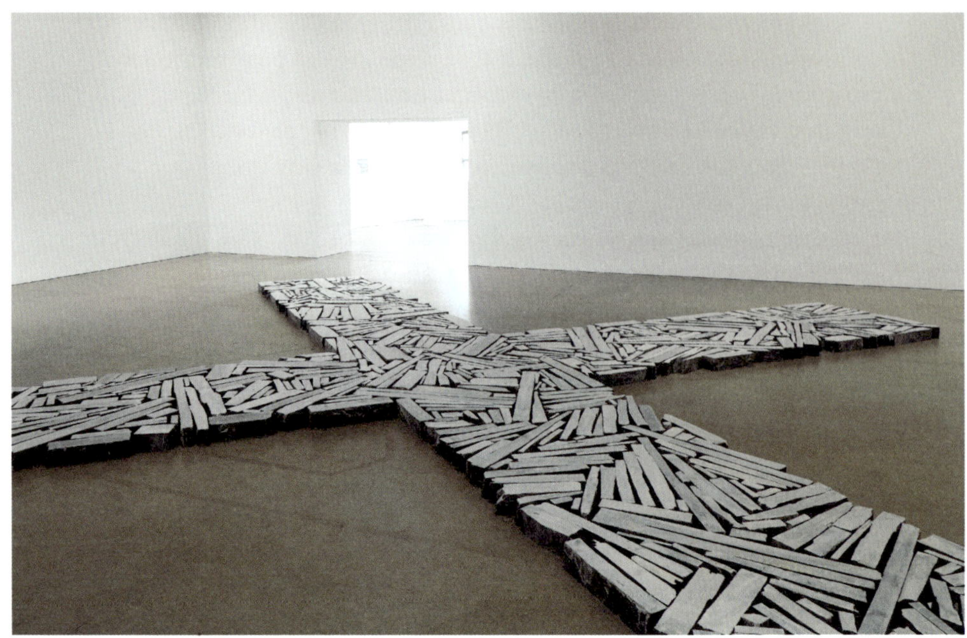

Time and Space 2015

Bristol 1967/2015 2015

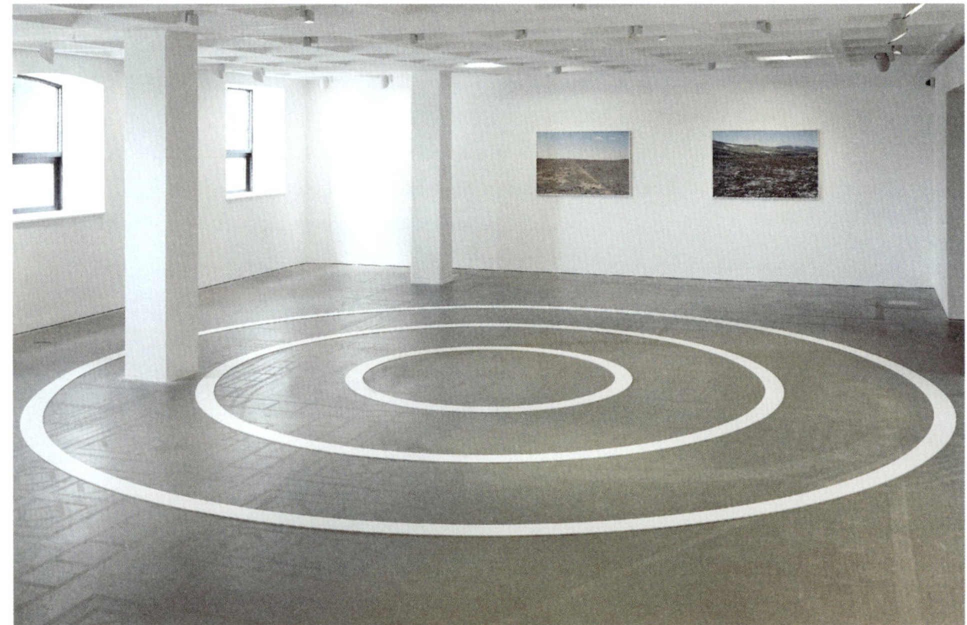

INDIA WINDSOR-CLIVE

He Walks the Lines – Richard Long: Time and Space

Arnolfini, Bristol, 31 July – 15 November 2015

All truly great thoughts are conceived while walking.

Friedrich Nietzsche, *Twilight of the Idols*, or, *How to Philosophise with a Hammer*, 1888

While wandering through the trees and dappled sunlight on a spring afternoon, Richard Long points to a young Japanese maple tree. He describes how it grew from a surviving offshoot after the original tree was destroyed by the 1987 hurricane, and how its brilliant colour inspired his *Red Walk* (1986), recording his encounters with the colour in the west of England. A revealing anecdote for the often enigmatic origin of his ideas.

In 1967, aged just 22, Long challenged the parameters of artistic production with *A Line Made by Walking* (1967). He photographed the mark made by repeatedly walking up and down in a straight line in a grass field. It presented walking as medium for art. A simple act with sophisticated ramifications.

Long began documenting journey as art. 'For me', he says, 'walking is about a way that as an artist I can be creative. To do things that have never been done before. We've been walking since we stood on two feet. But with some of my early walks I was almost certain no one had ever walked in a straight line across Dartmoor, even though people have crossed Dartmoor millions of times for different reasons.'

Since the early years he spent walking the River Avon and Dartmoor, Long has walked on every continent on the planet, from the high plateaus of Bolivia and forests of Canada to the Arctic and the Sahara Desert, always returning to Bristol, where he grew up, and where his new exhibition celebrates his home city's year as European Green Capital. His walks can last days, months, weeks, or just an hour.

Long's work is a coalescence of his ideas and the easiest locations to carry out these ideas, which happen to be some of the most spectacular landscapes on earth. He seeks out empty wildernesses, with stony, temperate deserts being his preference: 'It's a great pleasure to be alone in a big landscape. There are no distractions. You have the rhythm of every day, of walking, of getting tired, of finding a campsite, cooking a meal, sleeping. Life is reduced to a beautiful, simple, ritualised pattern.' He begins to describe his experience of walking: 'It's dynamic and sometimes it's challenging. It's contemplative and sometimes it's mind-expanding. Quite often while doing one walk I may have the idea for the next walk. One work leads to another. It's a state of mind.'

From photographing a circle of stones made on a mountain top to recording the phenomenological experiences of a walk in a few words, he reaches profound levels of understanding with clarity and consistency. Selective and refined, a minimalist tradition of truth to materials is met with evocative narratives about the beauty and the power of Nature: 'It's about being in the world and celebrating the world.'

Long's archetypal repertoire of lines and circles derives from his interest in the power of universal things. 'A circle doesn't belong to me: it belongs to everyone. Everyone can understand a pile of stones.' Long also states their practicality as the easiest marks to make, their positioning often dictated by the features of the landscape and whatever feels right, in the right place, at the right time. He finds beauty in simplicity. Whether they are planned, instinctive or left to chance, he creates formalised human marks in the landscape, each one an embodiment of time and trace.

Long often allows natural forces to play a role in his work. A great example of this is *Half-Tide* (1971), for which he made a cross of stones on a bed of seaweed at low tide. In the morning the tide came in and the cross appeared on the surface of the water where the stones were weighing the seaweed down. He also recalls the work entitled *Crescent to Cross* (1971), a walk from the centre of Islamic Spain, the Great Mosque of Cordoba, to the centre of the Spanish Christian world, Santiago de Compostela. During this walk he heard a cuckoo every day. It was these moments, rather than a preconceived idea, that then inspired an additional work titled *Cuckoo Walk* (2014). 'That's an example of getting a text work out of something which happened that I couldn't have foreseen – being an opportunist', he comments.

Long's work is a portrait of himself in the world, simultaneously biographical and anonymous. A sculpture may never be seen by anyone else, other than in a photograph Long takes to communicate his art to others. A passerby could come across a circle of driftwood or a line of stones in the landscape and have no idea who made it, when or why – only that it was made by a human. Or they might recognise it as being by the artist Richard Long and know its significance as art.

For Long, neither is necessary for the work, but rather adds to the duality of visibility and invisibility.

With walking, Long's statement of intent is 'to be an artist anywhere'. He doesn't have to have or bring anything to the place where he makes his work. His tools are his walking boots, a rucksack and an old Nikon single-lens reflex camera in a beaten leather case. His materials are in Nature. His studio is outside. With such an imaginative freedom as to how and where art can be made, he shows that 'sculptures can be above the clouds, not just in museums'.

Marking lightly on the earth's surface, Long's sculptural interventions in the landscape fall somewhere between making monuments and leaving only footprints. The elements of a man-made mark are assimilated back into Nature as soon as they are assembled; their creator's presence is as potent as his absence. Their transience, such as the delicate ice fragments in *A Circle in Antarctica* (2012), reflects the beauty and fragility in the balance of Nature. Each work is resonant of humanity's presence on the earth, not simply as onlookers but as participants. In Long's practice, walking becomes a sacred conversation with the land, a way of interacting with the world and engaging the senses. 'My work demonstrates how one can be connected to Nature and one's surroundings', he says. Or, as expressed in the gratifying accord Long strikes with the refrain to Johnny Cash's signature song, 'I Walk the Line', which Long quotes in his work *Reflections in the Little Pigeon River* (1970):

> I keep a close watch on this heart of mine
> I keep my eyes wide open all the time
> I keep the ends out for the tie that binds
> Because you're mine,
> I walk the line.

We continue to wander through the small woodland belonging to Long, once part of Bristol University's arboretum. It's a peaceful haven and a seedbed of creativity, a well-tended personal microcosm. We pass oaks, rhododendrons, a palm tree, wild garlic and a shell, before stopping to admire the soft bark of a 200-year-old Californian redwood. Long tells me there are sometimes deer in here. As we step back out into the open, there, on cue, is a deer staring right at us for a few moments before bounding off into the bushes. 'I paid him a lot for that', he smiles.

Resurgence & Ecologist, issue no.292, September/October 2015, pp.50–53.

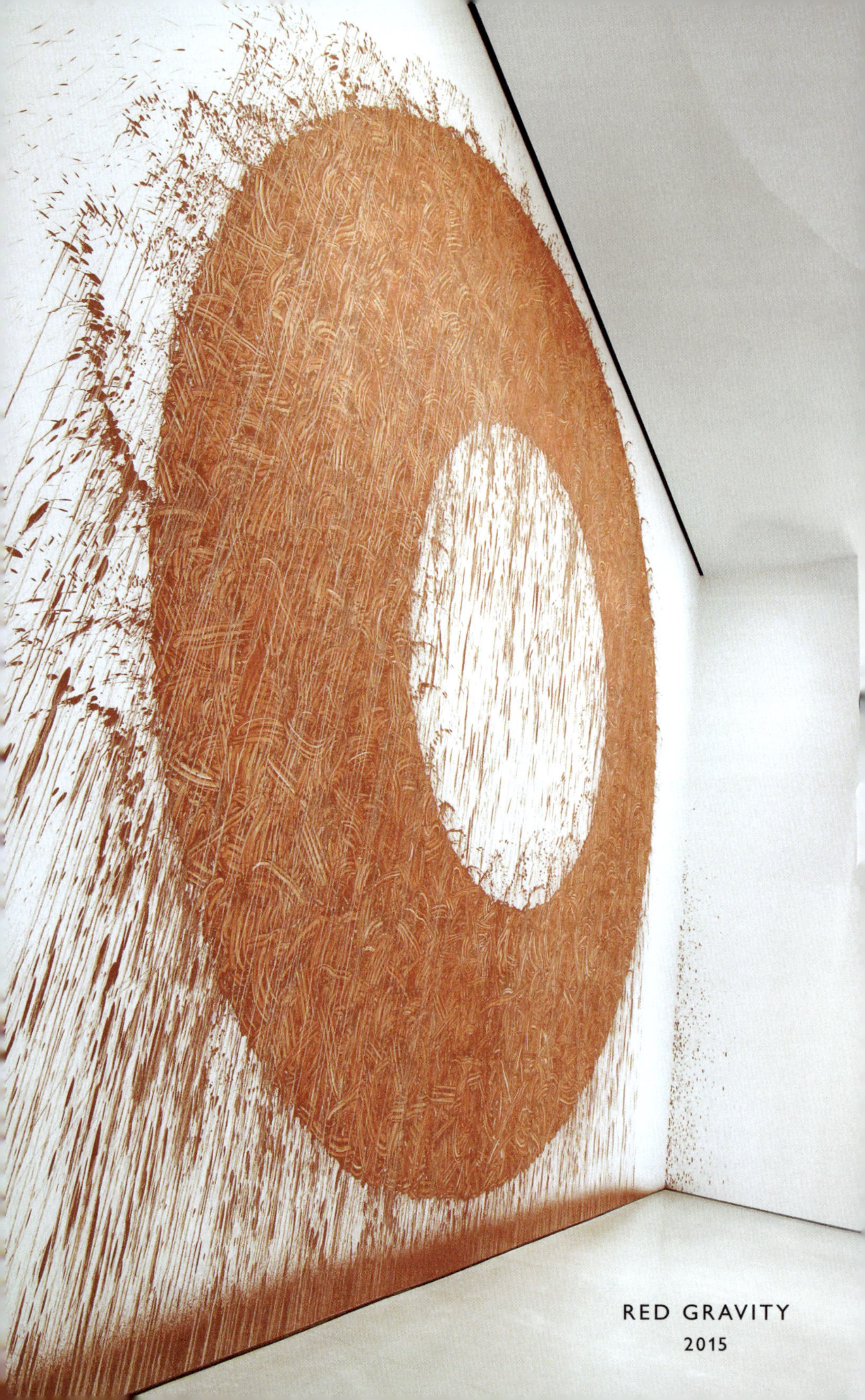

RED GRAVITY
2015

ANN MCCOY

Richard Long Crescent to Cross

Sperone Westwater, New York, 11 September – 24 October 2015

Entering the main gallery of Sperone Westwater, the viewer is dwarfed by *Red Gravity* (2015), a stunning, two-storey-high, circular red clay drawing filling the height and width of the main wall. A suspended glass balcony allows the viewer to see the top half, which enhances the work's scale. Made with clay and water, the giant circle bears the marks of the artist's fingers, and the surrounding spatters attest to the artist's quick energetic process. Since *River Avon Mud Circle* (1982), Richard Long has been making similar wall drawings. Much has been written about his art's grounding in direct contact with nature, the solitary activity of walking, his success in bringing outside inside, and his role in what Lucy Lippard called the 'dematerialization of art'. The work's simplicity and transcendental spiritualism have been discussed, referencing Zen Buddhism and Taoism. Like the ancient Chinese literati, Long has perfected an artform over time through repetition.

For this reviewer, there is another factor that explains the profound impact of Long's work. Long's postcards of Silbury Hill, and walks on Windmill Hill – a place where England's first inhabitants made alterations in the landscape – offer up a clue. We are deeply moved by Long's work because we glimpse a time 'before the fall', returning to the source of human development when man enjoyed a seamless relationship with nature. We are currently in the midst of the largest mass extinction since the Ice Age, and there is something calming about Long's work that is seated in unspoiled nature. His photograph and text work, *Windmill Hill to Coalbrookdale* (1979) – the birthplace of the Industrial Revolution – ends with no photos of rusted machine parts or industrial waste arranged in a line. Some of the few human references in Long's work are hand prints, like the *Mud Hand Circles* (1984), reminiscent of our Neanderthal ancestors' hand prints made of red ochre. There is poetic simplicity, strength and primal innocence in this work.

Werner Herzog's *Cave of Forgotten Dreams* (2010), a 3-D voyage into the rarely visited interior of the Chauvet-Pont-d'Arc Cave in southern France, also takes us into this realm. The cave-art era occupies a section of the timeline six times longer than the period from the Egyptian Old Kingdom to the present. Our bit, especially the last 300 years, has certainly not been a model for sustainability. What philosopher Jean Gebser calls the 'aperspectival' world, a time of the tribal 'we' and the anonymous 'one', forms the subterranean layer of our consciousness. Both Long and Herzog ask us to travel back to our human origins, and think about what we have lost with our technical frenzy. In an art world fuelled by rampant narcissism and materialism, Long's work provides relief and hope. Stones are placed and forgotten; the materials belong to no one. Although Long assured me he does hit a pub for a beer en route, or take advantage of the odd hotel, we imagine ourselves trekking alongside.

Crescent to Cross is a 'road walk' from the Great Mosque of Cordoba in Andalusia to the Cathedral of Santiago de Compostela in Galicia. A wall-text graphic on the gallery wall replaces photo documentation of the walk, a device he has used before. For Long, the photograph and the text have equal weight. We think of TE Lawrence's lonely treks to crusader castles in Arabia, or Sir Richard Burton's pilgrimage to Mecca – fellow Englishmen who also walked from Orient to Occident. Long's was not the historical pilgrimage route with bronze pavement plaques and flea-ridden hostels at allotted segments; he simply drew his own line on the map. The wall-text graphic on the gallery's upper balcony is the sole souvenir of this journey. We have no record of his thoughts along the way; his only agenda seems to have been traversing these points as others have done before. The wall text functions like a Rorschach inkblot: we are left to fill in the experience with our own imagination. With the current refugee crisis we are again seeing the Muslim east walking west into Christian Europe. For a non-political artist, a certain poignant synchronicity has occurred.

Two works on the gallery's upper floors, *Half Moon* (2015) and *Red Slate Line* (2015), are made with beautiful dark red slate from upper New York State. It is the colour of the slate that makes them especially memorable. Long started using pointed stones standing on end in works like *Standing Stone Circle* as far back as 1973, and line works on gallery floors date back to his art school days. Long has said that if you have a good idea it is worth keeping, and these works prove this to be true. In an art world obsessed with yearly trends, it is nice to see an old master like Richard Long bucking them. *Half Moon* completes this exhibition and makes the viewer again think of the crescent, but a crescent from New York State's geological time. The visual trek with Long through time and terrain is certainly worth the trip.

The Brooklyn Rail, October 2015, p.48.

CRESCENT TO CROSS

A ROAD WALK FROM THE GREAT MOSQUE OF CÓRDOBA TO THE CATHEDRAL OF SANTIAGO DE COMPOSTELA

A WALK OF 534 MILES IN 18 DAYS
SPAIN AND PORTUGAL SPRING 2014

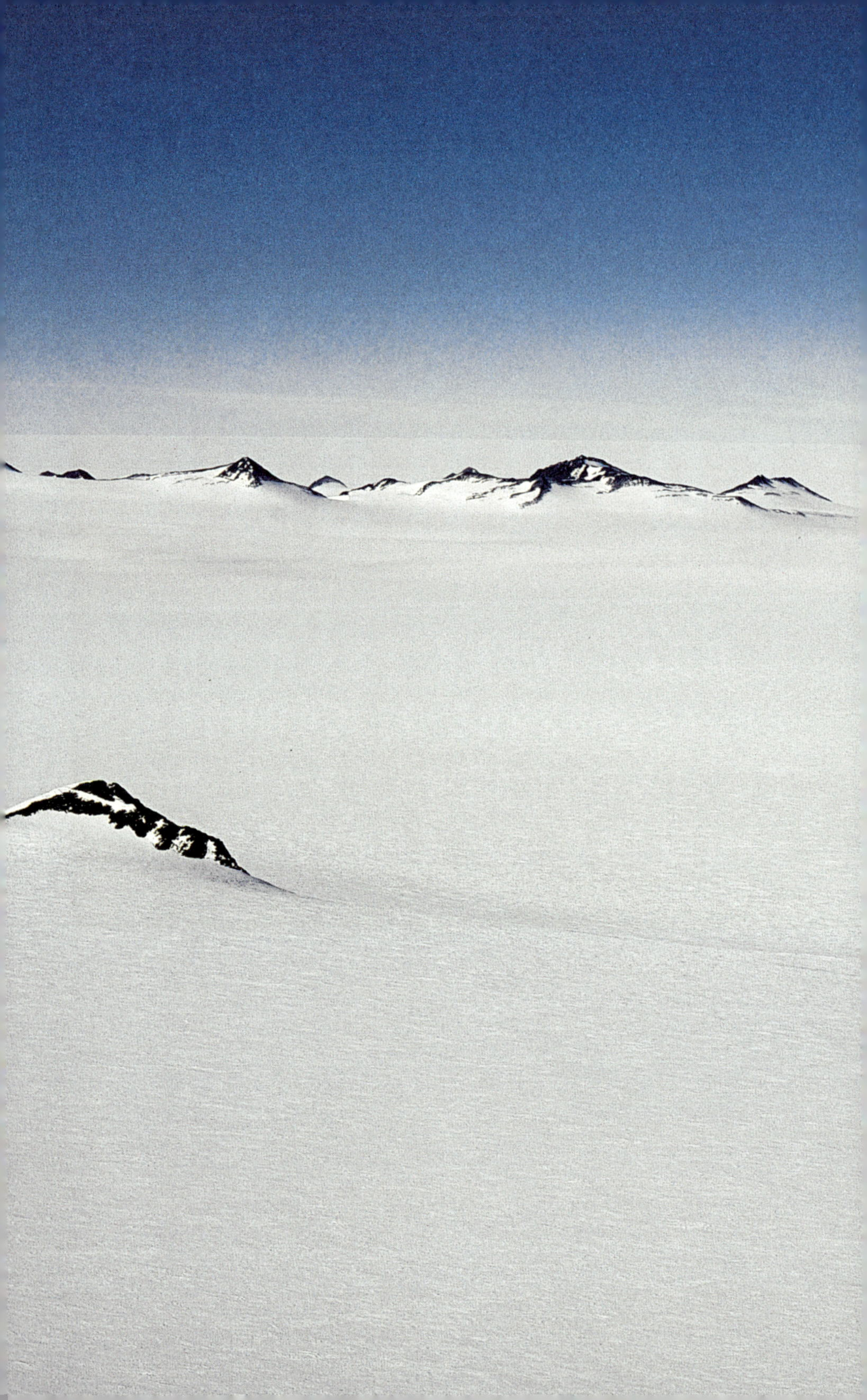

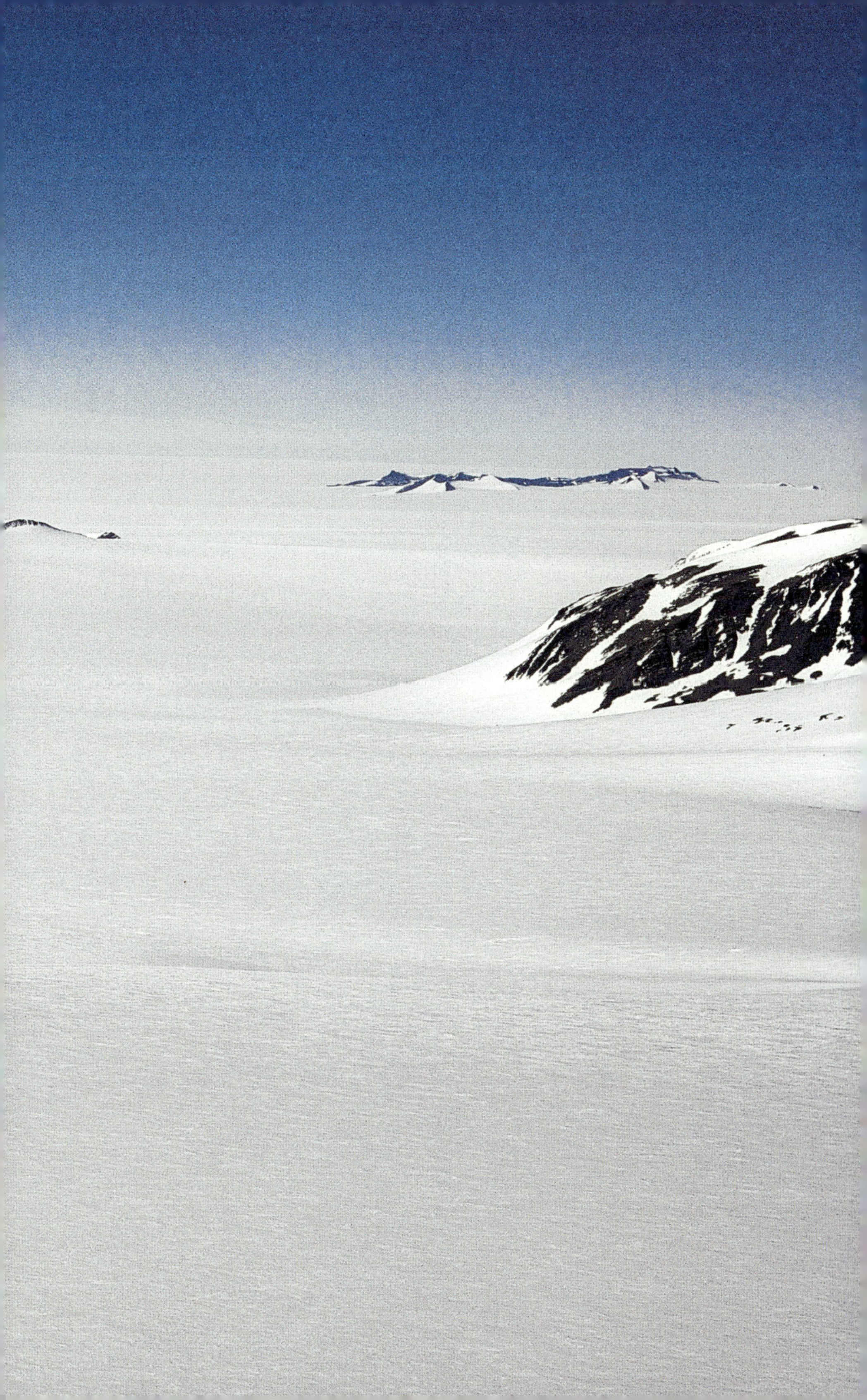

It is certain that the Britons were ignorant of the art of constructive masonry; for when the Roman legions left the British to their own resources, they advised them to build a wall between the two seas, across the island, to keep off their northern enemies. They indeed raised the wall as they had been directed; but not of stone, as having no artist capable of such work, but of sods [which] made it of no use.

ADAM BEDE

Published on the occasion of exhibition at
John Gibson Gallery, New York, 1969.

We were waiting two days for any type of vehicle to pass by going to Loitokitok 70 miles away. The Masai said there were lions along the route so we didn't start walking. Red dust blown from the dirt track covered all the grass around. So I began to walk two straight lines through the grass, brushing the dust away with my boots as I went.

Four days later we were climbing above Loitokitok, at 19,000, where the next sculpture began to take place.

Published on the occasion of exhibition at
Städtisches Museum Abteiberg, Mönchengladbach, 1970.

From a mountain top in Africa
To a Tennessee riverbed, brushing through hoar frost
Magic signs, secret journeys
A portrait of the artist touching the earth.

Published on the occasion of exhibition at
Whitechapel Gallery, London, 1971.

PREVIOUS PAGES
Antarctica 2012

THE BANKS OF THE OHIO
Appalachian murder ballad (Traditional). 1st verse

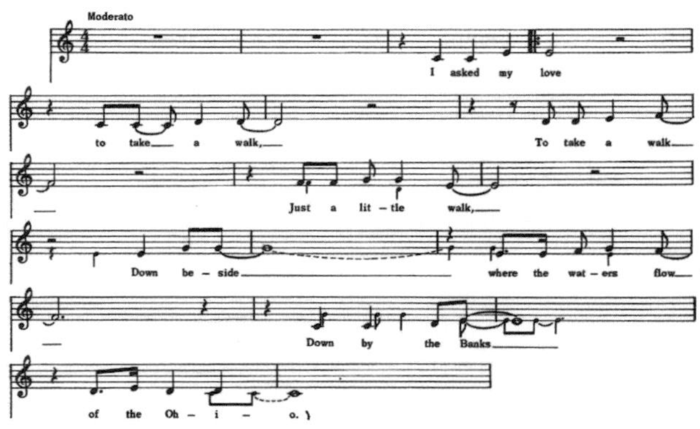

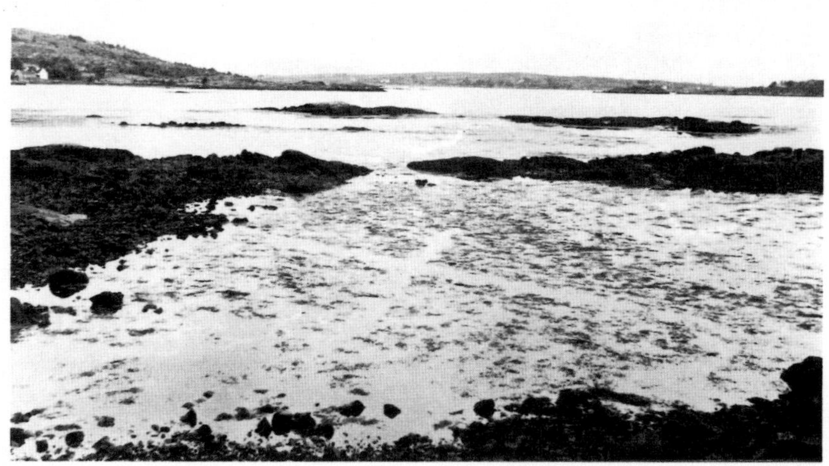

Half-Tide, Bertraghboy Bay, Ireland, 1971

17 · 58

Published in *Documenta 5*, exh. cat., Kassel, 1972

Five, six, pick up sticks
Seven, eight, lay them straight

I like simple, practical, emotional,
quiet, vigorous art.

I like the simplicity of walking,
the simplicity of stones.

I like common materials, whatever is to hand,
but especially stones. I like the idea that stones
are what the world is made of.

I like common means given the
simple twist of art.

I like sensibility without technique.

I like the way the degree of visibility
and accessibility of my art is controlled
by circumstance, and also the degree to which
it can be either public or private,
possessed or not possessed.

I like to use the symmetry of patterns between time,
places and time, between distance and time,
between stones and distance, between time and stones.

I choose lines and circles because they
do the job.

My art is about working in the wide
world, wherever, on the surface of the earth.

My art has the themes of materials, ideas,
movement, time. The beauty of objects, thoughts, places
and actions.

My work is about my senses, my instinct, my own scale
and my own physical commitment.

My work is real, not illusory or conceptual.
It is about real stones, real time, real actions.

My work is not urban, nor is it romantic.
It is the laying down of modern ideas in
the only practical places to take them.
The natural world sustains the industrial world.
I use the world as I find it.

My art can be remote or very public,
all the work and all the places being equal.

My work is visible or invisible. It can be an
object (to possess) or an idea carried out and equally
shared by anyone who knows about it.

My photographs are facts which bring the
right accessibility to remote, lonely
or otherwise unrecognisable works. Some sculptures
are seen by few people, but can be known about by many.

My outdoor sculptures and walking locations
are not subject to possession and ownership. I like the fact
that roads and mountains are common, public land.

My outdoor sculptures are places.
The material and the idea are of the place;
sculpture and place are one and the same.
The place is as far as the eye can see from the
sculpture. The place for a sculpture is found
by walking. Some works are a succession
of particular places along a walk, e.g.
Milestones. In this work the walking,
the places and the stones all have equal importance.

My talent as an artist is to walk across
a moor, or place a stone on the ground.

My stones are like grains of sand in
the space of the landscape.

A true understanding of the land requires
more than the building of objects.

The sticks and stones I find on the land,
I am the first to touch them.

A walk expresses space and freedom
and the knowledge of it can live
in the imagination of anyone, and that
is another space too.

A walk is just one more layer, a mark, laid
upon the thousands of other layers of human
and geographic history on the surface of the
land. Maps help to show this.

A walk traces the surface of the land,
it follows an idea, it follows the day
and the night.

A road is the site of many journeys.
The place of a walk is there before the
walk and after it.

A pile of stones or a walk, both
have equal physical reality, though
the walk is invisible. Some of my
stone works can be seen, but not
recognised as art.

The creation in my art is not in the common
forms – circles, lines – I use, but the
places I choose to put them in.

Mountains and galleries are both
in their own ways extreme, neutral, uncluttered;
good places to work.

A good work is the right thing in the right
place at the right time. A crossing place.

Fording a river. Have a good look, sit down, take off boots
and socks, tie socks on to rucksack, put on boots,
wade across, sit down, empty boots, put on socks and boots.
It's a new walk again.

I have in general been interested in using the
landscape in different ways from
traditional representation and the fixed view.
Walking, ideas, statements and maps are some means to this end.
I have tried to add something of my own view as an
artist to the wonderful and undisputed traditions
of walking, journeying and climbing. Thus, some
of my walks have been formal (straight,
circular) almost ritualised. The patterns of
my walks are unique and original; they
are not like following well-trodden routes
taking travellers from one place to another.
I have sometimes climbed around mountains
instead of to the top. I have used riverbeds
as footpaths. I have made walks about slowness, walks about
stones and water. I have made walks within
a place as opposed to a linear journey;
walking without travelling.

Words after the fact.

Published on the occasion of exhibition at
Anthony d'Offay Gallery, London, 1980.

My art is about working in the wide world, wherever. It has the themes of materials, ideas, movement, time. The beauty of objects, thoughts, places and actions. I hope to make images and ideas that resonate in the imagination, that mark the earth and the mind. My work is about my senses, my scale, my instinct. I use the world as I find it, passing through by design and by chance.

I like walking down the road; sleeping on the ground. I like both visible and invisible art. I make impermanent things with permanent ideas, or vice versa. I like common means given the simple twist of art. I like sensibility without technique. My talent as an artist is to walk across a moor, or place a stone on the ground. A good work is the right thing in the right place at the right time. A crossing place.

A circle, a line: they look good, they are abstract, they are common knowledge. They belong to everyone and equally to the past, the present and the future.

Art is one of the good things about human life.

I've got the stones if you've got the sticks.

Published in *Documenta 7,* exh. cat., Kassel, 1982.

Words after the fact

The source of my work is nature. I use it with respect and freedom. I use materials, ideas, movement and time to express a whole view of my art in the world. I hope to make images and ideas which resonate in the imagination, which mark the earth and the mind.

In the mid-sixties the language and ambition of art was due for renewal. I felt art had barely recognised the natural landscapes which cover this planet, or had used the experiences those places could offer. Starting on my own doorstep and later spreading, part of my work since has been to try and engage this potential. I see it as abstract art laid down in the real spaces of the world. It is not romantic; I use the world as I find it. My work is simple and practical. I may choose rolling moorland to make a straight ten mile walk because that is the best place to make such a work, and I know such places well. I like the idea of using the land without possessing it.

A walk marks time with an accumulation of footsteps. It defines the form of the land. Walking the roads and paths is to trace a portrait of the country. I have become interested in using a walk to express original ideas about the land, art, and walking itself.

A walk is also the means of discovering places in which to make sculpture in 'remote' areas, places of nature, places of great power and contemplation. These works are made of the place, they are a rearrangement of it and in time will be reabsorbed by it. I hope to make work for the land, not against it.

I like the idea that art can be made anywhere, perhaps seen by few people, or not recognised as art when they do. I think that is a great freedom won for art and for the viewer. My photographs and captions are facts which bring the appropriate accessibility to the spirit of these remote or otherwise unrecognisable works.

Time passes, a place remains. A walk moves through life, it is physical but afterwards invisible. A sculpture is still, a stopping place, visible.

The freedom to use precisely all degrees of visibility and permanence is important in my work. Art can be a step or a stone.

A sculpture, a map, a text, a photograph; all the forms of my work are equal and complementary. The knowledge of my actions, in whatever form, is the art. My art is the essence of my experience, not a representation of it.

My inside and outside sculptures are made in the same spirit. The urban and rural worlds are mutually dependent, and they both have equal significance in my work.

My work has become a simple metaphor of life. A figure walking down his road, making his mark. It is an affirmation of my human scale and senses: how far I walk, what stones I pick up, my particular experiences. Nature has more effect on me than I on it. I am content with the vocabulary of universal and common means; walking, placing, stones, sticks, water, circles, lines, days, nights, roads.

Published on the occasion of exhibition at the Arnolfini, Bristol, 1983.

A sculpture feeds the senses directly at a place.
A photograph or text feeds the imagination by extension to other places.
Each work is simple and contemplative.
A sculpture orders and concentrates materials.
A walk is a simple way to pass and order time.

Published as the private view card for exhibition at Abbott Hall Art Gallery, Kendal, 1985.

Notes on maps

A map can be used to make a walk. A map can be used to make a work of art.
Maps have layers of information; they show history, geography, the naming of places.
A map is an artistic and poetic combination of image and language.
For me, a map is a potent alternative to a photograph, it has a different function.
It can show the idea of a whole work, not a moment.
A map can show time and space in a work of art.
Distance, the days of walking, the campsites, the shape of the walking, can be shown in one concise but rich image.
In some of my works, I find the best places to realise particular ideas by first looking at a map.
A map can decide place and idea, either or both.
Maps can be read in many different ways, they are a standard and universal language.
I like to think my work on a map exists equally with all the other information on it.
On a long walk a map becomes a familiar, trusted object, something to look at endlessly, without boredom.
I can look at the planned future and the completed past.
A map is light.
A map could save my life.

Written 1994, first published in *Walking the Line*, Thames & Hudson, 2002.

Some notes on my work in mountains

My ambition when I climbed Mount Kilimanjaro in 1969 was to make a sculpture on the top. (In reality, the climb turned out to be more interesting than the work.) The highest I have been, 20,000 feet in Bolivia, was also the place at which I made a snow drawing, of a condor.

The idea behind *Throwing a Stone Around MacGillycuddy's Reeks* (1977) was to walk around a chain of mountains rather than to the top. In *Mountains to Mountains* (1980) it was to use the summits almost like stepping-stones along a walk, and in *Twelve Hours Twelve Summits* (1983) the idea was to spend a particular and ritualised amount of time (one hour) at each summit, so the rhythm of the stopping places was more the subject of the work, rather than the walking – positive and negative complementaries.

In the textwork *Pico De Orizaba* (1979) the idea was to record in words the different surfaces I walked over (up and down) while climbing the highest volcano in Mexico. One can read the words both up and down, just as every path goes both up and down (depending on the walker).

I liked the idea that in my *A Line in the Himalayas* (1975), made on the Khumbu Glacier below the Everest icefall, the sculpture would be on the move, slowly disintegrating and disappearing down the moraine, as soon as I had made it.

The sculpture *A Line in Japan* (1979) came about because – my original idea had been to make a mapwork recording a circular walk around Mount Fuji, following the snow line. However, as there was no snow on the mountain at all when I arrived, I had to follow a different idea.

I made the textwork *From Pass to Pass* (1984) partly because the reality of a walk in high mountains, for a non-mountaineer like myself, is to go from pass to pass. The passes are the lowest connecting points between the mountains, yet they become the highest points (the 'summits', the mental targets) along the walk from one valley to another. They are even marked by cairns and prayer flags.

I often think of my standing-stone sculptures, which are usually mountain works, as the culminating, celebratory (or last!) energy of the climb that has brought me to that place.

First published in *A chacun sa montagne*, Musée Jenisch, Vevey, 1995.

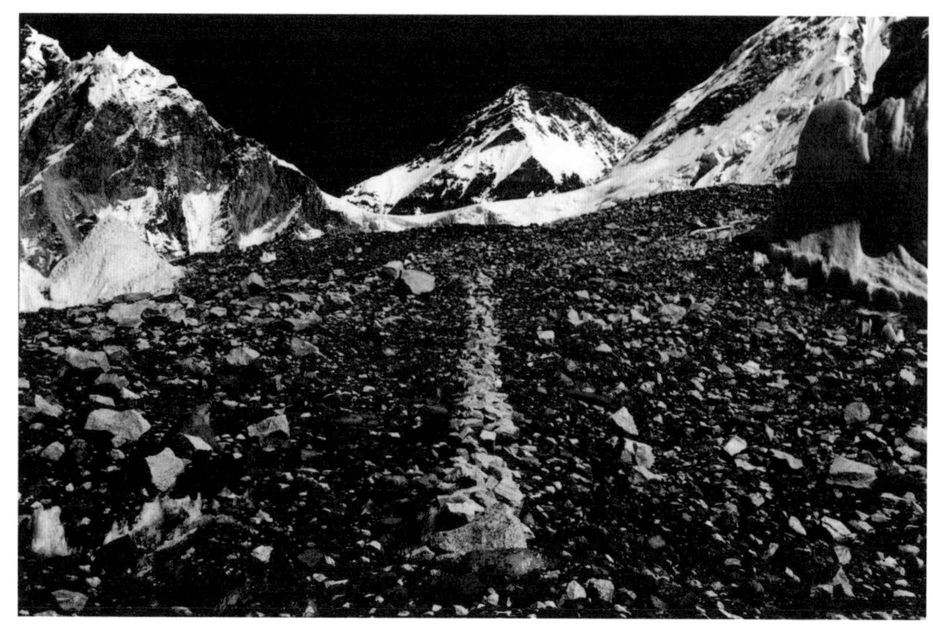

A LINE IN THE HIMALAYAS
1975

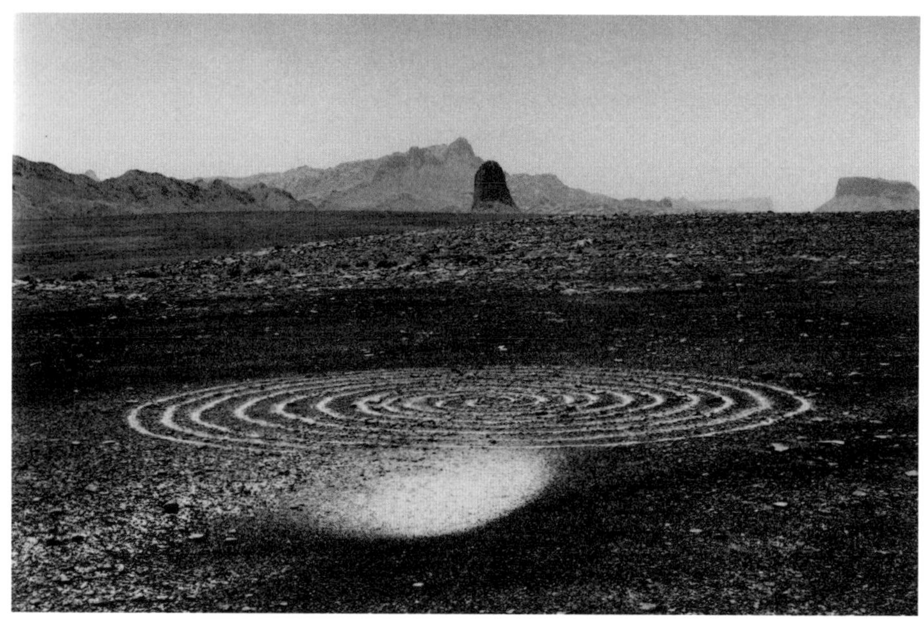

WHIRLWIND SPIRAL
THE SAHARA 1988

Notes on paths

A footpath is a place.
It also goes from place to place, from here to there, and back again.
Any place along it is a stopping place.
Its perceived length could depend on the speed of the traveller, or its steepness, or its difficulty.
Reversing direction does not reverse the travelling time.
A path can be followed, or crossed.
A path is practical: it takes the line of least resistance, or the easiest, or most direct, route.
Sometimes it can be the only line of access through an area.
Paths are shared by all who use them.
Each user could be on a different overall journey, and for a different reason.
Animals also make use of human trails, and vice versa.
A path is made by movement, by the accumulated footprints of its users.
Paths are maintained by repeated use, and would disappear without use.
The characteristics of a path depend upon the nature of the land, but the characteristics can be universal.
A long walk is often made by joining a selection of different paths together, one to another, to make one particular journey.
There is an infinite and cosmic variety of journeys, at all scales.
Around the world in different cultures, paths are marked in many different ways,
with cairns, signposts, milestones, prayer flags, shrines, menai walls, and other sacred or cultural markers.

Published on the occasion of the commission of *Footpath Line*,
Isla de Esculturas, Pontevedra, Spain, 1999.

Art as a formal and holistic description of the real space and experience of landscape and its most elemental materials.

Nature has always been recorded by artists, from prehistoric cave paintings to twentieth-century landscape photography. I too wanted to make nature the subject of my work, but in new ways. I started working outside using natural materials like grass and water, and this evolved into the idea of making a sculpture by walking.

Walking itself has a cultural history, from Pilgrims to the wandering Japanese poets, the English Romantics and contemporary long-distance walkers.

My first work made by walking, in 1967, was a straight line in a grass field, which was also my own path, going 'nowhere'. In the subsequent early mapworks, recording very simple but precise walks on Exmoor and Dartmoor, my intention was to make a new art which was also a new way of walking: walking as art. Each walk followed my own unique, formal route, for an original reason, which was different from other categories of walking, like travelling. Each walk, though not by definition conceptual, realised a particular idea. Thus walking – as art – provided an ideal means for me to explore relationships between time, distance, geography and measurement. These walks are recorded or described in my work in three ways: in maps, photographs or textworks, using whichever form is the most appropriate for each different idea. All these forms feed the imagination, they are the distillation of experience.

Walking also enabled me to extend the boundaries of sculpture, which now had the potential to be deconstructed in the space and time of walking long distances. Sculpture could now be about place as well as material and form.

I consider that my landscape sculptures inhabit the rich territory between two ideological positions, namely that of making 'monuments' or, conversely, of 'leaving only footprints'. Over the years these sculptures have explored some of the variables of transience, permanence, visibility or recognition. A sculpture may be moved, dispersed, carried. Stones can be used as markers of time or distance, or exist as parts of a huge, yet anonymous, sculpture. On a mountain walk a sculpture could be made above the clouds, perhaps in a remote region, bringing an imaginative freedom about how, or where, art can be made in the world.

Published on the occasion of exhibition at
Royal West of England Academy, Bristol, 2000.

Notes on works

A text is a description, or story, of a work in the landscape. It is the simplest and most elegant way to present a particular idea, which could be a walk, or a sculpture, or both.

Relationships are a fundamental theme of many works. I walk on a planet which circles the sun. Each day is a solar event. Time is measured in days, and walking time can be the measure of a country. *Water Walk* (1999) also measures distance by rivers. *A Line of 33 Stones A Walk of 33 Days* (1998) measures the days by stones. *A Circle of Middays* (1997) is a 12 day clockwise walk of 360 miles, being at a new point intersecting an imaginary circle at each midday. It is a textwork which is an abstract map and clock. It is an emblematic distillation of walking time, and daytime, and of the degrees in a circle.

Walking to a Solar Eclipse (1999) is about time and place. It makes use of a cosmic event, the perfect alignment of the Earth, Moon and Sun, as a unique moment which determines the destination of a walk. By contrast, in *Sincholagua Summit Shadow Stones* (1998), the shadow of the volcano in Ecuador could pass across my stone circle after sunrise many times a year.

From Uncertainty to Certainty (1998): this work is a narrative of a dispersed sculpture which uses language, stones, chance, walking and Dartmoor.

In my sculptures, a stone is a stone, and I also use other raw materials like dust, water and mud, only to show their own innate natures. Similarly, I present objective time and space through the measurement of my walks.

Another level of reality, however, is the subatomic world, where particles are in a flux of changing relationships between speed, mass,

WALKING TO A SOLAR ECLIPSE

STARTING FROM STONEHENGE
A WALK OF 235 MILES
ENDING ON A CORNISH HILLTOP
AT A TOTAL ECLIPSE OF THE SUN

1999

positions and time. In *An Exchange of Stones at a Place for a Time on Dartmoor* (1997) and *The Same Thing at a Different Time at a Different Place* (1997), I wanted to make works that were metaphors for things that happen in particle physics. A walk is an event in space-time, and I may carry, scatter, concentrate or place stones, or exchange their places along a walk, as required. My stones are like subatomic particles in the space of the world. These works represent parallel phenomena at a different scale. Our human scale actually exists somewhere nearer the outer boundary of the universe than the subatomic limit.

Speed of the Sound of Loneliness (1998) is about relative speeds, with the metaphor changing from the micro to the cosmic scale. The title is taken from a song written by John Prine and sung by the country singer Nanci Griffith.

The world is continually in geological movement. Continental drift is at the speed our fingernails grow, and parts of Britain have come up from the South Atlantic. Nothing in the landscape is fixed; nothing has its 'eternal' place. Stones are always moving along in rivers and glaciers, being thrown out of volcanos or clattering down mountains. Those works in which I move stones around are just another part of this continuum. The stones of *A Line of 33 Stones A Walk of 33 Days* (1998) constitute an artwork, but of course are still autonomously and anonymously in the world, now as before. Yet they all also happen to be where they are now through the mediation of a moving common denominator, that is, me doing a walk. Each stone represents an interface of scales – one small stone represents a day in a walk of 1,030 miles. Each stone represents a kind of measurement of Britain in relation to the speed of my walking and my route. Each stone has its geological history, yet perhaps momentarily, conceptually, symbolically or privately becomes 'something else' as well.

In *Walking Stones* (1995), by the action of a walk, stones get carried from day to day and from place to place. My work is another agent of change and placement. And walking is simple; stones are common and practical.

Published in *Walking the Line*, Thames & Hudson, London, 2002.

Akita Waterfall Line

My work is about nature.
The most important element of *Akita Waterfall Line* is water.
Together with oxygen, water is one of the most important elements on our planet.

There are three types of nature in this work.
One is the nature of human energy of the speed of my hand.
Next is the nature of water, liquidity of the mud.
Last is the nature of the gravity.

I make the top half of the work and nature does the rest.
I make the line and the gravity makes splashes.

One characteristic of all my mudworks is the contrast between the overall image and the micro details.
In the splashes, there is cosmic variety. Cosmic variety is one big feature of nature.
For examples, clouds, snowflakes, fingerprints, rivers, waterfalls, which never repeat.

Text adapted from a conversation with the artist on the occasion of the commission of *Akita Waterfall Line*, Sophie Home for the Elderly, Akita City, Japan, 2003.

Riverlines

Riverlines (2006) is a handmade work. I have made a 'cave painting' for a twenty-first-century building. It is made with a mix of mud from two rivers – the Hudson and the Avon. Both rivers flow into the same ocean. The River Avon, near Bristol, England, is my 'home' river, while the Hearst building is near the Hudson River.

In general, my work is about leaving or making my mark, with wide variations of permanence or visibility, like footprints or hand prints. In *Riverlines*, the raw materials of mud and water are directly mediated by my own hand and energy. Each line is roughly the width of my reach without the mud drying, so I could keep a continuous surface of wet mud as I came down each line, working with the ease of gravity, like a river falls from source to mouth. Each line is the 'same', each line is 'different', with the cosmic varieties of micro-scale like eddies on a river.

Rivers are one of the themes of my work. For example, I have made a 'straight' walk along a Roman road of the same length as the River Avon. I have walked across England carrying water from each river crossed and pouring it into the next river. I have used moorland riverbeds as footpaths. I have made a sculpture by throwing a line of stones into the Rio Grande from the edge of the canyon rim, from its start at river level to the height of the cliffs at 650 feet. I have walked cross-country between the mouths of two tidal rivers, measuring the walk relative to the tides by lunar time. I have made a book with its pages pulped with the mud of different rivers from around the world.

Rivers are powerful metaphors. The Ganges flows through Indian life and culture. The Mississippi carries the story of the United States in Mark Twain's *Huckleberry Finn*, and it was the 'Big River' of the song by Johnny Cash. It was an honour to make *Riverlines* for a masterpiece building.

Published in *Riverlines*, Ivorypress, London, on the occasion of the commission for the Hearst Tower, New York, 2006.

Slate Oasis

From there and here to the New York Vermont border
To a blue-green/red rockface to the Tatko family
To water snakes to slate mud to the Cairngorm Mountains
To White Water Line to A Disappearing Number
To the Idiot Wind to a Chakra blanket
To Penn Station to stone to stone to choice to chance
To a unique diminishing resource to a change of plan
To sedimentary time to a map of reverie
To sweaty gloves to infinite variety
To the cawing of crows (Mind Rock) to parallel worlds
To Autumn leaves to then and now.

Published on the occasion of the commission of *Slate Oasis* at the Institute for Advanced Study, Princeton, New Jersey, 2007.

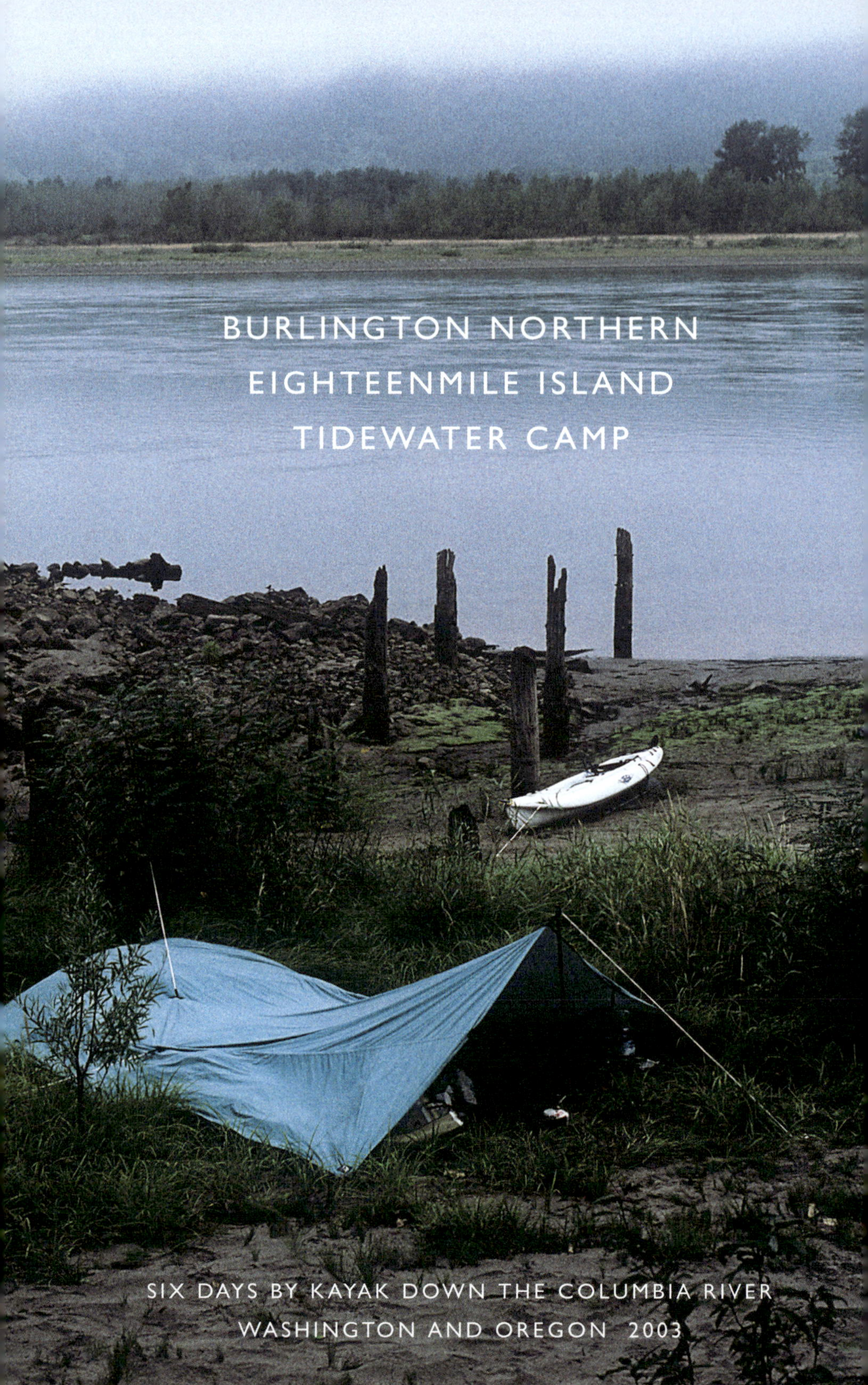
BURLINGTON NORTHERN
EIGHTEENMILE ISLAND
TIDEWATER CAMP
SIX DAYS BY KAYAK DOWN THE COLUMBIA RIVER
WASHINGTON AND OREGON 2003

From cave painting to here and now – human mark-making with what is to hand.

I

I was attracted to these ancient Chinese symbols mostly for the power of the images. The I-Ching, or the Book of Changes, comprises 64 hexagrams which are neither language nor abstract art but something in between. They are all based on variations of eight trigrams representing the natural elements. Their meanings are very open and poetic and universal, like mountain, tranquillity, river, change or wind. *Heaven* (2009), six solid lines, and *Earth* (2009), six broken lines, are the two basic images of which all the others are permutations. For me they represent the opposites and balances in nature, and in my work. Sky and ground. The complementary mental and physical aspects of my art – the intellect but also instinctive spontaneous primitive mark-making.

Heaven and *Earth* are made with mud mixed with a lot of water. Rivers run through my work and water is a major element of my art. My regular, local and best source of mud is the River Avon in Bristol, where I grew up. The mud is formed by the second highest tides in the world.

II

Nature has always been a subject of art, from the first cave paintings to twentieth-century landscape photography. I wanted to use the landscape as an artist in new ways. First I started making work outside using natural materials like grass and water, and this led to the idea of making a sculpture by walking. This was a straight line in a grass field, which was also my own path, going ‘nowhere’. In the subsequent early mapworks, recording very simple but precise walks on Exmoor and Dartmoor, my intention was to make a new art which was also a new way of walking: walking as art. Each walk followed my own unique, formal route, for an original reason, which was different from other categories of walking, like travelling. Each walk, though not by definition conceptual, realised a particular idea. Thus walking – as art – provided a simple way for me to explore relationships between time, distance, geography and measurement. These walks are recorded in my work in the most appropriate way for each different idea: a photograph, a map, or a textwork. All these forms feed the imagination.

III

I like the idea of making something from nothing.

In the mid-sixties I began to think that the language and ambition of art was too formal and orthodox. I felt it had barely engaged with the natural landscapes which cover our planet, or used the experiences those places could offer. Starting from my home territory and gradually spreading further afield, my work has tried to explore this potential. I see it as abstract art laid down in the real spaces of the world. It is not romantic; I use the world as I find it.

To make art only by walking, or leaving ephemeral traces here and there, is my freedom. I can make art in a very simple way but on a huge scale in terms of miles and space. My work can range from making a circle of stones, for example, to just placing a stone at every mile, or carrying a stone from one place to another, or simply making a work only by walking, with no intervention or displacement at all.

My work is completely physical and personal. I've walked or climbed to the place of each sculpture. I've made it with my hands (or feet) and energy at that time. To walk across a country from coast to coast, for example, is both a measure of the land itself – its size, shape and terrain – and also of myself, how long it takes me and not somebody else.

IV

From the beginning I have always made another category of work for indoor and gallery spaces. These are parallel to the works I make in the landscape. They could be made from collected driftwood, or stones from quarries, or mudworks made with my hands or feet on the floor or walls.

The outdoor and indoor works are complementary, although I would have to say that nature, the landscape, the walking, is at the heart of my work and informs the indoor works. But the art world is usually received 'indoors' and I do have a desire to present real work in public time and space, as opposed to photos, maps and texts, which are by definition 'second hand' works. A sculpture feeds the senses at a place, whereas a photograph or text work (from another place) feeds the imagination. For me, these different forms of my work represent freedom and richness – it's not possible to say 'everything' in one way.

I like the fact that every stone is different, one from another, in the same way all fingerprints, or snowflakes (or places) are unique, so no two circles can be alike. In the landscape works, the stones are of the place and remain there. With an indoor sculpture there is a different working rationale. The work is usually first made to fit its first venue in terms of scale, but it is not site specific; the work is autonomous in that it can be remade in another space and place. When this happens, there is a specific written procedure to follow. The selection of the stones is usually random; also individual stones will be in different places within the work each time. Nevertheless, it is the 'same' work whenever it is remade.

V

Dartmoor, in Devon, is my 'home' ground, a place I have used repeatedly in many ways since 1969. It is my prototype landscape, plateau-like, treeless, with plenty of water – perfect walking country. On much bigger scales I have recognised similar places around the world, like the tundra of Alaska, the pampas in Argentina or the steppes of Mongolia.

The idea for *Transference* (2003) came from a phenomenon in subatomic physics whereby a particle can act on the behaviour of another particle so as to create a symmetry of itself, over a relatively vast distance. So I first made a walk on Dartmoor recording various things. Then later on a completely different walk in Japan, I deliberately looked out for and could find certain things that were the same as on Dartmoor, or did repeat, or I could make them repeat, even in the same order of occurrence. It is about a symmetry of places, or events, on different sides of the world, and universal phenomena.

VI

Some of the ideas in my work are about relativity and measurement: of walking time to distance, or stones to distance, or places to sea level, or from river to river, for example. Most of my longer walks are measured by days and nights, by solar time. As the moon makes the tides, *Tide Walk* (1992), in contrast, is measured by lunar time. Since each tide is a 'wave' which travels around the coast, the tide level

T R A N S F E R E N C E

A THREE DAY WALK ON DARTMOOR

FOREST WHITE BUTTERFLIES CROSSING A STREAM
ANIMAL DROPPINGS SLIPPERY BOULDERS PEAT BOG
SLEEPING TOWARDS EAST HALF MOON YELLOW FLOWERS
A RIVER SOURCE FOOTPATH ORANGE MUD
A HILLTOP CAIRN WATERFALL BOOTS DRYING IN THE SUN
A SPICY THAI CAMP MEAL SLEEPING TOWARDS WEST DAWN CHOR
HEAVY DEW A CIRCLE OF STONES FOLLOWING A RIVER

DUPLICATIONS IN THE SAME ORDER OF OCCURRENCE
ALONG A SEVEN DAY WALK ON CHOKAI MOUNTAIN
HALF A LUNAR MONTH LATER

FOREST WHITE BUTTERFLIES CROSSING A STREAM
ANIMAL DROPPINGS SLIPPERY BOULDERS PEAT BOG
SLEEPING TOWARDS EAST HALF MOON YELLOW FLOWERS
A RIVER SOURCE FOOTPATH ORANGE MUD
A HILLTOP CAIRN WATERFALL BOOTS DRYING IN THE SUN
A SPICY THAI CAMP MEAL SLEEPING TOWARDS WEST DAWN CHOR
HEAVY DEW A CIRCLE OF STONES FOLLOWING A RIVER

ENGLAND AND JAPAN 2003

times between the English Channel and the Bristol Channel vary. So *Tide Walk* is about relativity, in that the tide will always be in a different state from the starting point of view of the walk compared to the end of it. It is like measuring the walk with two different clocks.

Hours Miles (1996) is a symmetry and balance between 'difficulty' and 'ease'. First I made a continuous road walk in 24 hours which came to 82 miles. Then I inverted the numbers and walked 24 miles in 82 hours.

Walking to a Lunar Eclipse (1996) uses a correspondence between sun and moon. It measures a walk from a midday high tide to a midnight cosmic event, the perfect alignment of sun, earth and moon. The walking miles correspond to the number of days in that year, a leap year.

The walks in this room are 'local', they crisscross the south and south-west of England. *White Water Line* (2009) demonstrates different types of energy. It uses china clay from the big clay pits near St Austell in Cornwall. This work represents the force of my hand speed, and the forces of water, chance and gravity. I make the top line of the image and nature makes the rest, revealing the cosmic variety of the microscale.

VII

Walking has enabled me to extend the boundaries of sculpture, which can now be deconstructed in the space and time of walking relatively long distances. Over the years my landscape sculptures have explored some of the variables of accessibility, solitude, isolation, permanence, visibility or recognition. I have used stones as markers of time or distance; they may be parts of a huge yet anonymous work. Stones can be added, moved, dispersed, exchanged or carried to make a work. My stones are like grains of sand in the space of the landscape and I can find them almost anywhere.

My work is about movement and stillness, the walking and the stopping places. Sometimes I make a sculpture when I stop to rest. I suppose my art covers a wide range, from works like these which could be practically unnoticeable or disappear in minutes, like a water drawing or dusty footprints, to a long-lasting work in a museum. The world is full of relatively permanent things like rock strata or the sea, but also transient things, like the life span of a butterfly, or the endlessly changing patterns of seaweed on a beach. I would like to think my work reflects and uses this rich complexity and reality.

VIII

My work really is just about being a human being living on this planet and using nature as its source. I like the intellectual pleasure of original ideas and the physical pleasure of realising them. A long road or wilderness walk is basically walking all day and sleeping all night. I enjoy the simple pleasures of well-being, independence, opportunism, eating, dreaming, happenstance, of passing through the land and sometimes leaving (memorable) traces along the way, of finding a new campsite each night. And then moving on.

Introductory texts written to accompany the exhibition
Heaven and Earth, Tate Britain, 2009.

My art is in the nature of things

I like the idea of making something from nothing

I can walk all day and sleep all night following an idea

I use the land without the need of ownership

My talent as an artist is to walk across a moor
or place a stone on the ground

My work is about movement and stillness
the walking and the stopping places
it can be either passing by or leaving a mark

I use intuition and chance body and mind
time and space

I use the world as I find it.

Published as a leaflet to accompany the exhibition
Heaven and Earth, Tate Britain, 2009.

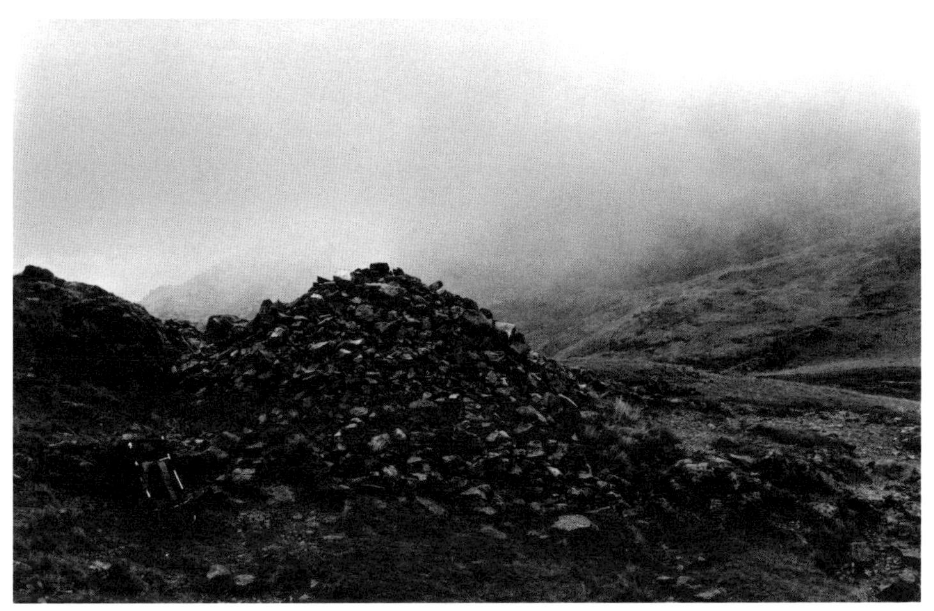

A THOUSAND STONES ADDED TO A FOOTPATH CAIRN
ENGLAND 1974

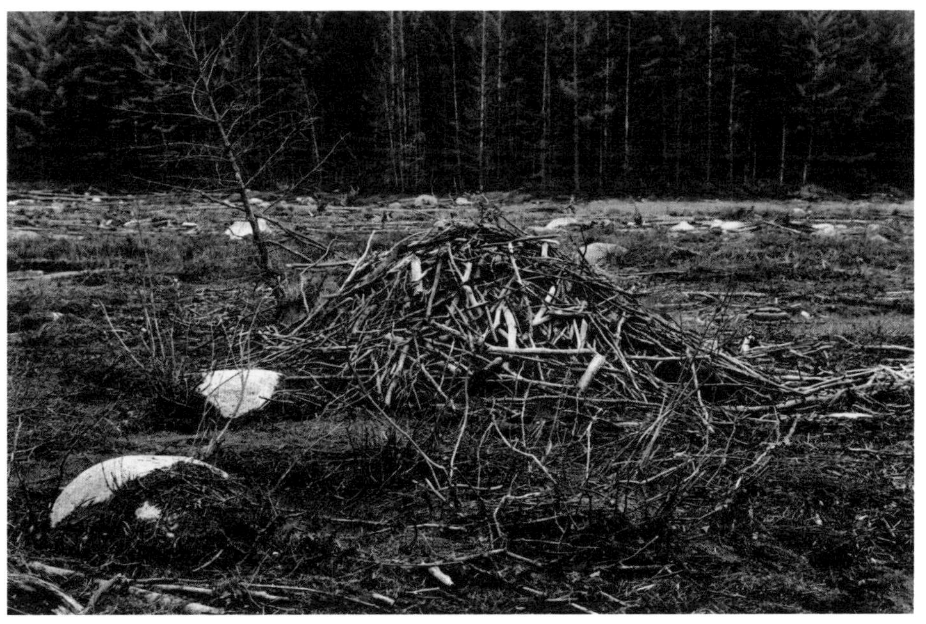

A HUNDRED STICKS PLACED ON A BEAVER LODGE
A SIX DAY WALK IN THE ADIRONDACK MOUNTAINS
THE FOOTPATH CROSSING BEAVER DAMS ALONG THE WAY
NEW YORK 1985

The infinite variety of fingerprints:
A continuum from the first art made in caves.
These works are handmade domestic objects
Marked with one moment after another.
My fingerprint is unique and each print of my
Finger is unique.

A magic touch,
A tender touch,
The human touch.

Published on the occasion of the exhibition
at Galerie Kamila Regent, Saignon, France, 2010.

South America was made on the first big overseas journey Hamish Fulton and I made together. We landed in La Paz and travelled in Bolivia, Peru and Chile for almost two months. I had preconceived the idea for a book, but not the particular places or images it might contain. We travelled by hitchhiking cars and communal trucks, on buses, on trains, by taxi, and by walking and climbing. We had a free and adaptable itinerary, often changing our plans on impulse or by circumstance. This fitted the general idea for the book, so that the great variety of places for the drawings occurred naturally, by chance, along the way. It is a book about movement, time, space, luck and opportunism. I had not seen the moon 'upside down' before. The positive /negative printing of the drawings comes from the characteristic of Indian weaving, and the cover drawing was influenced also by the traditional patterns of the blankets etc. we saw in the local markets.

Published in *South America*, Zédélé Editions, 2012.

In the nature of things:
Art about mobility, lightness and freedom.
Simple creative acts of walking and marking
about place, locality, time, distance and measurement.
Works using raw materials and my human scale
In the reality of landscapes.

The music of stones, paths of shared footmarks,
sleeping by the river's roar.

Published in 2011.

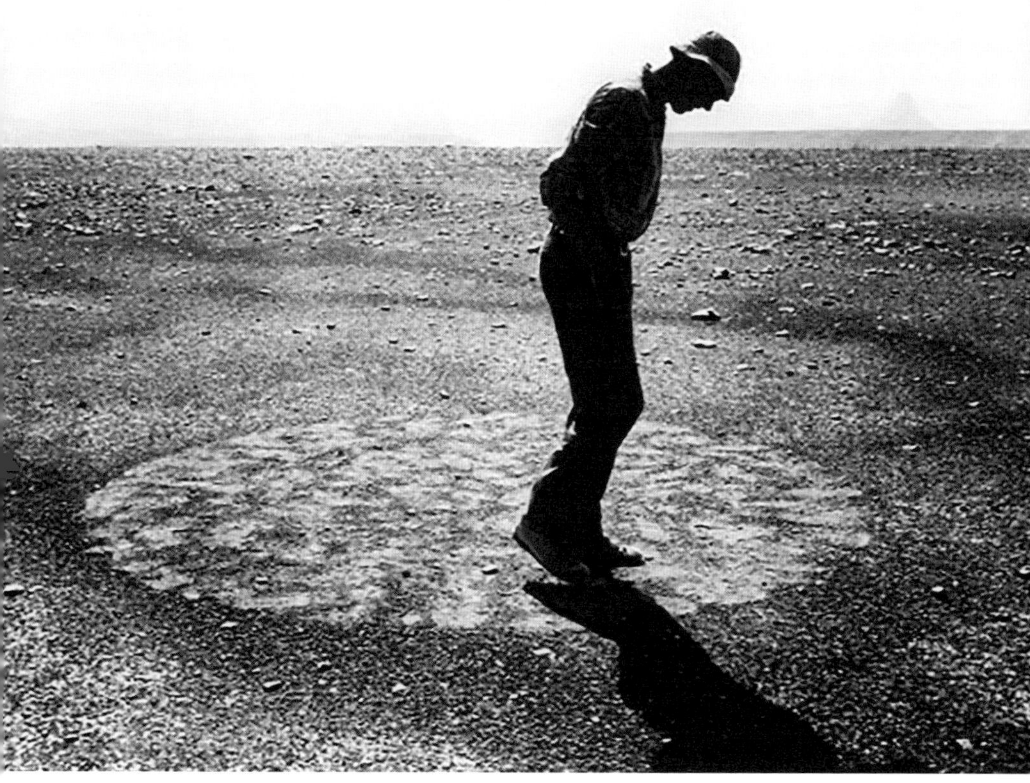

Richard Long, Sahara 1988

Walking as a medium enabled me to articulate ideas about time and space; space meaning distance. And walking was so simple and practical. I could do it on the country roads of England or in the public wilderness areas of National Parks. Walking represented independence and freedom, I could make art – I could be an artist – potentially, theoretically, anywhere in the world, just for the price of an air ticket. In 1969, I made a work on the top of Mount Kilimanjaro. On that trip, I also made a mapwork along the equator, *Line Dance* (1969), a zigzag walk from one hemisphere to the other. In those days, I did not feel the need of money, for the ownership or possession of land, or for the use of big machines to make my work. In that sense, it was a very different philosophy from American Land art. I was interested in scale, but not in mass, not in building 'monuments'. I could make the work *A Thousand Miles A Thousand Hours* (1974), just by walking.

In the 1970s, I had the idea to walk exactly one hundred miles, up and down, back and forth, in a straight line, in different landscapes around the world. The first was across the boggy mountains of the West of Ireland, the next the red outback of Australia, the next the High Plains of Alberta – walking on a sea of grass, and lastly in a bamboo forest in Japan. The idea was that the straight walk, the one hundred miles, stayed the same, but the places, the landscapes, changed.

For me, walking in wilderness landscapes is also the best way to find places to make sculptures along the way. I consider these works like the stopping places, or marks of passage. They are of the place, which is itself part of the locality. They are a sort of simple celebration of the place, like its stones, or the horizon, or the mist, and of me being there, at that particular time, possibly never to pass that way again. I sometimes think of these works as songs, like Hank Williams or Chuck Berry. I have said that a sculpture can be as far as the eye can see, meaning the stones could be aligned to a feature on the horizon, for example, or a passing cloud, at that moment, in relation to the viewer.

It is never my intention that these landscape sculptures remain permanently, or become known sites to be visited. Rather, that they are out there in the world, somewhere, perhaps to be seen by chance by locals, or even nobody at all. But nevertheless, they embody the spirit that art can be made anywhere, at any time, spontaneously, in solitude, in remote, empty places, which is still, in fact, the reality and characteristic of most of our planet.

Many of my stone sculptures in the landscape could be scattered by the elements, or animals. My line in the Himalayas, on the Khumbu Glacier, would naturally have broken up and disintegrated as the glacier moved down the valley like a slow river. Stones I place on roads could be seen, but not recognised or identified as art. Their meaning is only known in the narrative of a textwork. Nevertheless, the stones do not disappear, they are still out there in the world, anonymously, as they were before I used them, transformed only in the context of my art.

I am not a Conceptual artist, meaning I use real stones, I walk my walks, and they are made in real time. Nevertheless, ideas are very important, especially in the landscape works.

A FAVOURITE EXAMPLES IS:

A Thousand Stones added to the Footpath Cairn (1974)

Cairns are common to many footpaths the world over, to mark the way. They are made cumulatively and collectively, by passing travellers. I added exactly a thousand stones, as a sculpture, to an existing cairn, which will have been subsequently added to by countless others over the years. So this work becomes part of a social continuum.

TWO WORKS ABOUT THE SEA LEVEL:

1449 Stones at 1449 Feet (1979)
Sea Level Waterline (1982)

A line of water poured along the desert ground of Death Valley in California. Along a walk in Alaska, on the shore of the Bering Strait, I made a circle of driftwood on the Arctic Circle, one type of circle upon another, as it were.

SOME WALKS ABOUT IDEAS:

Throwing a Stone Around MacGillycuddy's Reeks (1977)

MacGillycuddy's Reeks are a group of mountains in the West of Ireland. I found a white marble stone and threw it from place to place, from throw to throw, on a walk around this ring of mountains, returning the stone to the place where I found it. An alternative to walking to the summits. A two-and-a-half-day walk and 3,628 throws of the stone.

A Cloudless Walk, France (1995)

An eastward walk of 121 miles in three and a half days from the mouth of the Loire to the first cloud. I started this walk with the intention to walk across France, but I noticed, as each day dawned and remained cloudless, I decided it would be a better, more unique or original idea to end the walk when I saw the first cloud. That's a good example of how opportunism, or being open to chance, or changing circumstances, can play a part in my work. By contrast, an example of a very pre-determined idea, and simply following it:

A FIVE DAY WALK

FIRST DAY TEN MILES
SECOND DAY TWENTY MILES
THIRD DAY THIRTY MILES
FOURTH DAY FORTY MILES
FIFTH DAY FIFTY MILES

TOTNES TO BRISTOL BY ROADS AND LANES
ENGLAND 1980

A sort of balance, or symmetry, between easy walking and relatively hard walking. My interest in time and movement: Walking in a Moving World. A six-day walk in Wales recording decreasing speeds, from passing across racing cloud shadows, to climbing over a glacial boulder moving at geological slowness.

Crescent to Cross (2012)

A walk from the Great Mosque of Cordoba to the Cathedral of Santiago de Compostela. An 18-day road walk in Spain and Portugal connecting two histories and religions.

I am interested in universals: stones, water, mud, hands, days, circles, symmetry, gravity, footpaths and roads. Walking is universal; we walked out of Africa for the first time as humans, on foot. Journeys are common to all people and cultures and yet it interests me to make walks that follow or realise original ideas, which are different from migrations or making journeys, or exploring, or being a nomad, or a pilgrim. Walking as art, in fact.

Using walking as both medium and measure, I have utilised or referenced many natural and cosmic phenomena in my work, like the equinox, the midsummer and midwinter solstice, sun and moon total eclipses, and tides – measuring some walks by lunar time as opposed to the days and nights of solar time. I have also used tidal bores or waves, the earth's magnetic axis, and metaphors for events on the subatomic scale. I have used stones to represent atomic particles. I have made a walk about the Japanese tsunami.

To consider what it means to make work in nature as an artist, I might think of two approaches, or attitudes. The first – to leave only footprints and take out only photographs. Alternatively – make more or less permanent objects or large-scale sculptures. I consider that my landscape works inhabit a rich territory between those two positions, they being a fluid mix of time, stones, space, movement, water, images and language.

It has always been my pleasure and intention to be *in* nature, whether walking down a country road, or in mountains or deserts, in all weathers, in rain, wind or snow, with my rucksack on my back, sleeping in my tent at night. On those trips, I feel the most energised, focused and creative. My work is my dialogue, physical and mental, with the world I live in.

Presented as a talk at the Abu Dhabi Art Fair, November 2014.

Battery Park

Battery Park is the first artwork I ever made in New York. In 1969 I was on the way to Ithaca for the exhibition *Earth Art* at the Andrew Dickson White Museum of Art at Cornell. I met John Gibson at a bar, and I showed him a few small black-and-white photographs of landscape works I had made in England, which I was carrying around in an Henri Wintermans cigar tin. John liked them and offered me a show of these pieces at the Gibson Gallery the next week. He suggested that, for the exhibition, I take my small prints to a poster shop and have them blown up. Printed and mounted on poster board, they comprised my first show. John suggested I go down to Battery Park to make the work pictured here. I dug up a long rectangle and made several undulations inside it. Using the excess soil, I formed a mound that I covered with sod.

Early on, I realised the world outside the studio was more interesting than what was going on inside it. People have been making impressions in the earth for thousands of years; in general, my work takes its place among many other man-made marks. I explore a rich territory between the Land art of monuments and machine-made earthworks and, at the other extreme, of leaving only footprints or temporary traces of passage.

Modern Painters, September 2015, p.37.

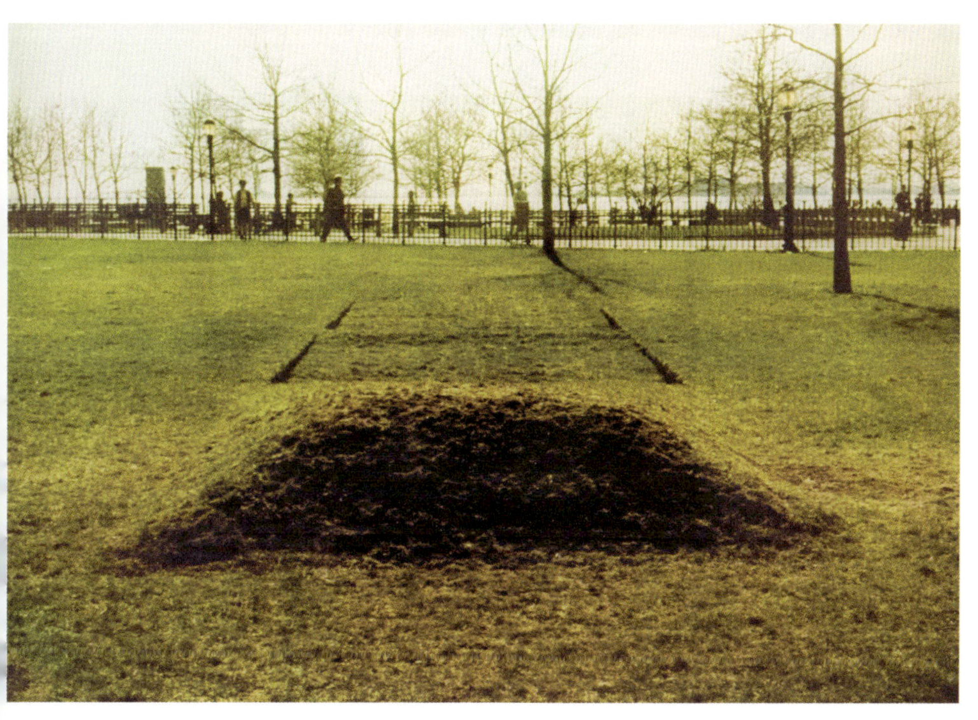

BATTERY PARK

1969

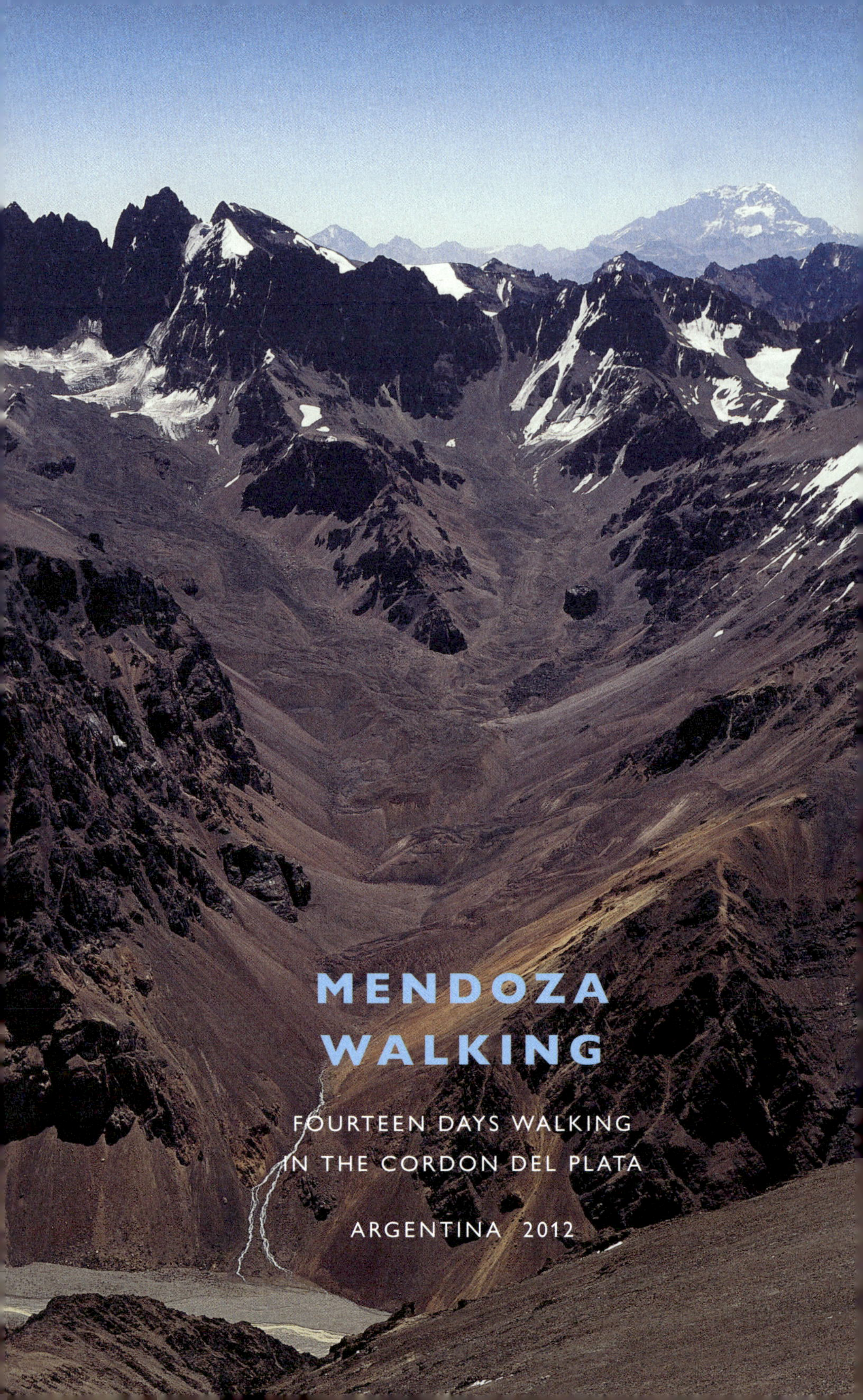
MENDOZA
WALKING
FOURTEEN DAYS WALKING
IN THE CORDON DEL PLATA
ARGENTINA 2012

A Line Made by Walking – words after the fact

The work originated through intuition.
After it was made I realised it could be the beginning of a journey – a life line.
In the next straight walk I made, the line in the grass became a line drawn on a map.
I had the idea before I arrived at the place. I took a stopping train going south-west out of London with no destination in mind. I got off at the first station in the first real countryside the train was passing through and found a suitable field easily and by chance.
The fact that over the subsequent years I have walked in straight lines for other reasons, over different distances, in different landscapes around the world, gives that work a real significance to a point of view which I have followed all my life.
Also at that time I was realising that to engage with the reality and space of landscape was the most satisfying and ambitious – physically and intellectually – way I could choose to make art.
Nature, the diversity of places, natural and cosmic phenomena, natural materials, movement, time and distance were to become my subject matter.

Bristol, 2015.

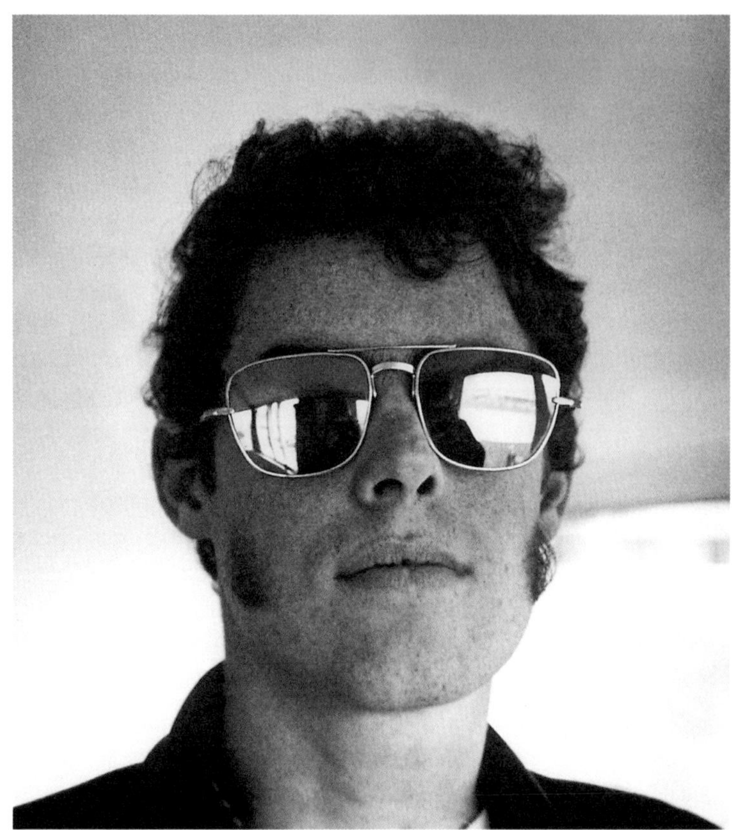

Richard Long circa 1970

Richard Long

Born 1945 in Bristol, United Kingdom
Currently lives and works in Bristol

Education
1962–65
West of England College of Art, Bristol

1966–68
St Martin's School of Art, London

SELECTED AWARDS

1988
Kunstpreis Aachen, Neuen Galerie – Sammlung Ludwig, Aachen

1989
Turner Prize, Tate Gallery, London

1990
Chevalier dans l'Ordre des Arts et des Lettres, Ministèire de la Culture, France

1995
Doctor of Letters, *honoris causa*, University of Bristol, Bristol

1996
Wilhelm Lehmbruck-Preis, Duisburg

2009
Praemium Imperiale Art Award for Sculpture, Japan Art Association, Japan

2010
Doctor of Letters, *honoris causa*, University of St Andrews, St Andrews

2012
Commander of the Most Excellent Order of the British Empire (CBE)

2015
Art Icon, Whitechapel Gallery, London

SELECTED SOLO EXHIBITIONS

1968
Richard J Long: Sculpture, Konrad Fischer Galerie, Dusseldorf, 21 September–18 October

1969
John Gibson Gallery, New York, 22 February–14 March
Sculpture, Konrad Fischer Galerie, Dusseldorf, 5 July–1 August
Richard Long: Exhibition One Year, Museum Haus Lange, Krefeld, July 1969–July 1970
Sculpture, Galerie Yvon Lambert, Paris, 5–26 November
A Sculpture by Richard Long, Galleria Françoise Lambert, Milan, 15 November–1 December

1970
Eine Skulptur von Richard Long, Konrad Fischer Galerie, Dusseldorf, 11 May–9 June
4 Skulpturen, Städtisches Museum Abteiberg, Mönchengladbach, 16 July–30 August
Dwan Gallery, New York, 3–29 October

1971
Galleria Gian Enzo Sperone, Turin, opened 13 April
A Sculpture by Richard Long, Art & Project, Amsterdam, 17 July–6 August
Whitechapel Art Gallery, London, 9–21 November
Museum of Modern Art, Oxford, 9–23 December

1972
Projects: Richard Long, Museum of Modern Art, New York, 14 March–17 April
Look the Ground in the Eye, Galerie Yvon Lambert, Paris, opened 3 May

1973
Lisson Gallery, London, 23 January–24 February
Wide White Space, Antwerp, 5 March–12 April
A Rolling Stone, Konrad Fischer Galerie, Dusseldorf, 29 March–25 June
Stedelijk Museum, Amsterdam, 7 December 1973–27 January 1974

1974
A Line of 164 Stones, A Walk of 164 Miles, John Weber Gallery, New York, 4–29 May
Scottish National Gallery of Modern Art, Edinburgh, 9 July–11 August
Lisson Gallery, London, 1–30 November
River Avon Driftwood, Konrad Fischer Galerie, Dusseldorf, 20 December 1974–19 January 1975

1975
River Avon Driftwood, Crossing Two Rivers–Minnesota/Wiltshire, Art & Project, Amsterdam, 18 March–5 April
Driftwood, Wide White Space, Antwerp, 15 April–16 May
Galerie Yvon Lambert, Paris, 24 April–20 May
Galerie Rolf Preisig, Basel, 12 June–12 July
Galleria Banco, Brescia, 2 October–16 October

1976
Stone Circles, Galleria Gian Enzo Sperone, Rome, 16 March–April
River Avon Driftwood, Konrad Fischer Galerie, Dusseldorf, 15 May–11 June
Wide White Space, Antwerp, 25 May–10 June
Stones, Lisson Gallery, London, 24–26 June
British Pavilion, XXXVII Venice Biennale, Venice, 18 July–10 October
Art Agency, Tokyo, opened 14 October
River Avon Driftwood, Arnolfini, Bristol, 23 November–24 December
Sperone Westwater Fischer, New York, 4 December 1976–8 January 1977

1977
The North Woods, Whitechapel Art Gallery, London, 25 January–27 February
A Stone Sculpture by Richard Long, Art & Project, Amsterdam, 8 February–5 March
Kamienne Kolo, Galeria Akumulatory 2, Poznan, Poland, 9 May–19 June
Galerie Rolf Preisig, Basel, 17 May–21 June
Lisson Gallery, London, 21 May–18 June
Kunsthalle Bern, Bern, 15 July–7 August
John Kaldor Art Project 6 [revised: *Kaldor Public Art Project 7*], National Gallery of Victoria, Melbourne, 8 December 1977–7 January 1978 and Art Gallery of New South Wales, Sydney, 15 December 1977–5 February 1978

1978
Driftwood Circle, Art & Project, Amsterdam, 10 January–4 February
Galerie Yvon Lambert, Paris, 2 February–3 April
A Canoe Journey Down the River Severn, Konrad Fischer Galerie, Dusseldorf, 11 March–7 April
Outback, Lisson Gallery, London, 2–20 May
Park Square Gallery, Leeds, 6–30 June
InK–Halle für internationale neue Kunst, Zurich, 19 July–31 August
Sperone Westwater Fischer, New York, 30 September–21 October

Ausstellungsraum Ulrich Rückriem, Hamburg, 21 October–12 November

1979
InK–Halle für internationale neue Kunst, Zurich, 19 February–8 April
The River Avon, Anthony d'Offay Gallery, London, 15 March–12 April
Galerie Rolf Preisig, Basel, 6 April–5 May
Recent Work by Richard Long, Orchard Gallery, Londonderry, 1–19 May
Chalk Stone Line 1979, Photographic Gallery, University of Southampton, Southampton, 11–29 June
Sculpturen en Fotowerken, Van Abbemuseum, Eindhoven, 29 September–28 October
Lisson Gallery, London, 9 October–16 November
Art Agency, Tokyo, 20 October–16 November
Museum of Modern Art, Oxford, 11 November –23 December

1980
Stone Circles, Karen & Jean Bernier, Athens, 1–29 March
Stones and Sticks, Art & Project, Amsterdam, 22 March–19 April
Fogg Art Museum, Harvard University, Cambridge, MA, 17 April–1 June
Sperone Westwater Fischer, New York, 26 April–17 May
New Work, Anthony d'Offay Gallery, London, 17 September–16 October
Low Water Circle Walk, Konrad Fischer Galerie, Dusseldorf, 8–29 November

1981
Sperone Westwater Fischer, New York, 10–31 January
Black and White Willow Circles, Graeme Murray Gallery, Edinburgh, 7–28 February
Konrad Fischer Galerie, Zurich, 8 May–6 June
Anthony d'Offay Gallery, London, 3 June–8 July
New Work, David Bellman Gallery, Toronto, 12 September–10 October
Centre d'arts plastiques contemporains, Bordeaux, 4 December 1981–30 January 1982

1982
Art & Project, Amsterdam, 23 January–20 February
Galerie Yvon Lambert, Paris, 13 February–12 March
Flow Ace Gallery, Venice, CA, 1–31 May
Sperone Westwater Fischer, New York, 25 September–23 October
National Gallery of Canada, Ottawa, 21 October 1982–9 January 1983

1983
Canadian Sculptures, David Bellman Gallery, Toronto, 19 March–16 April
Selected Works, 1965–1983, Arnolfini, Bristol, 26 March–7 May
New Works, Anthony d'Offay Gallery, London, 29 March–12 May
Century Cultural Foundation, Tokyo, 18 April–31 May
Art Agency, Tokyo, 20 April–31 May
Tucci Russo, Turin, 20 May–30 September
Konrad Fischer Galerie, Dusseldorf, 16 September–14 October

1984
Watermarks, Coracle Press, London, 7–31 January
Stone, Galleria Lucio Amelio, Naples, 14 January–6 February
New Works, Galerie Crousel-Hussenot, Paris, 10 March–15 April
Jean Bernier Gallery, Athens, 29 March–28 April
Concentrations 9: Richard Long, Dallas Museum of Art, Dallas 31 March–8 July
A Lapland Walk, Sperone Westwater, New York, 5 May–2 June
North Carolina Museum of Art (with Gilbert & George), Raleigh, 9 June–9 September
Butler Gallery, Kilkenny Castle, Kilkenny, 25 August–23 September
River Avon Mud Works, Orchard Gallery, Londonderry, 23 September–13 October
Muddy Water Falls, Anthony d'Offay Gallery, London, 16 October–16 November
Konrad Fischer Galerie, Dusseldorf, 20 October–30 November

1985
Buchmann Galerie, Basel, 26 January–9 March
From Pass to Pass, Anthony d'Offay Gallery, London, 4–29 June
Abbot Hall Art Gallery, Kendal, 6 July–1 September
Malmö Konsthall, Malmö, 20 September–24 November
Padiglione d'Arte Contemporanea di Milano, Milan, 29 November 1985–25 February 1986

1986
Palacio de Cristal, Madrid, 28 January–20 April
Oeuvres Récentes, Galerie Crousel-Hussenot, Paris, 12 April–13 May
Cleveland Museum of Art, Cleveland, 27 May–20 July
Sperone Westwater, New York, 6–16 September
Solomon R. Guggenheim Museum, New York, 12 September–30 November
New Works, Anthony d'Offay Gallery, London, 8 October–12 November

Porin Taidemuseo, Porin, Finland, 4 December –25 January 1987
White Foot Circles, Tucci Russo, Turin, 12 December 1986–14 March 1987

1987
Stone Water Miles, Musée Rath, Geneva, 7 May–21 June
Allotment One: Richard Long–Stone Field, Renshaw Hall, Liverpool, June–August
Donald Young Gallery, Chicago, IL, 23 October–28 November
Cairn, Cairn Gallery, Nailsworth, Gloucestershire, 7 November–5 December
Magasin–Centre National d'Art Contemporain, Grenoble, 13 December 1987–9 January 1988
Jean Bernier Gallery, Athens, 15 December 1987–9 January 1988

1988
Graeme Murray Gallery, Edinburgh, 7–28 February
Konrad Fischer Galerie, Dusseldorf, 20 February–30 March
3. Kunstpreis Aachen: Richard Long, Neue Galerie – Sammlung Ludwig, Aachen, 14 October–26 November
Anthony d'Offay Gallery, London, 22 October–26 November

1989
Kunstverein St. Gallen, St Gallen, Switzerland, 15 January–26 February
Jean Bernier Gallery, Athens, 23 February–27 March
Sperone Westwater, New York, 18 March–15 April
Footprints, Coopers Gallery, Bristol Old Vic, Bristol, 14 April–27 May
Tucci Russo, Turin, 21 April–20 July
Galerie Pietro Sparta, Chagny, France, 10 June–1 October
Collection Panza – Richard Long, Bruce Nauman (with Bruce Nauman), Musée d'art moderne de Saint-Étienne, Saint-Étienne, 30 June–6 September
Surf Roar, La Jolla Museum of Contemporary Art, La Jolla, CA, 20 August–15 October
New Works, Henry Moore Sculpture Trust Studio, Halifax, 25 October–10 December

1990
Arnolfini, Bristol, 20 January–25 February
Water and Stones, Anthony d'Offay Gallery, London, 26 January–24 February
New Work, Angles Gallery, Santa Monica, CA, 23 March–31 April
Galerie Tschudi, Glarus, Switzerland, 7 July–13 October
Turf Line, Konrad Fischer Galerie, Dusseldorf, 14 July–7 September
Tate Gallery, London, 3 October 1990–6 January 1991; and Tate Gallery, Liverpool, 23 January–3 March 1991
Magasin 3 Stockholm Konsthall, Stockholm, 5 October 1990–30 January 1991
Musée départmental d'art contemporain de Rochechouart, Rochechouart, France, 11 October 1990–6 January 1991

1991
Galeria Weber, Alexander y Cobo (with Hamish Fulton), Madrid, 5 February–30 March
Städtische Galerie im Städel, Frankfurt am Main, 21 February–12 May
Tucci Russo, Turin, 27 February–27 April
Walking in Circles, Hayward Gallery, London, 14 June–11 August
Sperone Westwater, New York, 19 October–16 November
Galerie Tschudi, Glarus, 23 November 1991–23 May 1992

1992
Jean Bernier Gallery, Athens, 23 January–21 March
Mississippi Mud, Angles Gallery, Santa Monica, CA, 9 April–9 May
Spring Circle and Other Works, Mead Gallery, Warwick, 6 June–4 July
Fundacio Espai Poblenou, Barcelona, 9 June –November
High Tide to High Tide, Konrad Fischer Galerie, Dusseldorf, 7 November–2 December

1993
65 Thompson Street, New York, 30 January–13 March
River to River, Musée d'Art Moderne de la Ville de Paris, Paris, 25 March–29 May
Georgia Granite Line, Cleveland Center for Contemporary Art, Cleveland, 2 April–27 June
Inkong Gallery, Seoul, 23 April–19 June
Wayside Stones, Anthony d'Offay Gallery, London, 25 June–12 August
Center for Contemporary Arts Santa Fe, Santa Fe, 22 October 1993–7 January 1994
Skulpturen, Fotos, Texte, Bücher, Neues Museum Weserburg Bremen and Forum Langenstraße, Bremen, 28 November 1993–13 February 1994
Galerie Tschudi, Glarus, 4 December 1993–28 May 1994

1994
Shenandoah/Neandertal, Konrad Fischer Galerie, Dusseldorf, 3 March–5 April
Kunstsammlung Nordrhein-Westfalen, Dusseldorf, 5 March–24 April

Books, Prints, Printed Matter, New York Public Library, New York, 26 March–25 June
Sperone Westwater, New York, 26 March–23 April
Museum Studies 2: Richard Long, Philadelphia Museum of Art, Philadelphia, 12 April–7 August
Palazzo delle Esposizioni, Rome, 4 May–30 June
Pier Arts Centre, Stromness, Orkney, 17 June–9 July
Tucci Russo, Turin, Italy, 1 October 1994–25 March 1995
22ª Bienal Internacional de São Paulo, São Paulo, 12 October–11 December
Stones, Clay, Water, Museum of Contemporary Art, Sydney, 21 December 1994–13 February 1995

1995
Peter Blum Gallery (with Alighiero E Boetti), New York, 5 February–5 April
Bündner Kunstmuseum, Chur, Switzerland, 11 February–26 March
New Work, Laura Carpenter Fine Art, Santa Fe, 11 March–22 April
La Sala de Exposiciones de la Diputación de Huesca, Huesca, Spain, 26 May–10 September
Önnur hæd, Reykjavik, Iceland, 5 July–31 August
Michael Hue-Williams Fine Art, London, 22 August–29 September
A Walk in Iceland, A Circle of Slate, A Walk in New Mexico, Anthony d'Offay Gallery, London, 13 September–14 October
Daniel Weinberg Gallery, San Francisco, 2 November 1995–13 January 1996
Walking Stones, Konrad Fischer Galerie, Dusseldorf, 16 December 1995–6 February 1996

1996
Setagaya Art Museum, Tokyo, 1 February–24 March; and National Museum of Modern Art, Kyoto, 23 April–26 May
Circles Cycles Mud Stones, Contemporary Arts Museum, Houston, 27 April–9 June
Here and There, Modern Art Museum of Fort Worth, Fort Worth, 5 May–7 July
Dolomite Stones, AR/GE Kunst, Bolzano, Italy, 10 November–30 November
Galerie Tschudi, Glarus, 29 October 1996–13 January 1997
Donald Young Gallery, Seattle, 7 November–21 December
Dartmoor Time, Spacex Gallery, Exeter, 26 November–21 December

1997
Wind Circle Memory Sticks, Wilhelm Lehmbruck Museum, Duisburg, 19 January–30 March
Ausstellungsgesellschaft Zollverein, Essen, 19 January–31 March
A Road from the Past to the Future, Crawford Arts Centre, St Andrews, 21 March–20 April
Benesse House Museum, Naoshima, Japan, 25 May–ongoing
More and Less: The Early Work of Richard Long, Henry Moore Institute, Leeds, 1 May–13 July
Sperone Westwater, New York, 20 September–8 November
Spazio Zero – Cantieri Culturali alla Zisa, Palermo, 1 November 1997–15 January 1998
Bristol City Museum & Art Gallery, Bristol, 20 December 1997–31 March 1998

1998
Kunst auf der Zugspitze, Bayerische Zugspitzbahn AG (in collaboration with Neues Museum Nürnberg), Nuremberg, 18 January–14 June
Richard Long omcirkeld, Witte Zaal, Ghent, 3–28 March
Anthony d'Offay Gallery, London, 28 April–18 June
Yorkshire Sculpture Park, Wakefield, 11 June–6 September
Galerie Tschudi, Glarus, 27 June–17 October
Galleria Tucci Russo, Turin, 19 September 1998–28 February 1999

1999
Every Grain of Sand, Kunstverein Hannover and Orangerie Herrenhausen, Hannover, 17 January–14 March
Platonic Walks, Bernier/Eliades Gallery, Athens, 4 March–21 April
Richard Long em Braga, Galeria Mário Sequeira, Braga, Portugal, 22 May–31 July
Centre for Artists' Books, Dundee, 18 September–17 November
Being in the Moment, Museum Kurhaus Kleve, Cleves, Germany, 4 December 1999–16 January 2000

2000
Two Thousand Fingerprints, Griffin Contemporary, Venice, CA, 22 January–4 March
Anthony d'Offay Gallery, London, 18 February–11 March
The Space of Time, Sperone Westwater, New York, 1 April–29 April
Fingerprint Stones, James Cohan Gallery, New York, 5 April–13 May
New York Projects (Public Art Fund project), Doris C Freedman Plaza, Seagram Plaza and New York City Subway, New York, 12 April–2 June
Royal West of England Academy, Bristol, 21 May–8 July
Guggenheim Museum Bilbao, Bilbao, 24 June–15 October
Richard Long im Schloss Leuk, Schloss Leuk, Leuk-Stadt, Switzerland, 20 August–21 October

Museo do Arte Moderna e Contemporanea di Trento e Rovereto, Trento, 2 September–5 November
Konrad Fischer Galerie, Dusseldorf, 14 October–25 November
River Avon Mud on River Avon Driftwood, Galerie Tschudi, Glarus, 2 December 2000–17 February 2001

2001
Mountain, Galerie Daniel Templon, Paris, 26 April–26 May
Sculptures, Galerie Tschudi, Glarus, 26 May–28 July
Museum Kurhaus Kleve, Cleves, 24 June–23 September
Heaven and Earth, Museu Serralves, Porto, 20 October 2001–6 January 2002
On Site: Richard Long, Milwaukee Art Museum, Milwaukee, 14 November 2001–3 March 2002

2002
Delabole–The Slate Quarry Show (with Kurt Jackson), Falmouth Art Gallery, The Moor, Falmouth, 4 January–2 February
02 02 02, Griffin Contemporary, Venice, CA, 2 February–2 April
Galerie Tschudi, Glarus, 16 February–20 April
New Art Centre Sculpture Park and Gallery, Salisbury, 18 May–22 September
A Moving World, Tate St Ives, St Ives, 13 July–13 October
Lake to Stones to Crows, James Cohan Gallery, New York, 9 November–21 December

2003
Hand Made, Galleria Lorcan O'Neill, Rome, 18 January–3 March
Konrad Fischer Galerie, Dusseldorf, 29 March–21 June
Here and Now and Then, Haunch of Venison, London, 11 June–30 August
Photographs from Wales, Iceland and New Mexico, Griffin Contemporary, Santa Monica, 18 October–20 December
Dialog (with Jivya Soma Mashe), Museum Kunstpalast, Dusseldorf, 13 September–22 November 2003

2004
Un incontro in India (with Jivya Soma Mashe), Padiglione d'Arte Contemporanea, Milan, 16 March–6 June
The Human Touch, Galeria Mário Sequeira, Braga, Portugal, 3 April–30 June
Kukje Gallery, Seoul, South Korea, 4 May–13 June
Sperone Westwater, New York, 10 September–23 October
The Music of Stones, Synagoge Stommeln, Pulheim, Germany, 19 September–28 November
Busan Museum of Art, South Korea, 16 November–13 February 2005

2005
Galerie Tschudi, Glarus, 2 April–28 May
Galleria Lorcan O'Neill, Rome, 9 April–21 May
In de Vitrines: Richard Long 60, Van Abbemuseum, Eindhoven, 30 August–23 September
Walking and Sleeping, Upstairs Berlin, Berlin, 10 September–5 November

2006
The Time of Space, Haunch of Venison, London, 3 January–10 February
The Path Is the Place Is the Line, San Francisco Museum of Modern Art, San Francisco, 21 January–25 April
Galleria Tucci Rosso, Turin, 11 February–30 April
Really, Really Simple: Richard Long–Opere dal 1978 al 2002, Villa Panza, Varese, Italy, 14 April–25 June
Lismore Castle Arts, Lismore, Ireland, 21 May–1 October
1 + 1 = 2 (with Roger Ackling), Von Lintel Gallery, New York, 7 September–7 October
Land and Line, Graves Gallery, Sheffield, 25 November 2006–24 February 2007

2007
Coal Ring, Kunstverein Ruhr, Essen, 1 May–17 June
Walking and Marking, Scottish National Gallery of Modern Art, Edinburgh, 30 June–21 October
Agadez (with Not Vital), Galerie Tschudi, Zuoz, 22 December 2007–22 March 2008

2008
Gravity, Galleria Lorcan O'Neill, Rome, 26 February–29 March
Neue Arbeiten, Konrad Fischer Galerie, Dusseldorf, 7 March–12 April
Musée d'Art Moderne et d'Art Contemporain, Nice, France, 31 May–16 November
Haunch of Venison, Berlin, 14 June–6 September
Spike Island (with Simon Starling), Bristol, 4 October–23 November

2009
Heaven and Earth, Tate Britain, London, 3 June–6 September

2010
Skulpturenpark Waldfrieden, Wuppertal, 25 February–9 May
A Thousand Stones, James Cohan Gallery Shanghai, Shanghai, 10 September–7 November
Artist Rooms: Richard Long, Ulster Museum, Belfast, 24 September 2010 - 27 February 2011; Abbot Hall Art Gallery, Kendall, 21 October–17 December

2011; The Hepworth Wakefield, Wakefield, 23 June–14 October 2012; The Potteries Museum & Art Gallery, Stoke-on-Trent, 30 November 2013–2 March 2014; and Burton Art Gallery & Museum, Bideford, 4 October 2014–10 January 2015
Galerie Tschudi, Zuoz, 22 December 2010–12 March 2011

2011
MC Gallery, Seoul, 18 February–2 April
Berlin Circle, Hamburger Bahnhof, Berlin, 26 March–31 July
Flow and Ebb, Sperone Westwater, New York, 6 May–25 June
Human Nature, Haunch of Venison, London, 27 May–20 August
Champ d'ocre, Chapelle Saint-Charles, Avignon, 2 July–16 October
Galerie Kamila Regent, Saignon, France, 4 July–1 August
Champ d'Ocre, Chapelle Saint Charles, Avignon, 23 August–16 October
Karoo Highveld, Iziko South African National Gallery, Cape Town, 9 November 2011–10 April 2012

2012
Text Works: 1990 to 2012, Galleria Lorcan O'Neill, Rome, 23 March–30 April
Flint Cross, Konrad Fischer Galerie, Berlin, 27 April–16 June
Works on Paper, SMAC Art Gallery, Stellenbosch, South Africa, 14 June–2 September
Galeri Artist, Istanbul, 7 September–3 October
Torre Pellice, Italy, 7 October 2012–24 February 2013

2013
Prints 1970–2013, Museum Kurhaus Kleve, Cleves, 21 April–30 June; Hamburger Kunsthalle, Hamburg, 14 July–20 October; and The New Art Gallery, Walsall, 15 April–21 June 2014
Rhine Driftwood Line, Museum DKM, Duisburg, Germany, 20 April–1 June
Hirose Collection 7, Hiroshima, 15 June–4 August
Drawings, Galerie Tschudi, Zuoz, 27 July–21 September

2014
Lisson Gallery, London, 23 May–12 July
Mendoza Walking, Faena Arts Center, Buenos Aires, Argentina, 28 June–28 July

2015
The Spike Island Tapes, Alan Cristea Gallery, London, 20 February–2 April
Time and Space, Arnolfini, Bristol, 31 July–15 November
Crescent to Cross, Sperone Westwater, New York, 11 September–24 October
Larksong Line, Galerie Tschudi, Zuoz, 19 December 2015–19 March 2016

2016
River Avon Mud, Galleria Lorcan O'Neill, Rome, 20 February–30 April
Gravity, Ivorypress, Madrid, 23 February–14 May
Cold Stones, Centro de arte contemporanéo de Málaga, Málaga, 13 May–21 August
Judd Foundation, New York, 1 October–17 December

2017
The Isle of Wight at Six Walks, Quay Arts, Newport, Isle of Wight, 8 April–1 July
Earth Sky, Houghton Hall, Norfolk, 30 April–26 October

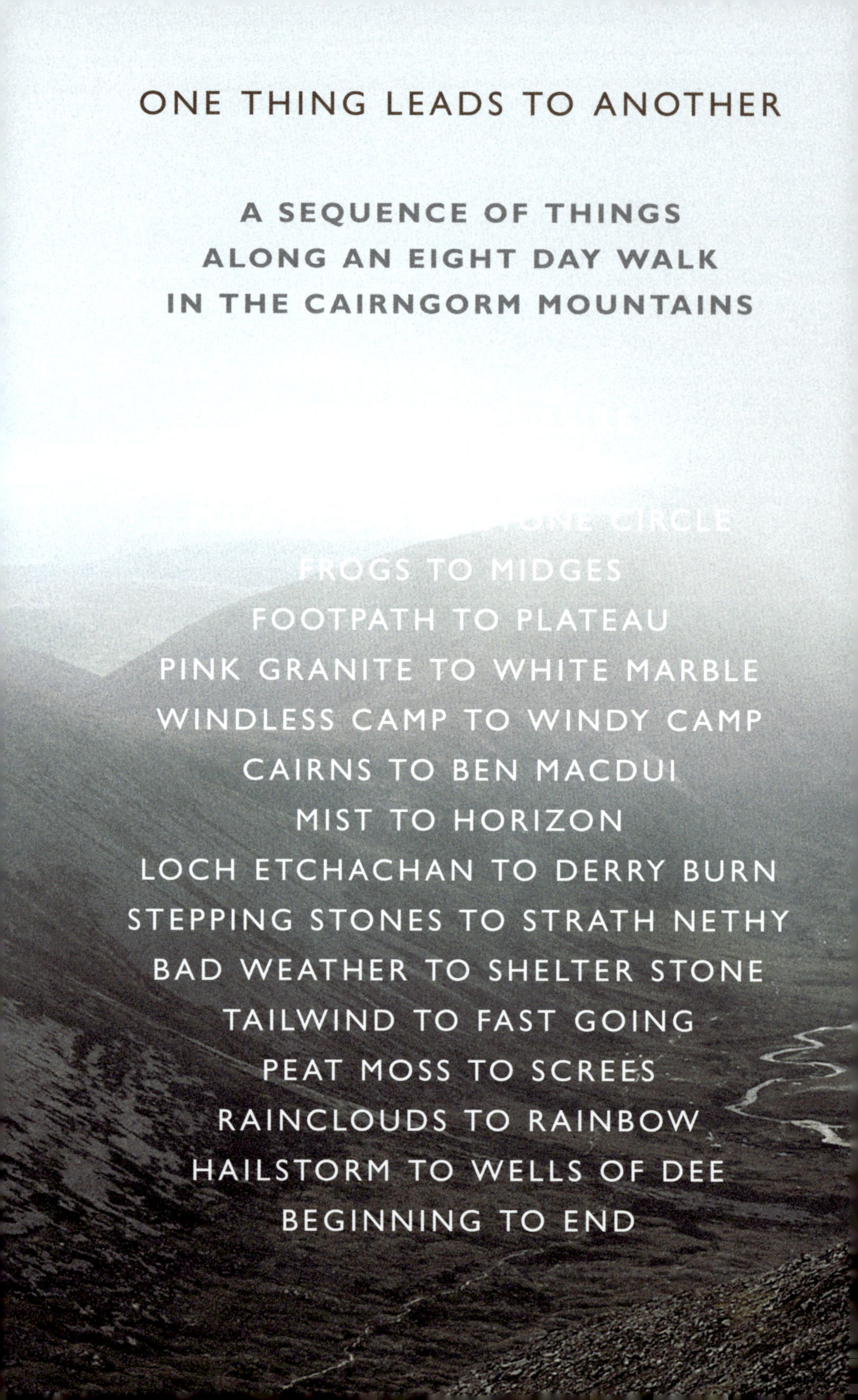

ONE THING LEADS TO ANOTHER

A SEQUENCE OF THINGS ALONG AN EIGHT DAY WALK IN THE CAIRNGORM MOUNTAINS

ONE CIRCLE
FROGS TO MIDGES
FOOTPATH TO PLATEAU
PINK GRANITE TO WHITE MARBLE
WINDLESS CAMP TO WINDY CAMP
CAIRNS TO BEN MACDUI
MIST TO HORIZON
LOCH ETCHACHAN TO DERRY BURN
STEPPING STONES TO STRATH NETHY
BAD WEATHER TO SHELTER STONE
TAILWIND TO FAST GOING
PEAT MOSS TO SCREES
RAINCLOUDS TO RAINBOW
HAILSTORM TO WELLS OF DEE
BEGINNING TO END

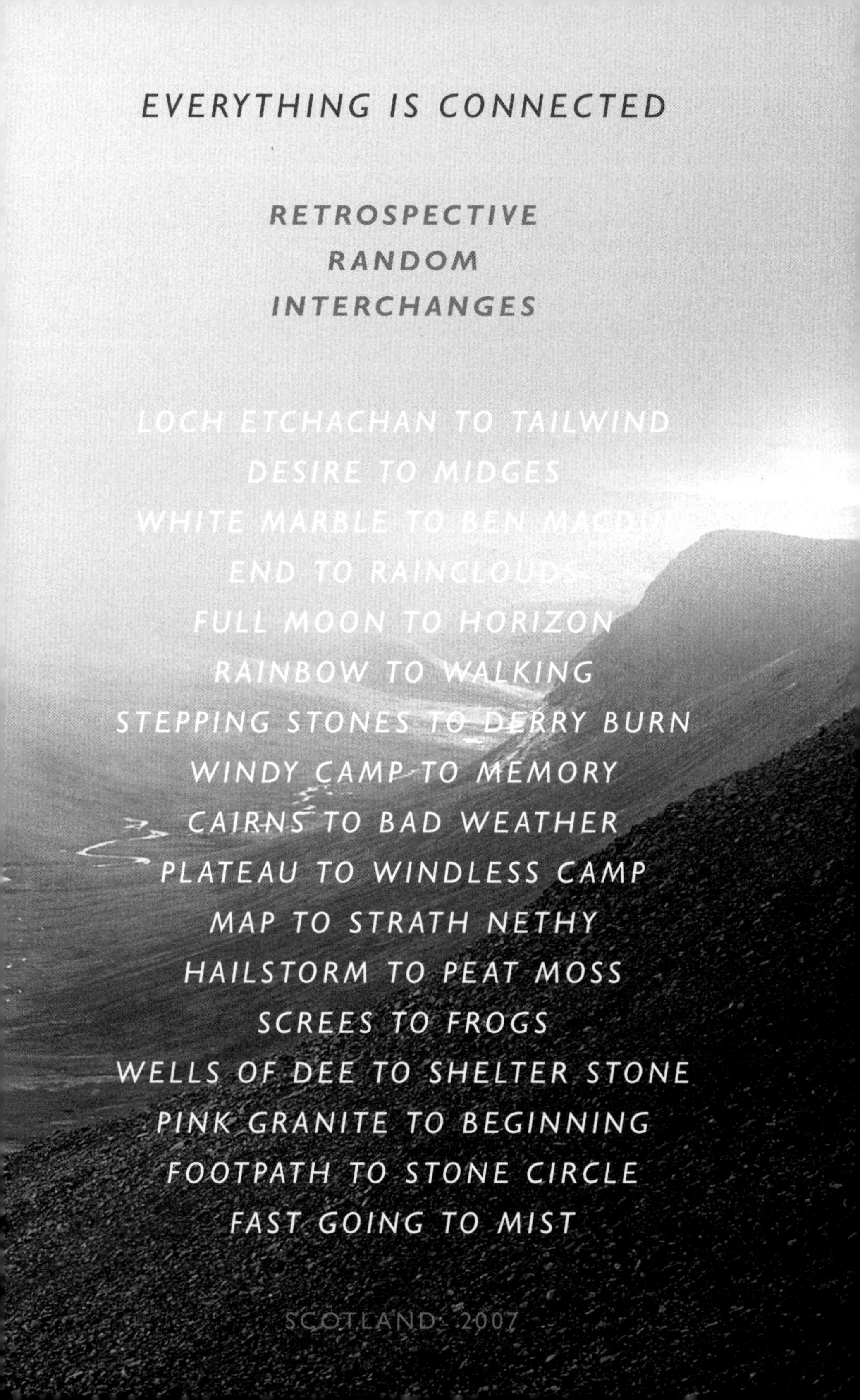

EVERYTHING IS CONNECTED

RETROSPECTIVE
RANDOM
INTERCHANGES

LOCH ETCHACHAN TO TAILWIND
DESIRE TO MIDGES
WHITE MARBLE TO BEN MACDUI
END TO RAINCLOUDS
FULL MOON TO HORIZON
RAINBOW TO WALKING
STEPPING STONES TO DERRY BURN
WINDY CAMP TO MEMORY
CAIRNS TO BAD WEATHER
PLATEAU TO WINDLESS CAMP
MAP TO STRATH NETHY
HAILSTORM TO PEAT MOSS
SCREES TO FROGS
WELLS OF DEE TO SHELTER STONE
PINK GRANITE TO BEGINNING
FOOTPATH TO STONE CIRCLE
FAST GOING TO MIST

SCOTLAND 2007

SELECTED GROUP EXHIBITIONS

1967
19:45–21:55, Galerie Dorothea Loehr, Frankfurt am Main, 9 September

1968
Young Contemporaries, Royal Institute Galleries, London, 30 January–27 February
Arte Povera piu azioni povere, Arsenali della Repubblica, Amalfi, 4–6 October

1969
Earth Art, Andrew Dickson White Art Gallery, Cornell University, Ithaca, New York, 11 February–16 March
One Month, Seth Siegelaub, New York, 1–31 March
Op Losse Schroeven: situaties en cryptostructuren, Stedelijk Museum, Amsterdam, 15 March–27 April; and *Verborgene Struckturen*, Museum Folkwang, Essen, 9 May–22 June
Live in Your Head – When Attitudes Become Form (Works – Concepts – Processes – Situations – Information), Kunsthalle Bern, Bern, 22 March – 27 April; Museum Haus Lange, Krefeld, 10 May –25 June; Institute of Contemporary Arts, London, 24 September–27 October
Land Art – Fernsehaustellung I, Fernsehgalerie Gerry Schum/Sender Freies Berlin, Berlin, 10.40 pm, 15 April (32 min)
July, August, September 1969, Seth Siegelaub, New York, July–September
Prospect 69, Städtische Kunsthalle, Dusseldorf, 30 September–12 October

1970
Tabernakel, Louisiana Museum, Humlebæk, Denmark, 24 January–22 February
Evidence on the Flight of Six Fugitives, Museum of Contemporary Art, Chicago, 28 March–10 May
18 Paris IV. 70, Rue Mouffetard, Paris, April
Information, Museum of Modern Art, New York, 2 July–20 September

1971
Guggenheim International Exhibition 1971, Solomon R. Guggenheim Museum, New York, 12 February–25 April
The British Avant Garde, New York Cultural Center, New York, 19 May–29 August
Sonsbeek 71, Arnhem, 19 June–15 August
Road Show: A New English Enquiry (British Council touring exhibition), Museu de Arte Moderna, XI São Paulo Bienal, São Paulo, opened 4 September

1972
De Europa, John Weber Gallery, New York, 29 April–24 May
Documenta 5, Kassel, Germany, 30 June–8 October
The New Art, Hayward Gallery, London, 17 August–24 September
Actualité d'un bilan, Galerie Yvon Lambert, Paris, 30 October–14 October

1973
Contemporanea, Parcheggio di Villa Borghese, Rome, November 1973–February 1974

1974
Carl Andre, Marcel Broodthaers, Daniel Buren, Victor Burgin, Gilbert & George, On Kawara, Richard Long, Gerhard Richter, Palais des Beaux-Arts, Brussels, 9 January–3 February
Sculpture Now: Dissolution or Redefinition, Royal College of Art, London, 11–22 November

1975
Artists Over Land, Arnolfini, Bristol, 26 August –20 September

1976
Arte Inglese Oggi 1960–1976, Palazzo Reale, Milan, 26 February–16 May
Andre/Le Va/Long, Corcoran Gallery of Art, Washington, DC, 11 December 1976–30 January 1977

1977
Skulptur Projeckte Münster, Westfalisches Landesmuseum für Kunste im Kulturegeschichte, Münster, 3 July–13 November
Rosc '77, National Museum of Ireland and Hugh Lane Gallery of Modern Art, Dublin, 21 August–30 October
Probing the Earth: Contemporary Land Projects, Hirshhorn Museum and Sculpture Garden, Washington, DC, 27 October 1977–2 January 1978; La Jolla Museum of Contemporary Art, La Jolla, CA, 27 January–26 February 1978; Seattle Art Museum, Seattle, 23 March–21 May 1978

1978
Peter Joseph, David Tremlett, Richard Long at Newlyn, Newlyn Orion Galleries, Newlyn, 17 January–17 February

1979
Un Certain Art Anglais, Musée d'Art Moderne de la Ville de Paris, Paris, 19 January–12 March
Hayward Annual 1979, Hayward Gallery, London, 19 June–27 August
Skulptur: Matisse, Giacometti, Judd, Flavin, Andre, Long, Kunsthalle Bern, Bern, 17 August – 23 September

1980
Andre, Dibbets, Long, Ryman, Louisiana Museum, Humlebæk, Denmark, 19 January–24 February
Pier + Ocean, Hayward Gallery, London, 8 May –22 June; Kröller-Müller Museum, Otterlo, 13 July–8 September
Roger Ackling, Hamish Fulton, Richard Long, Michael O'Donnell: Four Temporary Works Situated in West Penwith, Cornwall, England, St Ives September Festival, St Ives, September

1982
Documenta 7, Kassel, Germany, 19 June–28 September
Kunst wird Material, Nationalgalerie, Berlin, 7 October–5 December 1983
ARS 83, Ateneum Art Museum, Helsinki, 14 October–11 December

1984
The Critical Eye/I, Yale Center for British Art, New Haven, 16 May–15 July
Terrae Motus, Villa Campolieto, Ercolano, Italy, 6 July–31 December
Rosc '84, Guinness Hop Store, Dublin, 24 August –17 November
1965 to 1972 – When Attitudes Became Form, Kettle's Yard Gallery, Cambridge, 14 July–2 September; and Fruitmarket, Edinburgh, 6 October–25 November
The British Art Show: Old Allegiances and New Directions 1979–1984, City of Birmingham Museum and Art Gallery and Ikon Gallery, Birmingham, 2 November–22 December; Royal Scottish Academy, Edinburgh, 16 January–24 February 1985; Mappin Art Gallery, Sheffield, 16 March–4 May 1985; Southampton Art Gallery, Southampton, 18 May–30 June 1985; Art Gallery of Western Australia, Perth, 19 February–24 March 1985; Art Gallery of New South Wales, Sydney, 23 April–9 June 1985; and Queensland Art Gallery, Brisbane, 5 July–11 August 1985

1985
The British Show, Art Gallery of Western Australia, Perth, 19 February–24 March; Art Gallery of New South Wales, Sydney, 23 April–9 June; and Queensland Art Gallery, Brisbane, 5 July–11 August
Hayward Annual 1986, Hayward Gallery, London, 15 June–7 July

1986
Entre el Objeto y la Imagen, Palacio de Velázquez, Madrid, 28 January–20 April; Centro Cultural 'la Caixa', Barcelona, 3 June–15 July; and Museo de Bellas Artes de Bilbao, Bilbao, 29 July–20 September
Bodenskulptur, Kunstverein Bremen, Bremen, 29 April–15 June
Landscape: Place, Nature, Material, Kettle's Yard Gallery, Cambridge, 12 July–31 August

1987
The Unpainted Landscape (Scottish Arts Council touring exhibition), Maclaurin Art Gallery, Ayr, 10 January–7 February; Pier Arts Centre, Stromness, 7–28 March; Scottish Gallery of Modern Art, Edinburgh, 11 April–17 May; Artspace Galleries, Aberdeen, 30 May–24 June; Collins Gallery, University of Strathclyde, Glasgow, 7 July–8 August; and Crawford Centre for the Arts, St Andrews, 21 August–20 September
Wall Works: Richard Long, Michael Craig-Martin, Annette Messager, Marion Möller, Matt Mullican, Sol LeWitt, Cornerhouse, Manchester, 14 November–31 December
A Quiet Revolution – British Sculpture Since 1965, Museum of Contemporary Art, Chicago, 23 January–5 April 1987; Museum of Modern Art, San Francisco, 4 June–26 July 1987; Hirshhorn Museum and Sculpture Garden, Washington, DC, 10 November 1987–10 January 1988

1988
Starlit Waters: British Sculpture 1968–1988, Tate Gallery, Liverpool, 28 May–4 September
Donald Judd, Richard Long, Kristjan Gudmundsson, The Living Art Museum, Reykjavik, 4–19 June
Sculpture in the Close, Jesus College, Cambridge, 20 June–31 July
New Sculpture/Six Artists, Saint Louis Art Museum, St Louis, 23 September–30 October

1989
Magiciens de la Terre, La Grande Halle and Centre Pompidou, Paris, 18 May–14 August
Furkart, Hotel Furkablick, Furkapasshöhe, Switzerland, July–September
2nd Istanbul Biennial, Süleymaniye *İmareti*, Istanbul, 25 September–31 October

1990
The Journey, Lincoln Cathedral, Lincoln, 17 June–12 August

1991
La sculpture contemporaine après 1970, Fondation Daniel Templon – Musée Temporaire, Fréjus, France, 4 July–29 September

1993
Gravity & Grace: The Changing Condition of Sculpture 1965–1975, Hayward Gallery, London, 21 January–14 March

1996
Swinging the Lead, The Old Leadworks, Bristol, 24 May–22 June
Sculpture in the Close, Quincentenary Exhibition, Jesus College, Cambridge, 22 September–29 October

1997
Géographiques, FRAC Corse, Corte, Corsica, 21 June–13 September

1999
Richard Long, Sebastian Smith, Serge de Hildebrandt, Chantier Naval Opéra, Antibes, 26 July–3 September

2002
Wüste, Hessischer Landesmuseum, Darmstadt, 28 April–27 October

2003
Go(gh) Modern, Van Gogh Museum, Amsterdam, 27 June–12 October
The Last Picture Show: Artists Using Photography 1960–1982, Walker Art Center, Minneapolis, 12 October 2003–4 January 2004; UCLA Hammer Museum, Los Angeles, 8 February–9 May 2004; Museo de Arte Contemporanea de Vigo, Vigo, Spain, 28 May–19 September 2004; Fotomuseum Winterthur, Zurich, 26 November 2004–13 February 2005

2004
Intra-Muros, Musée d'Art Moderne et d'Art Contemporain, Nice, 26 June–14 November
Turning Points: 20th Century British Sculpture, Tehran Museum of Contemporary Art, Tehran, 24 February–2 July

2007
Turner Prize: A Retrospective 1984–2006, Tate Britain, London, 2 October 2007–6 January 2008; *History in the Making: A Retrospective of the Turner Prize*, Mori Art Museum, Tokyo, 25 April–13 July 2008

2008
Blood on Paper: The Art of the Book, Victoria and Albert Museum, London, 15 April–29 June

2010
With a Probability of Being Seen. Dorothee and Konrad Fischer: Archives of an Attitude, Museu d'Art Contemporani de Barcelona, Barcelona, 15 May–12 October
25 Jahre Galerie Tschudi, Galerie Tschudi, Zuoz, 24 July–11 September

2011
Modern British Sculpture, Royal Academy of Arts, London, 22 January–7 April

2012
Encounter: The Royal Academy in the Middle East, Cultural Village Foundation – Katara, Doha, Qatar, 6 December 2012–6 March 2013

2013
Uncommon Ground: Land Art in Britain 1966–79 (Arts Council Collection touring exhibition), Southampton City Art Gallery, Southampton, 10 May–3 August; National Museum of Wales, Cardiff, 28 September 2013–5 January 2014; Mead Gallery, University of Warwick, 18 January–8 March 2014; and Longside Gallery, Yorkshire Sculpture Park, 5 April–15 June 2014

2014
Body & Void: Echoes of Moore, Henry Moore Foundation, Perry Green, 1 May–26 October

2015
Five Issues of Studio International, Raven Row, London, 26 February–3 May
Space and Matter, Sperone Westwater, New York, 29 June–31 July

2016
Conceptual Art in Britain 1964–1979, Tate Britain, London, 12 April–29 August
It's Me to the World, Modern Art Oxford, Oxford, 19 August–18 October

AMAZONAS
ANCESTORS
MACHETE
ANIMISM
ZILLIONS
OXYGEN
NEGRO
ANTS
SUNSETS

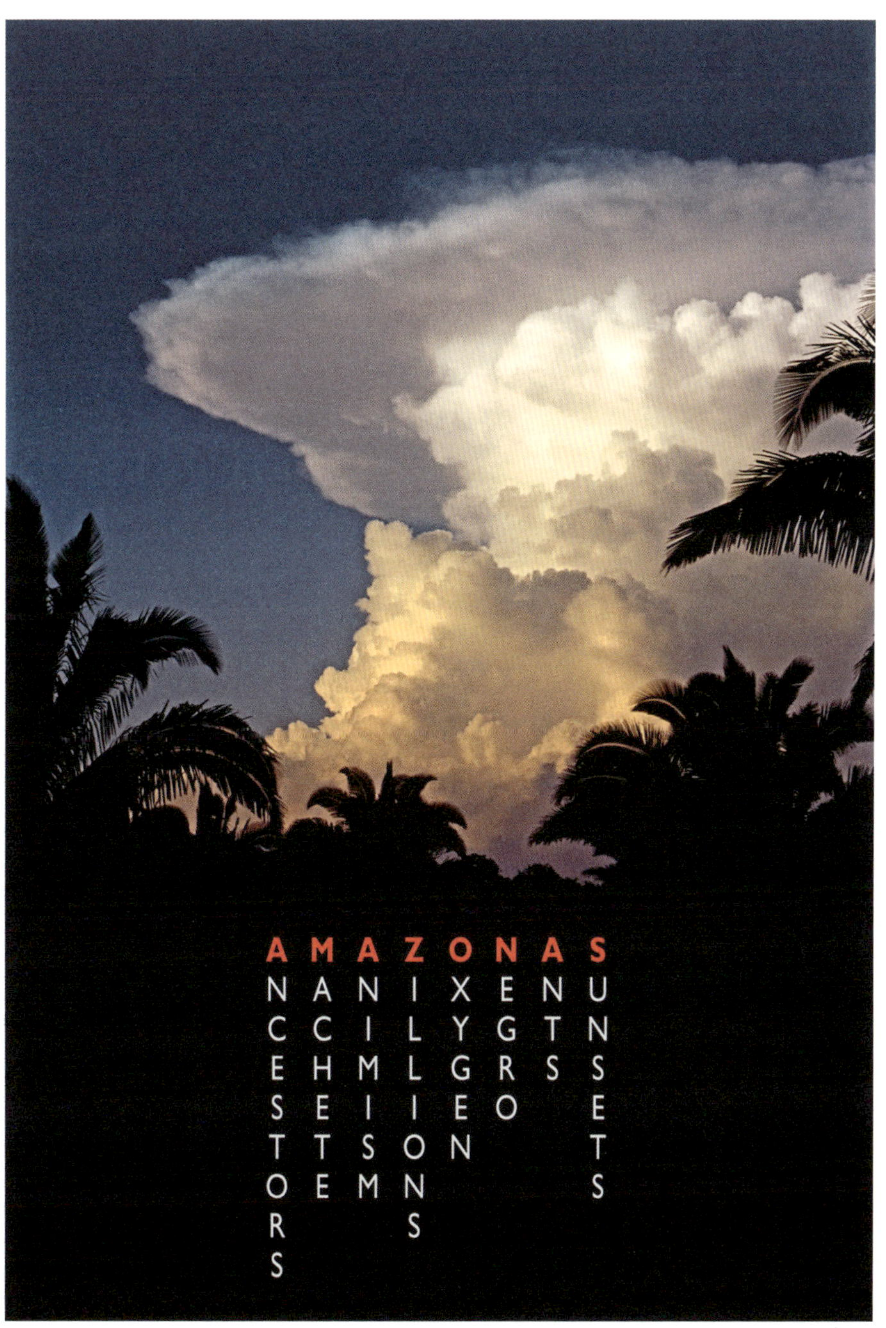

2016

PHOTOGRAPHIC CREDITS

Unless otherwise stated all photography is by Richard Long.

Julian Andrews p. 60 (both)
Stuart Bunce/Spike Island p. 8
Brian Cleckner p. 278
Hamish Fulton, pp. 38, 124–125, 154–155
Guggenheim Museum, Bilbao, pp. 202–203
Philip Haas, p. 319
Denny Long, p. 328
© Richard Long. DACS 2017, p. 61
Hervé Perdriolle, p. 217
Tate Library and Archive. Photo: Tate Photography, pp. 140, 142, 143, 145, 240, 244–245
Robert Vinas, Jr., p.286
Ursula Wevers, p.18
Stuart Whipps, p. 282
Whitechapel Gallery Archive. Photo: Nicholas Logsdail, p. 29
Whitechapel Gallery Archive. Photo: Brian Shuel, p. 30

Every effort has been made to trace the copyright holders of photographs reproduced. The publisher apologises for any omissions that may have inadvertently been made.

Published in 2017 by Ridinghouse

Ridinghouse
46 Lexington Street
London W1F 0LP
United Kingdom
ridinghouse.co.uk

This publication was made possible with contributions from Lisson Gallery, London; Sperone Westwater Gallery, New York; Galerie Tschudi, Zuoz (Switzerland). Special thanks are due to Karsten Schubert; Joanna Thornberry and Angela Westwater.

Distributed in the UK and Europe by
Cornerhouse Publications
c/o Home
2 Tony Wilson Place
Manchester M15 4FN
United Kingdom
cornerhousepublications.org

Distributed in the US by
RAM Publications
2525 Michigan Avenue Building A2
Santa Monica, CA 90404
United States
rampub.com

ISBN 978 1 909932 30 2

British Library Cataloguing-in-Publication Data
A full catalogue record of this book is available from the British Library

Exhibition chronology by Dorothy Feaver
Copyedited by Sarah Auld
Proofread by Eileen Daly and Sophie Kullmann
Designed by Philip Lewis

Set in William Text
Printed and bound in Italy by Verona Libri

OVERLEAF
River Avon Mud Drawing 1990

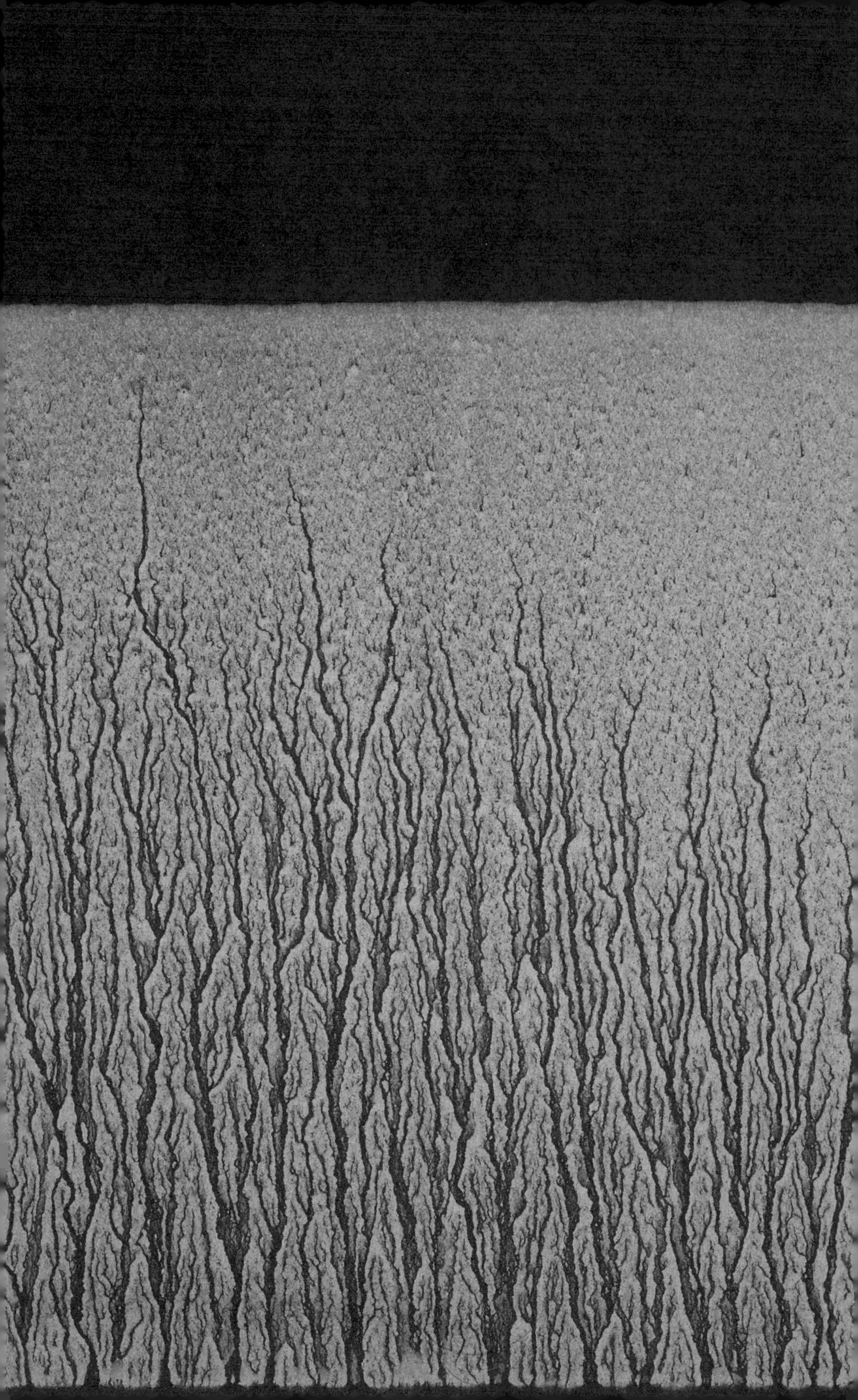